In Your Face

In Your Face

Professional Improprieties and the Art of Being Conspicuous in Sixteenth-Century Italy

---

DOUGLAS BIOW

Stanford University Press
Stanford, California

Stanford University Press
Stanford, California

This book has been published with the assistance of the Gladys Krieble Delmas Foundation and a University Co-operative Society Subvention Grant awarded by the University of Texas at Austin.

Printed in the United States of America on acid-free, archival-quality paper

Library of Congress Cataloging-in-Publication Data
Biow, Douglas.
In your face : professional improprieties and the art of being conspicuous in sixteenth-century Italy / Douglas Biow.
p. cm.
Includes bibliographical references and index.
ISBN 978-0-8047-6215-1 (cloth : alk. paper)—ISBN 978-0-8047-6216-8 (pbk. : alk. paper)
1. Italy—Civilization—16th century. 2. Personality and creative ability—Italy—History—16th century. 3. Artists—Italy—History—16th century. 4. Authors, Italian—16th century. 5. Eccentrics and eccentricities—Italy—History—16th century. I. Title.
DG445B57 2010
709.2'245—dc22
2008053118

Typeset by Bruce Lundquist in 10.5/12 Bembo

To
Thomas James Biow
and
David Christopher Biow

Behold, then, our brains where they go churning, behold where one loses time, and where the days get wasted: in fingering through papers, turning pages, consuming eyesight, exhausting the tongue, upsetting the stomach, tiring the brain, and going mad with all this blessed reading and writing!

—Anton Francesco Doni, *La libraria*

Contents

Prologue

AN ESTABLISHED, WORLDLY ARTIST with a virtuosic command of numerous visual idioms repeatedly pummels, over a period of days, a model he has slept with. Another male artist with a notorious temper and a capacious imagination unleashes his pent-up fury by snubbing a man of repute who has access to enormous riches and deeply entrenched institutional support, and who has commissioned him to complete a work of art of tremendous size and inventive scope, the likes of which no one has ever envisioned before. A renowned writer presumably engages one of his many followers to attack, if not kill, a protégé who has irked him in countless ways. Yet another writer of the same pugilistic and narcissistic stripe makes every effort to humiliate a rival in print as he seeks to claw his way to recognition and, he hopes, fame—his vengeful, competitive nature knowing no bounds.

Surely all these instances can be construed as cases of glaring professional impropriety. And arguably that is what makes them in part so fascinating. We expect professional artists and writers to behave one way, ideally with polite restraint and a polished demeanor; but we are sometimes taken with them when they behave in another manner, outlandishly. Witness the plethora of tabloids, our contemporary hunger for sensationalism, our cult of naughty (if not criminal) celebrities. Bad behavior, in the end, is often more fun to read about than good manners. Consider Norman Mailer's lurid stabbing of his second wife, Adele Morales, with a penknife back in 1960, at the outset of a decade full of larger-than-life, eccentric, countercultural characters.

Yet interestingly enough the instances cited here are drawn not from the present or recent past but from a far more distant one—a past that is often lost to us today and that requires some effort of the imagination if we are to retrieve and appreciate it fully. They come from sixteenth-century Italy, more specifically from the lives of Benvenuto Cellini, Michelangelo Buonarroti, Pietro Aretino, and Anton Francesco Doni—from the likes of the men who furnished us with some of the masterpieces of Western culture, such as the vault of the Sistine Chapel and the *Perseus* in the Loggia dei Lanzi in Florence, at the dawn of the early modern era.

Historically this is significant, for if the sixteenth century in Italy constitutes a period when professional propriety was being codified in an intense, accelerated, and often sophisticated manner in a number of widely printed and influential treatises written primarily by humanists to meet the demands of a society increasingly dominated by court culture, it also constitutes a period when male writers and visual artists seeking some measure of recognition from the cultural elite positioned themselves, or were positioned by others, as occasionally lacking professional propriety on the grand scale. More specifically, the Italian sixteenth century seems to be a period when people took a broad interest in the professional propriety *and* impropriety of its writers and visual artists. And some writers and visual artists seemed intent both to explore issues of decorum and to violate it in complex ways in their art and writings as a means of expressing selfhood in general and their own selfhood in particular. In concentrating on matters related to professional impropriety, this book explores modes of representation as reflecting primarily "attitudes" and "states of mind" about selfhood, not so much demonstrable "facts" about what people actually did or did not do. If this book maintains, for instance, that there was a rise in the representation of writers and visual artists lacking professional propriety in sixteenth-century Italy, it does not, for a host of reasons, seek to document (in the sense of reliably and systematically quantify) the rise of writers and visual artists *themselves* lacking professional propriety during the period.

Moreover, although this book claims that the sixteenth century in Italy provides us with more intense, widespread, and grandiose instances of writers and visual artists being represented or representing themselves as lacking professional propriety than in the earlier Renaissance, it does not claim that there existed a generational shift in representations of such violations of socially accepted norms of comportment. In this respect, this book, as it unfolds for the most part chronologically, addresses a period change in modes of representing selfhood in the context of notions about proper and improper conduct, but not incremental changes within the period itself. More locally, and personally, this book brings together two longstanding interests of mine, namely, professionalism and propriety, which I explored in *Doctors, Ambassadors, Secretaries: Humanism and Professions in Renaissance Italy* and *The Culture of Cleanliness in Renaissance Italy*. With this book I have at once telescoped and magnified these combined interests by concentrating on the sixteenth century, admittedly with some forays into the very end of the fifteenth century.

The landmark study that describes many of the sort of people I have in mind in this book, at least in the visual arts, is that of Rudolf and Margot

Wittkower, *Born Under Saturn: The Character and Conduct of Artists, a Documented History from Antiquity to the French Revolution.* As valuable as the Wittkowers' book has been for cultural history generally, I do not subscribe to their notion that the artists they identified as "eccentric" in the period emerged as a product of social alienation, first because I tend to associate the concept of social alienation with full-blown, advanced, open-market economies and I see no evidence for this in the Italian Renaissance; and second because I see no evidence that there was a pervasive, full-fledged, open "art market" operating at a significant economy of scale. Instead I see primarily guilds, workshops, and a vigorous patronage system at work for visual artists in the first three quarters of the sixteenth century in Italy, which is the period largely covered in this book. For much the same reason, I find untenable Arnold Hauser's reading of the underlying causes of the mannerist style, explored in his *Mannerism: The Crisis of the Renaissance and the Origin of Modern Art.* John Shearman, in his brief yet elegant *Mannerism*, is more descriptive than analytical about mannerism, which he encapsulates coyly as the "stylish style," so he does not attempt to account for its causes, as Hauser did by concentrating in a separate section of his book on "Alienation as the Key to Mannerism," for instance. But Sherman's reading of mannerism, at least as it seeks to capture the broad outlines of a visual style, is more universally viable, even if less intellectually daring in its scope.

In any event, the Renaissance sensibility of "eccentricity" that the Wittkowers found in a number of visual artists working primarily in sixteenth-century Italy, and that the Wittkowers attributed to the social "alienation" experienced on the part of the artists they discussed, bears little resemblance to the Romantic, modern, or postmodern notion of eccentricity in the arts, which is indebted in scholarly literature to the concept of social alienation, social critique, and social disembeddedness associated primarily with full-fledged open, impersonal, capitalist market systems of industrialized nation states and now with economic globalization, postcolonialism, and post-capitalism. More persuasive with respect to the sixteenth century, I believe, is the probing analysis offered by the eminent cultural historian Peter Burke in *The Italian Renaissance: Culture and Society in Italy*, who argues that the behavior of the sort of eccentric visual artists identified by the Wittkowers in the period in question collectively bore "a social message." According to Burke, these eccentrics, whom he does not discuss as being socially alienated, sought to demonstrate through their behavior that they were truly "free"—a concept of self-determination, however, that we might label today an enabling illusion as we look back at the period and view with suspicion Burckhardtian notions of "individualism" in the Italian Renaissance. Scholars today, including Burke, are more inclined to talk about degrees of "agency" instead of degrees of desire for freedom.

Furthermore, most of the writers and visual artists examined in the individual chapters of this book have been viewed as mannerist in one sense or another, and two of them, Baldassar Castiglione and Michelangelo, have been held up as paradigmatic figures of the High Renaissance. Yet this book makes no attempt to investigate any of the writers and visual artists discussed in it in the context of High Renaissance or mannerist styles in any programmatic way. And I make no apology for this. To engage in a discussion about how this or that writer or visual artist was or was not mannerist would seem to me to sidetrack the book, which already covers a great deal of disciplinary ground, into a number of debates and subissues, not the least of them being whether there was such a thing as mannerism, and by extension what the potential social and cultural causes of mannerism may have been. More to the point, mannerism—which I employ only as a descriptive term—is about a stylistic shift, *not* a behavioral one (even if the term derives from the literature of manners), and in this book I am above all interested in examining the connections among character, conduct, and creativity in sixteenth-century Italy. After all, High Renaissance and mannerist writers and visual artists could be deemed decorous and indecorous, seemly and unseemly, highly conformist and aggressively nonconformist. There is nothing, I contend, strictly High Renaissance or mannerist about "them," only their "style" of writing or visual art. Vasari, for instance, was typically viewed as polite and well mannered in his own time, and Bandinelli sometimes brutish and ill mannered, if not a downright menace; but *both* Vasari and Bandinelli are usually designated today, at least by scholars who embrace the concept of mannerism, as mannerist artists. Neither of them strikes me as particularly "alienated" socially within the courts of sixteenth-century Italy, to which they were bound for most of their professional lives, or economically from the means of production of their art making, over which they wielded a great deal of control. For the purposes of this book, then, mannerism is an artistic *maniera*, not a manner of purportedly being in the world. Indeed, mannerist artists adopted arguably all sorts of manners of being in the world, as did Renaissance and baroque artists before and after them, from Masaccio to Caravaggio, Raphael to Bernini.

Additionally, in using the topic of *the conspicuous* thematically as an organizing principle in this book, my aim has been to focus on the basic Renaissance concern with "self-fashioning"—a concept about which I have something to say in the Introduction—by examining figures who stand in stark opposition to those who imagined it in terms of moderation, limitation, and discretion, as a matter of becoming part of an elitist, essentially court society in sixteenth-century Italy, where they had to stand out, but where their conspicuousness also had to be underplayed at all times. The heroes (or some might deem antiheroes) of this book are consequently those who appear to have violated such norms by promoting themselves aggressively, and by effectively using writing or the styling of visual artifacts to memorialize their assertiveness and intractable delight in parading themselves as transgressive and insubordinate on the grand scale within the dominant culture of their time. Hence, by focusing on writers and visual artists of this sort, I have sought to construct a version of the Italian Renaissance that is neither the luminous, balanced, suave, and elegant one of Castiglione's and Vasari's courts (which was once in scholarly fashion not so long ago in the academy) nor the dark, oppressive, conspiratorial, and traumatic one of Niccolò Machiavelli's and Francesco Guicciardini's princely states (which is far more in scholarly fashion now), but instead one that exists in the verbal and visual culture of the period and that defines the "self," which for many scholars is evolving in this period in a novel and forceful way, through its various habits of being aggressively conspicuous.

Lastly, the phrase "in your face," positioned boldly in the title, has no obvious equivalent in Italian during the period covered in this book; yet, despite being an anachronism, it seemed to capture the spirit of the sort of aggressive performative selves I discuss in it, so I have adopted it, albeit sparingly in the body of the book, as a way of expressing through modern idiomatic English a way of thinking globally about a variety of egregious styles of behavior in the past and how they were represented in a variety of venues, from treatises to biographies, autobiographies to letters, poems to prose satires. In sixteenth-century Italy other terms in the vernacular would have come to mind in verb, noun, or adjectival form: *bravare*, *gridare*, and *lamentare* for what it meant to make a noise to get one's way; *prepotenza*, *oltraggio*, *dispetto*, *scandalo*, *affronto*, *ingiuria*, *diffamazione*, *insolenza*, *maldicenza*, and *vilipendio* for actions and behaviors that offended and pushed other folk around; *temere*, *terribile*, and *terribilità* for fierce, temperamental, and immoderate behavior and intensity; *paragonare* and *giostrare* for competitive activities in the arts; and *strano*, *astratto*, *pazzo*, *selvatico*, *stravagante*, *fantastico*, *bizzarro*, *capriccioso*, *bestialità*, *fantasticheria*, *stranezza*, and *bizzarria* for eccentric comportment and the sorts of people who exhibited such comportment, which could occasionally be taken, in the best of circumstances, as a sign of remarkable talent and genius, characterized respectively by the terms *ingegno* and *divino*.

Certainly Italians of the period possessed no shortage of ways of insulting one another, vigorously expressing disapproval, or using language as an assertive performative act, as Elizabeth Horodowich has most recently demonstrated in *Language and Statecraft in Early Modern Venice*; and as Peter Burke, Lauro Martines, Guido Ruggiero, Robert C. Davis, and Thomas and Elizabeth Cohen (among others) argued not too long ago. "In your face," however, seemed to me more broad-based and open-ended than anything else I could come up with as an all-encompassing catch phrase, and thus less liable to lead the reader toward a single restrictive mode of what could be deemed improper. I am, in the end, concerned throughout this book with a plurality of professional improprieties and not any one in particular as the men discussed in it sought to express themselves and acquire, as best they could, status. As always, variety characterizes much of the Italian Renaissance. This is true with regard to the sort of larger-than-life personalities and their manifold, and indeed sometimes idiosyncratic, professional improprieties examined in the core chapters of this book. It is also true regarding how visual and verbal artists could express themselves, and potentially get in other people's faces, through a variety of means in distinctively verbal and visual forms and terms: in the case of writers through presentation manuscripts, pamphlets, letters, diatribes, harangues, burlesques, romances, novellas, pasquinades, poems, dramas, how-to books, encyclopedias, treatises, satires, commentaries, and the like; in the case of visual artists through paintings, goldsmithing, ceramics, sculpting, drawing, architecture, presentation drawings, portraiture, self-portraiture, and print, among so many other forms and modes of representation.

THIS BOOK COVERS A LOT OF GROUND and cuts through a number of disciplines, primarily literary studies, history, and art history, and I am grateful to several scholars for helping me work my way through them, though I, of course, take full responsibility for all mistakes and shortcomings. In particular I should single out at the outset a number of scholars from my home institution. First and foremost I thank (yet again) my long-time friend and colleague Wayne A. Rebhorn, who read an early draft of this manuscript—a draft that required a great deal of patience on his part to get through in its original cumbersome, rough-hewn state. I thank him, as always, for his time, perspicacious eye, and acumen. No one, it seems to me, is better at seeing the forest for the trees. My friend and colleague Louis A. Waldman provided much generous help, both in looking over the manuscript at an early stage and in talking to me about ideas that surfaced in connection to art history. Alison Frazier sharpened chapters with her knowledge about the history and manufacture of books, and Ann Johns intervened in just the right way in the chapter on Michelangelo. Daniela Bini came to my aid in trying to come up with the best translations possible, especially when it came to Doni's colorful prose, which often left me flummoxed.

A number of other scholars assisted me greatly. John Watkins read through the entire manuscript at an early stage and offered helpful insights, encouragement, and cautionary words of advice. John Jeffries Martin nudged me with great editorial skill in my reading of Aretino. Stephen Campbell read an early version of the book, forced me to rethink it completely, and commented on the revised Introduction; he will find some of his salient observations plunked (agreeably so, I hope) wholesale into my text. Tom Willette gave his expert advice on two chapters, made all the difference in the world in my reconceptualizing the Introduction, supplied me with spades of information that I have done my best to incorporate wholesale into the text and notes, and urged me along as I poached on his field; I am especially grateful to him for helping me reframe the thesis and think my way through a number of thorny issues. Megan Holmes made superb suggestions for improving the Introduction and Michelangelo chapter, and I have incorporated them, word for word (and here with gratitude), directly into the body of my text. Paul F. Grendler read through the Introduction and the second and fifth chapters, offered important observations, and saved me from making a number of errors. Tom Cohen helped out greatly with the Introduction, and Giorgio Masi, a pioneer in Doni studies, generously furnished me with his most recent work on Doni's manuscripts, which allowed me to correct some of my datings in the appendix. Harald Hendrix cautioned me about overstating Doni's financial success, offered valuable insights into the complex problem of explaining why Doni turned to manuscript production in his later years, and furnished me with the information and wording for thinking about the circumstances that led Doni to abandon Venice in 1555.

Both the historians Guido Ruggiero and Paula Findlen made excellent suggestions for refining the manuscript in their readings for Stanford University Press. My thanks as well to Ken Albala, Michael J. B. Allen, Julia Hairston, Timothy Moore, Roberto Muratore, Antonella Olson, Matteo Palumbo, Guy Raffa, Deanna Shemek, and, once more, Wendy Nesmith and her ILL staff. I would feel amiss if I also did not mention with sadness the recent passing away of Eduardo Saccone, a distinguished scholar and gentleman of *buone maniere*, who first introduced me to the riches of the Italian Renaissance many years ago when I was a graduate student at Johns Hopkins University, and who always greeted with warmth (and perhaps some puzzlement) the books I wrote and sent him over the years. My daughter, Simone Biow, an elegant and accomplished writer now pursuing her degree in college, has always been a source of enormous encouragement in my work; she is just about the only member of my family who has read at any length what I've written (she even read through the revised Introduction to this book), and she has, believe it or not, assured me that she has done so (at least at times) with pleasure.

I am especially grateful to two foundations and my home university for financially assisting me in the writing and researching of this book: the John Simon Memorial Guggenheim Foundation for a yearlong fellowship; the Gladys Krieble Delmas Foundation for two separate summer research fellowships, one of which allowed me to travel and view Doni manuscripts;

and the University of Texas at Austin, for a special research grant, a yearlong faculty research assignment, and the ongoing research funding awarded me from my professorship. Daniela Bini, the chair of my home department, and Randy Diehl, the dean of liberal arts at the University of Texas at Austin, generously covered the costs of procuring images from various sources and the rights to reproduce them in this book. Albert R. Ascoli, William Kennedy, John Jeffries Martin, and Wayne A. Rebhorn at one time or another wrote on my behalf for at least one of these fellowships, and I am grateful for all their help. An earlier version of Chapter 1 appeared in the special issue "Toward a New Diplomatic History" in the *Journal of Medieval and Early Modern Studies* 31 (2008), 35–55; an earlier version of Chapter 2 appeared in *The Renaissance World*, ed. John Martin (Oxford: Routledge, 2007). I presented early versions of Chapter 3 at Trinity University and Chapters 3 and 5 at the University of Michigan (Medieval and Early Modern Studies Colloquium), where I profited from our discussions. I am indebted to Emily-Jane Cohen at Stanford University Press for her sustaining interest in this book and sound editorial advice, as well as to Sarah Crane Newman, Judith Hibbard, David Luljak, and Tom Finnegan for their patience, assistance, and good judgment.

Finally, since this book focuses exclusively on men who were represented as extremely colorful characters in their own time, it seemed only fitting to me to dedicate it to two male companions in my life, neither of whom will probably read any of the words placed above or below this sentence, but who are certainly colorful characters in their own right: my brother, Tom, and my son, David. If I ever manage to write another book, it will be dedicated to my daughters, Simone, Erica, and Giulia, who have now all grown up into young adults, who at times endured over their early lives my own idiosyncratic ways of behaving, and who will always have a special place in my heart.

Note on Translations

IT IS STANFORD UNIVERSITY PRESS'S POLICY to minimize citations of the original foreign language. All the poetry in Italian in the body of my text, however, appears with the original; prose in Italian is always translated in the body of my text, with words or phrases occasionally highlighted in the original. Titles of sixteenth-century printed books or manuscripts in Italian appear with the original titles and are not translated, except on rare occasions. Unless otherwise indicated, all translations are my own.

In Your Face

Introduction

THIS BOOK IS IN LARGE MEASURE about how the improprieties of a group of writers and visual artists in sixteenth-century Italy were encoded in their works of art. In the process it addresses the performance of gender as it examines exclusively men who ostensibly lacked professional propriety in a period when professional propriety was being codified in a number of influential and widely printed treatises and in social practice. Men, and virtually men alone, adopted—according to the stories told about them and how they represented themselves—a host of strikingly aggressive and indecorous strategies of self-presentation and self-promotion.[1] Writers and visual artists adopted these strategies in sixteenth-century Italy perhaps to advance their careers, in part by trying to attract attention by appearing eccentric and noteworthy, but also because it was in their nature to do so, and most important from a historical perspective because they could. Indeed, an underlying argument of this book is that various historical factors permitted writers and artists to behave egregiously during the period in question. One factor was the growth of the print industry, which allowed a number of writers—specifically what scholars have dubbed the polygraphs (*poligrafi*) writing in the vernacular—to distance themselves from court culture (which had proven such a fruitful avenue for career advancement for many writers) and survive somewhat independently of it, directly or indirectly, through the print marketplace.[2] A closely related factor was the development of a vigorous patronage system, which created wider opportunities for artists than previously existed and gave them the possibility of reaching a level of fame not attained in the fourteenth and fifteenth centuries.[3]

Finally, and more broadly, this book is about the changing relationship of writers and artists to court culture from the very end of the fifteenth century to the last quarter of the sixteenth century. During this period, the papacy—after having largely quelled the threat of conciliarism, subdued baronial rule in Rome, and increased its coffers through various financial mechanisms—began to commission works of art on a truly grand scale as a major European court, along with sustaining, albeit not always in a lavish manner, the careers of writers of broad appeal and renown. So too did a number of powerful dukes and princes in their courts across Northern Italy, as well as cardinals who housed impressive courts of their own in their enormous palaces centered in Rome.[4] Collectively the courts in sixteenth-century Italy, which varied widely in size and function, poured money into the verbal and visual arts, and writers and visual artists in search of work and fame responded on a grand scale, occasionally attaining through their efforts a sort of pan-European celebrity status.[5]

Some of the principal concerns addressed in this book may be best explored in a preliminary fashion by looking at the visual arts in sixteenth-century Italy, where there would seem to have been no dearth of artists lacking professional propriety in a society so dominated by court culture. Consider, for instance, the mannerist artist Giorgio Vasari (1511–1574) and the book that helped make him famous as a writer, *Le vite dei più eccellenti pittori, scultori e architetti* (1550, revised and enlarged 1568). Vasari's *Vite* not only presents us with a range of (mostly Tuscan) artists for reflection. It also presents itself as a sort of thesaurus of the then current language used to describe their personalities and normative and nonnormative habits of comportment. Vasari, as is known, worked well in court culture and used it to his advantage.[6] Though the cantankerous, fastidious goldsmith and sculptor Benvenuto Cellini (1500–1571) mocked Vasari for having long, uncut fingernails,[7] Vasari seems to have embodied universally the role of the polite (in the sense of not simply clean but also elegant, polished, and well-mannered) court artist.

Vasari's self-portrait, which resembles Raphael's portrait of Baldassar Castiglione (1478–1529), works hard to ensure that we will view him in this manner (Figures 1 and 2). It represents Vasari, who by then had already published the first version of his *Vite* (1550), as a gentleman. Elegantly robed, he displays a gold chain about his collar as a sign of his elevated status, but this assertion of distinction remains understated. The chain, with the pendant dangling from it, is prominent, but not too prominent. The decorous manner of its presentation thus assures us that Vasari is a gentleman, for a gentleman in the court does not call too much attention to himself. There is nothing flamboyant about Vasari here, nothing that would lend the impression that he is about to make an abrupt, aggressive, or exaggerated gesture. Even his fingernails, despite Cellini's assertion to the contrary, are clean, tidy, and nicely cut. Exhibiting proper *politia*, a period term "signifying both refinement (as in aesthetic excellence) and civility (as in politic behavior),"[8] Vasari's poised hands show no sign of his having labored with the paintbrushes that rendered Michelangelo Buonarroti (1475–1564) so filthy as he worked on the Sistine Chapel, or the tools of the trade that, according to Leonardo da Vinci, besmirched the bodies of sculptors, those messy mechanical workers who chipped away at stone and churned up dust.[9] Moreover, Vasari's hands, far from being the "small dirty hands" Cellini deprecatingly asserted them to be, are long, elegant, and thin-fingered.[10] They are the proportioned, uncalloused hands of a gentleman of the court. Likewise, the elegant slivers or swaths of white that emerge about Vasari's wrists and neck serve to frame and highlight, but do not immoderately call attention to, two of the most important features of a courtier: his face, which registers his character and power of mind, and his hands, which enact that character and power through unobtrusive gestures. His beard is fashionably but not foppishly trimmed, and he has enough hair on his head to warrant not having to cover it with a stylish hat, as the balding Castiglione was instead constrained to do in his portrait.

All in all, Vasari's self-portrait visually rehearses Castiglione's concept of *sprezzatura*, the ideal behavior of studied nonchalance and "coolness." Vasari, like Castiglione, thus appears before us in this portrait as a suave gentleman who will fit perfectly within the court. He is tempered, balanced, and thoughtful. If the three-quarter pose and the slight turn in the eye suggest that Vasari is shifting his attention from the artistic work at hand to the viewer, we may assume, from his tight-lipped mouth, that he is also waiting to be spoken to, as a courtier often should be, yet open to discussion. He may even be inviting us into conversation about the architectural work he touches lightly, while retaining all along a sense of quiet, respectful dignity within his own space as he is stylishly figured into the picture plane with calculated aplomb.

As a writer, Vasari put these qualities of the polished courtier into practice. His *Vite* serves not only to talk about and weave together the character, conduct, and creativity of artists,[11] often with the aim of establishing formal contrasts and parallels among the individual lives with sometimes great narrative license. Vasari's *Le vite* also serves to ingratiate the author as writer and artist within the Medici court. Time and again, Vasari makes it evident that the visual arts flourished and reached their apex in Florence, in part through the influence of the Medici family in general, and now through the patronage of Cosimo I, who occupies the position in *Le vite* of the perspicacious overseer of the talents of the individual members associated with his court—one of whom, of course, is the moderate and temperate Vasari.[12] If excellence has prevailed in the arts in Florence in particular and Tuscany in general, it is in part because such patrons as Cosimo I have recognized, as

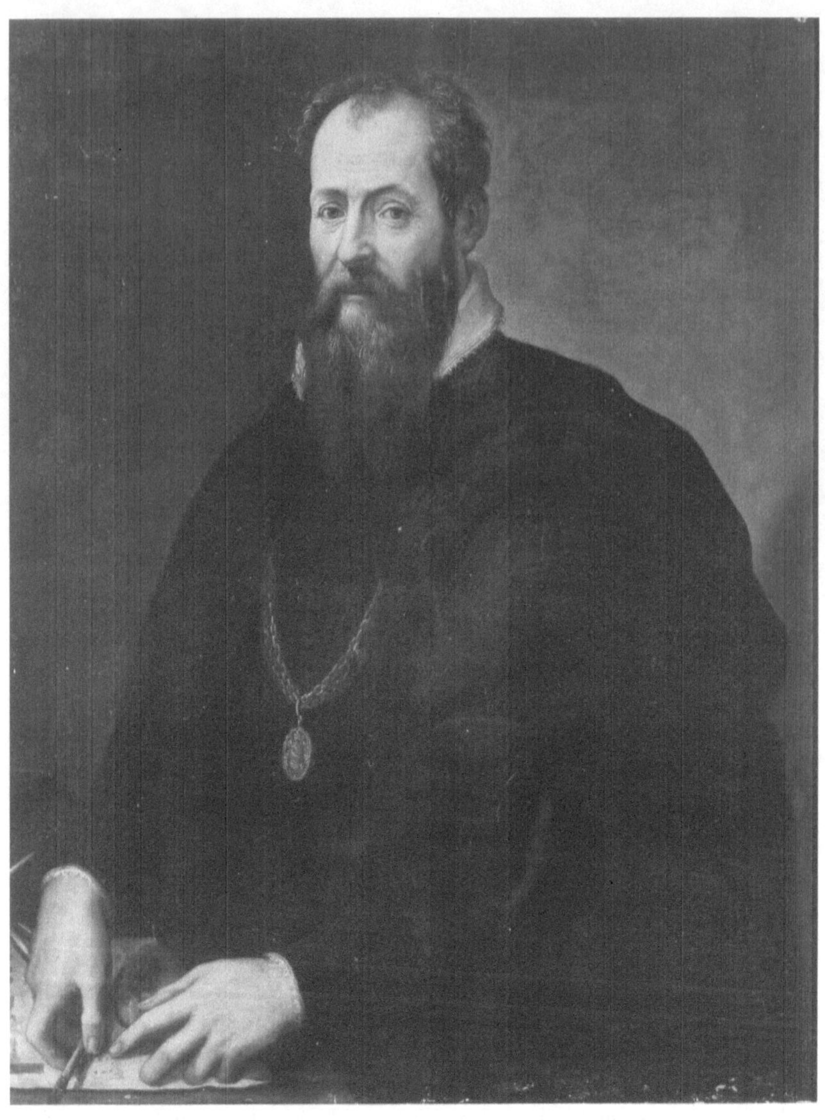

FIGURE 1. Giorgio Vasari (1511–1574). *Self-Portrait*, ca. 1566–1568. Uffizi, Florence. Photo courtesy Scala/Art Resource, New York.

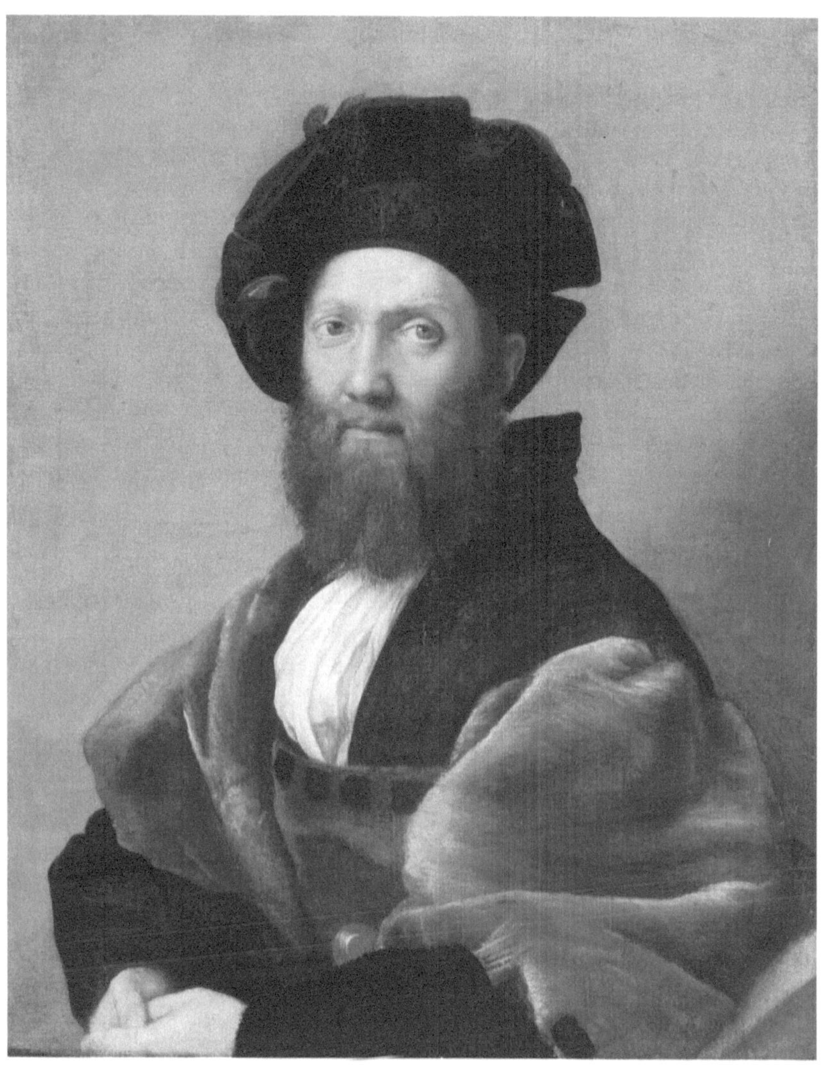

FIGURE 2. Raphael (1483–1520). *Portrait of Baldassar Castiglione*, ca. 1514–1515. Louvre, Paris. Photo courtesy Réunion des Musées Nationaux/Art Resource, New York.

well as nurtured, that excellence. It goes without saying that a number of qualities prized in the court, and elegantly dramatized in Vasari's portrait, are valued throughout *Le vite*, among them *piacevolezza, costumezza, grazia, gentilezza, cortesia, pulitezza, belle maniere, buona creanza, bontà, modestia, gravità, nobiltà, graziosità, diligenza, quietezza, giocondità, arguzia, destrezza, providezza,* and *prudenza.*[13] In advocating these qualities of character, moreover, Vasari is not only displaying a keen awareness of the positive features of many artists and seeking to elevate their (and consequently *his*) cultural status at a time when court culture dominated Italy. He is also keen on connecting personality and performance, conduct and creativity. In this context, and especially in the second edition of *Le vite*, Raphael stands for Vasari as the supreme example of the courtly artist whose conduct—his grazia, which rendered him so pleasing (*grato*) to his patrons in court culture—also found expression in his artistic representations: the grazia of the faces, postures, and gestures of the genteel people imaged in his works of art, as well as the grazia of his own maniera, which is exhibited in the suave, understated way he handled *colorito* and rationally worked out his *disegno.*[14]

Vasari privileges the comportment associated with court culture, but he also reveals that other qualities of character—qualities that were by no means prized in the court—underpinned the conduct of accomplished artists and found expression in their art. Some of these other qualities of character that he has in mind are associated with artists who were supposedly, in a word, downright weird. And there were allegedly enough of these oddballs out there, painting and sculpting and goldsmithing, that we can say they did not constitute a fringe group, either before or during Vasari's sixteenth century, at least as he represents them in *Le vite.*

The Tuscan painter Piero di Cosimo (1461–1521), for instance, epitomizes this group in some respects in *Le vite.*[15] As Vasari describes him (and we should bear in mind that Vasari as a storyteller is often given to exaggeration for the purposes of narrative enhancement and moral edification), Piero di Cosimo was scatterbrained to the point where he would lose his train of thought altogether—hardly a good quality in the court, where one had to prove oneself adept at conversation. He loved "solitude" as he went about "imagining/fantasizing about things" (*fantasticando*), building "castles in the air" (575–77). He was reclusive, absentminded, and withdrawn. In the terms of Giovanni della Casa's etiquette treatise, the *Galateo* (1558), which appeared well after Piero lived but encapsulated and codified the tenets of court conduct already in practice and shared by men such as Vasari, Piero lacked the ability to accommodate himself to the needs and wishes of others. He also exhibited strange habits of hygiene: he had developed, for instance, a peculiar love for disorder in the upkeep of his own garden, which, according to Vasari, reflected in its "surly, unsocial" (*salvatico*) character Piero's own messy, inhospitable "nature" (577). His "bestiality" (crude, uncultivated behavior, his *bestialità*; 577) made him appear "weird" (or strange, odd, literally "crazed": *pazzo*; 577). He was "capriccioso" (bizarre, unpredictable, capricious; 577), "stravagante" (odd, eccentric, idiosyncratic; 577). He ate only when he was hungry, and his eating habits left much to be desired. He was also neurasthenic. He got angry at flies. The crying of babies bothered him. Somebody's coughing would prove immensely irritating. When the sky thundered loudly he'd wrap himself up in a cloak and huddle in a dark corner, with all the windows shut tight. In a phrase, as Vasari puts it, "he arrived at such a strange state by living through such strange ways/fantasies" (581). None of these qualities, we can assume, would recommend Piero as a model for Vasari's court culture of sixteenth-century Italy. His bestialità would situate him not in the "conversable space" of the court palace, which required constant engagement, interaction, polish, tidiness, moderation, reserve, affability, and availability, but more appropriately in the woods.[16] Best to let this man, in all his strangeness, run wild, it might seem, much as he left his garden go to seed and rot.

As an example, Piero was not alone in his habits of "living strangely" in *Le vite*. In Vasari's own time, Sodoma (Giovanni Antonio Bazzi, 1477–1549) represents yet another peculiar man whom Vasari has to reckon with. He was "withdrawn, absent-minded" (*stratta*; 1057) and "bestial," according to Vasari, conducting himself "oddly" (also perhaps crazily, *pazzamente*; 1057) in old age. Sodomy, to be sure, cannot be enlisted as an anticourtly practice, but Sodoma's habits of living "with little honor" (1058) explains how he acquired his salacious nickname and elicits some reproach from Vasari, if only because those habits of comportment exceed the good Aristotelian mean that makes for calculated negligence in the court, the coolness of sprezzatura; as Vasari reports, because "he always had about him boys and young men without beards, whom he loved beyond measure [*fuori modo*], he acquired the nickname Sodoma, about which, far from being bothered or disdainful, he gloried in, writing about in stanzas and *capitoli*, and singing to them on his lute with great ease" (1058). Everyone has vices, we might assume, but it is wise not to parade them around so blatantly and inopportunely, so fuori modo.

Along with that, Sodoma seems to have possessed the strange habit of collecting all sorts of animals, which he lodged in his house and allowed to roam about freely. If Piero di Cosimo puzzlingly loved a home garden that looked like wilderness, Sodoma, a man of some affectation (*affettazione*), loved a house that looked like a veritable zoo. Likewise, Jacopo Pontormo (1494–1556), another artist of Vasari's own time, proved himself such a recluse that he never went to a party, much less graced with his presence "other places where people gathered together" (1026). He refused to let anyone serve him food, ostensibly for fear that he would have to keep even minimal company with another human being, or for that matter let anyone cook for him, no doubt for the same reason.[17] More important, amid all the examples of odd or uncouth men that can be adduced from *Le vite* (and there are many of them, including such luminaries as Masaccio), Vasari's one great hero in his narrative, Michelangelo Buonarroti—who combined in his excellence the three main branches of artistic endeavors (painting, sculpture, and architecture) and who represented the culmination of these arts since the time of the ancient Greeks—proved to be one of the most anticourtly, indecorous figures of Vasari's own time, a man conspicuously lacking professional propriety on all accounts.

What was Vasari to do? How could Vasari, the polished court artist advocating courtly habits of comportment in *Le vite* and in a society so dominated by court culture, explain the presence and excellence of these sometimes bizarre, uncouth, anticourtly figures? Vasari, to be sure, fudges, sometimes ignoring faults (as he does, for instance, in the case of Rosso Fiorentino), at other times taking people to task as he embellishes his narrative of artists' lives for often rhetorical, structural, and edifying purposes. But one key to Vasari's handling of the issue lies in the word *fantasia*, which he enlists in his discussion of Piero di Cosimo. As Vasari makes evident, a man such as Piero had fantasia in excess, a capacity to invent with unrepressed creative copiousness to the point where he became too distracted to follow a simple line of thought.[18] "That man," as Vasari observes, "was sometimes so taken with/absorbed in what he was doing that, while talking about something, as it customarily happens, at the end of talking [about it], a person [that is, the interlocutor] had to go back to the beginning [of Piero's discussion] and tell him about it, since his brain had gone/wandered off to another fantasy [*fantasia*] of his" (576). Fantasia, which should be construed as "an intellectual power responding to objects of sense" as well as a mental faculty of invention capable of creating "second worlds,"[19] perhaps arises from competition, which is a necessary condition of artistic excellence in *Le vite*.[20]

But one also gets the sense in *Le vite* that fantasia derives from nature, as the product of someone tapping into an innate gift, and from effort, as the product of someone diligently exercising a particular part of the mind conventionally thought in Renaissance faculty psychology either to reside, along with the *sensus communis* and *imaginatio*, in one of the three ventricles of the brain, or to function in a Platonic vein as a "species of 'insane' inspiration."[21] Fantasia, like competition, was of enormous value to Vasari, much as it was, though in different ways, for Cennino Cennini, Antonio di Pietro Averlino (Filarete), Giorgio di Francesco Martini, and Leonardo da Vinci before him. It would therefore seem that an artist such as Piero di Cosimo, as reportedly odd as he was in his absence of professional propriety, can be excused on many accounts if he has fantasia in abundance, though Vasari makes it clear throughout his *Le vite* that he does not want fantasia to be allowed to run free, unbridled.

Fantasia is labile and dangerous. It is as allied to the senses of the body as it is to the intellect, as connected to appearances as it is to essences, as rooted in indecorous and superfluous monstrosities as it is to perfect, ordered, rationally conceived beauty. Associated with boldness, daring, and risk taking, fantasia must therefore be rigorously controlled by reason. Fantasia itself consequently doesn't make for genius. One needs something special for that, which eludes easy definition and remains something of a mystery in *Le vite*, something akin to the humanists' notion of *ingenium*.[22] But without fantasia, and without proper, disciplined training and rigorous control of it through the rational art of good disegno, one cannot, it often seems in *Le vite*, be a genius. In this sense, then, fantasia is essential for invention, which Francesco Salviati, for all his professional improprieties (at least according to Vasari),[23] excelled in as a painter; Salviati was, Vasari insists, "rich, abundant, and most copious in his inventions of all things and universally skilled in all parts of painting" (1165). Michelangelo, of course, had a surfeit of fantasia, almost problematically so.[24] He is the model daring artist in *Le vite* whose fantasia proved so immense and fertile that it boggled the mind of the viewer who tried to take in the multitudinous forms of the human body that he worked out and displayed in often vast dimensions and in at times scandalous variations, thereby rendering the great Michelangelo in the eyes of his contemporaries at once divine and undivine, awe-inspiring and offensive.[25] Fantasia, in this sense, is not a guarantee of genius, but it is often in Vasari's *Le vite* a precondition for it.

In reading *Le vite*, moreover, one gets the impression that if an abundance of fantasia can justify odd behavior—the sort of behavior evinced in such men as Piero di Cosimo—it also contributes to that behavior, or at the very least it goes hand in hand with it. At first glance, the argument may seem circular, but it is not: odd behavior for Vasari does not produce fantasia, but excess in fantasia may give rise to odd behavior. More than anything else, the argument that connects fantasia to genius and strange behavior is self-mystifying. If you have fantasia, you may or may not behave oddly, just as you may or may not be a genius; if you behave oddly, you may or may not have fantasia, just as you may or may not be a genius. The best way to determine if someone is a genius is to look at the body of work produced. Acting oddly may therefore bring you to the attention of people and thus lead them (potential patrons) to believe through inference that the artist has fantasia in abundance and therefore is of value, perhaps even a genius.

Sometimes in *Le vite* it almost appears that artists in the late fifteenth and sixteenth centuries are, to be prosaic about it, knocking themselves out in Italy to appear odd, just to get noticed.[26] But in the end it is the quality of the art produced that matters for Vasari. Such, for instance, was the case with Sodoma: "On account of his oddities [*pazzie*] and because he had the reputation of being a good painter [*buon pittore*] Giovan Antonio [Bazzi] right at that moment came to the attention of Agostino Chigi, the very rich and famous Sienese merchant, who happened to be in Siena" (1059). Sodoma's "pazzie" aside, those oddities that helped bring him to the attention of some influential patrons such as the astonishingly rich Chigi would not have afforded him, by their very nature, a privileged place as an artist of repute, much less of genius, in Vasari's *Le vite*, had Sodoma not also been deemed a "buon pittore." For Vasari is interested in uncovering true excellence, whether it be manifested in the work of a chaste person or a sodomite, a saint or a sinner, someone exhibiting or lacking politia, just as he is interested in distinguishing the value of an excellent maniera, the special quality of a strong, personal distinctive style, from rote maniera, a general period style that anyone of middling talent can pretty much adopt. Some viewers may therefore mistake bizarre behavior for competence, or even for a sign of genius. Worse, some artists may perform in odd ways in order to attract attention and seek to be viewed as adventurous artists brimming with fantasia, which would have constituted a move in a decidedly wrong direction for Vasari. But in the end it was the product that mattered. Hence, for Vasari much could be accounted for and much excused if the product and overall body of work were of exceptional quality. And Vasari is concerned most of all in talking about that body of work and in locating, as the title of his book declares, "excellence."

There were certainly excellent artists for Vasari who would have done well to curb their behavioral excesses. Such was the case with Vasari's near contemporary, Baccio Bandinelli (1493–1560), whose portrait (Figure 3), along with his unexemplary conduct as an arrogant and abrasive man as it is summarized by Vasari, may serve as a fitting end point to this survey, however compressed, of the Vasarian conception of the proper role and behavior of the artist in sixteenth-century Italy.[27] Unlike Vasari, Bandinelli, who in his churlishness has been characterized as "Michelangelo's evil twin,"[28] displays in his sophisticated portrait an absence of understatement, a sweeping rejection of the values of Castiglione-styled sprezzatura, of studied negligence and equipoise and grazia. Everything about Baccio in his portrait is overt. In the language of this book, it is in your face. Rather than recalling Raphael's suave, paradigmatic portrait of Castiglione (Figure 2), Bandinelli's full-length self-portrait pointedly and ostentatiously echoes Michelangelo's Libyan sibyl on the Sistine Chapel ceiling, with its crossed legs twisted and arched feet placed in a strained pirouette. Bandinelli's body evinces a mannerist *figura serpentinata*, though without arguably the exquisite grazia of Pontormo's

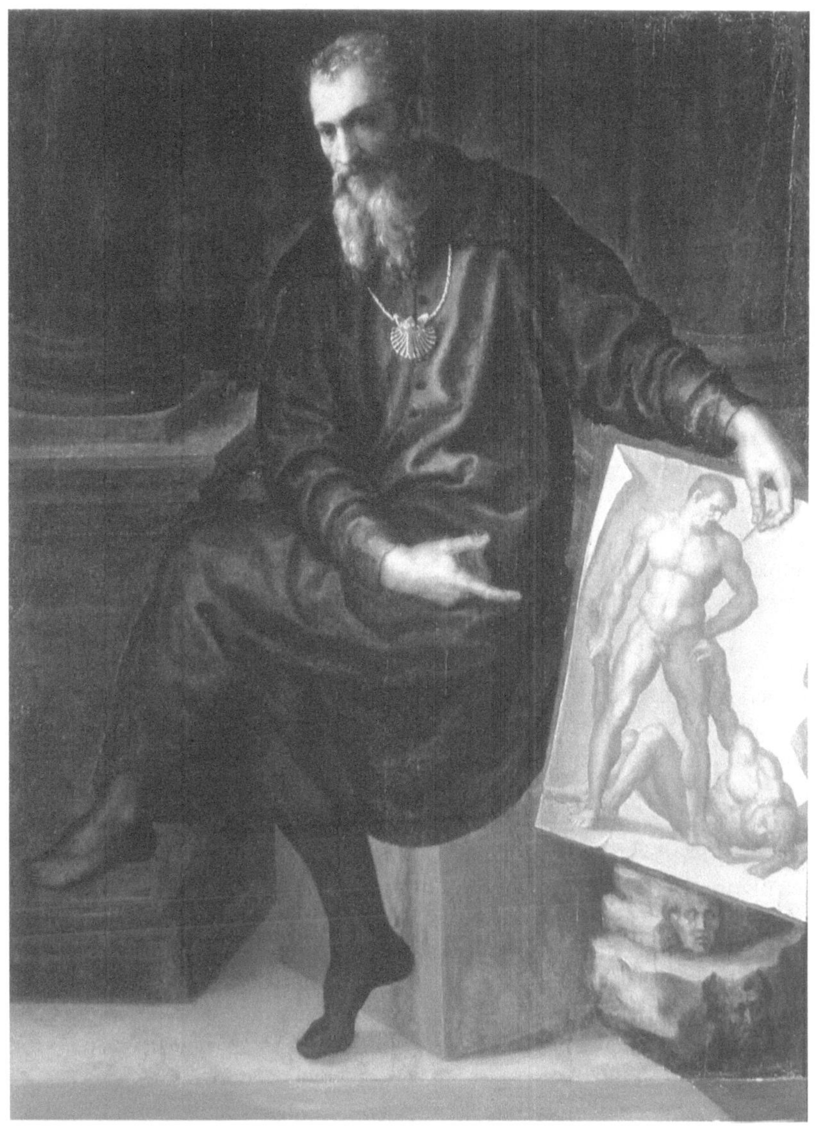

FIGURE 3. Baccio Bandinelli (1493–1560). *Self-Portrait*, ca. 1540–1550. Courtesy Isabella Stewart Gardner Museum, Boston.

supple figures. Bandinelli's gestures are all too blunt, even histrionic. And the highlighted shell pendant, which hangs on a gold chain and declares his induction into the chivalric order of St. James, rests as a material sign of honor on his smock far too conspicuously to be overlooked for a second; it is in some respects even more prominent in its placement and lighting than his head and hands, the instruments of enlightenment and thoughtful activity privileged in Vasari's far more restrained self-portrait. There is certainly no Raphaelesque suavity about this painting, or the manner of the man as he is represented. Bandinelli's hands do not rest as Vasari's do in gentlemanly equipoise; they actively point. And what they point to are Bandinelli's accomplishments as an artist, not his accomplishments as a gentleman, who should never gesture so immoderately or immodestly.

This is not, then, a man of the arts engaging us in conversation, as Vasari appears to do in his portrait, but one who aims to impress the viewer—his peers, his patrons, posterity—at all costs as a professional who has mastery over all sorts of arts as he engages in a sophisticated and assertive manner in a *paragone* (competition) with others. For unlike Vasari as he represents himself in his portrait, Bandinelli does not acknowledge us; we are supposed to acknowledge him. He has something to profess, and he means to do so boldly, openly, and aggressively. He indicates not with one hand but two, just to drive home the point that disegno lies, as well it should in both Vasari's and Bandinelli's school of thought, at the foundation of good art.[29] And the portrait enacts that principle by encoding Bandinelli's mastery over the arts of painting, drawing, and sculpture as we look at the colorful painted canvas, the painted "red chalk" design on the paper he points to, and the painted sketch for the statue of *Hercules and Cacus*—a statue that Bandinelli had by that time already constructed (1527–1534), though significantly in different form than the one depicted here. As a result, Bandinelli, ever the insistent pedagogue, here self-consciously indoctrinates us into his artistic process of invention as a sculptor with a full grasp of disegno in the very moment that he appears to us in this painting as a finished product of that process of invention in another medium—the medium, that is, of paint, which can even serve Baccio here in an innovative manner to double for red-chalk drawing.[30]

Moreover, the self-portrait enacts, in a by no means subtle yet still sophisticated manner, Bandinelli's rivalry with Michelangelo, whom, as Vasari observed, he labored to surpass in an ongoing agon. After all, it was Bandinelli and not Michelangelo who won the commission for the *Hercules*, which was to be a companion piece for Michelangelo's "gigante," the colossal *David* placed in a privileged position in Florence's Piazza della Signoria. In this regard, the complex, multileveled painting dramatizes—yet again, all too emphatically and aggressively, as Bandinelli points with both hands to the drawing—why Bandinelli received the commission. Bandinelli, he would have us understand from the demonstrable gestures, was simply superior in the art of disegno; everything Michelangelo could do, Bandinelli can do better.

If Bandinelli is bending over backwards to be recognized in his self-portrait (and he is certainly twisting himself about into an uncomfortable, Michelangelesque pose in order to be recognized as a gifted, versatile artist in the mannerist vein), we can say from a Vasarian viewpoint that Bandinelli's strategy of aggressively calling attention to himself in his life, as Vasari recounts it in his narrative, backfired; he lost clients over the course of his career thanks to his abrasive comportment, which on occasion could become brutish.[31] From the vantage point of some ungenerous connoisseurs of art, Bandinelli's strategy of aggressively calling attention to himself was unmerited; he was neither at the level of Michelangelo nor even as good an artist as the charitable Vasari made him out to be—a negative assessment that has now rightly come under much scrutiny and scholarly revision.[32] From the vantage point of this book, however, Bandinelli's strategy is fascinating. His in-your-face comportment, which Vasari viewed as arrogance and Benvenuto Cellini perceived as a strategy for masking incompetence, may not have assisted Bandinelli in endearing him to others in the long run, or in catching the eyes of potential patrons, in the way that Sodoma's pazzie seem to have rendered him at least in passing a curious figure of interest for the banker Chigi and Vasari himself.

But Bandinelli's absence of professional propriety, even as it perhaps hindered his career within the court and was largely viewed as negative, does come through in Vasari's *Le vite* as a mark of Bandinelli's artistic intensity. Structurally, Bandinelli's professional improprieties in *Le vite* acquire a positive valence in the way that, *mutatis mutandis*, Michelangelo's abrasive comportment does. For Vasari, there were some artists, such as the inimitable Michelangelo, who behaved with professional impropriety because that was who they were. In this regard, Michelangelo's behavior was not a prudential performance put into place to garner approbation or condemnation; nor was it a manner of acting in the world in order to impress people with a bold and unsurpassed maniera. In Michelangelo's case, his professional impropriety was a sign and a consequence of his intensity and devotion to art, as was his inclination to seclude himself. He shunned company and refused to marry in order to devote himself all the more completely to the perfection of his craft, spiritually wedding himself, much as an ascetic might do, to his work in both body and soul.[33] Similarly, Bandinelli, Vasari leads us to believe, aspires to this same sort of intensity and devotion in his rivalry with Michelangelo, though he remains in Vasari's estimation outclassed in matters of fantasia, disegno, and ingegno, as virtually everyone else does in *Le vite.*

The situation for a number of writers allegedly lacking professional propriety was markedly different from that described by Vasari for visual artists. Consider, for instance, the polygraphs, the adventurers of the pen, who wrote in the vernacular and used the press as a means of securing a livelihood as best they could and for broadcasting themselves to the world.[34] These polygraphs, who often attacked court culture but also sought to profit from it through patronage, were selling not just a product—the books they wrote, translated, printed, plagiarized, or pirated—but themselves as phenomena worthy of keen readerly interest. In the process of selling themselves and seeking a stable basis of operation within the print marketplace, a number of the polygraphs also occasionally squabbled conspicuously among themselves in intense, vitriolic ways. As Vanni Bramanti has pointed out:

> The great diatribes and the ruthless fights among many writers, the unpredictable shifts from affectionate friendships to violent aversions . . . : all this needs to be appreciated according to the absolute need to survive at all costs, an exigency that these characters ineluctably had to face all the time. In the writing activities of the great editorial houses of the time, among them the Giolito and Marcolini presses in Venice, and the Giunti and Torrentino in Florence, the waters could not have been too still, so that among those engaged in those presses . . . there was always the possibility of a personal attack suddenly erupting and coming to the surface.[35]

In the case of the polygraphs, competition sometimes meant getting in one another's face. To be sure, as they engaged in verbal battles, the polygraphs of the sixteenth century exhibited obvious affinities with the humanists of the fifteenth century, who could occasionally become a cantankerous and combative lot, from Lorenzo Valla to Angelo Poliziano, George of Trebizond to Poggio Bracciolini.[36] However, the squabbles among the polygraphs, which never resulted in direct physical blows (as far as we know),[37] were presented to a broad-based public through the medium of print. Moreover, unlike the squabbles among the humanists of the previous century, those among the polygraphs were transmitted to the public not in classicizing Latin, the restrictive language of the cultural elite, but in a rough-and-ready vernacular, a popularizing language accessible to a large base of potential readers eager to take advantage of the flourishing book market and interested presumably in the "lives" of these colorful men. The squabbles among the polygraphs in this way were arguably far more conspicuous than those of some of the more pugnacious humanists of the previous century.

Unlike earlier generations of writers, then, and unlike those of their own generation, the polygraphs of the midsixteenth century exhibited exaggerated habits of aggression and impropriety on the grand scale. Though they knew how to be deferential and decorous, and though they could form lasting friendships and durable work-related associations, they could also be downright nasty when they wanted to be—fiercely, egregiously, and publicly so. Print culture, of course, became the principal vehicle through which polygraphs expressed themselves and, in the process, gave expression to their professional improprieties occasionally in their various posturings.

But there were also many authors in sixteenth-century Italy, we should bear in mind, who staged their identities as difficult, odd, or off-putting in the vernacular without ever exhibiting the highly aggressive, indecorous comportment displayed by these men in the immoderate *personae* they occasionally constructed for themselves. Ariosto, for example, presented himself as crazed in his *Orlando furioso*, sane only, as he blithely put it with gentle irony, in "ludic intervals." But in comparing himself to Orlando, the berserk, jilted protagonist of his poem, Ariosto is playing a suave, literary game. And the figure of the courtly poet within the romance hardly comes off as overly aggressive and mean-spirited, even if he momentarily flies off the handle from time to time, as in his tirade against women.

Conversely, a number of men of reputedly polished professional propriety who worked in the courts wrote verse and prose—some of it tongue-in-cheek, some of it elegantly modeled on the classics—that could perhaps make even a few of the polygraphs blush for their improprieties. One could be, that is, like Petronius, the great "arbiter" of good conduct, elegance, and taste, and still the author, as Petronius was, of the *Satyricon*, of scandalously hostile, satirical writing, and no one would conflate the two, the man and the work. But that does not seem to have been the case with the polygraphs, who were selling so much of themselves as figures of keen readerly interest, especially, but not only, in their vernacular letter collections, for which Pietro Aretino (1492–1556), truly a unique model figure among the polygraphs, first created such a vogue. The personae the polygraphs created with their letters, and the sorts of posturing they engaged in as they presented themselves in various guises in print, were occasionally ones of professional impropriety, the personae and posturing, in Ariostan terms, of the often aggressive, feared, mean-spirited "scourge." Ortensio Lando (ca. 1512–ca. 1553) characterized himself, for instance, as a difficult, quarrelsome man, while Nicolò Franco (1515–1570), a polygraph of undistinguished origins, savagely attacked Aretino, his erstwhile mentor, who no doubt benefited from the negative attention bestowed on him and certainly knew how to return Franco's savage jibes in kind.[38] Ludovico Dolce (1508–1568) and Girolamo Ruscelli (ca. 1504–ca. 1565) squabbled intensely for a while.[39] Venom, in short, flowed freely among the polygraphs.

In this context, it is important to point out that there is a reason women writers, so many of whom began to acquire a public voice in the vernacular in sixteenth-century Italy, do not occupy a role as protagonists in this book. Historically, one of the problems facing women writers at that time was the need to curb the appearance in print of being too aggressive. They needed to elevate themselves in the public eye and thereby acquire greater respect and acceptance, so as not to appear, in the best of circumstances, indiscreet through the personae they created, and in the worst of circumstances brazen. Like men seeking recognition in print, women writers aspiring to be embraced by the elite tended to accept the culturally determined constraints placed on their behavior as they represented themselves in their writings. However, unlike men, aspiring women authors did not deviate in their writings in egregiously indecorous ways from the norms defined by those constraints.

In other words, no woman of artistic merit occupied a position in society that can even remotely be considered equivalent to that of Pietro Aretino or Anton Francesco Doni (1513–1574). There was no female "scourge of princes" lashing out at, tormenting, and provoking vindictively the powerful. No high-profile woman of artistic merit in the sixteenth century tried to destroy another in print with such venom and vengeance, ultimately with the aim of burying that person's name forever, as Doni indignantly did. Even Veronica Franco (1546–1591), one of the most talented and outspoken women of her generation, operated in the most decorous of ways. In fact, it was Franco's poetic interlocutors who behaved with impropriety as they antagonized her.[40] She, conversely, behaved in a manner that made her appear all the less a *cortegiana* and far more a *donna nobile*, a woman of talent and acute poetic sensibilities who commanded respect and displayed proper decorum. A woman by no means deluded about the nature of her profession, and one who could evidently make men go wild with desire, Franco was capable of recasting in a personal idiom the untoward remarks hurled at her by her detractors. She did so in a manner that elevated her in the eyes of everyone. Coopting the language of her antagonists to make it poetically her own, she made the cortegiana a figure of refinement and, by extension, herself a figure of professional propriety. She thereby downplayed the typical notion of the cortegiana as a woman who put her body on conspicuous display for sale to the best bidder.[41] Far from being part of the market and a commodity herself with carnal goods to give in a commercial exchange for cash, she is figured as a woman of moderation and courtly comportment engaged in an economy of refined, honorable gift giving.

We might therefore ask: What historical developments are characteristic of the polygraphs? Historically, these men, who viewed themselves in Paul Grendler's terms as critics of their world, were not dismantling their society from within and laying bare its material and economic contradictions and tensions in the manner articulated by Georg Lukács in his classic study of critical realism in the bourgeois novel.[42] They were hardly "alienated" from the means of production as they worked directly or indirectly in the marketplace of print, no more than the visual artists whom we have so far examined were in any way alienated from their means of production within a guild or vibrant patronage system, however much they might have felt caught at times between the workshop and the court and competing allegiances to patrons. Quite the contrary, the polygraphs, who critiqued social mores rather than matters of material production, were ineluctably wedded to the market system, the very system that critical realist authors sought to dismantle more than three centuries later in its full-blown, capitalist state in modern, industrialized Europe.

Indeed, the polygraphs, who for the most part came from modest backgrounds,[43] aimed to earn a living both directly and indirectly through the market, however economically precarious the career opportunities offered them might actually turn out to be, and however much they might have felt the need to supplement their income through other means of employment. Virtually all of the polygraphs sought some measure of prosperity and fame, if not also social status, patronage, and legitimation, through the commercialization of language in the massive book market ofVenice. Aretino, however, occupied a distinct and unusual place within that heterogeneous group and benefited primarily from court and patronage allowances to subsidize his lavish and generous lifestyle in his house on the Grand Canal.[44] In any event, the untoward behavior that the polygraphs periodically manifested in their popular writings can be construed as symptomatic of the new competitive realities facing men who by and large aimed to survive off the commercialization of language, either directly or indirectly, and not the patronage system of a *specific* court to which they might be attached in some sort of service, if indeed they could successfully attach themselves to one.

Speed, *prestezza*, not the tedious work of polishing (*limando*) prose or verse over a prolonged stretch of time, also defined much of their mode of production, for they often had to get their work out there quickly for public consumption.[45] Aggressivity within the print marketplace—not idealized, restrained courtly comportment in a Castiglione-like ducal palace—defined in a number of instances their mode of presenting themselves in the "real" world. They were competing often enough not for the honor and privilege of being physically close to a prince and at his service at a specific court, but professionally with each other for recognition within the print marketplace and for the kinds of relationships they could potentially foster from afar with powerful figures through print.

To be sure, the polygraphs sometimes benefited from patronage and the acts of gift giving associated with courtly culture (hence the endless parade of fulsome dedications one finds in their books). They also accrued honor, as Aretino in particular did, by being associated with court culture and enjoying the protection and munificence of powerful men. In Aretino's case, the protection and munificence came from such truly powerful men as Charles V and Francis I, among others. But despite the privileged status and legitimation they might attain through association with court culture, much of their basic survival—with the notable exception of Aretino—depended on the thriving book industry, to which they were inevitably bound, and to the commercial republic of Venice, where they lived and worked for extended periods. Unlike Castiglione's courtier, then, polygraphs putatively worried not so much about appearing effeminate generally in their practices of verbal deception, or in appearing to be subordinate to an autocratic ruler within the court.[46] They worried about appearing too much like prostitutes as they engaged, even at some distance removed in the case of Aretino, in a market economy of exchange within the book industry in the commercial capital of republican Venice.[47] Indeed, in a calculated defensive strategy of deflection and rhetorical inversions, they might sarcastically claim, as Aretino did as he embraced fully the new medium of print, that it was the courtiers who were the real prostitutes (*puttane*), the true insidious parasites feeding off and infecting society at large. More often than not, they might effusively praise, as Doni and Lodovico Domenichi (1515–1564) did, the cultural power and possibilities of print, while recognizing all along the pitfalls, ruses, and risks associated with it.

Unlike polygraphs, visual artists—with the exception of those who mobilized the technique of printing to further their success and disseminate a visual vocabulary[48]—worked in an entirely different environment, though polygraphs and visual artists might ultimately have been vying for recognition from the same people through their artifacts and in their search for legitimation, patronage, and fame. Whereas polygraphs worked directly or indirectly in a diffused, pervasive, and thriving "market" of commercialized print, no comparable market operating on a similar economy of scale and openness existed for the sort of visual artists dedicated to painting and sculpture discussed in this book, which focuses primarily on the first three quarters of the sixteenth century in Italy.[49] Different social and economic pressures than those governing the polygraphs conditioned the habits of comportment of visual artists of painting and sculpture as they have come down to us.

In this respect, it is all the more remarkable that many visual artists were able to prosper despite their purported lack of professional propriety, precisely because so many of them seeking recognition and engaging in rivalries with one another were bound, in one form or another, to court culture for substantive commissions, as Michelangelo, Cellini, and Bandinelli were. Aretino, for instance, made a point of distancing himself gradually from court culture not too long after arriving in Venice, even as he benefited financially from allowances from courts, although it is evident from his largely successful sojourns in Rome and Mantua that he could function well in actual courts if he wanted to.[50] Aretino's rejection of the court came about not because he could not be a part of it or thrive in it but ideologically, because he couldn't stand court culture, if we can take his pronouncements sincerely, and materially, because he had a career alternative available to him through (though not exactly in) the print marketplace, even if Aretino made every effort to appear courtly in his insistence that he was merely presenting people with gifts and seeking only gifts in exchange for his artistic labors. The substantive gifts he received, we need to bear in mind, always elevated both him *and* the giver, conferring honor on both; the givers accrued honor within this economy of exchange of cultural capital for their munificence and perspicacity, the recipients for their priceless talent and devotion to their art. But after 1527, once he left Mantua, Aretino hardly budged from the commercial Republic of Venice, and he never failed to lambaste the court in his withering attacks. Similarly, Doni, Aretino's close follower and eventual *bête noire*, made a modest living as a polygraph in the print marketplace of Venice for a number of years, and perhaps he did better than most,[51] though the house he claims he owned, as he tried to present himself on the opulent, flamboyant model of Aretino, was probably unassuming, and there is no evidence that he owned property in the country, other than his house in Monselice, which was totally ruinous and of no financial consequence.[52]

Despite all his best efforts, Doni was not, unlike Aretino, able to win a position at court. And he tried desperately from the mid-1550s to the 1560s to find a position at court or to win some sort of significant court patronage, first through Aretino (who refused to help him, which seems to have led to their falling out) and then, when that effort failed miserably, by sending off to potential patrons carefully crafted presentation manuscripts, which Doni composed, copied out, and illustrated in his own hand as valuable gifts designed to gain favor. To be sure, over time some polygraphs were constrained for economic reasons to abandon Venice and periodically pursue positions at court, and some, such as Domenichi, were far more adept at finding stable remunerative employment than others.[53]

That the frequently off-putting Doni was denied a position at court, even if he could be gracious and well-mannered in print when he wanted to be, is not surprising, especially given the impressive number of writers competing with one another for such positions and the patronage of a pope, cardinal, prince, king, or duke. Court privilege, which Aretino participated in yet turned his back on, brought with it status, honor, reputation, and legitimacy, though not always much lucre. Many sought court privilege in sixteenth-century Italy—the "charlatan" surgeon, physician, and writer Leonardo Fioravanti, for instance, who worked in the ambit of polygraphs in commercial Venice, labored unsuccessfully to win a position at the court of Cosimo I—but not everyone could secure such a position, whether or not they possessed pulitezza, grazia, and buone maniere.[54] Yet Doni, who did not fare well in finding a place at court, had another option open to him, even if he chose not to avail himself of it after the late 1550s, and even if he made things difficult for himself in Venice through his untoward behavior. In theory, he could always take advantage of the print marketplace, which had initially produced some financial well-being in Venice and made his career possible. This option of being connected to a market that operated at such an economy of scale, however precarious those job opportunities within the print marketplace of Venice might have been, was not available to visual artists invested in producing sculptures and paintings, and particularly those aiming to do so in a grand manner. In this regard, the fact that so many visual artists lacked professional propriety, as Vasari recounts the stories of their lives, but managed to do well in sixteenth-century Italy as painters and sculptors tells us much about the individual talents of a select number of these "excellent" artists and the sorts of needs that propelled patrons in the court to put up with people who certainly did not seem to fit well into court culture. Such artists, we might infer, if Vasari's narratives reflect some kernel of truth about their lives, must have been considered exceptionally good, and the appetite of patrons for their works must have been great.

In *Le vite* some of these artists ostensibly did better than others. As Vasari observes, his dear friend Francesco Salviati would have been far more successful had he comported himself differently, attempting to apply himself more sweetly to conversation,[55] whereas Sodoma's "pazzie" seemed to endear him, at least in passing, to Agostino Chigi. By contrast, Sodoma, who was knighted by Leo X, also ended his days in poverty, according to Vasari, on account of his "bestialità." Cellini could have borne some of Vasari's advice, though he would never have taken it from Vasari. Michelangelo, we know from documents, did remarkably well financially, eventually amassing a small fortune, and he never lacked for commissions from patrons. Indeed, Michelangelo was so swamped with commissions that he never finished many of them. But given his temperament, Michelangelo, who was eventually emancipated from guild regulation by papal intervention, lived uneasily with court culture and the patronage system of the courts to which he was bound for much of his life. Typically he locked horns with those for whom he worked. No one really wanted him around, and unlike the gracious and gregarious Raphael or Donato Bramante, who operated so smoothly within court culture and displayed the requisite politia, Michelangelo did not enjoy the company of his patrons (except, we are led to believe, during the very early years of his career when he was associated with the Medici household). Over the long run, had Michelangelo not been as talented as he was, and had his terribilità of character not matched the awesome terribilità of his inventions and inspiring artistic accomplishments, he could have ended up, like the incorrigible Cellini, without commissions and out of favor with the court, or like the immoderate and bestial Sodoma destitute and impoverished at the end of his life.

ALTHOUGH THIS BOOK is in large measure about how the professional improprieties of a select group of writers and visual artists in sixteenth-century Italy were encoded in their works of art in complex ways, it focuses on a performative practice, a mode of behavior: the art of being conspicuous, with "art" here understood in its broadest sense to mean everything from talent and knack to empirically acquired skill. To this end, this book begins in the first chapter with a model of discretionary comportment both of and for court culture in sixteenth-century Italy. Specifically, it focuses on Castiglione and his work as a diplomat in order to explain what it meant, in theory and in practice, to be conspicuous and yet deftly inconspicuous in the courts of the period. The first chapter also explores how strategies for being conspicuous changed dramatically in the late Renaissance as some writers became more and more openly indecorous and manifestly aggressive in print, particularly after the Sack of Rome. Those strategies for being inconspicuously conspicuous also coincided, significantly enough, with an unprecedented outpouring of books on proper conduct and professional propriety, from Castiglione's own influential *Cortegiano* (1528) through della Casa's *Galateo* (1558) to Stefano Guazzo's *Civil conversazione* (1574), as well as in a host of treatises written over the course of the first three quarters of the sixteenth century on how to become a proper secretary, cardinal, or ambassador.

The remaining chapters, which constitute the core of the book, examine men who stood as exemplars of a very different form of comportment. The second chapter focuses on Aretino, perhaps the most obnoxious in-your-face man of the sixteenth century, whose fame rested partly on his ability to frighten others into submission by threatening that he would chastise or embarrass them in public with his sharp, irreverent tongue. The third chapter discusses Michelangelo, who stood for many as a towering model of untoward comportment among artists in his generation, even though Vasari, Michelangelo's most ardent early champion in print, made every effort to account for his professional improprieties by casting him as the Redeemer of art. The fourth chapter examines Cellini, the Florentine goldsmith turned sculptor who immortalized himself by telling the story of his life not only as an artist but also as a belligerent, forceful, and at times fiercely arrogant man. The fifth chapter focuses on the Florentine polygraph Doni, who earned the reputation of being a contentious man with a taste for violating decorum and who was famous, at least in part, for taking on the inimitable, not-easily-defeatable Aretino in a caustic public attack. Accordingly, if one great model for professional propriety in a society dominated by court culture was Castiglione's landmark *Cortegiano*—a treatise that explored how to be at once strategically conspicuous and inconspicuous within the court—Aretino, Michelangelo, Cellini, and Doni, we shall see, represented themselves and were represented as having deviated at times with a vengeance from those courtly norms established by Castiglione.

Although the topic of the conspicuous as it is explored in this book may seem to cover a discontinuous range of phenomena as it finds expression in the works of Castiglione, Aretino, Michelangelo, Cellini, and Doni, it fundamentally has to do with habits and practices of self-presentation, be it Castiglione's discreet signaling of his prowess as a diplomat; the endless self-advertisements of professional writers such as Aretino and Doni, whose careers depended on the print industry; or Michelangelo's and Cellini's self-conscious mythologizing of their brash, contumacious characters when dealing with patrons, rivals, and peers in the visual arts. Rather than trying to narrow down the topic of the conspicuous to a single limited, and limiting, definition, however, I have preferred to let it acquire additional meanings and density as we move from chapter to chapter, as well as from one generation of writers and artists to the next. The purpose of test cases, after all, is to eschew uniformity and appreciate complexity while acknowledging family resemblances.

Hence Michelangelo's legendary acts of being aggressively conspicuous have much to do with his habits of self-presentation, his famed, off-putting terribilità. But when understood in the context of Michelangelo's lack of grazia and tremendous powers of fantasia, they also have to do with a particular psychological disposition—a disposition that finds itself manifested and magnified in his works of art in themes of intense, creative absorption. Similarly, Cellini's acts of being aggressively conspicuous have much to do with a driving need to surpass others (especially Michelangelo) and acquire recognition through self-presentation, much as Cellini's archrival Bandinelli sought to do in a sophisticated manner in his self-portrait. But they also serve to provoke wonder, the passion of *meraviglia* that had become such a self-proclaimed or underlying goal of much Renaissance literature and art.[56] In the verbal arts, Aretino's acts of being aggressively conspicuous in print speak to his yearning to acquire celebrity status through carefully crafted presentations of himself. But they also address his longstanding desire to outdo the consumption practices of court culture, the very courts he critiqued, by embracing both the popular and the elite. Likewise, Doni's acts of being aggressively conspicuous in print speak to his quest for recognition on a truly grand scale through his self-presentations. But they also reveal a need to transfer himself into objects of his own creation in the hope of acquiring through them everlasting fame—in his instance through widespread dissemination and preservation of his name and achievements in the form of mechanically reproduced books.

Unfolding for the most part chronologically, this book is also divided into three sections, each with a distinct thematic focus serving as a heuristic device to aid the reader in locating connections among the authors and visual artists discussed. The first section concerns diplomacy, the second food, and the third objects. The first section consists of one chapter examining closely Castiglione's seminal *Cortegiano*. To show how Castiglione always knew how to stage himself inconspicuously in the very moment that he called attention to himself and to his excellence as an outstanding diplomat, Chapter 1 considers not only the nature of diplomatic work as it is encoded in the *Cortegiano* (a treatise dedicated to forming the "perfect courtier") but also the many letters that Castiglione wrote while he was the papal nunzio to Spain (1525–1529).

The second section, focused on men who were part of Castiglione's generation, concentrates on the topic of food. It begins with Chapter 2, which covers virtually all of Aretino's major works. This chapter explores both Aretino's own habits of eating, which he offers to us in his voluminous letters as representations for consumption by his readers in the marketplace of print, *and* the eating habits of his fictional characters as they are dramatized in works of imaginative literature, particularly his first comic play, the *Cortigiana*, and two scurrilous dialogues about food, sex, and prostitution. The second section concludes with Chapter 3, which concentrates above all on Michelangelo's *Bacchus*, the irreverent, "unclassical," yet classical sculpture produced originally for one of the most powerful patrons in Rome, Cardinal Raffaele Riario.[57] The *Bacchus*, which I here present as a pivotal and proleptic work in Michelangelo's early career, addresses the topic of intense, inward absorption in the figures of the inebriated wine god and the hungry satyr, both of whom can be seen reveling in their own states of sensual consumption as they cherish the food they stare at and hold in their grasp.

Turning to two exemplars taken from the next generation of artists and writers, the third section of the book concentrates on objects. These men were also the rivals of those in the second section. It begins with Chapter 4, which focuses primarily on Cellini's monumental *Vita*, an innovative book written toward the end of his life and remaining in manuscript form for 159 years after his death. Cellini's *Vita* tells the story not only of his life as an artist but also of his life as a wonder-eliciting maker of objects for a public obsessed with collecting things of all sizes and value in an increasingly courtly world defined by conspicuous consumption. The third section ends with Chapter 5, which primarily concerns Doni's *Libraria*, a book about books—indeed, the first such book about books in Italian literature. My argument is that Doni, who had already had his own press in Florence for a year, is obsessed with the topic of fame and immortality as they are forged through print. For Doni, who failed to find a position at court, only print can make us truly conspicuous. Indeed, only print can proliferate versions of us throughout the world according to Doni and thus keep us eternally and materially present before other people's eyes.

Methodologically, this book also engages two competing, but by no means antithetical, models in current scholarship for conceptualizing the production of Renaissance writing and visual art. On the one hand, scholars have argued over the past decade and a half that what made possible and in some ways defined the Renaissance in general was "appetites." At the most basic level, the concept of appetites underpins a demand-side notion of the Renaissance that privileges examining shifts in habits of consumption as a way of understanding the uniqueness of the period.[58] According to this reading, the Renaissance occurred first in Northern Italy because in the late fourteenth and fifteenth centuries and after there was a great deal of concentrated money to spend on art; a fierce, competitive desire to consume art in impressive quantities; a dynamic economic system and social structure prepared to meet that immense desire for consumption through the fluid distribution of wealth; and the development on the part of consumers of "values, attitudes, and pleasures in their possession of goods so that these things became the active instruments for the creation of culture, not just the embodiment of culture."[59] Moreover, in this analysis the sixteenth century in particular witnessed increasingly widespread attention to the ostentatious display of conspicuous consumption in Italy and thus to the lavish expenditures that defined the aristocracy, court, and papacy, including massive feasts and elaborately staged festivities. This hunger for consumption also extended to tiny and medium-sized durable items, from paintings to pottery, that were purchased on a grand scale to furnish houses, palaces, churches, and private chapels. We are dealing in the sixteenth century in Italy with a society that had to produce art objects, ranging from colossal sculptures to stage sets to the tiniest of jewels, in sufficient quantities to meet this extensive demand. Furthermore, that demand for art, which so fueled the Renaissance generally, found expression in the sixteenth century in all sorts of venues, from book buying and manuscript hunting to the competitive yearning for fame on the part of patrons, artists, and writers through consumption and production of material culture. A central character of the Italian Renaissance, then, which flowered in the sixteenth century, was, according to this reading, a deep, insatiable, almost Faustian hunger for durable, worldly goods of all sorts and shapes—a hunger that can perhaps be viewed genealogically as having distantly given birth to our own age of rampant, and often crass, consumerism.

On the other hand, scholars for a very long time have been arguing that what defined and underpinned the Renaissance was, instead, "ideas," not appetites. It is all well and good to say that appetites fueled the Renaissance, but this understanding takes us only so far in allowing us to appreciate the distinctiveness of the period. It does not help us understand why certain forms of expression took the form they did and thus gave rise to the Renaissance as the Renaissance. The economic and social historian Richard Goldthwaite, for instance, can explain how palaces and churches were built in Florence through a close understanding of the construction industry and the guild system, even to the point where he meticulously calculates the calories an average worker needed to consume to work a full day. He can also explain convincingly the economic conditions that made possible the accumulation of wealth and thus the impressive consumption of art needed to fill up those houses, palaces, private chapels, and churches, all of which would have required collectively a plethora of durable goods to furnish them adequately, from paintings to sculptures to books to hope chests to tiny votive offerings.[60] But he cannot explain through an examination of the economic and social conditions that made possible the accumulation of worldly goods, or through the identification of new consumption habits that emerged in Italy for the first time in the Renaissance, why palaces took the shapes they did, why patrons preferred certain styles of art, and why different artists strove to represent reality in their specific manner. He cannot (nor does he aim to) explain the privileging of one "style" over another, which is what marked so much of the Renaissance in Italy. Economic and social historians invested in a demand-side interpretation of the Renaissance can explain the conditions for a certain type of lifestyle, in which a new relationship with objects potentially appeared for the first time in the West and the creation of a new sort of culture of consumers emerged, but they have not been able to account for the particular choices made by patrons regarding their style of living and their preferences for specific styles of art, which is what makes the Renaissance, as a period style, the Renaissance. Only the impact of certain ideas at the expense of others in response to those worldly goods in a Renaissance of avid consumers "on an extended shopping spree," as Randolph Starn has jovially put it, can adequately explain why both patrons and artists made certain choices about the objects furnished and often cherished.[61]

This book operates on the assumption that ideas are central to much of the art of the period and that appetites, the raw hunger to consume on an impressive scale, fueled the production of this art. However, this is not a book about appetites *per se*, though it is concerned at times with the material conditions that made possible this aspect of the Italian Renaissance. This is not a book about how much anyone did or did not really consume, but about how *ideas* related to appetites took shape and are represented in works of visual and verbal art, in often complex ways and as a matter of intellectual and aesthetic concern. It is also concerned not just with durable goods but also with nondurable products for consumption. Hence, in the section devoted to food, I am not particularly interested in what Aretino and Michelangelo actually ate (though sometimes information to that effect does come into play in the individual chapters). And I am not concerned with trying to ascertain whether Michelangelo or Aretino ate what they claimed they did when they bought or received gifts of food. Rather, I am interested in how these men represented the idea of food and consumption in their works and how this representation served to construct and reflect a certain type of identity. Similarly, in the section dedicated to objects I am not particularly concerned with the material conditions that fed the hunger for objects of all types, shapes, and sizes in Renaissance Italy, from books (of the sort that the polygraph Doni spent part of his life making and writing) to jewelry (of the sort that the goldsmith-turned-sculptor Cellini spent much of his life fashioning, and eventually boasted about having crafted in an impressive quantity to meet an enormous consumer demand). Rather, in this book I concentrate on the representation of the appetite for objects (visual art objects of all sorts, as well as books as collectable, durable goods), and how Doni and Cellini responded to the demand for those objects by writing and behaving, or appearing to behave, in certain ways. My concern, then, is with representations of selfhood, with the understanding, of course, that representations are always "facts" in and of themselves and that they can have historical importance and impact, much as the "documents" used to establish the veracity of certain events in the past are always in and of themselves representations open to rhetorical analysis.

In this respect, the overall aims of this book fit well within the sort of inquiry that has animated much discussion of so-called Renaissance self-fashioning, though with some reservations and qualifications regarding the "New Historicist" approach to the concept. For instance, I do not view the "self" in the Italian Renaissance, a period that ranges roughly from 1350 to 1600 for the purpose of this study, as an empty cipher onto which familial, political, social, educational, and economic forces have freely inscribed themselves, thus rendering the self merely the product of those forces and thereby completely vitiated of "agency." Indeed, there is sufficient evidence from the work of social and cultural historians, from Ronald Weissman to John Jeffries Martin, Guido Ruggiero to Elizabeth Horodowich, Peter Burke to Lauro Martines, that the self in the Italian Renaissance, far from being a mere shackled historical and discursive construct, was, as Thomas Greene aptly put it long ago, "flexible." In particular the self, these and other scholars have come to insist, was embedded in a host of social activities, from politics to gossip to money lending, all of which required negotiation of competing, interpersonal social obligations in a manner that enhanced selfhood, rather than completely determining it. At the same time the self could express itself imaginatively not only through the established, classical virtue of "prudence," but also, just as important, through the newly theorized, burgeoning virtue of "sincerity." It was at once "porous" and open to influences, as well as "layered" and complex in its overall constitution. And the self, as it mediated between the interior and the exterior, stood in Renaissance Italy at the center of what one scholar has called "consensus realities" of local and extended communities, networks, and affiliations in which identities were "to a great degree based upon a performance of self and a negotiation of self with the groups with which a person interacted."[62] It should be clear that in taking this stance with regard to self-fashioning I am not advocating a return to the Burckhardtian, essentialized notion of the "individual" emerging with "free, unfettered subjectivity" in the Italian Renaissance, any more than I am attempting to mystify the Renaissance self, though I do maintain that some Italian writers and artists labored to mystify their innate abilities and ingegno even as they sought to lay bare their strategies of professional know-how through a language of demystification.[63]

Additionally, what distinguishes the nature of self-fashioning in Renaissance Italy, and what marks it off, for example, from that of medieval Italy, is not only the sheer quantity of it but often enough the quality of it, as selfhood found truly widespread expression in the writing and art that has survived in abundance from the period. Dante Alighieri, to take a familiar example, investigated expressions of the self within an overarching theological framework in his *Divina commedia*, much as he explored the development of the self in his *Vita nuova*, again adapting the evolution of selfhood to the Christian model of *imitatio*. Certainly a number of Renaissance writers, from Petrarch to Ariosto to Tasso, looked to Dante as a way of conceptualizing the self, especially as the self finds expression in and through moments and periods of "crisis" or through the posturing of a new type of authorial voice. And one can argue strenuously along with Albert R. Ascoli for the prescient modernity of Dante's creative, authorial presence.[64] But one never finds in Dante's works, much less those of any extant major author of the Italian Middle Ages, writings that even begin to approach the far-reaching protean treatment of selfhood explored, say, in Machiavelli's letter to Vettori, where the number of roles adopted by a single person in the brief course of a single day are so fluid and manifold and contradictory as to mark a decisive break with prior, established patterns for expressing and modeling selfhood.[65]

Something new is taking place here, much as something new appears to be forming in the writings of Petrarch about the nature of selfhood, whether or not we choose to view Petrarch as marking for historiographical purposes the beginning of humanism, as has traditionally been the case, or prefer to apply pressure to that concept, as Ronald Witt has done, and situate him as an extension of, if not in fact a reactionary deviation from, early forms of humanism.[66] To be sure, in the end we can attribute the shift from a medieval to a Renaissance notion of selfhood—a shift that we should by no means view as smooth, monolithic, uniform, or teleological in nature—to a number of contributing factors, some of which would no doubt bear more weight than others for most scholars: a new conception of historicism and novel analytical approach to the classical past; the development of philology; changes in professional needs and modes of notarial writing; shifts in family structures and relations; the birth of humanism; the restructuring of educational practices; perhaps even the changing nature of "appetites" in the period and the creation of new habits of consumption. Yet, however we account for this shift in the notion and expression of selfhood as we move from the Middle Ages to the Renaissance in Italy, it does appear from the work of historians, art historians, and literary scholars that the shift did indeed take place. Historically this is significant in and of itself, whether or not we can come up with a universally acceptable, unifying explanation that can account adequately for "why" it took place.

This book, then, addresses the basic concern of Renaissance self-fashioning by examining men who were represented, or represented themselves, as flouting on the grand scale the niceties of decorum in sixteenth-century Italy. It is these men, who violated the widely accepted and increasingly codified norms of decorum, who are the heroes of this book, rather than such courtly luminaries as Pietro Bembo, Ludovico Ariosto, Donato Bramante, and Raphael, who moved through society with breathtaking sprezzatura, or even those who sometimes wrote salacious or indecorous verse or prose but were known generally for being polished, decorous courtiers, such as Annibale Caro. It goes without saying, moreover, that authors emerging from low and popular culture were sometimes anticonformist and aggressively conspicuous in their anticonformism in Renaissance Italy, from the Florentine barber poet Burchiello, who entertained people in his shop, to the impoverished Bolognese blacksmith turned poet Giulio Cesare Croce, who entertained people on the street. We would naturally expect this to be the case. It is quite another matter, however, to see authors and visual artists who aspired to be part of court culture, or embraced by the cultural elite in some measure, behaving in such untoward ways and often refusing to back down when facing their social superiors.

Adhering to decorum was universally perceived as a crucial tool for social advancement and for surviving in elitist Renaissance Italian culture, as della Casa advised in his etiquette treatise, the *Galateo*. Discretion (*discrezione*), understood as a prudential virtue, as a way of being "discreet" in the eyes of others, assisted ambitious people in a world where it was important not to stick out too much in tightly woven and intensely gossipy communities. Discretion indeed allowed one to enhance one's position in the eyes of others, as Francesco Guicciardini advised in his *Ricordi*, a series of personal reflections and maxims that he put together for himself and his family. Seeking the Aristotelian mean between extremes aided one in being virtuous and thus in acquiring recognition from the prince whose favor one desperately sought to gain in the court, as Castiglione advanced in his landmark *Cortegiano*. Needless to say, for della Casa, Guicciardini, and Castiglione fame was a necessary good, as were ambition and family pride and self-promotion, but being *too* conspicuous in an effort to be recognized was not. It was important for these authors, as it was for so many others, to control affect and the aggressive physical presentation of the self. However, behavior that was conspicuous, aggressive, and indiscreet—a matter of getting in another person's face and exhibiting professional improprieties from time to time—also offered a viable way of presenting the self in sixteenth-century Italy, and some sought to do so on the grand scale.

In this light, we may consider in closing the writer Torquato Tasso (1544–1595), who, albeit insane at times, can function in this book as a proleptic counterexample to both Castiglione, the man of emblematic tact and propriety in the period, and Aretino, Michelangelo, Cellini, and Doni, the four privileged heroes of professional impropriety. Although Tasso was a brilliant and polished courtier, he sometimes lacked professional propriety, most notably in 1579. In that year, just five years after the death of Doni, the professional poet in the service of Duke Alfonso II found himself taken from the presence of his patron, escorted to prison, and placed in a solitary cell for an indefinite period.[67] This man, great humanist poet that he was, had already gotten in other people's faces once too often. On one occasion (the one occasion, we might posit, in which he should have been tossed out of the court), Tasso acted like a maniac: he attacked one of the duke's own ministers, assaulting him with a knife. But in 1579, Tasso went one step too far when he blurted out insulting remarks about the duke, which only a person who had lost his wits would have ever dared do in the absolutist courts of late-Renaissance, post-Tridentine Italy. Even worse for Tasso, his disruptive and indecorous outburst occurred during the period surrounding the celebrations of Alfonso II's wedding to Margherita Gonzaga, when the center of attention was supposed to be the duke and his bride, *not* the court's prized poet, who surely managed to get all eyes focused on him as a result of his untoward behavior. To be sure, despite all the research done on Tasso and his life, it is still not clear what particular event provoked this outburst. But whatever the specific cause, the gist of Tasso's complaint is clear. Tasso felt neglected, even slighted, and this in its turn led him to make one of the biggest blunders of his life.[68]

At first glance, it is odd that Tasso would have ever managed to displease the duke so much as to warrant imprisonment. Even a cursory glance at any of his major writings, from his dialogues to his epics to his letters, reveals a man who showcased his need to subordinate himself at every turn, though in the case of the *Gerusalemme liberata* it is possible to reconfigure this act of subordination in literary and psychological terms as constituting a covert strategy on Tasso's part to reacquire mastery over his superiors through the cunning creation of an all-powerful, authorial voice. Tasso presents himself, for instance, as just a needy servant in his *Gerusalemme liberata*, but he then occupies the position of an omniscient God. He frames himself as Alfonso's son in need of guidance, but then he patronizingly guides Alfonso as if the duke were all along in need of edification.[69] From a slightly different vantage point, in which identity is always construed as a fiction constructed through a necessarily endless process of differentiation, we can perhaps say that the differences without (the opposition between the superior prince and the inferior poet) are really foils for the differences within (Tasso displaces his own irreconcilable, repressed conflicts inside himself onto others so that he can create differentiation and thus, arguably, an identity).[70] Still, subordination, at least on the face of it, would seem to be the name of the game for Tasso, who was well aware in post-Tridentine Italy that there were inferiors and superiors in the world. And Tasso was also aware that those superiors could lop off the heads of inferiors or, at the very least, toss them into prison. Above all, Tasso was aware that superiors always had to be obeyed.

Nowhere does Tasso make his understanding about the hierarchical structure of the court more evident than in his dialogue on the court itself, which he composed while in prison, and thus while he was yearning, as is evident in all his letters from that period of his life, to be restored to the duke's good graces. In the *Malpiglio overo de la corte* (1585), which draws on Castiglione's *Cortegiano* while revising it dramatically to fit the more oppressive tenor of the time, Tasso observes that the function of the courtier in late-sixteenth-century Italy is not to stand out and speak his mind but to obey every command without a qualm. The courtier, who must prudently dissimulate in order to survive within the tense atmosphere of the court, has in effect become a tight-lipped secretary, as secretarial treatises defined the profession during the late sixteenth century.[71] Tasso's courtier knows the autocratic power of the potentate. To get ahead he must dutifully, silently, and inconspicuously obey without hesitation. This subordinating courtier is, and always will remain, an inferior, despite the greatness of the mind he possesses:

> Neapolitan Stranger: The courtier's prudence, then, will consist in carrying out the prince's orders.
>
> Giovanlorenzo Malpiglio: So it seems to me.
>
> [...]

N.S.: Then a courtier who expresses his inferiority by obeying promptly and agreeing humbly makes himself pleasing to his prince.

G.M.: I agree.

N.S.: But since the intellect is by nature to rule, it seems that the man who possesses superior prudence ought not to be considered inferior for any reason. And this is why princes usually hate any greatness of mind. When a courtier has greatness of mind, which sometimes happens, he ought to cover it modestly, not show it off with pride [172–75].

Even if we imagine that Tasso is revealing through this fictional exchange the covert truth of the courtier's superiority, a superiority conferred on the courtier because he *knows* that he must cover up his greatness of mind in order to please the prince with all apparent humility, the fact remains that the prince, who necessarily conditions the courtier's comportment, is the person in power. And thus the prince ineluctably forces the courtier into acquiring some knowledge of himself as a subject as the courtier self-consciously subjects himself to the autocratic power of the court. The prince alters the courtier's perhaps natural drive to display his greatness of mind, his yearning perhaps to be "sincere" and express his inner feelings through the language of the heart, but the courtier prudently redirects that drive for public recognition and personal expression into highly self-reflexive acts of calculated subordination and self-effacement.

Unlike the courtier described in Tasso's *Malpiglio*, the men explored in the core chapters of this book were ostensibly everything but subordinate (and, parenthetically, most of them also often liked having a good laugh, unlike the mirthless Tasso). Moreover, if Tasso himself proved to be just too conspicuous for the duke at times, and if he acted with reproachable professional impropriety on occasion, he can be excused in some measure. Mentally he was not well. And if his manic impulses led him sometimes to act out both inappropriately and too conspicuously by showing off rather than decorously concealing his feelings and greatness of mind, Tasso's judgment always led him to temper his aggressive impulses and show respect for his place, the place of others, and the order of the cosmos, at least when he was in full possession of his wits. One of Tasso's great talents, which he perfected at an early age as an eager and accomplished student of the court, was to make amends so that he could return to the court from which he originally came and to which he felt so bound from his early childhood on.

Aretino, Michelangelo, Cellini, and Doni, it would seem, behaved differently. In full possession of their wits, they enjoyed putting themselves out there, engaging in a good fight. No one would take them down; not a prince, not the pope. If they were imprisoned, they'd escape, as Cellini described himself doing with flashy, self-aggrandizing drama. They were represented, and repeatedly represented themselves, as stubborn, intractable, and sometimes obnoxious men, all of them lacking, at one point or another, professional propriety. Woe to you if you should ever incur the wrath of Aretino; a flood of vituperation would drown you. Much the same can be said of Doni, who lambasted Aretino and tried to bury under vindictive sarcasm his erstwhile friend Lodovico Domenichi to the point of near oblivion. Cross Cellini in some manner, and rest assured (he repeatedly seems to warn us in his autobiography) he will denounce you vehemently, fly into a state of wild destructive rage, or stab you in the gut. Michelangelo's wrath and bad temper were, of course, legendary, part and parcel of his terribilità. True, these men knew well the rules of decorum when they needed to ingratiate themselves, and they could deploy the art of dissimulation to try to slip out of the clutches of people trying to pin them down, just as they understood, and could and did indeed employ, the language of courtly grazia, sprezzatura, and *bon giudicio* (good judgment). Nevertheless, so often their aim was not to be decorously conspicuous in the manner of Castiglione or Vasari, but aggressively and indecorously conspicuous in their professional improprieties. And it was to that end that these men, who lived in a society dominated by court culture, dedicated much of their art.

PART ONE

Diplomacy

CHAPTER 1

Baldassar Castiglione and the Art of Being Inconspicuously Conspicuous

Prologue

"Now finding myself in Spain. . . ." So begins a sentence early on in the first paragraph of Baldassar Castiglione's "Letter to the Reverend and Illustrious Signor Don Michel de Silva, Bishop of Viseu," which forms the preface to the *editio princeps* of his *Libro del Cortegiano*, printed in Venice in 1528 by the heirs of the Aldine press.[1] Castiglione wrote this new preface while in Spain, as is evident from the phrase just quoted. But what he fails to mention in this letter—and purposely so—is that he was Clement VII's official resident ambassador to the court of the Emperor Charles V when he wrote it in the spring of 1527. This position, to which Castiglione was appointed on July 19, 1524, was an important and prestigious one. Being the pope's ambassador to Charles V, his *nuncius apostolicus*, was no small task. It involved daily meetings; a constant sifting through reports and rumors; the need to appear knowledgeable even while largely clueless about what was going on in the privy cabinets of the courts in Spain and Italy; little time for domestic affairs; constant attention to diplomatic details and personal monetary problems; a great deal of formal staging, orations, and presentations; the careful weighing of words so as not to appear, as one French ambassador did, both rude and threatening before the emperor; and the voluntary offering of advice to the pope back home and the proffering of advice when asked for it. Last but not least, at stake was the great peace of Christendom, as Castiglione never failed to mention in his letters. Being the papal nunzio to the court of Spain was a position of profound influence, and it was not bestowed lightly on him. Castiglione understood the importance of the position, as he makes plain in letters to both the Marquis Federico Gonzaga and pope Clement VII,[2] and he hoped he could use the office to help bring about positive change in a dangerous political climate. With the emperor threatening to invade Italy and the king of France captured and then, once released, still bent on securing tracts of Italy for himself, Castiglione did his best to work for universal tranquility during a period of tremendous instability.[3] Peace and the good of humankind were as important to him when he was an ambassador in Spain as they had been earlier when he was writing the *Cortegiano*. "And to be always at war," Ottaviano Fregoso remarks in the fourth book of the *Cortegiano*, "without seeking to arrive at the end which is peace, is not right" (311, 438). Castiglione expresses much the same concept over and over again in his letters sent to Italy while ambassador in Spain. "Certainly I will use everything," he wrote in one instance, "that I think can be put to use in order to work for the universal good of all [*al bene universale*], and since God has granted me the grace [grazia] that the emperor and these other lords respect me, I will do everything in my power to see to it that all my efforts aim to this end" (P 2.107).

As prestigious as this ambassadorial position was in early-sixteenth-century Italy, Castiglione does not give us any information about his work in Spain in the *Cortegiano*, either in the overarching preface to the book, where one might expect it to appear, or in the individual prefatory remarks framing the four separate books that make up the larger completed work we read. Instead, in the preface to Don Michel de Silva and the opening remarks to each book, Castiglione talks about matters that have to do with language, literary and rhetorical models, fashion, the distorted perspective afforded through aging, the passing of time, the influence of the body over perception, youth, ideal human proportions, the nature of fortune, accusations of effeminacy within the court, women, decorum, custom, envy, the uses and abuses of nostalgia, the death of beloved friends, the passing away of a cherished and laudable woman, the beauty and centrality of Urbino, the future of Urbino, and the glory of the ducal palace of Urbino. Nowhere, however, does Castiglione state that he occupied, and was still occupying, one of the most important and influential posts in Christendom. In fact, the only explicit glimpse we have of Spain itself, despite Castiglione's lengthy sojourn there, comes in the five words cited at the opening of this chapter. Nevertheless, my claim is that Castiglione's ambassadorial service in Spain is important, for it forces us, at the very least, not only to rethink the preface to Don Michel de Silva (who was once a long-time ambassador from Portugal to the court in Rome) but also, more generally, the role of professional expertise in the *Cortegiano*. In the broadest terms, thinking about his ambassadorial work reveals that Castiglione differentiated in some measure between professional roles and goals in the *Cortegiano*. Courtiers working at the court of their prince at home in Italy did one thing, while courtiers working as ambassadors representing the prince in another court away from home did quite another, even though many of their duties overlapped. Both the courtier at home and the courtier as ambassador away from home offered advice, for example, but the advice delivered came in differing contexts and environments, with the two acting out fundamentally divergent roles professionally in relation to the prince.

Specifically, with regard to the *Cortegiano*, my argument is this. By situating the conversations that took place in Urbino during the period when he was abroad as an ambassador in England, Castiglione means for us to recognize that he was both selected and "elect." After some deliberation, Duke Guidobaldo of Urbino specifically chose to send Castiglione there. And he chose Castiglione because he was the best and most honorable person for the post, which required a man of learning, respect, tact, and dignified social standing. Castiglione had proven himself a fine orator, and Guidobaldo could rest assured that he would be well represented by his eloquent and refined courtier.[4] Being chosen for this task literally sets Castiglione apart. Indeed, it sets him right outside the confines of the enclosed circle of the courtiers gathered together in the evenings in Urbino. However, because Castiglione's ambassadorial work places him outside the scope of discussion of the courtiers, which aims to elevate the courtier at home as an intimate counselor and educator of the prince, Castiglione avoids calling too much attention to himself. On the one hand, his aim in mentioning that he was sent away as ambassador is to be conspicuous, for he would surely have us view him as worthy since he was the person chosen to represent the duke. On the other hand, Castiglione also aims to avoid being *too* conspicuous, for it would only invite invidious comparison in a book in which all the courtiers are seen as potentially equal during the course of the evening games. In the *Cortegiano* each courtier must be viewed as worthy as the other, coming from numerous parts of Italy to form by geographical union a conceptual consensus through dialogue.[5] Moreover, being too conspicuous would only undermine (1) the underlying aim of the book, which is to elevate the courtier as an independent, autonomous figure within the court, an educator who can forcefully challenge the prince; and (2) the harmonious, integrated structure of the book, which is focused on a closed group in a single emblematic court and not those who work outside it at various courts about Europe. Ambassadorship therefore is not—nor can it be—the subject of the *Cortegiano* even as (or arguably precisely because) Castiglione is engaged in ambassadorial work within the fiction of the text. If, then, Castiglione later omits mentioning his role as the papal nunzio in Spain in his new prefatory letter, it is not because he deemed it unimportant, but because ambassadorial work just did not fit conceptually or formally into the scope of the *Cortegiano*. Ambassadorial work is thus superfluous to the *Cortegiano* as a whole and cannot fit into the book in a central way, yet it remains crucial to the book's structure, since ambassadorial work is precisely what Castiglione was doing when he was off in England (as the conversations he "records" ostensibly took place) and when he was off in Spain (as he wrote the final authorized preface shortly before the Sack of Rome).

Before considering these matters, however, it would be best to review some events in Castiglione's life, particularly those that have to do with his work as a courtier and diplomat, as well as his training to become one.[6] Born in Casatico near Mantua in 1478, Castiglione descended from a family of repute. He therefore possessed the lineage and, what is more, the financial means to pursue a career as a courtier. His schooling in Milan at the Sforza court, which attracted a number of luminaries, involved him in a humanist education, so it is hardly surprising that his writings reveal a close understanding of Cicero's *De oratore*, Quintilian's *Institutio oratoria*, Plutarch's *Lives* and *Moralia*, Xenophon's *Memorabilia* and *Cyropaedia*, Aulus Gellius's *Noctes atticae*, Homer's *Iliad*, Aristotle's *Ethics* and *Politics*, Plato's *Republic*, *Symposium*, and *Protagoras*, and the poetry of Catullus. As is to be expected, Castiglione's Latinity was excellent, and he read and wrote widely in the vernacular. His diplomatic work extended over a broad period, beginning in roughly 1505 with his aborted attempt to represent Guidobaldo at the court of the Marquis Francesco II Gonzaga (his former lord, who had cooled toward Castiglione once he left Mantua) and ending with his years as the nuncius apostolicus in Spain. After Guidobaldo's death in 1508, Castiglione remained at Urbino and served the new duke, Francesco Maria della Rovere, who appears as the young prefect in the *Cortegiano*. Working diplomatically for della Rovere over the next several years, he was sent to Rome as the resident ambassador of Urbino in 1513. Later, he worked for Federico Gonzaga and served him as the resident ambassador of Mantua in Rome in 1519 and 1522. Castiglione's diplomatic work took him far and wide, from England to France to Spain, but much of it took place in Rome, where he forged a network of connections and kept in touch with friends, old and new. No trace of Castiglione's diplomatic work, however, ever found its way directly into the *Cortegiano*, which he painstakingly revised once he began to write it shortly after 1513. He completed the first version in 1514–1516, the second in 1520–1521, and the third, which gave the book its final four-part shape, in 1521–1524.[7] Significantly, Castiglione's greatest influence on others came not through his important diplomatic work, through which he had hoped to make a lasting difference by reconciling the emperor and the pope after the Sack of Rome, but through his book, which Charles V claimed to keep by his bedside along with the Bible and was widely translated and imitated throughout the European Renaissance.[8]

The Cortegiano: *Courtiers and Ambassadors*

In the *Cortegiano*, Castiglione is not at all interested in particulars as far as particulars are concerned. As a writer he is not, that is, interested in caressing the details, as Vladimir Nabokov once put it, so that the particulars might stand out and call attention to themselves in all their self-referential, literary glory. Like Plato, Aristotle, and Cicero, three classical authors whose writings served as major models for the composition of the *Cortegiano*, Castiglione is instead interested in particulars as subordinated (though necessary) parts of an integrated, harmonious whole.[9] This is true, for instance, with regard to Castiglione's notion of the courtier's person as it relates to both ethics and aesthetics (97–98, 147–48). Moreover, that Castiglione ultimately privileges the whole over the part is also true with regard to his notion of sprezzatura, for what is at stake is ultimately a gestalt, a total, comprehensive effect.[10] Sprezzatura involves, among other things, an ability on the part of the courtier to make people think a far greater ability lies concealed from public view, an ability that remains untapped but nevertheless, were it to be put into action and revealed, would naturally find a proper end in a perfected, complete performance.[11] The courtier's sprezzatura is therefore recessive in the very moment that it is suggestive of a larger whole. Once we see a courtier ride a horse brilliantly, then we assume that he rides well all the time, since we are inclined to seek the harmonious whole from a particular. In this respect, it is essential that nothing stick out too much and thereby call attention to itself too conspicuously, for that would only undermine either our ability to grasp the whole from the particular or, just as important, our ability to seize freely with our imagination a whole extrapolated from the particular that is calculatingly revealed to us for public viewing. A sliver of whiteness revealed at the edge of a courtier's sleeve or collar in a Renaissance painting stands in for the presumed whiteness and general *pulitezza* of the entire clean shirt concealed beneath the covering garment. Psychologically, for Castiglione, our imagination simply works toward completeness as we—or the viewers taking in the courtier's performance—fantasize about "something more than what you will see" (130, 187).[12] We must therefore make every effort as courtiers to ease the natural working of the mind of the observer in that regard by carefully limiting and selecting what we expose to view. This is the case not only when it concerns the courtier's behavior as he exercises sprezzatura, but his ideal physical shape as well. Consider, for instance, the bald head. In a phrase, Castiglione would have us understand, we should be careful if or how we show it.[13] In some instances it will only invite us to fantasize that the rest of the courtier's body happens to be less than perfect. Best to dissimulate, or, to use the terms of Torquato Accetto, best to dissimulate honestly. The classic formulation of this concept in the *Cortegiano* occurs early on in the first book, not long after Count Ludovico da Canossa has articulated the notion of sprezzatura as the art of hiding art (46, 68).

To reveal only the right amount of oneself, be it with regard to one's abilities or physical qualities, requires some forethought on the part of the courtier, and it necessitates a balancing act of competing desires. On the one hand, the courtier desires to be recognized; on the other, he does not want to be *too* recognized. The courtier, after all, aims to be seen; one of his principal efforts is dedicated to attracting "the eyes of the bystanders, as the lodestone [attracts] iron" (100, 150). He must strive to be "outstanding" (*eccellente*; 38, 56). He must visibly surpass the French by leaps and bounds in what they are best at, the Spaniards in the natural talents of their professed skills. Only by being seen can the courtier catch the eye of the prince and acquire his favor (grazia), which is what the courtier really desires, even more than the collective approval of other like-minded courtiers, who may claim him as one of their own and look on warmly as they watch him put sprezzatura into action. "You may also take it to be implied in our rule," Federico Gonzaga observes, "that whenever the Courtier chances to be engaged in a skirmish or an action or a battle in the field, or the like, he should discreetly withdraw from the crowd, and do the assigned and daring things that he has to do in as small a company as possible and in the sight of all the noblest and most respected men in the army, and especially in the presence of and, if possible, before the very eyes of his king or the prince he is serving" (99, 149). Nevertheless, in the process of trying to "feed his spectators' eyes with all those things that it will seem to him may give him added grace" (99), and in the process of excelling beyond the bounds of everyone else so that he is literally outstanding, the adroit courtier does not want to be *too* recognized, for that would only destroy the overall impression of a well-constructed, complete person—the courtier's *integrità* and professional propriety.[14] So Castiglione observes in the *Cortegiano* in a number of cases how we must avoid "ostentation above all things" (34, 47). One must therefore be, in essence, inconspicuously conspicuous, evident in the crowd but not too evident, noticeable but not too noticeable. Excessive conspicuousness, for this reason, is aligned with affectation (affettazione), which destroys the overall effect that the courtier wishes to convey about himself. "How much more pleasing and how much more praised is a gentleman who bears arms, and who is modest, speaking little and boasting little, than another who is forever praising himself, swearing and blustering about as if to threaten the whole world—which is simply the affectation of wanting to appear bold. The same holds true in every practice, rather, in anything in this world one might do or say" (*anzi in ogni cosa che al mondo fare o dir si possa*; 45, 66).

In anything in this world one might do or say, it bears emphasizing. The single blemish of affectation, like a brazenly bald head, only invites the prince—

as well as competitive courtiers adept at uncovering defects in others with their keen ears and sharp eyes—to assume that the rest of the courtier is perhaps similarly blemished. If you stick out too much, you get known for being just too known. Hence, as Federico Fregoso summarily observes in the dialogue,

> let [the courtier] have the discretion and good judgment to know how to bring people adroitly and opportunely to see and hear what he considers himself to excel in, always seeming to do this not for ostentation, but casually as if he were begged by others than because he wishes it. And in everything that he has to do or say, let him, if possible, always come prepared and ready, but give the appearance that all is done on the spur of the moment. But, as for those things in which he feels himself to be mediocre, let him touch on them in passing, without dwelling much upon them, though in such a way that one might believe he knows much more about them than he shows, like certain poets who have sometimes suggested the most subtle things in philosophy or other sciences, and instead they understood very little about them [136–37, 195].

Here as elsewhere in the *Cortegiano*, less is always more, as the courtier borrows his strategy of performance and professional propriety from both poetry and rhetoric and, through sprezzatura, balances the need of being seen and not too visible, of being recognized and not ostentatious, of showing off a talent and not being viewed as a show-off, of exhibiting himself and not being an exhibitionist, of being outstanding and not physically standing out too much. This is the courtier's craft, his *arte* of being inconspicuously conspicuous as he manipulates our desire to imagine a complete, integrated whole through the calculated and suggestive unveiling of only a part of his abilities.

Now, to say that Castiglione himself, the man in flesh and blood who actually wrote and rewrote the *Cortegiano* over roughly a ten-year period, was known as a dazzling courtier of marked professional propriety is also to say that he consciously aimed to be known. Castiglione worked hard to position himself so that others would recognize him. This is the man, after all, who felt compelled to employ the false modesty topos at the outset of the *Cortegiano* in order to insist, as he puts sprezzatura into action, that the portrait conveyed in his book was not in any way a self-portrait, as Vittoria Colonna, waxing eulogistic, had suggested it was in a letter.[15] Clearly someone could mistake Castiglione for the perfect courtier fashioned in the book. That this was done on at least one occasion tells us how highly Castiglione was esteemed and how well known he was as a superb courtier (and we may reasonably doubt that Vittoria Colonna was alone in her assessment, even if we accept that people were inclined to make all sorts of inflated, ingratiating statements in their letters). Needless to say, Castiglione would have us know how highly he was esteemed at the outset of the *Cortegiano*, just as he would have us know that some people could and did take him as the embodiment of the perfect courtier. To borrow from the language of the *Cortegiano*, "In my opinion it all consists in saying things in such a way that they do not appear to be spoken to that end, but happen to be so very apropos that one cannot help saying them; and to always seem to avoid praising one's self, yet do so" (34, 48). Castiglione may protest that he should not be taken (or mistaken) for the perfect courtier, his only task therefore having putatively been to paint a verbal portrait of himself while looking at the mirror, but readers may still persist, rightly or wrongly, in seeing him as precisely that perfect courtier. "Indeed," Castiglione avers through the voice of Count Ludovico da Canossa, "even if he knows that the praises bestowed upon him are true, let him not assent to them too openly, nor concede them without some protest" (71, 111). It is best to accept conspicuous praise inconspicuously, with grace and without the slightest hint of affectation. This form of behavior, modeled on the classical virtue of *mediocritas*, constitutes a salient mark of professional propriety within the "new" profession of the courtier explored by Castiglione in his book.[16]

Indeed, Castiglione worked hard throughout his life, as he did in his book, to control his self-presentation and avoid appearing too conspicuous. He wore the right hat to cover his baldness, as is evident in Raphael's portrait of him (Figure 2). And from what we know, as he grew older and perhaps naturally grayed in places, he never conspicuously dyed his hair, which would have elicited only scorn and laughter, as it does when the courtiers mock Morello da Ortona for precisely that reason: elderly men should not try too hard to disguise the passing of their years (107, 160). Instead, Castiglione cut a figure in just the right way, with maximum professional propriety and politia, even to the point where he would go into enormous debt to appear "just so" to everyone else.[17] He worked hard at his appearance and manners and abilities not just because he wanted to be welcomed by other courtiers as one of their own, accepted into their fold and counted as a fine, upstanding, honest courtier. True, as a number of scholars have observed, sprezzatura functions as a signaling device among the courtiers themselves so that they may function as a sort of professional group, a team.[18] *They* know that the courtier with grazia has labored hard to achieve the proper total effect. *They* can see the particular for what it is: a pose struck, for instance, to impress in just the right way, so that the grazia of the courtier comes off as a *je ne sais quoi*, as something natural, when instead it is highly confected. The other courtiers can detect all this and approve of his actions, as they might a winning performance in the theater. But ultimately the grazia of the courtier, as numerous scholars have also observed, serves to win the grazia of the prince, not the favor of the other courtiers. The courtier separates himself from the crowd and does something noticeable to "feed the spectators' eyes" because he wants to seize the attention of the prince. He wants that attention so that he can be taken into the prince's graces, serve him, and by serving have influence.

Having influence is the ultimate guiding aim of the courtier, the "final cause," in Aristotelian terms, of all that he hopes to accomplish. This notion lies at the heart of the professional scope of the *Cortegiano*, though it comes through forcefully only in the belatedly added fourth book, which has a Platonic flourish to it but nevertheless remains still fundamentally Aristotelian in outlook.[19] It is in the final, culminating book that Castiglione, always concerned with both praxis and theory, investigates most openly some of the professional concerns of the courtier. In the fourth book we are told that the courtier has a purpose in a profession that Castiglione had already envisioned, as early as his first preface, as new. In Aristotelian terms, there is a teleology to the courtier's existence, an end toward which all his efforts must strive. In one sense, the courtier is supposed to be a sort of *maestro di scuola*, who teaches the prince how he should conduct himself. In this respect the courtier has a profound influence on the development of the prince, an influence not unlike the pedagogical molding that took place in the humanist classroom as individuals were ideally shaped into moral citizens, though the edifying process now occurs in the court with a grown, mature man, not a young, impressionable boy.[20] However, as the prince's instructor (which, Amedeo Quondam rightly argues, remains a central theme of the *Cortegiano* from the earliest to latest versions),[21] the real professional aim of the courtier is to be an advisor. Broadly conceived, the *Cortegiano* is about how best to acquire the ear of the prince so as to give him counsel. More specifically, it is about how one can gain access to the prince through all sorts of strategies of comportment so that one can then offer counsel, influence events, and have a role in the shaping of the world of which one is always a part. Again, it bears repeating: the end, *il fin*, of the courtier is to serve his prince, but his larger aim is to serve the prince in order to have leverage so that the courtier, in all his wisdom, can influence world events. If the courtier must learn to dance well to win the grace of the prince, so be it; if he needs to be an instructor to teach the prince how to follow virtue, so be it. All these "ends" serve a larger end, the "final cause," which is the courtier's desire to shape the world for the better by counseling the prince to rule well. This is imperative, we learn, for at the moment bad princes abound. Hence, even though nothing of real consequence happens if someone—an affected courtier who lacks grazia, for example—sings poorly or dances clumsily, we face dire consequences if a prince actually fails to govern well: "Take note that ignorance of music, of dancing, of horsemanship, does no harm to anyone. . . . But from not knowing how to govern peoples there come so many woes, deaths, destructions, burnings, ruins, that it may be said to be the deadliest plague that one can find on earth" (292, 415). In the short run, then, the courtier's failure in performing well before the prince makes little difference; but in the long run his failure to guide the prince properly makes all the difference in the world. Only the good courtier, who has won the favor of the prince through all his strategies of ingratiating himself, can help avert disaster, which makes his daily comportment critical to his overall professional success:

I say, then, that, since the princes of today are so corrupted by evil customs and by ignorance and a false esteem of themselves, and since it is so difficult to show them the truth and lead them to virtue, and since men seek to gain their favor by means of lies and flatteries and such vicious ways—the Courtier, through those fair qualities that Count Ludovico and messer Federico have given him, can easily, and must, seek to gain the good will and captivate the mind of his prince that he may have free and sure access to speak to him of anything whatever without being annoying [293, 417].

There is, however, yet another important role for the courtier. This role is represented by the absent presence of the writer himself, who reminds us that he did not attend the festive conversations that took place over four days at Urbino. At that very moment, in the early spring of 1507 when these discussions were occurring in a sort of Platonic symposium, Castiglione was ostensibly on a diplomatic mission for Duke Guidobaldo within the fiction of the dialogue. Castiglione had in fact already returned home by that time, but no matter; the slight deviation in actual chronology works to Castiglione's advantage and his narrative purpose. The duke, in fact, chose Castiglione to be sent to the court of King Henry VII in England to receive on his behalf the Order of the Garter. At this event Castiglione had to be knighted, for only a knight could enter into the distinguished company of honored men and receive the Garter in another's stead. Furthermore, it is clear from Castiglione's letters that as he began to think about the possibility of being selected for the mission, he was fully aware of the great honor that would be bestowed on him if he were chosen to travel to England on behalf of Guidobaldo. Indeed, early on he seems eager to learn if he will be selected. "As to what you say of my probable journey to England," Castiglione confides to his mother, Luigia, with whom he so often corresponded over the course of his life, "I know nothing. My lord has not mentioned it to me, either with his own lips or through anyone else. All I know is that someone will have to go. Who it may be, I have not the least idea" (C 1.129).[22] A day later, on March 3, 1505, in yet another letter to his mother, Castiglione reveals himself to be suddenly more confident that his talents and birth would make him the proper and logical choice to be sent on such an important embassy:

As for going to England, I don't know anything else about it except that my Lord Duke must send a person, and has even told someone that he wants me to be the one. And when I go over the gentlemen of his household and their different offices, it is not hard for me to believe that the journey falls to me [*non mi è difficile credere che la andata tochi a me*]. The reason for sending someone there is for the confirmation of the privileges of the Order of the Garter that His Excellency is to receive from His Majesty the King, an order something like that of St. Michael in France. For this task it is necessary to send him a man of reputation, capable of solemn ceremony, and accepted by His Majesty the King, and much honored [*A questo bisogna mandarli homo da cunto, e cum gran solenità e acettato da la Maiestà del Re e molto honorato*]. It would take long to narrate about it all, for this order is established with great ceremony. So that if it should seem to His Excellency to choose me for this, I will not refuse it, for it is a most honorable thing, one from which I may also hope to profit, for I know I would go there with strong backing [*cum gran favore*; C, modified, 1.129–30, R 57–58].

Given the honor associated with this post (an honor that rewarded him with the title of knight), it may seem strange that Castiglione chose not to discuss the work of diplomacy, and more specifically the work of the ambassador in the *Cortegiano*. After all, this was the work in which Castiglione was engaged when the events in the book ostensibly took place, so it would seem only appropriate for the nature of ambassadorial duties to appear as at least one aspect of the professional concerns of the courtier. More to the point, ambassadorial work was typically one of the courtier's principal duties, one of the ends toward which he labored in the new profession being described by Castiglione. In Aristotelian terms, which are the terms that drive much of Castiglione's thinking about the notion of ends, it would have made perfect sense for Castiglione to have taken the time in the fourth book to discuss ambassadorial work since this was one of the expected abilities of the courtier. Princes often called on courtiers of good standing to represent them outside the confines of their realm. To be sure, as James Hankins has observed, it was a goal toward which Castiglione's own humanistic, rather than philosophical, education would have ineluctably led him: "He was trained to be an orator both in the Renaissance sense of the word—i.e., an ambassador—as well as in the Ciceronian sense. As a Ciceronian orator he would aim to be a statesman, 'a good man skilled in speaking,' *vir bonus dicendi peritus*, but also a man of broad general culture."[23] Ambassadorial *techne* would have therefore certainly made an apposite topic of conversation in the added fourth book, where the professional ends of the courtier are so openly investigated. In the process, Castiglione could have perhaps taken the opportunity to draw yet again on Quintilian and Cicero. Why, then, does Castiglione refuse to talk about ambassadorial work? This was the very work he was employed in at the time the conversations took place in Urbino in the early spring of 1507, at least in the fiction of the narrative. Ambassadorial work was precisely the kind of work for which Castiglione, like so many other courtiers engaged in the discussion, had been broadly prepared to do in the *studia humanitatis*.

First, we need to bear in mind that Castiglione does in fact want us to give some consideration to the work of the ambassador, even if he elided it in the discussion of the courtiers at Urbino. In framing the book, he could have used the opportunity to absent himself from the discussions among the courtiers in any number of ways, but he made a point of doing so during the period when he was engaged in ambassadorial work, even fudging the facts to do so (he was actually already home, as we have seen, when the discussions putatively took place). Thus Castiglione reminds us, if only obliquely, of the critical role of the courtier as ambassador by absenting himself within the dialogue as an ambassador. Second, in representing himself as the prince's ambassador while these conversations take place in the evenings at Urbino, Castiglione reminds us that, of all the courtiers present, he was the one considered worthiest of representing the duke. He was the chosen person of great professional propriety and requisite politia and should therefore be considered—even as he demurs in the preface—special. As with the art of sprezzatura, the mere mention of his embassy to England is enough to conjure up Castiglione's overall excellence. He may or may not be the perfect courtier that Vittoria Colonna suggested he was in a letter, but he was evidently deemed the worthiest courtier to represent the duke on such a special, ceremonial mission. Third, in functioning as an ambassador, though absent, Castiglione literally re-presents the prince abroad. According to standard diplomatic theory and practice, the ambassador representing a potentate functioned as a stand-in. In a real sense, he was the potentate's "other" body, as inviolate as if he were the prince himself.[24] Consequently, much like ambassadors today, Castiglione had diplomatic immunity (a diplomatic immunity that was not always observed at the time) because he was, in effect, the potentate himself. Hence, when Castiglione resided in England, he was treated *as if* he were Guidobaldo himself, as a functional double. When the English royalty regaled Castiglione with gifts, they bestowed those gifts on Castiglione himself, but also, at the same time conceptually through him, on the duke. When the hosts in England arranged a dinner to celebrate Guidobaldo's induction into the Order of the Garter in an elaborate ceremony, Castiglione sat in the place of honor, as if he were the duke himself who had received the Order of the Garter. When he ate, the food filled his body literally, but symbolically it filled the body of the duke. There was, then, no difference in the way he was treated than if he had been the duke himself. Yet it is worth remembering that Castiglione was not the duke in the very moment that he symbolically occupied his place and space as the duke's ambassador.

These considerations can help explain why Castiglione, even though his brief stay in England was an extremely positive experience, eschews the topic of ambassadorial work in his discourse—that is to say, why, in a real sense, he makes it both conspicuous (we are told he is away as the duke's ambassador) and inconspicuous (this fact is introduced only marginally in the book). In a court such as the one in Urbino, it was essential professionally for the courtier not to upstage another courtier too much. Arguably this would elicit envy, but also, and more important, other courtiers would view it as a sign of affectation and thus an act of professional impropriety. The courtier, to be sure, should call attention to himself but, as we have seen, not ostentatiously or obtrusively.

Things are significantly different for the ambassador, however. The ambassador, who is no longer in the presence of the prince, has already won the prince's favor. He is not looking to serve but considering *how* to serve in a manner that will best leave a positive, lasting impression, so that others will approve not only the ambassador but also, above all, the prince. Every move the ambassador makes can be interpreted as a shadow gesture of the prince's intent. If the ambassador speaks well, he speaks well as if he were the prince. If he behaves poorly, the prince's prestige suffers. When representing the prince in diplomatic affairs as his ambassador, then, the courtier does not need to think about the risks of upstaging other courtiers. Professionally, he must in essence be careful not to upstage the prince as he acts out the role of being his functional double. As the prince's representative, he therefore needs to calculate matters slightly differently than if he were back home at court. He is acting always on someone else's behalf as if he were that person, prepared to give counsel; but he is not, in the end, that person.

Theoretically, then, one of the worst mistakes an ambassador can make, beyond engaging in out-and-out treason or simply botching the job altogether, is to foreground himself at the risk of eclipsing the potentate for whom he stands in. Professionally, as an ambassador away from his court it is good to speak well, but the oratorical performance must always be viewed as belonging to someone else. The ambassador must always be viewed as the particular that reveals the whole—although the "particular" in this case does not point to the courtier himself but to his prince. Any error on the ambassador's part, any cause for censure, would reflect badly on the prince. And errors, we know from Castiglione, are something people love to seize on, "as men sometimes take so much delight in reproaching" (3, 4). As Castiglione warns even more forcefully in the second book: "For, truly, we are all by nature more ready to censure errors than to praise things well done; and many from a kind of innate malice, even when they clearly see the good, strive with all effort and care to discover some fault [*errore*] or at least something that seems a fault" (97, 147). One false slip by the ambassador, one simple act of professional impropriety, and not just his but more important his *prince's* reputation goes down the drain. The prince suffers the censure as if it were his own.

The *Cortegiano* therefore does not, and cannot, address matters of ambassadorial work because those matters take us far beyond the professional concerns that Castiglione means to address and resolve within the purview of his book. With its artful focus on a circumscribed group in a closed circle in Urbino, a group so taken with itself that the members forming a tight, self-enclosed collectivity are even capable of forgetting the passing of the night as they keep each other entertained with their verbal games,[25] the *Cortegiano* sets out to cover the role of the courtier as a subordinate who should nevertheless be viewed in his new profession as an essential part of a harmoniously working, self-regulating, and mutually edifying court.

So essential is the courtier to the construction of this ideally harmonious, integrated whole that the prince must take the courtier into consideration *at all times* if he is to persevere and prosper. The courtier at home is not the stand-in for the prince, though the choice of courtier will always tell us something about the prince's judgment and the sort of man he is. Rather, the courtier at home is the prince's intimate with whom he can exchange ideas and from whom he can freely seek advice. It is therefore essential in the *Cortegiano* that the courtier at home not be the prince's voice, his literal *portavoce*, much less his body doubled in so many figures sent to courts about the world, much as ambassadors, each bearing the word of the prince, might fan out across the realms of Italy, France, Spain, and England as specular embodiments of the prince. Instead, in the *Cortegiano*, with its focus on the ideally harmonious workings of Urbino, it is essential that the courtier appear as an independent thinker who can challenge the prince to view matters differently on occasion and thus, in the best of circumstances, persuade the prince (if indeed the prince is predisposed to receive advice, as good princes are) to follow the best possible path and thereby live a virtuous life:

> The aim [il fin] of the perfect Courtier, which we have not spoken of up to now, I judge is to win for himself, by means of the accomplishments ascribed to him by these gentlemen, the goodwill and the mind of the prince whom he serves that he may be able to tell him, and always will tell him, the truth about everything he needs to know, without fear or risk of displeasing him; and that when he sees the mind of his prince inclined to do something inopportune, he may dare to oppose him and in a gentle manner avail himself of the favor [grazia] acquired by his good accomplishments/qualities, so as to dissuade him of every evil intent and lead him to the path of virtue [289, 412].[26]

Much of the *Cortegiano* therefore serves to make a case for the courtier's position as one of near equality with the prince, even if the two men, within the established hierarchy of the court, can never be equal.[27] The *Cortegiano* is a descriptive, rather than prescriptive, treatise that makes a case for a group insisting on its own professional jurisdictional claims, and in doing so it offers a view that elevates the courtier in what Castiglione openly terms a "new profession" in an earlier, discarded preface.[28] This is not parity, but it is tentatively and suavely approaching it.

In this light, any talk about the function of the courtier as an ambassador would only remind us more openly of what the courtier at home should *not* be. The courtier in his new profession should be not the prince's advocate, his functional double far away, but an independent advisor and interlocutor at home. The courtier is not standing in for the prince. In the best of circumstances, he is instead standing right next to the prince. He is not the absent presence of the prince sent to deliver or gather information or offer counsel from afar, as the ambassador was, but his own self-styled, fully embodied presence situated beside the prince ideally in a fruitful, horizontal dialogue of exchange. Hence, just as the work of the prince is absent from the *Cortegiano*, so the work of the ambassador, whose displaced presence abroad sets him outside the confines of the closed circle of men and women in the duchess's quarters, must remain absent from the discussions as well. Put differently, if, as scholars have argued, Castiglione gradually stages in the *Cortegiano* a tension between the prince and the courtier precisely because the courtier does not wish to be viewed as a mere extension of the prince but a near equal to him (while still always remaining a subordinate), then it is understandable why Castiglione would have been loathe to include any discussion of ambassadorial work in his book. That work, the work of the ambassador as "orator," would only highlight the degree to which the courtier, at least when operating outside the confines of the court as an ambassador, was in fact an extension of the prince, his portavoce, his mouthpiece, even as he dutifully engaged in counsel.

Consequently, if the topic of ambassadorial work on the part of a courtier in his new professional role were to arise in the *Cortegiano*, the tension between the prince and the courtier would then arguably be displaced onto a tension between two competing visions of the courtier: on the one hand, the courtier who functions as the instrument of the prince (as his portavoce, even as he gathers news and interprets it for the prince and furnishes the prince, when asked, with advice in a potentially constant give-and-take); and on the other hand, the courtier who functions as an independent instructor of the prince (as his counselor, educator, and challenging interlocutor). Both men, to be sure, have influence in the world, and both serve to advise, but they have influence and advise in different ways. Castiglione's concern, at least for the moment in the *Cortegiano*, is with the influence of the courtier as a part *within* the functioning totality of the ideally complete court at home. Castiglione can therefore allude to ambassadorial work by reminding everyone where he, in the fiction of the dialogue, was when the festive discussions took place at Urbino. But, like the prince whom he was bodily representing as an ambassador in England, ambassadorial work must remain functionally absent in the *Cortegiano* in order to make a space for the new profession of the courtier. Someone, after all, has to stay home at court to tell the prince how to rule because, as Castiglione avers, so many princes are flattered by self-serving sycophants and "have the lack of what they would most need to have in abundance: namely, of someone to tell them the truth and make them mindful of what is right" (290, 413). We might summarily say, then, at the risk of adopting the anticourtly rhetoric of overstatement, that the figure and function of the ambassador are rendered structurally essential to the working of the court as the Italian sixteenth-century court is defined in the *Cortegiano*, even if the figure of the ambassador and his diplomatic work are necessarily absent, for the most part, from the treatise's professional purview.

Castiglione: The Courtier as Ambassador

Castiglione's election as the ambassador to receive the Order of the Garter in England on behalf of Guidobaldo marked one of the highpoints of his work as a courtier in Urbino. It was, after all, the occasion of his knighting; his experience in England, albeit brief and largely ceremonial, proved extremely felicitous, despite a few initial setbacks. However, the greatest moment of Castiglione's investment in the court occurred later, not while he remained at home working within the court as the prince's advisor at hand. Nor did it occur in his first important ambassadorial mission, when he went to England to represent Guidobaldo and was received so warmly. It occurred in his last ambassadorial mission, when pope Clement VII asked him to be the papal nunzio to the court of Emperor Charles V in Spain—during the time, that is, when Castiglione was writing the preface that sent his *Cortegiano* off into the world, a book that describes (rather than prescribing) how one should be a perfect courtier in a world where none in practice existed. Castiglione's understanding of diplomacy, however, had obviously changed in the intervening years, between his trip in 1506 to England, where he remained long enough to send a few letters home, and his trip in 1525–1529 to Spain, where he died. The ambassador who sent the *Cortegiano* to Venice to be printed was clearly no longer the young ambassador who is only marginally present in the same book. Now, barely a year before his death, as he was sending the *Cortegiano* off to Venice with the new preface, Castiglione could count himself a seasoned diplomat knowledgeable in the ways of the world. Up to that moment, Castiglione had represented his lords in a variety of circumstances, be it in the service of Guidobaldo of Urbino, Francesco della Rovere, or Federico Gonzaga. On three occasions, he served as a resident ambassador to Rome for broad periods, and he worked unstintingly for his superiors. However, when Castiglione was asked by the pope to represent the church officially as the resident ambassador to the greatest and most powerful emperor, Castiglione achieved a new high-water mark in his career, as is evident in the letters he sent both to Gonzaga and to the pope himself. The position, once offered to him in 1524, was not one he could refuse. But it was also one that would cause him enormous pain.

Castiglione's experience abroad in Spain was in some ways highly pleasurable. Like many Italian Renaissance humanists who worked as resident ambassadors, Castiglione used his time abroad as an opportunity to establish yet more contacts with other humanists and thereby further his connections in a community of like-minded and highly literate men. He might lament the absence of old friends, but he could also consider himself blessed to have as a companion while abroad such a man of distinguished background and intellectual heft as Andrea Navagero, the Venetian resident ambassador to the same court. Being a resident ambassador thus permitted Castiglione, as it had permitted such men as Ermolao Barbaro before him, to widen his horizons and broaden his own appeal in the communitas of distinguished thinkers invested in the studia humanitatis.

It also brought Castiglione into contact with other cultures, which in turn allowed him to enrich his understanding of foreign perspectives and arguably process those perspectives through the cognitive filter of his humanism. Not only did Castiglione learn much about Spain, marveling over the objects, people, and places that he saw, but he also learned much about the discoveries in the New World. Much of the excitement at being edified through contact with new people and things comes through in his familiar letters sent back home from Spain. Moreover, Castiglione was received well wherever he went, winning the favor and trust of the emperor. To be sure, his embassy cost an enormous sum of money, but it was money no doubt well spent in his mind. Being the pope's ambassador to the great court of Spain was an important position, the sort Castiglione had always yearned for professionally in order to make a difference in the world. This was the kind of service he had dedicated his life to, and it should therefore be viewed as the fulfillment of his diplomatic career and work as a courtier.

Nevertheless, Castiglione's experience as the resident ambassador to the great court of the emperor was also frustrating. Much of the time while he was in Spain, Castiglione found himself in darkness, laboring, as he put it memorably in one letter, "with his eyes shut" (P 2.6). What he meant by this expression is simple enough. He was not receiving adequate information from the papacy on what was going on back home and therefore did not know what policies he should present and pursue before the emperor. This complaint appears often in Castiglione's letters, even to the point of becoming a painful refrain. "I am very confused," he observes with frustration in one letter, "nor do I know well how to act" (P 2.5).[29] Over and over again, he expresses his anxiety as he waits for letters (P 2.37–38), and he fears that he will be left here as if "abandoned," forgotten, as if he were not even "in the world" (P 2.55). "I alone am without letters," he laments (P 2.61). "We are all in extreme anxiety waiting for the letters," he complains in another instance, "and I above all" (P 2.35). At times diplomacy feels just like guesswork (P 2.117). "I have the greatest fear about erring," he confesses, "which could easily happen to a person much more sage than I, especially in not having news regarding the will of the master" (P 2.115). He would act accordingly, he insists, if only the will of the pope were clarified (P 2.115).

This must have been a trying period in Castiglione's professional life. Time and again he reveals that he knows something terrible is at stake. He sees the danger of wars and disaster looming on the horizon. He fears matters will go dreadfully not just for the pope but also for Italy. He wishes, as he makes evident, to work for "universal peace" (P 2.3). What, then, does the ambassador do if he's not receiving news yet wishes to work for peace and universal well-being for the parties involved? How does he act if he's working, as Castiglione frankly put it, with "eyes shut," in "extreme confusion," in great "doubt"? How can you positively influence world events if you're groping in the dark? In one sense, to use the terms of the *Cortegiano*, the ambassador, like the courtier, has to face tough choices, do his best, and use his "good judgment" (bon giudizio). He must therefore rely on the familiar precept of rhetorical aptness articulated by Federico Fregoso toward the beginning of the second book: "Let him consider well what he does or says, the place where he does it, in whose presence, its timeliness, the reason for doing it, his own age, his profession [in this instance, it happens to be the profession of the ambassador], the end at which he aims, and the means by which he can reach it; thus, keeping these points in mind, let him act discreetly in whatever he wants to do or say" (98, 148).

At the same time, the ambassador must also in many instances dissimulate, as Ermolao Barbaro urged in his treatise on ambassadorial work, *De officio legati*, the first such treatise composed by a humanist.[30] So Castiglione, for instance, observes in a moment of painful frustration on not receiving news: "And in the meanwhile I will dissimulate what it seems to me I can dissimulate, and I will always have my eye on serving his most Holiness" (P 2.117). In another sense, like all ambassadors Castiglione must traffic in news, though news that is suspect. He must constantly listen to gossip, the circulating, always shadowy, unreliable rumors of the court. Using his discretion (discrezione), which for Francesco Guicciardini was the supreme skill needed to succeed as an ambassador, Castiglione must try to sift through diverse and conflicting pieces of information and figure out, in the absence of any solid information from the Vatican, what is actually going on back home and how he is supposed to perceive it all.

Gossip therefore becomes a critical motif of Castiglione's letters while in Spain, along with how difficult it was for him to separate truth from falsehood. Every statement uttered by someone else, as it floats about unmoored from its uncertain origins, is suspect. One must, of course, always measure the source (on occasion the information comes from the French, and as Castiglione observes, this makes it all the more unreliable).[31] However, since there is often no other information available beyond the gossip that circulates, there is no alternative other than to take it into consideration. "Even so," he observes in one instance, "the ambiguity and the diversity of the opinions is very great" (P 2.52). Ambiguity and diversity of opinions: these are two of the complex factors that Castiglione had to take into account all the time as he patiently and prudently sifted through the rumors that circulated. Gossip, as Elizabeth Horodowich has observed, was essential to the free-flowing movement of social relations in the Venetian politics of the Renaissance.[32] So it was as well for the ambassador abroad caught up daily in matters of consequence on the world stage. Gossip was, for much of the time, Castiglione's only information, such as it was. If an ambassador was a man sent to "lie abroad," as the quip had it, one of Castiglione's major tasks, as a self-interested ambassador abroad, was to figure out from all the lies transmitted through court gossip what was worth considering and reporting.[33]

We will probably never fully know why the Vatican kept Castiglione in the dark at such a trying and delicate time in European diplomacy for the papacy. Indeed, just as we can never fathom "the dark innermost recesses" (125, 182) of the minds of any one person,[34] as Castiglione sententiously observes in the *Cortegiano*, so we can never really access the minds of those who failed to send news to Castiglione when he was an ambassador in Spain. Perhaps it is just in the nature of a large and cumbersome bureaucracy to mess things up. Even today (or especially today), with high-tech mechanisms for dissemination of information in the blink of an eye, information does not always seem to flow through its channels across agencies to the proper people in the right place. The Vatican in early-sixteenth-century Italy probably fared no better, especially given the rather cumbersome and unreliable mail service at its disposal. Yet again, perhaps the papacy just mistrusted Castiglione at times and therefore failed to keep in touch with him as regularly as he wished. This was not uncommon. Or perhaps the papacy might have even feared that Castiglione was no longer adequately representing the position of the Vatican, that he was getting just too close for comfort to the emperor.

This was indeed a problem that ambassadors faced when they lived abroad for some time. They needed to get close to the source in order to acquire information, but getting close also potentially jeopardized the appearance of being sufficiently detached and objective. To make matters worse, Castiglione, who was proud that the emperor showed in him great faith and trust,[35] had his entrenched enemies back at court in Rome, men who viewed him with suspicion as too pro-Spanish—an issue that comes through unequivocally in his letters, which occasionally read as arguments for, rather than about, the emperor. Time and again Castiglione lauds Charles V's virtues, his love of peace, and his love for the pope. In any event, whatever the reason for the Vatican's reticence in contacting Castiglione and supplying him with the news he longed to receive in order to operate successfully, what Castiglione must have learned as a seasoned ambassador in Spain from 1525 to 1529 was, in effect, precisely what Francesco Guicciardini learned as a fledgling ambassador in Spain more than a dozen years earlier.[36] Castiglione learned, painfully enough, that ambassadors are often kept in the dark; that they are forced to operate with "eyes shut"; that perhaps they are meant to be kept in the dark for reasons the ambassador will never know; and that they cannot, at any given moment, choose not to act because they are always on stage (not only before the potentate to whom they have been sent but also before other ambassadors who are observing their individual performance and calculating what information they can glean from it). And of course he learned that they must traffic in lies, rumors, and gossip and use their "bon giudizio," "discrezione," and available talents at "dissimulazione" in order to succeed as best they can. As Castiglione puts it succinctly in one letter, "I involve myself as ably as I can" (P 2.61).

In the eyes of Clement VII, as is well known, Castiglione did not succeed in his job, at least during the middle period of his four-year stay, and the pope's stinging rebuke of Castiglione was one of the lowest moments of an entire career of distinguished diplomatic service marked by what he no doubt imagined to be unassailable professional propriety. While he was abroad in Spain, both Spanish and German mercenary forces (most of the latter being Lutheran) invaded Rome, where they tortured many of the clergy and ransacked buildings. The outraged Clement VII managed to escape and secure himself in Castel Sant'Angelo, where he remained unscathed but fearful for his life for ten months. When word of the traumatizing event reached Spain, Castiglione was crestfallen, just as so many other humanists were, in Italy and throughout Europe.[37] But soon enough, Castiglione had another reason to feel devastated when Clement VII, still effectively imprisoned in Castel Sant'Angelo, blamed much of what had occurred on Castiglione. That accusation, which arrived in a letter sent to Spain from Rome on August 27, 1527, occasioned Castiglione's direct response to the pontiff in a remarkable letter sent about four months later, on December 10, 1527. In his letter, Castiglione acknowledges the pope's displeasure in no uncertain terms, saying the pope "believes that those disasters occurred much to my blame," because he had allegedly "trusted too much" the emperor and his promises (P 2.148). These were not idle accusations. Clement VII was incensed, and he saw fit to take out his displeasure on the ambassador who had won the emperor's trust. The pope saw his ambassador, as Castiglione reports the matter, as acting with "imprudence" and "negligence."[38]

If we can say that Clement VII chose the right person for the job of ambassador when he selected Castiglione, we can also say that he certainly chose the wrong man to accuse of ineptitude and treachery. While standing in for the pope as ambassador, Castiglione, a man with a strong sense of self and professional propriety, was not afraid to stand up for himself.[39] Far from being a pushover, he resiliently pushed back, reminding the pope, with all the grazia and sprezzatura at his command, that he kept the pontiff informed even when not informed himself: "It seems to me that to write every day [to me] about what one was to do regarding every event, which I waited for from Rome, was more fitting than what Rome might have waited for from me [in my letters]. . . . But it is impossible to obtain from others [in this case what Castiglione sought from Rome] more than others want to give" (P 2.150–51).[40]

In the *Cortegiano*, the book that was finally sent out to print not long after the Sack of Rome, we learn over and over again that it is important to excel and be seen excelling, though it is still essential not to be too conspicuous in doing so. To this effect, Castiglione urges, the courtier must stand out; yet, he warns, "let him accompany his every movement with a certain good judgment and grace, if he wishes to deserve that universal favor which is so greatly prized" (38, 55–56). Castiglione did excel. He did stand out from the crowd and was thus "outstanding," both in the confines of the book, as the chosen ambassador who is absent from the discussions, and outside the confines of the book, as the one who could be taken (or easily mistaken) as the perfect courtier. And as an outstanding individual, as one who seems, even from the critical vantage point of the present, as just too good to be true, Castiglione was not afraid to take a stance, as his tenacious response to the pope's rebuke demonstrates.

But in responding to the terrified pontiff, whose wrath he had incurred, Castiglione also always achieved the balance and equanimity that marked the courtier he described in his book as one who could "temper his every action with a certain good judgment and grace." He maintained his cool. Even as he continued to stand in for someone else while ambassador to Spain, and even as he found himself unjustifiably accused by that very person of misconduct and ineptitude and thereby shamed and disgraced, he remained himself, the person who was morally upright, in search of service, and in search of having an influence in the world through that service. Even as he was in the position of losing the "universal favor which is so greatly prized," he valued himself by responding with the requisite sprezzatura and professional propriety.

It is in the overall context of his work as an ambassador that we may return to the preface Castiglione wrote for the final authorized publication of his *Cortegiano*, which was in the spring of 1527, just a few months before the Sack of Rome and thus before he received the pope's stinging letter of rebuke. It is altogether astonishing that Castiglione never mentions his ambassadorial service in Spain at all. It was as if, beyond the offhand passing phrase "finding myself in Spain," the years in which Castiglione toiled on behalf of an unresponsive papacy had vanished into thin air.

But perhaps not quite vanished. For the choice of the destinee of the new dedication is also, I submit, telling. It is suggestive, in the terms of the language of sprezzatura, at hinting through only the particular of the name at a larger, concealed whole. The name "Don Michel de Silva, Bishop of Viseu," brings us back to Portugal. And in turning to that part of the world, the name of the dedicatee brings us back to Castiglione's presence and work in Spain. Additionally, the name reminds us, or at least it reminds those in the know within the then-tight-linked world of diplomacy, that Signor Don Michel de Silva had once been a longstanding, influential ambassador in Rome, where he and Castiglione first met.[41] It is thus merely through the hint of a name that Castiglione perhaps aimed to remind us, deftly, without the slightest affectation, that he now labored, just as his destinee had once labored, as an ambassador on the grand stage of world events during a most momentous and transforming period in European history. And as the book goes off to Don Michel de Silva, whom we may envision as a specular image of the ambassadorial author himself, it bears all of Castiglione's hopes for a better world, "because," as he observes before he sent the new preface off from Spain, "without a doubt, things are in great danger in Italy" (P 2.18). Those things in danger affected not just Castiglione and his friends but, to be sure, the very institutional structures that allowed him to prosper and fashion his identity as a man of impeccable worth, politia, and unassailable professional propriety.

Epilogue

Shortly after Castiglione passed away (pained no doubt by the earlier accusations leveled at him after the Sack of Rome), a great funeral procession followed his body to the Cathedral in Toledo, where he was buried in full royal ceremony. Charles V, the emperor's distinguished court, and many illustrious members of the church were in attendance. Charles V reportedly said of Castiglione that he was "one of the best *caballeros* of the world," and the emperor sent a letter to Clement VII, written in his own hand, lamenting Castiglione's death and commending him once more to the pope.

Castiglione's untimely death, caused by one of the many ailments he suffered over the course of his years, marked the end of his distinguished career as a courtier and, as we have seen, as a diplomat working tirelessly in the service of the pope. His death, on February 8, 1529, also marked in many ways the passing of an age. A number of people mourned Castiglione. But with the advantage of historical hindsight we can also say that the elegiac sentiments expressed by various writers in their sadness about Castiglione's death can be viewed as part and parcel of a deeper mourning for a time gone by. The Sack of Rome, often viewed as a watershed moment in early modern European history, changed things dramatically for Italian humanists, traumatizing a number of them and dispelling a great deal of optimism.[42] Along with that, a whole new political and social order gradually came into being in Italy not long after Charles V's invasion and the definitive defeat of the French. Florence, which managed to reconstitute its Republic in 1527, finally became a princedom in 1531, and by 1537 Cosimo I became duke (eventually the Grand Duke of Tuscany in 1569), thus forever quashing republican aspirations in a city that had inspired so many great thinkers to ponder the nature and virtue of republican institutions. Spanish hegemony in the peninsula soon consolidated and reinforced absolutist regimes, and the church, which tolerated all sorts of broad-minded and inquisitive thinking, now with the tacit support of the emperor vigorously pursued after 1540 a policy of ferreting out heretics, combating Protestantism, and prohibiting books heretofore widely available.

A whole new crop of professional writers connected directly and indirectly to the marketplace of print also came to the fore in the period after the Sack of Rome. Pietro Aretino called himself and was dubbed, interestingly enough, "secretary to the world"—*not*, it is worth emphasizing, "ambassador to the world" or "courtier to the world."[43] From his palace along the Grand Canal in Venice, with its glorious view of all the workers toiling about in the marketplace and with the incandescent sunsets shimmering off to the west, Aretino was not representing anyone else as a secretary to the world, and he didn't want to. Nor, for that matter, could we imagine any prince really wanting Aretino to represent him, though Aretino's fame and influence did aid the Venetian Republic and thus accounts, in some measure, for the support he received there and the favor that Doge Andrea Gritti bestowed on him. For when Aretino called himself a secretary, he meant it in a specific, self-serving way. He was the "keeper of secrets" of the world through the network of connections he had managed to forge directly through print and indirectly through the print marketplace. Moreover, rather than being inconspicuous about it, he was all-too-conspicuous. Far from keeping those secrets as a tight-lipped secretary ideally should, he bandied them about in a manner that only reaffirmed his position as an independent, anticourtly, antidiplomatic figure. Styled the "scourge of princes" by Ariosto, he was the very opposite of a good secretary, much as he was the very opposite of what would have made a good (much less a "perfect") courtier, even if he had thrived as a courtier for a number of years as yet one more of the *enfants terribles* of early-sixteenth-century Italy.

After he left Mantua in 1527, Aretino did not aim to serve anyone in particular in the courtly world of sixteenth-century Italy. He looked at the court with unabashed hostility both before and after he definitively left Rome, and he deemed those who worked in the court to be inveterate dupes, sycophants, idiots, or pedants. He also held the church and its minions in the papal court in disdain. Unlike Castiglione, who vigorously defended the church in his response to Alfonso Valdès,[44] Aretino, who loved to get in people's faces, argued that the Sack of Rome was, albeit a shame, in many ways well deserved. The church, as a seedbed of sin, got what was coming to it, and Aretino, that "scourge of princes," had foretold that it would occur. For him, as he put it in the second version of his *Cortigiana*, Rome was not the *caput mundi* but the *coda mundi*. With that image, and with Aretino's habit of seizing the basest possible common denominator, we can also guess what he really had in mind in the crude terms he loved to deploy. If one lifted up the tail and looked behind it, together with the church and its court, Rome was full of unseemly matter.

Aretino, as we shall see in the next chapter, had his virtues, but not uniformly modesty or temperance. He also lacked Castiglione's education, social rank, and above all his ability to maintain aplomb. As a diplomat and an ambassador, Castiglione sought to achieve the balance of standing in for someone who had to stand out and yet still remain himself, the person who, as he so poignantly put it, was a "worthy, sincere, and truthful man" (P 2.60), despite all the notable pressures placed upon him. This was a man who, as he rendered evident in his letters sent from Spain, could offer advice while still working under extreme diplomatic duress, constrained time and again to pursue policies with his "eyes shut." Whether abroad or at home, Castiglione constituted the model of the courtier of professional propriety. Aretino, for the life of him, could not behave the way Castiglione did for any length of time; nor would he have wanted to. We can see this evident in how the two men responded to others' rebukes. When Castiglione found himself attacked, he delivered sententious remarks. He eased the pope into seeing the world through his vision and thus enabled a superior within the court to envision sympathetically the justified vision of an inferior. By contrast, Aretino, when attacked, responded with thunderous ire. He provoked, he spat venom, he used every possible word to bludgeon others with the stick of his opinions. And he did so with the greatest pleasure and on the grand scale. In short, Aretino loved to get in another person's face, striving to be, unlike Castiglione, aggressively conspicuous. Thus, where Castiglione's response to the pope's rebuke becomes a testament to his equanimity, poise, and respect and consequently reminds us all the more why Castiglione was chosen to serve in such an important diplomatic position as a person of unparalleled merit and professional propriety, Aretino's response to any sort of rebuke reveals his love of the inflammatory. He hungered for attention through print culture (much as he hungered for food, a subject we explore in the next chapter). Aretino is the man, after all, who initially acquired fame through his ribald and openly offensive *pasquinate*; who freely stepped on the feet of the esteemed, including popes; and who loved the limelight as he sought to render himself the most famous person of his age—often enough through acts of egregious professional impropriety. Like Castiglione, Aretino had exposure and was widely known throughout Europe, but in a way that Castiglione, "one of the best *caballeros* of the world," would have scorned had he lived long enough to witness it.

PART TWO

Food

CHAPTER 2

Pietro Aretino and the Art of Conspicuous Consumption

An Appetite for Things

When the servant Guardabasso in Pietro Aretino's comic play of 1542, *Lo ipocrito*, claims that half of the thieves in the world "die of hunger," he voices a cliché to explain in broad sweeping terms how poorly household members, at least within the fiction of the drama, were being treated. At the same time, he responds indirectly to his old and crotchety master, the curmudgeon Liseo, who claims that "whoever wants to be poorly served should have lots of household workers" (*assai famigli*; 1.1).[1] Liseo, Guardabasso would have us understand, is dead wrong. It is the members of the household who are instead poorly served by those they serve. And it is significant that in registering his complaint, Guardabasso—whose name, in keeping with his moody querulous nature, means "look down"—centers his thoughts on hunger, even to the point where he fantasizes about people (albeit thieves) in a state of famished devastation. For food, if not actually the fear of dying of hunger, is often on their minds.

Early on in the second act of the play, for instance, Liseo notes that he would like to see Guardabasso, along with his two other servants, taken care of in a "better life." Yet if that were to happen, Guardabasso responds, he would just like something substantial to eat—some down-to-earth, hearty, nourishing food that sticks to the ribs and plugs up the pit of the stomach. "If you want us to have a better life," he replies, directly echoing his master's words, "it is necessary that sometimes there be meatballs, and at times little livers, and often tripe with some cheese to plug up the belly" (2.3).[2] For their part, Guardabasso's cohorts in the service of Liseo—Malanotte and Perdelgiorno, whose ludic names mean roughly "Bad Night" and "Waste Away the Day" (or perhaps Miss One's Chance?)—fantasize about some of the food they've seen being sold on the street, and how they would love to fix it up for a sumptuous banquet all their own:

> Malanotte: Tell me, what did you think of those capons that that guy was selling?
> Perdelgiorno: Well, I didn't see the most visible ones.
> Malanotte: Were they expensive?
> Perdelgiorno: Rather, a good buy in great abundance.
> Malanotte: Did you think about doing them up boiled or roasted?
> Perdelgiorno: One should be done boiled, because the noodles, which you need to wrap up the capons, make a feast worthy of a duke. And also there's the fat to use up for the broth.
> Malanotte: To do what with?
> Perdelgiorno: To smother up all over the other capon; the broth keeps the capon, while it is all covered with cloves as it is turned on a spit, nice and soft from the constant basting. That way the grease of the fat penetrates the capon right to the bone, so that it just melts in your mouth [2.8].

So famished is Perdelgiorno that in one instance his thoughts turn instinctively, as if drawn to the topic by a persistent gnawing in the belly, to the presence or absence of food according to the fortunes and whims of the masters. More often than not, fortune is on the wane, the masters feel the pinch in the purse, and the *famigli* are sadly left with barely edible food: "sour desserts," "strong wines," "bread like a rock," and "meat for a cat" (4.14).

Guardabasso, Malanotte, and Perdelgiorno in Aretino's *Lo Ipocrito* are, as servants are wont to be in Renaissance drama, hungry for attention, honor, and respect. In this way they are like so many other figures of household help represented in works of imaginative literature of the Italian Renaissance. But, above all, they are hungry for some food, the sustenance that forms the basis of existence so that people like Guardabasso can get on with life, let alone have a "better life." And there is perhaps every reason they should be hungry, as we can gather from a reading of Piero Camporesi's *Land of Hunger.* Not only did Italian Renaissance literature dwell on the topic of hunger, especially with increasing frequency in the sixteenth century, but hunger itself was a matter of real, daily, historical concern—or so Camporesi passionately claims. "The 'plague of God,' the 'rabid hunger,'" he observes, "cannot be dated with exactitude, but from as far back at least as the second half of the sixteenth century one gets the very bitter impression that, for two centuries and a half, hunger weighed upon the whole of Italy like a terrible nightmare."[3] In times of famine the rank and file suffered terribly, especially in areas dominated by the Spanish after the 1530s. Records of the period, for instance, show that in Milan "the people were starving in 1536 because they could not afford to buy," and great mercantile cities such as Venice saw periods of extreme shortage.[4]

However, it is also important to note that economic and social historians have not always seen the Italian Renaissance as a period of such hard times. Richard Goldthwaite, for instance, has argued that both skilled and unskilled workers employed in the construction industry (at least in the case of Florence, where a building boom took place in the fifteenth and sixteenth centuries) were paid well enough to feed themselves and their families, and some could put a substantial margin of wealth between them and the poverty line.[5] Goldthwaite's calculations may seem somewhat pedestrian to the eye of literary and cultural scholars as he takes into consideration the amount of calories typical workers would have burnt, then calculates how much basic food (meat, wheat, etc.) they could have bought with their wages according to the changing value of money over time, and finally concludes that the accumulated archival evidence, however scanty, suggests that workers after the Black Death in Florence were better off than before. Nevertheless, Goldthwaite's calculations, along with Brian Pullan's about the standard of living of Venetian artisans and Massimo Montanari's more broad-based appraisal of food consumption in Italy and Europe,[6] certainly have the virtue of cautioning us when it comes to approaching the topic of hunger and appetite in the Italian Renaissance. They remind us that when we use literature as evidence, it is always difficult to tell what is real and what is imaginary. There is hunger, which was certainly experienced by people in the Italian Renaissance (not the Machiavellis, Castigliones, or Guicciardinis of the world, to be sure), and then again there is hunger in literature, a commonplace (in rhetorical terms, a topos) as old as Homer's description of Odysseus's famished crew gorging on the forbidden, slaughtered cattle of the sun god Helios.[7]

This chapter, which focuses on Aretino and his interest in styles of consumption, deals with the intersection of the real and the imaginary when it comes to the topic of hunger and food. For if Aretino's characters are hungry, so, it is important to recognize, was Aretino—or at least the Aretino he imaginatively and self-consciously *represented* in his letters. Indeed, in one letter he compares himself to a pregnant woman with all sorts of cravings that he has to satisfy, in that particular instance by consuming the gift of the "liver sausages" sent him (6.94). Like the characters in his irreverent play *Lo Ipocrito*, Aretino represents himself as having an immense, almost insatiable, appetite for food, an appetite that found expression not only in his letters, which rendered him a public figure of notorious repute and created a vogue for such collections in the vernacular, but also in his works of imaginative literature, beginning with *La cortigiana* and extending on to his scurrilous dialogues and later comic plays. When it comes to food, what distinguishes Aretino was not only his imagined gargantuan appetite—a "bestial appetite" (6.140) that was not at all parasitical in nature, he would have us believe, like the appetite of those household servants satirically described in *Lo Ipocrito*—but also his fantasies about the art of consumption in his poetry and prose.

Put differently, if, as Ken Albala has observed in his study of eating habits in the European Renaissance, dietary literature with all its restrictions and prohibitions "must have generated a considerable amount of anxiety and guilt" for many people, Aretino in the self-presentation of his letters seems little affected or troubled by it all. He remained, he gives us to believe, supremely free of all those "fears, prejudices, and preoccupations" that the dietary literature addressed or discursively created and that in time began to find their way into the visual arts in sixteenth-century Italy in complex ways.[8] Aretino ate heartily and with gusto, if we can at all trust what he had to say about his appetites, and he certainly enjoyed talking about consumption as well. Moreover, in a culture in which numerous types of food could be shunned because they retained lingering associations with the lower classes (garlic was traditionally the food of the peasant, the *villano*, for example, just as salad was characteristically considered a low food), Aretino liked to say he ate everything that came his way with an egalitarian delight.[9] Ideologically, he had no socially rigid "food system." Hence, if "food pressures . . . are a barometer of social differentiation," as Albala points out, Aretino consciously aimed to flatten out social distinctions through his talk about his eating habits and his appetites.[10] He was, according to his vigorous self-mythologizing, open to all types of food associated with all strata of society, much as, to connect at the outset of this chapter two aspects of pleasure central to Aretino's life, food *and* words, he was open to all types of linguistic registers, from the popular to the elite. Aretino self-consciously portrayed himself as a great and conspicuous consumer with an enormous appetite. By doing so, he inevitably offered himself up artfully as a figure worthy of consumption in print for the widest possible public.

Furthermore, in focusing on Aretino and the topic of consumption, this chapter examines a critical transitional period in Italian history: the period between the Sack of Rome in 1527 and the midsixteenth century. Historically, Aretino's concern for consumption figures into the period just before Camporesi indicates that the "nightmare" of famine took hold of much of Italy; Aretino died at midcentury, at which point, Camporesi claims, people began starving across Italy. At the same time Aretino's concern for consumption would seem to overlap conceptually with the same period described by Camporesi within the realm of the imaginary, which focused so resolutely on the topic of hunger. Aretino indeed addressed in a bold and determined way the themes of hunger that would dominate popular writings composed after midcentury.

Additionally, in focusing on the second quarter of the sixteenth century, this chapter addresses a period when Italy gradually came to be dominated by court culture and when writers such as Aretino, in search of fame and income, felt obliged to take up some sort of position ideologically in relation to court culture. Even such cities as Florence, long a bastion of republicanism, finally succumbed definitively to Medici autocracy in the 1530s. Aretino, who lived early in his life in the ambit of the courts of Rome and Mantua, and then, after 1527, permanently in commercial, republican Venice, witnessed this change and looked at it with unabashed hostility. For him courts were not only changing for the worse as they adopted increasingly elaborate rituals. The court, especially from the vantage point of the sanctuary of Aretino's house in Venice from 1527 on, was debased through and through. It was a place of ignominious skinflints, where people prostituted themselves for social advancement. For this reason, Aretino's interest in consumption figured squarely into his ongoing rivalrous and contentious relationship with the court, and in particular with Castiglione's *Cortegiano*, which offered up such a singularly positive and often nostalgic view of court culture in the early sixteenth century.

Furthermore, Aretino's interest in consumption, when measured against the alternately niggardly or overly ostentatious meals at the court, allowed him to advance his own aggressive, competitive agenda to assert himself in the foreground in relation to others as an author of importance within the print marketplace, and thus, even if he was no longer part of a specific court, a person worthy of being known by people from all strata of society. The art of consumption that Aretino applauded was central to the art of the sixteenth century poligrafo, the adventurer of the pen,[11] who could exist outside the court and survive off the gifts of others, as well as the fruits, literal and figurative, of his prolific and supremely versatile writings in the vernacular. This art of consumption belonged to the marketplace of print that Aretino was eventually indebted to once he left Mantua in 1527, even as he sought to distance himself from the marketplace by maintaining the appearance of being courtly—or, at least, of being capable of appearing to be courtly when he wished to be.[12]

That food figured so prominently in the writings of a major critic of the court should not strike us as entirely surprising. As Mikhail Bakhtin argued long ago in *Rabelais and His World*, the gargantuan consumption of food within the imaginary in the European Renaissance, with its attention to both the sensuous and the copious, had much to do with carnival.[13] An unrestrained, stuffed body irrepressibly eating virtually anything and everything in sight patently announced the body of carnival as a sign of popular culture. And that culture, along with focusing on the bottom part of the human form (especially the genitalia and the anus), relentlessly identified food with sex and sex with food. Aretino embraced much of that in his art of consumption in his plays, dialogues, and letters. In those varied literary forms we find a carnivalesque focus on the tavern; the *copia* of food in popular feasts with an undifferentiated mass of people engaged in ribald acts of consumption; the voluptuous sensuousness of food; the unashamed pleasures of food as if it were sex; the oral pleasures of talking about food in the copia of language; the mixing of high and low foods in a manner that upsets conventional food hierarchies (much as Aretino brilliantly mixed up high and low linguistic registers in his writings); and the irreverent manner in which a religious vocabulary is employed to describe massive quantities of food, as if the cornucopia of food on display were something truly sublime and worthy of devotion.

By approaching consumption in this way, Aretino in one sense acknowledges the value of festive popular culture, so much of which is bound to the market and would have been viewed as improper in the court. Appetites are indeed important, Aretino would have us remember, and we should never forget that for a minute. In another sense, however, Aretino critiques elitist, court culture. Men such as Castiglione voicing the ideology of the elite failed to take into account the importance of bodily appetites. More important, when Castiglione and others like him do discuss bodily appetites, they do so grudgingly, and their guiding assumption is that the mean, rather than the extreme, is virtuous.[14] Men such as Castiglione were simply too concerned with matters of professional propriety to stage conspicuously in their writings the importance of real bodily appetites.

On the other hand, as Norbert Elias observed in *The Civilizing Process* and Peter Burke in *Popular Culture in Early Modern Europe*, one way in which the elite in the early modern period in Europe increasingly differentiated themselves from the rest of society was through the refinement of their habits of the consumption of food.[15] Less, in a real sense, was more, though abundance, it is important to stress, was still displayed and prized in the court. The body of elitist culture, especially as it was codified within the courtly world of Castiglione's *Cortegiano*, should ideally be agile, thin, trim. The courtly body was not one that consumed massively, or revealed itself to be one that ate indiscriminately or immoderately with uncontrolled appetites. It was not, in a word, a "fat" body in its ideal form, as any portrait by Bronzino testifies.

To be sure, at first glance there would seem to be little in Aretino's writings that advocated such an elitist view of consumption. Aretino, pictured often as a rather heavy-set man himself, nevertheless embraced aspects of an elitist approach to the consumption of food. He did so in several ways. First, when he received food as a gift, he often highlighted the status of the friend or acquaintance who gave it to him. Those gifts were always signs of social elevation; they were the rewards he received for being a valuable person who had achieved not only fame but also status. Often enough those gifts came from people of distinction in a recognizably stratified world, and he emphasizes the fact that they are gifts, not payment in kind connecting Aretino to profitable market exchanges. Those gifts of food elevate not only Aretino as the recipient of them but also the giver of the gift. They are therefore to be taken as symbols of honor for all the members concerned. Second, Aretino often boasted of the high status of the company he kept when he dined. He sometimes chose to dine privately in his house with men of worth, as he was quick to present his prandial companions. Third, he understood the honor bestowed on him by having such a cornucopia of food at his disposal. Aretino did not need to be at the court to partake in festive rituals of conspicuous consumption as acts designed to foster and cement loyalties, for he could hold those feasts for himself and others on his own, he boasts, and he could do so selectively for his friends in bonds of mutual trust and loyal, private companionship. Fourth, he publicized his habits of consumption in print, therefore fashioning himself as a man of importance and stature, even as he critiqued court society. He availed himself, that is, of the marketplace of print to disseminate and magnify his presence to a vast public, but he did so, he liked to claim with some sleight-of-hand, without really being part of the marketplace at all.

In this way, through his art of consumption Aretino retained some version of courtly distinction and professional propriety as a writer bound in some measure to the marketplace of print. He acquired status and reputation, and not just fame, through his own publicized consumption of so much valuable food bequeathed to him as honorable gifts. But he also violated the codes of courtly distinction, undermining the professional proprieties associated with it, in order to embrace carnival in his self-presentation and critique aspects of the court he found hypocritical and, underneath it all, devoid of value. Much as Aretino would continuously and prominently display the gift of the valuable gold chain he received from Francis I in 1533 as a tangible mark of honor, so too Aretino repeatedly flaunted the gifts of food he received and consumed as a sign of his distinction in a world where hunger was real, where popular culture fantasized about conspicuous consumption, and where such consumption indeed served an important social function of reinforcing loyalties and acknowledging social position in the restricted, controlled, and highly stratified context of courtly culture. Aretino, in brief, wanted readers of his voluminous letters to know that he possessed what popular culture bound to the marketplace desired and what elite culture bound to the court had in abundance: massive quantities of every type of food. Yet he possessed that food, he also wanted everyone to know, in a way he could control to his own end: with the people he wanted to dine with, in the environment of his own choosing, and in Venice, the distinguished republican city he praised and called home. This is the privilege not of popular culture but of the elite, a man protected by the powerful Doge Andrea Gritti

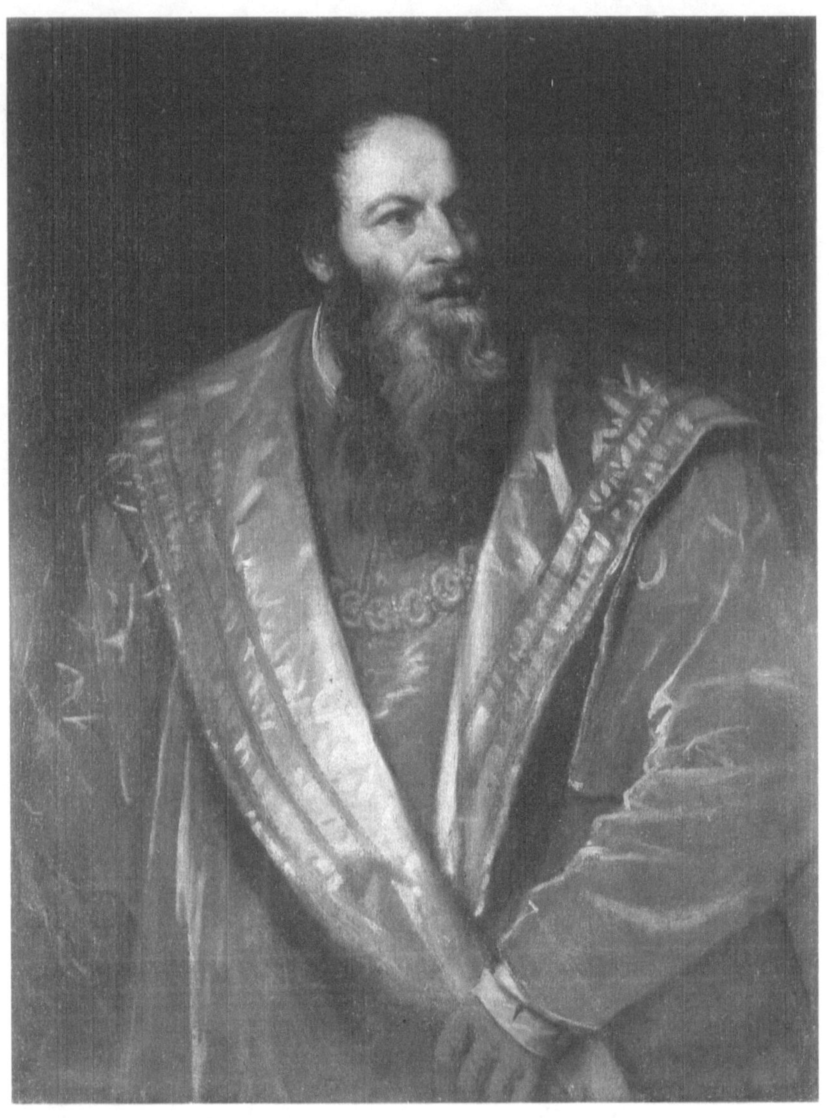

FIGURE 4. Titian (ca. 1488–1576). *Portrait of Pietro Aretino*, ca. 1545. Palazzo Pitti, Florence. Photo courtesy Scala/Art Resource, New York.

and favored by such esteemed and powerful men as Francis I, the king of France, and Charles V, the Holy Roman Emperor.

In this respect, thinking about and representing the conspicuous consumption of food permitted Aretino to align himself with popular culture and find real value in it and the marketplace with which it is often associated; yet it also allowed him both to maintain a sense of distinction that aligned him with the elite and to distance himself from the very body politic of popular culture he appeared to embrace so openly in his writings. Somewhat as in Titian's portraits of him (Figure 4), Aretino presented himself through his habits of consumption in his letters as the concealed body of carnival. In Titian's portraits, for instance, Aretino is massive and corpulent, with his huge cheeks and enormous beard and bulging frame taking up the entire canvas. At the same time, however, Aretino presented himself as a body festooned with the trappings of the elite, just as in Titian's portraits he also wears expensive robes and, most notably, bears prominently the distinctive gold chain bestowed on him as a gift of honor by King Francis I.

The Appetite of the Parasite: Courtly Consumption and the Hunger of Prostitutes

Early in his career, while he was still associated with the papal court in Rome and critiquing court culture from within it, Aretino offered a striking impression of how important food was to him within the context of the imaginary. In his first comedy, *La cortigiana* (1525/1534)[16]—whose ambiguous title can be read as "The Courtesan," "The Courtiers' Play," or "Courtly Matters," and which is deliberately titled to echo and parody Castiglione's *Cortegiano* then circulating in manuscript form—hunger animates in particular Rosso, the main parasite, who expresses a longing for food that gives him little respite. When, for example he is sent out to procure a gift of food for his master, the foolish Parabolano, Rosso takes it on himself to steal some lampreys from a Florentine fishmonger hawking food along the street; then, later in the day, we see Rosso leaving a tavern licking his fingers, having in the meanwhile feasted on the purloined food with Cappa, a friend and fellow companion in the trickster's intrigue (2.1). Food, we are bluntly told by Rosso, is not a substitute for sex and all the attendant social conventions that govern the getting or fantasizing about it, including the longings and sighs and desires for "sweetness," the Petrarchan *dolcezza*, for instance, that makes even clear, fresh waters acquire in the *Canzoniere* a special, memorable taste. Quite the contrary, sex, in Rosso's mind, is a sorry substitute for the real sweetness of life, which is nothing other than the savory taste of food. Similarly, if "civet" is customarily used to enhance one's standing in the world by making one seem more appealing through scent, food is not a substitute for such social status and acceptance, Cappa avers. Social status is instead a substitute for a basic longing that animates us all: the desire to be surrounded by immense quantities of succulent, odoriferous food. In the end, it seems, all you have to do is set up a tavern by a perfume shop, and everyone will drop the civet and run for the spits dripping with fat. For it is in the tavern where one finds acceptance. It is in the tavern where the hunger of ambition—viewed here as an ersatz lure in life, since the true aim is to be well fed—actually gets satisfied and one can rest in peace. It is in the tavern where one can fashion an identity that matters in the world and consequently acquire, as Rosso puts it, "a name." Indeed, as far as Rosso is concerned, there is absolutely no point in seeking to achieve glorious deeds worthy of a triumphal homecoming if you can satiate the craving for recognition by having your fill at the tavern.

Moreover, it is in the tavern, not the humanist's schoolroom, where children were disciplined and thus educated into acquiring habits and attributes that would serve them well in life and secure them a reputation. Similarly, it is in the tavern where everyone can entertain at least the illusion of being an equal and thus feel like a lord, the master of his or her own destiny. The tavern is consequently for the comical Rosso, as it is for the hilarious, corpulent Shakespearean Falstaff, the place of full-fledged "agency." And, as Rosso irreverently announces at the outset of the second act, it is in the tavern, the earthly "paradise," where one consumes the food that matters. That is because the tavern *is* quite literally paradise for Rosso, where lampreys—stolen lampreys nicely cooked—are deemed angelic sustenance. The tavern is consequently the place of earthly, rather than atemporal, "joy," the embodiment of all things that anyone could possible crave both now and forevermore. In this way Rosso's and Cappa's inflation of their own bellies comes with a corresponding deflation of virtually all societal norms, hierarchies, and cultural expectations. Everything of standard, accepted value in Renaissance Italy is systematically and comically overturned and deemed wanting, a lackluster substitute for the cornucopia of food. In the tavern, amid all that material food, the spiritualized reflection of the self in the beloved does not seem to matter, any more than does the fulfillment of coition, the making of a name for oneself through self-presentation, the longing to achieve triumphant deeds, the security of position in a transparently hierarchical world, the search for distinction in the world through a fashionable education, and the joy of eternal life in heaven where those who are blessed feast on celestial ambrosia and are forever fulfilled. In Rosso's and Cappa's carnivalesque view of things, food is the great reward, and hunger is the great equalizer.[17] The belly, and thus the body with its appetites, triumphs.

In thinking about *La cortigiana*, we need to bear in mind that Aretino was a courtier in Rome during his time there, a "familiar," for instance, in the house of Agostino Chigi,[18] and much of the play—indeed, the essence of it—focuses on highlighting in an exaggerated way the flaws of the court, including the calculated stinginess of patrons when it comes to parceling out food. We hear this from no less than Flaminio, one of the few loyal, temperate courtiers in the play. Flaminio has become so disillusioned with the way he has been treated that he ends up counseling an elderly man, Sempronio, to spare his son any extended contact with the court, which is so full of ignominious cheapskates, he laments, that one can barely scrape by with the sorry crumbs one receives (2.5). The debased court, we learn from Flaminio, has lost the art of affably eating food, an art that once accompanied communal meals in festive gatherings of conspicuous consumption, thereby bringing together lords and servants in a bond of trust and mutual respect. In the old days, we learn from the nostalgic Flaminio, there was always plenty to eat, whereas now, amid the squalor of the incorrigible skinflints, one "has to look after his own fire and water" (2.5). Now the mothers of the lords, with a watchful greedy eye, "keep the keys of the wine cellars and ration the food—so much on feast days, so much on regular days" (2.5). "They even count the bowls of soup!" Flaminio plaintively exclaims. Worse, we later learn from the ever-hungry Rosso, the physical space in which the servants are constrained to eat is so revolting that they lose their appetite for the paltry, uninviting food that is served. "If you could see once the table all set up," he confides to the bawd Aloigia in a *tour de force* scene of disgust:

> and then had to eat the food that was on it, you'd be frightened to death yourself.
>
> Aloigia: I've never happened to see one.
>
> Rosso: The moment you set foot inside the small dining area, it doesn't matter whose it is, you find yourself in a tomb so dark it'd make a graveyard seem more cheery. In the heat of the summer it's boiling, and in winter the words freeze in your mouth. The stink's so fierce it'd take away the strong scent from civet perfume. That's where the plague comes from, nowhere else! Shut up the servants' messes, and presto! Rome would be cured of the plague.
>
> Aloigia: Merciful heavens!
>
> Rosso: There are more colors on the tablecloth than on a painter's smock. It's washed in the pigs' tallow that's left over at night from the candles—although most of the time we eat in the dark. And the bread's as hard as enamel. You can never wash your hands or your face. We eat St. Luke's mother at every meal.
>
> Aloigia: You eat Saints' flesh?
>
> Rosso: Even the crucified! No—when I said we eat St. Luke's mother I meant the way they paint them: he's an ox and his mother's a cow.
>
> Aloigia: Ha, ha, ha!
>
> Rosso: That beef they feed us is older than creation, and it's cooked so badly, abstinence itself would lose its appetite.

Aloigia: They should be ashamed!

Rosso: Morning and night always the same cow! The broth they make of it makes lye-water taste like sugar.

Aloigia: Aagh!

Rosso: Don't throw up yet—there's worse! They always put cabbage, cabbage roots, and squash in the soup—just when it's ready to be thrown out, I mean; otherwise, forget it. It's true, in place of fruit—as a refreshment—they give us a couple of chunks of buffalo cheese, which sits in your stomach like a lump of glue that'd kill a statue.

Aloigia: Jesus! [5.15]

Small wonder that the tavern becomes for Rosso a worldly substitute for paradise and eating well constitutes the best form of revenge against the parsimonious patrons. Rosso can aggressively and sadistically act out the role of the parasite within a comedy that laughs at his antics and the people he mocks and tricks, but for the duration of the play Rosso cannot act in a manner that will fundamentally alter his lifestyle or make his master truly suffer. His days are numbered. He is, and forever will remain, a hungry man in search of food. The penniless and famished Rosso is stuck in a stratified world where the success of mobility is measured in part by the habits of consumption; hence, he will never be able to get enough. In this way he is not just a stock comical figure with an appetite, but also a perennial figure *of* appetite.

Though courtiers were always lamenting about compensation, there are reasons to think that Aretino, an inveterate complainer with a gift for hyperbole and purplish prose, had cause to complain about courtly life in Rome as he cast his cold satiric eye over life in the papal city he eventually came to deplore. And there are reasons to believe that perhaps not everything here in Flaminio's and Rosso's descriptions of the poor conditions in which household members are fed should be taken as unalloyed, literary exaggeration. As Aretino put it in one of his early letters, "what my friends eat in my house," which is to say his house in Venice, "is worth more than all that I ever hoped for in the court" (1.98).[19] Servitude did not come easily to Aretino,[20] anymore than it did to the polygraphs who emulated him, from Ortensio Lando to Anton Francesco Doni. And he griped about servitude throughout his life. However, there is no evidence that Aretino himself was as hungry as the querulous household help in his comic plays (or that he was treated as poorly as they) when he was in the company, for instance, of the astronomically wealthy banker Agostino Chigi, whom he lauded in one letter for the dinners that Chigi orchestrated and that amazed Pope Leo X.[21] There is no evidence, in short, to assume that Rosso and Flaminio are voicing the author's own sorry personal experience as the member of a household, though there is no reason to discount that he had witnessed hardship in the court at Rome.

Moreover, judging from the surviving early literature on *scalchi* in Renaissance Italy, which is to say the literature devoted to "the head of a rigidly departmentalized bureaucracy" in households (whose job it was to see that everyone in the "famiglia" was fed),[22] there would seem to be little basis for such a stinging complaint on Aretino's part about the eating habits of the court generally in sixteenth-century Italy.[23] Cristoforo di Messisbugo's *Banchetti composizioni di vivande e apparecchio generale* (1549), describing the dazzling and immense banquets prepared for the d'Este court from the 1520s to the 1540s, can give us some idea of the expenses that princes, including Roman ones, were willing to take on in order to accommodate the household and guests in festive celebrations. Food overflowed at sumptuous banquets such as the ones described by Messisbugo (he has little interest in the food that any housewife could cook: beans and the like). And even if only a part of that food concocted for the feast made its way downstairs, as it were, there must have been enough to keep the household help from feeling famished.[24] In the d'Este palace there were plenty of people to feed, and for the most part the household help—everyone from the Guardabassos to the Flaminios of the courtly world—were probably fed well enough, be it at the master's table or in the small dining area, the *tinello*, in acts of shared loyalty and in a manner that reinforced social hierarchy.

In any event, it is hardly accidental that the term customarily used to describe a person in a Renaissance Italian household, be it in the Florentine *catasto* or Messisbugo's accounts, was a *bocca*, a mouth.[25] A person, for all intents and purposes, was in Florentine tax declarations and Ferrarese account books a mouth—not a mouth that necessarily spoke, protested, pleaded, and poeticized,[26] but a mouth that consumed, in one form or another, food. And there were sound reasons for defining a person in such a reductive, material way at times, thereby making the masticating orifice that consumed (rather the verbalizing orifice that communicated and displayed loyalty through conversation over the breaking of bread) function in those instances as a part for the whole. The amount of money spent to feed a person was, in truth, among the greatest sums any household had to absorb in its overall budget in Renaissance Italy, be it a large household like the one governed by Messisbugo in his account books or small ones like those Goldthwaite had in mind when talking about unskilled and skilled workers in the Florentine construction industry.[27] Things, to be sure, were no different in the Chigi household or the papal court where Aretino labored and witnessed from time to time feasts of lavish consumption. If Aretino was in purely reductive, materialist terms a bocca in Rome, it is probably safe to say that he was a bocca decently fed, even if in time he would turn out to be a bocca that ridiculed in his plays and satires the courtly world he left behind. Indeed, in time he would turn out to be, as his friend and editor Francesco Marcolini remarked in a letter, one of the most generous, hospitable people in Venice, a city of patrician merchants increasingly known in the sixteenth century for its extravagant opulence instead of famous restrained frugality.[28] According to Marcolini, Aretino, for all intents and purposes, transformed his house into a tavern and freely offered up food to the famished hangers-on, the Rossos and Guardabassos of the world:

The hospitality of your house, which is always open to everyone, keeps on going, so that it was not a marvel if on the first of May 1533, a band of foreigners thought that your house must be a tavern, such as it was, especially on seeing many people coming out and saying proudly that they had drunk the best wine in Venice. And they climbed the stairs and sat down at the table and called for a salad; and when it had been served with other dishes as they wished, and wanting to leave, they called for your Mazzone, whom, being young, handsome, blond, big, fat, happy, and pleasing, they thought was the innkeeper. When one of the companions asked him what they owed for dinner, the good Mazzone, seeing himself treated as an innkeeper and thinking that they were making fun of him, set about them with his fists, whereupon from the insults that you hurled at them, along with some of your blows, the gallant companions realized that you were the master of the house, and not a gentleman housed at an inn, as they had thought. And realizing the good companions that they dined like emperors, it didn't cost them anything other than a large "thank-you," and having done that to their advantage, they left laughing [B 28].[29]

Though there is no plausible correlation between Rosso's hunger as a servant within the play and Aretino's own experiences as a courtier in Rome, there is a history behind Rosso's hunger—an ancient literary history, that is—in the figure of the parasite in Roman and, to a lesser degree, Greek comedy. Unlike Rosso in Aretino's play, however, the parasite in Roman and Greek comedy was not a servant but a free person who had lost his fortune through profligacy, or perhaps never had a fortune to begin with, and who openly and boastfully lived off others. A stock character of Greek and Roman comedy, the parasite was a flatterer, although at other times (usually in Plautus, less often in Terence and the Greek comedies) he was outrageously hungry. Sometimes he was presented lightheartedly, but often he suffered terribly, though hilariously, because he failed to get someone to feed him.[30]

Aretino could have adopted the figure of the famished parasite indirectly from the modern avatars of classical comedies, the *commedie erudite*, the regular comedies, which were so popular in sixteenth-century Italy. A host of other literary models potentially subtend Aretino's figure of the hungry servant. Many of them no doubt derive their inspiration directly or indirectly from Boccaccio's *Decameron*, the great thesaurus of colorful characters for Renaissance comedy, which gives us quasi-professional gluttons such as Ciacco (resuscitated from Dante's hell) and numbskull hunger artists such as Calandrino (with his traditional peasant fantasies of cornucopian lands full of mountains of parmesan cheese, vines bound together by sausages, and streams of wine). Moreover, with his ear for the nuances and argot of popular culture, Aretino could have accessed the figure of the famished servant from street theater, the kind of theater that would eventually give rise to the figure of the parasite in the *commedia dell'arte*, who transforms everything into a comestible and seems to live in the grip of a deep, primordial hunger. Beyond that, as Camporesi has argued, much of the cultural imagination of the early modern period—a period that runs for Camporesi from Dante to the late seventeenth century—centers on the theme of hunger generally, with the Bolognese Giulio Cesare Croce representing the great popular singer of the theme at the end of the Italian Renaissance.[31]

But when Aretino drew on the tradition of the hungry parasite, he was not only echoing or borrowing from works of imaginative literature. He was also taking as one of the central targets of his attack Castiglione's *Cortegiano*, the seminal etiquette text that had been in circulation in manuscript form while Aretino was composing his *La cortigiana*, even if it did not appear in print until 1528. Castiglione talks about many things in his treatise as he discursively fashions the perfect courtier through the collective contributions of a group of courtiers gathered together in Urbino. Revealingly, however, one of the things Castiglione's courtiers do not talk about at any length is food, other than to insist that courtiers should avoid engaging in debased forms of physical competition while consuming it. Such degraded competitions take place when courtiers, thinking to prove themselves jovial by behaving as if they were in a tavern rather than a prince's palace, irreverently fling "soups, sauces, jellies, and every kind of thing in one another's faces" and then laugh about it, or when they "vie among themselves and lay wager as to who can eat and drink the most vile and nauseating things; and they concoct things so abhorrent to human sense that it is impossible to mention them without the greatest disgust" (134, 192).[32] Beyond these forms of base competitive behavior, which are loathsome not only because they privilege the cravings of the body but also because they exemplify immoderate behavior (a cardinal sin in the *Cortegiano*), Castiglione's courtiers, who must typify professional propriety, have nothing to say about food other than to insist that courtiers "ought not to profess to be a great eater or drinker" (135, 194).

By contrast, Aretino has come to set the record straight. Food matters. And when it comes to eating, the virtue of moderation in the court, where people aim to be inconspicuously conspicuous, is the luxury of those who can ascertain with a high degree of predictability when their next meal is coming to them and that, in fact, they will be sitting at a well-stocked table when they do sit down to eat. It's not enough to get close to the master whom one aims to serve dutifully so that one can influence world events. Intimacy with the prince means little if you're not getting decently fed. Similarly, the honor of being close to the prince and his distinguished company at the dinner table, a bocca consequently rendered of particular social value, is undermined if there's nothing edible on your plate. And the pleasures of sharing food in court culture as a way of communicating and cementing relationships, to curry loyalty in a sort of social act of communion and love, is thoroughly subverted if there is a paucity of food, or if everyone in the court feels starved. Men and women of all ranks of society felt bound to the person who fed them and with whom they ate, but presumably they felt this way if they were in fact getting properly fed.

La cortigiana was not Aretino's only parodic attack on Castiglione's *Cortegiano*. In his two sets of *Dialogues* (1534–1536), Aretino's most extended parody of the genre of how-to books[33] (the most famous at the time being, of course, Castiglione's *Cortegiano*), the experienced and worldly Nanna aims to fashion her daughter Pippa in the second set of dialogues into a professional prostitute who will acquire fame. She will be the perfect prostitute, as it were, for a society bent on producing the perfect courtier, as well as the perfect secretary, perfect ambassador, and perfect cardinal.[34] In addition to the expectation that Pippa must never clean her teeth with a napkin, chew "in a filthy manner" (188, 314), or say dirty things in polite company (better to let a tooth fall from your mouth, she warns, than let drop a dirty phrase; 187), Pippa as a professional must never "be seen or heard peeing, easing [her] bowels, or dabbing [her] face with a handkerchief" (188, 315). Like the fools in Shakespearian drama, Aretino's Nanna and Pippa (along with Antonia, yet another impish character in the dialogues) function as foils. They are figures who highlight both the virtues and vices of the dominant culture they manipulate to their own advantage.

In this case, Nanna and Pippa take advantage of the virtue of employing good manners in order to win a place in society at the very moment that they bring to the foreground the vices of greed, opportunism, and self-serving power that underpin the use of good manners for the purpose of making money and advancing a "career." They thus reveal that others who fashion themselves for social advancement through professional proprieties are also whores in their own way, as Aretino makes evident a number of times in his dialogues. "Indeed," Nanna bluntly observes in the dialogue, "Maestro Andrea used to say that whores [puttane] and courtiers [cortigiani] can be put on the same scales" (149, 256). Like courtiers, whose habits of presentation give them a mark of distinction, thereby determining where they belong both in society and at the dinner table, prostitutes in Aretino's dialogue must always be careful about how they consume—much as, a few decades later, Giovanni della Casa will dictate in his *Galateo* how people of stable social standing must eat with proper decorum at the table.[35] In Aretino's satire, which he composed not while a courtier in Rome but instead as a professional writer living in Venice, it is the *posture* that matters, the *show* of representing good manners and appearing to care about cleanliness and politia, even if one's predisposition would be to feast like a pig at a trough in an act, at least within Castiglione's court, of obvious professional impropriety.[36]

Pippa must be told not to consume great quantities of wine even if she is thirsty, or for that matter to consume food conspicuously at the dinner table, because her predilection, we can assume, would be to eat heartily and without much consideration for the feelings of others who have sat down to dine (187, 314). We can safely make this assumption about Pippa's undisciplined eating habits not only because she must be told what *not* to do—the expectation therefore being that she would otherwise do what she is not supposed to do and would consequently offend decorum by conspicuously sticking out amid the gathering—but also because everyone in Aretino's dialogues, including the interlocutors, thinks about consuming food. This is certainly true at the very beginning of the work. It is hardly accidental that what partly initiates the discussion at the opening of the first dialogue is Antonia's admiration of Nanna's ability to buy all sorts of food, since she has profited so well over the years from being an adept prostitute. "You can afford the most fantastic delicacies" (*godi fin del latte della gallina*; 5, 77, literally the "the milk of the hen"), she observes with some envy.

Food is on Antonia's mind, just as it is on the minds, as well as in the bellies, of the people described in the dialogues. It is food, for instance, that people gorge on right away, as Nanna describes the first hours of her life after having entered the convent as a young girl—all, it turns out, in preparation for her eventually becoming a prostitute. No sooner has the door been shut behind her, cutting her off from her family, than the sisters of the entire convent, with countless monks and friars attending, settle down to "one of the most delicate feasts" possible, with "the sort of food," Nanna assures us, "that the pope in person has never tasted" (11, 82), though the habits of consumption here described leave much to be desired and have more to do with street behavior than the presumably refined comportment of the Holy See. Being in the convent is no different than being in the marketplace of Piazza Navona, we learn, with garrulous men and women squabbling and picking at the food. One piggish friar worked his jaws so much as he ate large quantities of food that "he had his cheeks bulged out like a man blowing a trumpet"; then, to polish it off, "he put his mouth to a bottle and guzzled it all down" (12, 82). "I could not describe all the wine they guzzled and the pastries they devoured" (30, 98), Nanna remarks with incredulity as she describes the postcoital hunger of a group within the convent. Another ravenous friar, after delivering a sermon from the pulpit, "did with the wine, refreshing himself, what horses do with water, devouring pastries with the voracity that a nasty donkey gobbles the tendrils of a vine" (48, 112). In the meantime luscious capons were being cooked in preparation for yet more feasts to come (34, 101).

The pleasures of the life of the convent, we learn at the outset of the dialogues, are first and foremost the pleasures of the table. And the pleasures of the consumption of food continue through Aretino's dialogues, whether we are talking about Nanna indoctrinating others into the highly sexualized life of the convent, the sexual delights and peccadilloes of adultery in marriage, or the sexually lucrative work of prostitution. Humans are beasts, we are given to understand, and the beast must be fed, both inside and outside the convent. As a recently married woman, whose lack of virginity has been cleverly disguised, Nanna and a friend, she recalls, feasted on a "light supper" that included no less than "a thousand small dishes—livers, sweetbreads, chickens' feet and necks, a salad flavored with parsley and pepper, nearly a whole capon, olives, red apples, goat's-milk cheese, quince jelly to settle our stomachs, and candies to sweeten our breath" (72, 168–69). As it is for the lascivious married woman, so it is for the prostitute exercising her profession. Pippa may be warned by Nanna not to consume lavishly and conspicuously, but in the end eating this way is fun. Eat as much as you want, she is advised professionally, when you are with old men, for old men can't perform very well, if they can perform at all, and they take pleasure in seeing young women eat, so young women might as well take pleasure in consumption. "At dinners like this," Nanna recommends, "you can gorge yourself without standing on ceremony" (194, 319). Moreover, a prostitute needs to think about setting aside food on occasion for a later time. It's important not just to eat but to store up large quantities of comestibles. Appetites come and go, and though one can get one's fill at a meal it's important to think about the days that follow. Hence, have the competing clients pay for the meals royally, with the aim of having a plethora of leftovers (265, 374).

At the same time, the hunger described in the *Dialogues* is not only for food *per se* but also for sex envisioned as a form of food, as a type of consumption that propels people to behave in such a way that they can hardly have enough, with the exception perhaps of the prostitutes themselves who only yearn for sex as one might a light snack, *uno sfizio*, to put it colloquially, because their lust is so regularly fed. Things are different for virtually everyone else, however. Far from a snack, sex is a feast. "But the joy he derived from shoving it into and pulling it out of every hole and aperture," Nanna informs us, "are gentilities; the height of it was to see a herd of flunkies, undercooks, and hostlers rush out of the vineyard house with the growl that famished, chained dogs make as they pounce on the food like monks on a plate of broth" (300, 441). "What a feast!" Antonia exclaims on hearing about one person after another aggressively stuffing it (the "it" being in one instance first a glass dildo already used as a utensil for eating food and then a male member) smack into the "oven" of yet another person, so that they all looked like a "spit of damned souls" (26, 94). Women who are unresponsive and lack the talent of taking on many positions offer a man who tastes them about as much savor as one "gets from broad bean soup cooked without oil or salt" (16, 86). On occasion sex is so fulfilling that one can lose an appetite for food itself (24); it occurs, predictably enough, to Nanna. In another instance, the coy appearance of chastity on the part of the prostitute may make an aroused client so frustrated that she appears to him as an appetizer that only redoubles his desire for a full meal (120, 235). Various sexual activities, moreover, sometimes bring to mind different sorts of dining tastes. Anal intercourse, for instance, is so appetizing, Antonia insists, that it is deemed "a choice tidbit that people fight for more than lamprey. It's a dish for gourmets" (*È una vivanda da gran maestri*; 37, 103).

Finally, Aretino takes delight in finding various ways of talking about sex as food. One option would be to be blunt. In fact, Aretino explains why it is important to be to the point and avoid the niceties of indirection, the kinds of indirection that are required by decorum and constitute the modus operandi of courtiers in Castiglione's treatise in their acts of refined professional propriety:[37]

> Wetnurse: It's a strange thing that one cannot even say ass, cunt, and prick.
> Midwife: A hundred times I have wondered for what reason we must be ashamed to mention that which nature is not ashamed to create.
> Wetnurse: I have thought about that too, and even more: it seems to me that it would be more honest to show the prick, cunt, and ass than the hands, mouth, and feet.
> Midwife: Why?
> Wetnurse: Because the prick, cunt, and ass do not curse, bite, or spit in one's face as mouths do. They don't kick like feet, or lend themselves to false oaths, belabor with clubs, steal, and murder like hands [367, 536].

No doubt Aretino finds irreverent satisfaction in just saying things as they are, in not beating around the bush; he surely takes pleasure in offending decorum here, much as he does elsewhere, beginning in his literary life with the *sonetti lussuriosi* and the pasquinate.[38] But the pleasure of talking about sex, and in this instance the parts of the body that are repeatedly deployed in the dialogues as the privileged instruments of sex (that is to say, the prick, the cunt, and the ass), is the pleasure in finding various and sundry euphemisms for the activity.[39] And in keeping with the close connection established in the text between the hunger for food and the hunger for sex, many of those euphemisms have to do with food. A woman has cheeks like milk and honey, much as they are conventionally represented in elevated Petrarchan love lyric. But in keeping with the contrary genre of carnival songs, where food lasciviously doubles as body parts, a woman also has a vagina that is a "granary" (114, 230), an ass that tastes of "mint and wild anise" (89, 182), and a "you-know-what" that is full of "honey" and tastes sweeter than the sugar sold by the sugar merchant who himself hungers for the prostitute's services. Similarly, a man boasts of having between his loins a veritable "sausage" (73, 170), and he is capable of satisfying a woman with a piece of "larded bread" (59, 159).

If the variety of sexual positions and sexual lovers serves to arouse an appetite, so too linguistically the variety of ways that Aretino finds to talk about sex complements his notion about the importance of variety in increasing the appetite. We don't always want to eat homemade bread, Nanna observes, any more than we want to dine at home all the time, for "to vary foods stimulates appetite" (61, 160);[40] it keeps the juices flowing. Furthermore, the variety of ways of talking about sex as food feeds the underlying principle in the *Dialogues* that a well-told and well-informed narrative is itself a form of feeding. Consequently, the response on the part of the listeners—or readers saying the words out loud—is to yearn for that narrative full of calculated digressions and variations with a stimulated appetite, like a famished child groping for the breast. "I'm waiting for you to get to the heart of your story," Antonia informs Nanna, "like babies waiting for the wet nurse to shove her tit in their mouths. It seems to me that your dawdling is more painful than the day before Easter is to someone peeling eggs after having fasted through Lent" (19, 88–89). The oral pleasure of sex mirrors the oral pleasure of verbalizing sex.

When it comes to matters of consumption, then, nothing in Aretino's *Dialogues* comes to us in moderation, and everything serves to offend decorum, in particular the decorum advanced in such books of professional self-development as the *Cortegiano*, which Aretino here deliberately parodies with characteristic satirical vengeance. Hence, if Castiglione's notion of conspicuous consumption revolves around objects of distinction and taste, from the elegant palace of Urbino, which is viewed as the most beautiful and distinguished in all of Italy, to the duke's study, which is stocked full of expensive books and is elaborately decorated with refined and edifying images,[41] Aretino's notion of conspicuous consumption revolves around fulfilling one's appetite for both sex as food and food as oral pleasure to such an extent that people are inspired to behave in the most immodest and immoderate of ways. Appetite, Aretino reveals, is a strange thing. It can get the better of us and lead us to behave in a debased manner. When clients are properly cajoled and manipulated to a point of absolute frustration, for instance, their appetite can even lead them to eating a prostitute's excrement and swallowing her period, or just as bad, consuming the scabs of her syphilis:

> Nanna: I won't deny that [a whore] uses every possible art to blind them, making them eat our excrement, and our periods too. There was one—I won't even mention her name—who, in order to get one [of her lovers] to pursue her, gave him a flock of the French disease-crusts to eat, since she had plenty to spare.
>
> Antonia: How awful! [141, 250]

Appetite has no bounds in Aretino's dialogues, no zero degree of debasement.

At the same time, it is important to have an appetite and to recognize that one has an appetite, Aretino also seems to warn, for there is no denying the demands—indeed sometimes the most immoderate demands—of the body. In this light, if no one talks at any length about food in the *Cortegiano*, it is not just because talking about food (God forbid talking about the pleasures of sex!) would offend decorum by addressing so openly matters that have to do with satisfying the body rather than the mind, which are matters more appropriate to the marketplace than the court. No one talks at any length about food in the *Cortegiano*, we might reasonably posit, because talking about such a matter would simply mean stating the obvious in a manner that would undermine the virtue of sprezzatura (the art of understatement, nonchalance, and studied coolness) that is so suavely put into practice in the text itself with great professional propriety. We should, in short, just generally assume that these laudable, happy courtiers, whose sexual appetites are sublimated through talk about gender and gentle yet tense skirmishes with each other about women,[42] are being well fed day in and day out at the dinner table in a manner that cements their relationships in bonds of mutual loyalty and friendship. Surely we should assume this is the case at the beginning of book 2 of the *Cortegiano*, when, before the courtiers have all gathered together in the late evening with the duchess to continue their games, "the Prefect desired that they should eat, and took all the gentleman to supper" (95, 145).[43] However, this was not always the case in the sixteenth century, Aretino warns. The court, to be sure, is just what Castiglione describes: a place of show and prudential performance. In this way it is not only ideal but also very real. But according to Aretino the life of the courtier is far different from anything Castiglione ever presented: "Ours was a fine world, in the old days, and my good godfather Motta gave me a neat comparison. 'Nanna,' he told me, 'today's whores resemble today's courtiers [cortigiani], who, if they wish to live in pomp and plenty, are forced to steal; otherwise they'd die of hunger. And for one courtier who has bread in his coffer, there are hordes that scrounge for crusts" (287–88, 431–32).

In the *Dialogues*, as in *La cortigiana* and *Lo Ipocrito*, once more Aretino invites us to witness the sorry state of the court. In truth, courtiers are a hungry lot, he would have us believe, and they are not just hungry for respect, honor, and distinction, as Guardabasso, Malanotte, Perdelgiorno, and Rosso make clear. Like prostitutes, and the parasites in classical and contemporary Renaissance literature, they are simply hungry for food as well. To be sure, Aretino's comparison and representation is more literary imagination and satirical characterization than anything else, but it was a colorful and ribald exaggeration that offered to the public at large a constructive yet irreverent counterpart to Castiglione's image of the court as an enviable place of perfected moderation with its decorous habits of consumption, professional propriety, and finely controlled appetites. When viewed as a sort of over-the-top, preemptive strike against the court and the practices of courtiers, moreover, these satirical characterizations allowed Aretino, who profited so much from print culture, to deflect attention away from his ever appearing to have prostituted himself as a writer by commercially participating, if only indirectly, in the marketplace of print. Characteristically, one of Aretino's strategies for asserting his own professional propriety was by sabotaging the propriety of others. As a writer living indirectly off the marketplace of print, Aretino's offense, which paradoxically just rendered him all the more conspicuous, was often strategically his best defense.

Food for Thought: Aretino's Art of Consumption

If there is a fictional figure in the European Renaissance generally who embodies in the cultural imagination of the period what it means to have an enormous appetite for things, it would have to be Christopher Marlowe's Faustus, the man who is willing to give up everything, even his own soul, so that he can sate his desire. He knows everything, but he must have more. His desire is for an absolute, a sort of anguished demand. But to single out an actual living-and-breathing person who embodied in the cultural imagination of the period through his calculated representations of himself what it meant to have an enormous appetite, one could do no better than choose Aretino, a man who positioned himself as happy to have his home in Venice mistaken for a paradisiacal place of plenty where capons were eternally stuffed, sausages dripped fat from spits, and the booze flowed freely. In one instance, for example, early on in his life in Venice, as he wrote off a letter of thanks to Girolamo Agnello (the brother of the Mantuan ambassador) for the keg of wine sent him, he describes how his house was turned into a sort of tavern and, through the offering of the delectable wine bestowed on him to others, he acquired fame. Wherever anyone "eats or sits or walks," he reports to Agnello, elevating the giver as he elevates himself,

> one doesn't talk about anything other than my perfect wine. For which reason I am better known on its account than I am on my own. I'd be undone if such a solemn

drink didn't come. And it seems to me a good thing that it is on the lips of every harlot and of every tavern-crawler, for love of its savor which bites and kisses at the same time. My eyes fill with tears as I think, pen in hand, about those little tears placed on the eyes of those who drink it. So you can imagine what it will do to me upon seeing it leap with sparkling color in a well-washed goblet of pure glass [C 34, 1.72].

Aretino loved food, and he loved receiving it in a culture where gift giving constituted a privileged form of making and reinforcing connections, as well as exchanging and building honor.[44] For in giving a gift, Aretino reminds his dear friend Jacopo Sansovino (the sculptor and architect with whom he often dined), "one sees the love of him who sends it, the thoughtfulness of him who brings them, and the delight of him who receives them" (C 287, 5.323).[45] It is not only essential, therefore, that people like Girolamo Agnello supply Aretino with gifts of food and that, in receiving these gifts, Aretino cements relationships within extended networks of influence and patronage as a matter of simulated, ritualized, courtly conduct. It is also essential that Aretino in his letters aggressively advertise, in printed works that indeed become public documents, how these gifts advance his standing, his own sense of distinction, and his sense of privilege and entitlement. They are essential to his notion of selfhood as he crafts it in his letters.

Hence his letters, which propelled him into fame, are full of expressions of gratitude for the gifts of food he receives. He receives *confetti* on a number of occasion, along with lots of peaches, some so wonderful that it seemed to him, upon "eating them, to have eaten the fruit" (*pomi*) that would have made Adam forget about the taste of the apple (1.233). He gets massive quantities of olives and olive oil, hares and veal, and thrushes so good that Titian, upon sniffing them, even cancels a dinner engagement to feast on them, he informs Count Manfredo di Collalto in 1532 (C 39, 1.84–85). There are truffles and oysters that stimulate the appetite, strawberries that are crimson, perfumed, and savory, as well as cucumbers, figs, muscat grapes, apricots, melons, plums, artichokes, squash, beans, suckling kids, jellies, almonds, citrons, and fish (herring, shrimp, and carp, among others). There are mushrooms that he consumes in abundance, chickens, a fair amount of spiced bread, turkeys, pear-shaped lemons, cheese, caviar, fennel (not a lot of it, but what comes is tasty, some "sott'aceto"), salami (one of which was stolen from him), snails, salads of all types, mixed in such a way that the "bitterness and bite" of one kind matches another, "making of all a mixture so suave that it would satisfy satiety itself" (88, 1.307). And there are gallons, one can deduce, of wine, muscatel and Trebbiano among others. Some of the wine is so good that the guests in Aretino's house, he records in a letter to the Lucchese priest Meo Franci, "seemed like a gaggle of gabblers who had collected around the wine barrels at Empty Talk Inn—the kind who trying to make a thousand mouthfuls and a thousand sips out of a stalk of fennel and a small glass of Trebbiano, lick their tongues against and then away from their palates with the same sort of 'laf lof' that the fingers of servants do when they thrust them into a pie" (C 165, 2.250). He cannot contain himself with gratitude on receiving "the gift of sugar that comes in loaves, in powdered form, in slabs, and in liquors" (1.461).

Quantity also matters, "since man by his nature celebrates in seeing an abundance of food" (1.176), he remarks to the Venetian gentleman Marc'Antonio Venier. Abundance, *abbondanza*, pleases the eye and the appetite, as is evident in so many paintings in the Italian Renaissance.[46] Consequently, nothing is finer than being sent an enormous cheese, he tells us, the sort of cheese that can elicit stupor, like the one Count Lodovico Rangone, the future governor of Friuli, ostensibly sends him in 1550:

> As for me, I believe that from the udders of how many of the herds of cattle and the flocks of sheep that Apollo ever looked upon, would have come, in their whole lifetime, enough milk to make a cheese as enormous as the one that your and my Gian Tomaso Bruno made me a gift of in your name. When I saw it, the admiration it aroused in me agrees with the appetite which its abundant beauty evoked, so that I will go about enjoying it (with never-ending astonishment) as long as it lasts and to the great honor of your courteous and caring lordship [C 300, 6.62].

Aretino's worth is therefore measured not only in the nature of the gift and its provenance. (What gift is sent and who sends it are always critical and telling pieces of information that he needs to share with his reader, to build up both himself and the giver of the gift as people of esteem and honor.) Aretino's worth is also significantly measured according to the amount of the gift, its "copia," as he put it in one letter. The cheese is stupefying in its grandeur, and so it is right that Aretino, in keeping with his notion of gift giving as an expression of shared love and honor, should receive it. The cheese is larger than life, and so, conspicuously, is Aretino as he represents himself. And, as we learn in another instance, he really adored cheese, or so he claims. On one occasion he tells how he took the rare measure of cautioning his household help, whom he usually treats, he insists, with decorous familiarity and generosity, not to dare touch his recent, coveted gift of cheese, about which he finds himself compelled to break out in Latin—certainly a false boast since Aretino's Latinity was abysmal (4.159). "In the meantime," he insists in his letter of 1547 to the Veronese knight Gherardo Boldieri, "I ordered the housekeepers, whom I hold as ladies [*madonne*], that insofar as they held dear their roguish shoulders, they should not dare to taste even a mouthful; and tasting some of that cheese later, I sang out in a disorderly way [*isquinternai*] more praises to the sheep who gave birth as such beasts to that cheese" (4.159).

Aretino ate not only a lot but also all sorts of foods, he maintains. He didn't limit himself to the types of food customarily associated with the elite, but also the foods that were typically considered low: "Certainly my spirit, if I had the means, would like to feast in royal grandeur, but my mouth, although it is still able to enjoy tasty dishes, takes its nourishment from simpler, country/peasant food [*vivande villane*]. If it is a sin, then, to devour a whole salad, and with it a whole onion, I am done for, because I find in such things a delicate flavor, much richer than what those kitchen hawks who hovered around the table of Leo [X] ever tested" (C 76–77, 1.266). He presented himself as refusing to disdain the "rude and rustic fare" (C 268, 5.68). Even his dreams bring him to a fantasized tavern; citing his own *La cortigiana* in a letter of 1537 to Count Gian Iacapo Leonardi, the Urbanese ambassador to Venice, he observes: "To quote Cappa: 'He who has not ever been in a tavern does not really know what heaven is like'" (C 111, 1.385).

To be sure, Aretino was perfectly capable of praising the simple life, in which "you eat to live and do not live to eat" (C 135, 2.53), as he puts it to the Tuscan sculptor Simone Bianco in 1538, but in the same context he felt compelled to furnish us with the names of all sorts of food available to anyone living the so-called simple life: salads, sausages, omelets, roast pork, wine, eggs, fish, capons, and broilers. Nothing pleased him so much as food, he would have us believe over and over again, and no food was too good for him (or, which really seems to be the issue, too debased). Onions have a place at his dinner table, as do fine peaches and savory wines. In particular, wine—indeed a steady supply of it—gives him "the same pleasure that sends others in ecstasy" at the service of a sensual "love" (C 266, 5.39). To this effect, Aretino has only words of mockery for the advice of doctors, who would limit the range of foods available for consumption according to the particular complexion of the individual (something that the other famous Aretine, Francesco Petrarca, had little tolerance for when he was, conversely, informed not to drink water but wine instead to preserve his health).[47] As far as Aretino is concerned, he has solid, material evidence that the doctors must be quacks when it comes to limiting his intake of food (4.253). His own body, and his own tolerance for the food he consumes, tells him directly and unequivocally that he should just keep consuming what and exactly as he does.

This was not a man, then, who would like us to believe that he disdained the pleasures of consumption of any sort of food, or that he suffered little the prohibitions and admonitions of doctors. As a result, he was, he claimed, prepared to break out into song on tasting a thrush, and he asserted elsewhere that he was astounded that poets have not sung extended praises of salad (C 88, 1.307)—something that Ronsard would later do. He was also ready to discourse on the types of olives with the pedantry of a learned gourmand: "Spanish olives," he opines, "are ostentatiously large. Bolognese olives, not being juicy—as indeed Spanish olives are not juicy either—retain some of the bitterness that comes to them from the tree" (C 117, 1.392). This was also a man, we are led to believe, who could attack the food sent him with ravenous pleasure. He had, as he put it, a "bestial appetite" (*appetito bestiale*), and he consumed food with "ravenous pleasure" (*famelico gusto*; 6.140–41). But it is important to stress that Aretino's habits of consumption as he represents them are simultaneously high and low, elitist and popular. His body, often portrayed by Titian, has the look of a man who has lavished attention on his table, but it is also a distinguished portly body, as allied to the world of the refinement as it is to the marketplace and tavern. This is not strictly the body of carnival but of the high and low *combined*. Aretino's habits of consumption are the locus of a synthesis as much as they are wide-ranging and all-inclusive. He was happy, he insisted, with both the food of the elite and the food of the tavern, and he could transform his house into a setting appropriate for the one and the other.

The pleasure Aretino takes in what he eats also has much to do with where he is eating, he maintains. It matters supremely, as he represents his acts of eating, that he is consuming his food at his own house, and not at the court. What made the food of the simple life arguably satisfying, for instance, was that one consumed it in one's own domain, even if home might happen to be a fantasized rustic hut. Needless to say, in his letters, which were written and published while he lived in commercial, republican Venice, the court remains the privileged locus of anticipated indigestion (C 136, 2.53). His praise of the simple life may be a literary exaggeration, but his contempt for the court and praise of dining in his own house with food freely given to him was not. "Courts eh? Courts ah?" he writes to Giovanni Agnello from Venice in 1537, "It is better to eat bread and jests than the smell of viands on a silver platter. . . . Just as there is no stronger suffering that reaches that of a courtier [cortegiano] who is weary and has nowhere to sit down, who is hungry and may not eat, and who is overcome by sleep and yet must stay awake, so there is no contentment that can reach mine, who can sit down when I am worn out, eat when I am hungry, and sleep when sleep assails me" (C 99, 1.353). By contrast, bread simply tastes better when it is consumed at one's own home, where it is free of servitude and where servants are treated decently, as if they were sons and daughters. In his house, he would have his readers believe, people are urged to return as if to a "tavern" where the bread is never "locked up" and "the wine is never watered down" (C 252, 4.270). Eating must also be done in company, for anyone who dines alone is just "gorging himself like a wolf" (*ingordigia di Lupo*; C 266, 5.38). It is always a delight to feed others, those who are friends and those in need. His house is always a "mensa del carnasciale," he rejoices in a letter to Marc'Antonio Venier, a place of festive consumption (1.176), as well as a place of refined dining among the cultural elite.

In this way Aretino's home becomes a sort of clearinghouse, a distribution center as allied to the market as it is to select aspects of the court. The food sent him doesn't just fill his body—and his body did indeed gradually grow to the point where he was viewed and could view himself as fat (C 1.228). The food sent to him also fills the bodies of others, he would have the readers of his letters know. Deliver a gift of food to Aretino and a larger, communal body is being fed, both in private elitist settings and more open-ended ones in his own home. In this respect, Aretino in his letters occupies the status that Alberto Capatti and Massimo Montanari have attributed to the figure of the cook in their history of Italian cuisine: "a key player or pivot in the dynamics of intercultural exchange."[48] What is more, Aretino seeks to represent himself as embodying that process of intercultural exchange in his acts of conspicuous consumption.

How then, is the reader supposed to take in all this conspicuous consumption, digest it, as it were, as a matter of appetite? In keeping with vernacular and humanist writings in the Italian tradition, which explicitly establish a high-minded connection between literature and food, beginning with Dante's *Convivio* and then extending on to the writings of such distinguished humanists as Leonardo Bruni, we are invited to think of Aretino's letters about the consumption of food in terms of literary digestion as well.[49] However, if Dante and Bruni are offering us up knowledge and virtue through their works as food, Aretino seems to be offering us something else, something far less spiritual and morally edifying. He seems to be offering up himself as someone privileged and honored who receives so much food and conspicuously consumes so much of it.

"Tell me what you eat and I will tell you what you are," Jean Anthelme Brillat-Savarin observed pithily in his nineteenth-century *The Philosophy in the Kitchen*.[50] In Aretino's case, as we have seen, we know a lot about what he purportedly ate, and thus a lot about who he would like us to think he was as a man who could combine both the high and the low and also share all his food with his friends. And what we get when we read about his habits of consumption is Aretino himself conspicuously put forward in all his egregious anticonformist corporeality. His letters about consumption speak to his peculiar, larger-than-life mode of conspicuous self-fashioning. His food *is* his personhood, his embodied essence. In this respect, in buying and acquiring Aretino's letters we are invited to consume through the marketplace of print culture the popularized arch-consumer in literary form, participating, if only at a distance once removed, in the kind of consumption for which Aretino created a name for himself. As he put it to the Forlivese gentleman Bernardino Teodoli in 1538, consuming his letters was like gathering cherries to eat: "I will say that I do not marvel at all over the fury that at Rome was displayed about my book of letters, because just so children also show themselves to be when they see the first cherries of the season" (*nel vedere le prime ciriege*; 1.523). We may or may not be fully aware when we read Aretino's descriptions of his habits of consumption that our desire is someone else's, but we can still take pleasure in that mediated desire, mystified or demystified as it may be.

Moreover, and more important, the consumption of prose about wine and salads and olives and peaches and spiced bread and fennel is the consumption that we have all along been looking for as readers engaged in the marketplace of print through our own appetites for his books, which we are invited to buy and consume as worldly goods. We are putatively interested, after all, in the flow of words, the representations and posturing, not the cornucopia of actual, referenced food put on display. Aretino's art of consumption in this regard encapsulates the narrative strategy of his letters as a collection, a *raccolta* to be taken symbolically as a harvesting, as he presents us with six separate volumes (the last printed posthumously) that privilege variety in subject matter and style, just as he privileges throughout his works a variety in foods and their preparations. Hence, even though the true etymology of the word *satire* would not be disclosed until the first decade of the seventeenth century,[51] it is nevertheless not too anachronistic to think of Aretino's letters—and by extension many of his works in general—within the context of that elusive genre, as a dish that is offered up with a variety of foods to be tasted. And the foods he offers up in his letters are as allied to the marketplace as they are to the court. For with his letter writing, the gifts of food Aretino has received and shared are in their turn offered back to the public at large in representations of food that are shared in a language everyone can understand. And all this is done, Aretino is quick to point out, outside the confines of the court full of hungry, parasitic hangers-on and, as he also insisted, in a manner in which he could never be accused of directly, much less grossly, prostituting himself through the new, highly instrumentalized medium of print.[52]

One oral pleasure in this way feeds another. Consumption of food leads to literary production about food, and consequently—if the reader is willing to engage Aretino's art by buying it and buying into it—back to material consumption once again. Aretino's art of consumption, then, is not strictly an art of food (for that, one can read in the period everything from carnival songs to collections of *novelle*) any more than it is the art of edifying readers through literature imagined as food (for that, one can read Dante's *Convivio* or Bruni's Ciceronian letters). Instead, Aretino's art of consumption is ultimately the art of conspicuously consuming massive quantities of food, so that we may begin to think about how we become, through the process of reading all his varied letters in the vernacular, consumers ourselves. In this way, as in so many others, Aretino makes us conscious of our bodies, our habits of consumption, and our endless and unpredictable appetites for things in a culture so deeply invested in not just the art of eating but also, as he makes plain, the art of eating well.

CHAPTER 3

Michelangelo Buonarroti and the Art of Conspicuous Absorption

A Meal for Michelangelo

E. M. Forster once remarked that characters in novels don't need to eat food.[1] People need to eat food so that they can stay alive (after all, they have bodies), but fictional characters in novels don't need to eat food because they are not in any way biologically alive (simply put, they don't have bodies—a point so obvious it hardly seems worth stressing). In any event, characters don't need to eat food in novels; people do. It's as simple as that. And it's as simple as that, we may argue by extension, if we apply Forster's remarks about food in novels to literature at large, including classical literature. Homer's and Virgil's heroes eat, for instance, but no sensible reader would be puzzled if they arrived at the end of their epics and discovered that Odysseus, Achilles, or Aeneas had never consumed food with their companions when they sat down to meals at carefully orchestrated banquets or when they disembarked in new places and needed to fill their bellies as quickly as possible. The point, of course, is that Odysseus, Achilles, and Aeneas do eat, but they do not *need* to eat food in order for the reader to accept their viability as characters ("flat" or "round" characters, as the case may be). We are willing, that is, to suspend not our belief in them as characters but our understanding of the biological functions and needs of the human body. Moreover, if Odysseus, Achilles, and Aeneas eat, which is in fact the case, it is because the conventions associated with the genre of epic demand that they eat. We enter a work with a set of conventions associated with it, or we are indoctrinated into those conventions by the authors themselves. Thereafter we just move along, accepting what comes our way, if indeed we are willing and eager to move on. Readers, for instance, have always marveled over Dante's ability to make us believe that the wayfarer is journeying through the otherworld with his entire body—they have even gone so far as to measure the distances within hell and the sizes of the giants guarding the frozen lake of Cocytus—but no one (or at least no one in his or her right mind) has asked if the wayfarer has been consuming food during his roughly seven-day voyage from hell to heaven.[2] Surely at some point he must have gotten hungry. Conversely, readers are inundated with details about how much Gargantua eats in Rabelais's mock epic, but no one seems to stop and ask how he could have consumed so much food.

Unlike Aretino, Michelangelo (Figure 5), whose thoughts about food are partly the subject of this chapter, did not intend to publish his letters. He certainly never intended them to be construed as a sort of literary supplement for food, as a source of personal profit accessed indirectly through the marketplace of print, or as a way of giving an interested public vicarious entry into a well-heeled lifestyle of leisure amid the elite in a world of conspicuous consumption. Michelangelo's letters are instead the direct, and sometimes hurried, expressions of a man—a very private, thrifty, busy, and solitary man, who was often concerned (good Florentine male that he was) with accounting for every measure of his material wealth. Inevitably, one of those concerns centered naturally enough on the important worldly possession of food—a topic, as we have seen, of keen interest to Aretino. "I've received a pack-load of Trebbiano for which I'm grateful," he informs his nephew Lionardo in 1548, while in Rome. "Nevertheless, I tell you not to send me anything else unless I send and ask you for it, because I'll send you the money for what I want" (2.93).[3] And then, just a few letters later, toward the end of January 1549, Michelangelo writes to Lionardo: "The cheese you've sent me—I've had the letter—but I haven't yet had the cheese" (2.97).[4] Why not? Why indeed, we learn: because the cheese has been stolen. "I believe the muleteer," he writes, "who brought it has sold it to someone else, because I sent to the Customs for it several times. The said muleteer has invented a thousand tales and talked so much that he must have made off with it—so I make no doubt he's a rogue. So don't send me anything more; because it's more a nuisance than use" (2.97).[5] Concerned as he always is with every last item of his material wealth, Michelangelo, who by then was a well-to-do man, takes pains to uncover the whereabouts of his missing cheese by sending Urbino, his personal assistant, to track it down at the Customs House. Eventually this is what he learns toward the beginning of February 1549: "The men at the Customs say that the carrier either sold it at the inn, or left it in Florence, because here they don't put less than five barrels of cheese in bond and the Customs consign all these directly to their owners. It must be that the said carrier himself is an out-and-out glutton, because he did everything he could to avoid Urbino, until he left" (2.98).[6] The loss of this barrel of cheese seems to have upset Michelangelo, just as it grated on him when he thought

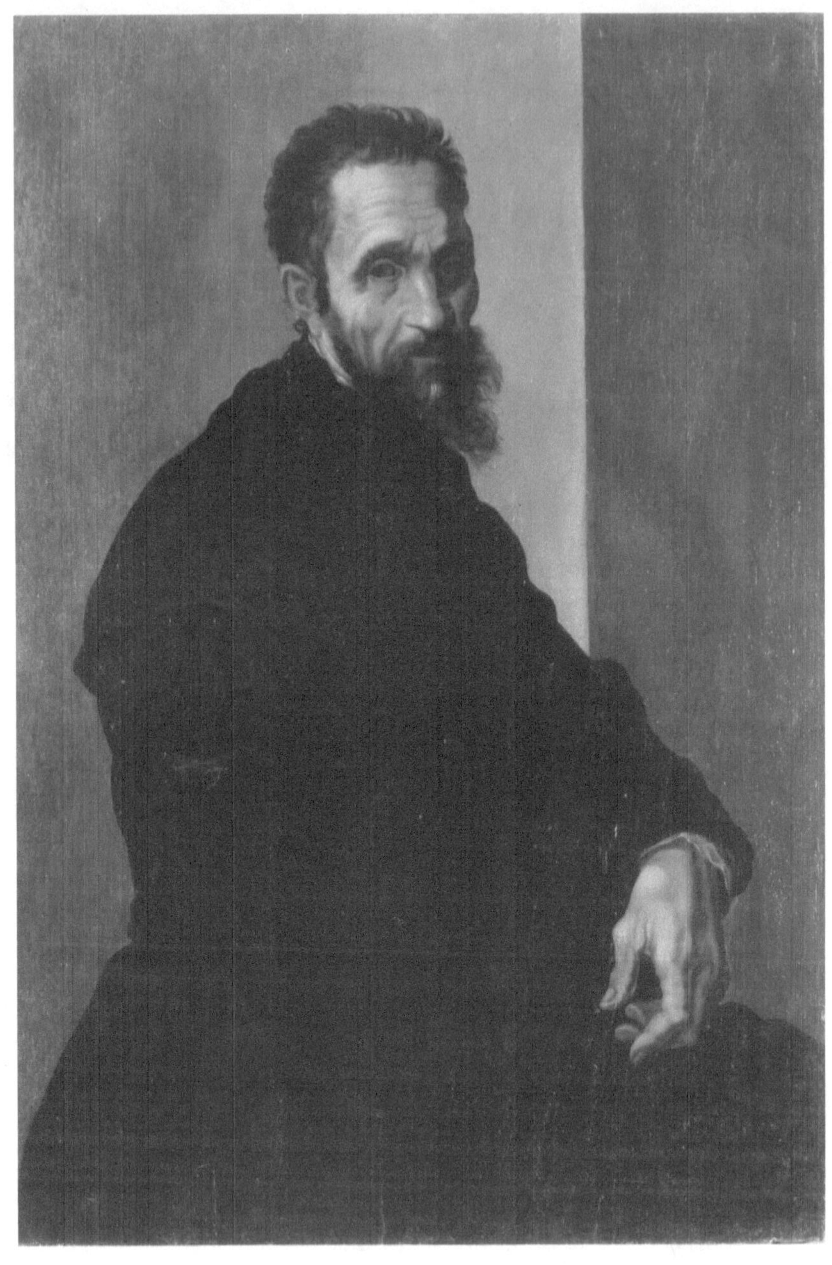

FIGURE 5. Jacopino del Conte (1515–1598). *Portrait of Michelangelo*, ca. 1540. Casa Buonarroti, Florence. Photo courtesy Scala/Art Resource, New York.

he was cheated at other times, such as nearly a year earlier, in May 1548. "I got the barrel of pears," he writes,

> which numbered eighty-six. I sent thirty-three of them to the pope; he thought them excellent and was very grateful for them. As for the barrel of cheese, the Customs say that the carrier is a scoundrel, and that he never brought it into the Customs, so that when I find out that he's in Rome, I'll see that he gets what he merits—not on account of the cheese, but in order to teach him what it means to show little respect for people [2.91].[7]

We will never know if Michelangelo captured the thief and taught him a lesson or two, much less recovered the cheese, but we can rest assured that if he had managed to lay hands on him the carrier would have no doubt received the brunt of Michelangelo's legendary wrath for absconding with his goods. His famed terribilità, which has defined for many his character *and* his art, manifested itself in all sorts of ways, whether facing down a pope in an unprecedented act of professional impropriety by throwing planks at him, transferring his intensity into his larger-than-life art, losing his temper with members of his sometimes ungrateful family, or just hunting down a scoundrel who had made off with some of his cheese.[8]

If Michelangelo was occasionally concerned with having food and with accounting for its whereabouts in his letters, he was not, conversely, concerned at all with consuming food or taking much pleasure in it. His abstemiousness marks him as the precise opposite of his contemporary Aretino, just as, physically, his leanness stands in stark contrast with Aretino's corpulence. Michelangelo's abstemiousness indeed comes through not only in his letters but also in the writings of others about him. True, his letters reveal that he likes marzolini cheese (which was oval shaped, usually running around five hundred grams, and freshly made from sheep's milk), and he seems to consume much Trebbiano wine (which he freely shares with such men as the pope, as he does his pears).[9] But his comments about either his habits of consumption or his pleasures in consumption in his letters are rare.[10] This is a man who would not suffer the torments of gluttony either in Dante's Inferno or Purgatory. Quite the contrary. He and others commenting on his habits of consumption discuss how noticeably abstemious he is, to the point that it seems he doesn't eat at all. In 1531, for instance, Michelangelo fell ill, "for he works much," we are candidly told by a concerned third party observer, Giovan Battista Mini, and as a result the great Michelangelo "eats little and badly" (C 3.329). Earlier, while laboring intensely in Bologna for Julius II, Michelangelo himself claims in a letter of 1507 that he could "barely snatch the time to eat" (1.39, C 1.52). "I haven't even time enough to eat as I should" (1.54, C 1.101), he declares in yet another letter, this one of 1509, while working on the chapel vault. And once more, to his father, in a letter composed not long after completing the Sistine Chapel, while he is still lingering in Rome and finishing up a number of affairs, he observes: "I must tell you that I do not think I shall be able to come home this September, because I'm being pressed in such a way that I haven't time to eat" (1. 87, C 1.143). Even Michelangelo's biographers—both Giorgio Vasari and Ascanio Condivi—make a point of commenting on the great artist's habits of shunning the consumption of food when he was at work. In particular his pupil Condivi, whose biography Michelangelo had such a large hand in, makes this trenchant observation: "[Michelangelo] has always been very abstemious in his way of life, taking food more out of necessity than for pleasure, and especially while he had work in progress, when he would most often content himself with a piece of bread, which he would eat while working" (Cv 106, Cdv 62–63).[11] In an effort both to incorporate Condivi's observations into his enlarged *Vite* (first published in 1550) and to correct mistakes made by him and Condivi in their respective narratives, Vasari observed that "when he was a young man, in order to be intent on [by which Vasari means "fully absorbed in"] his work" (*per istare intento al lavoro*), Michelangelo used to content himself "with a little bread and wine." And he was still doing the same when he grew old, Vasari further reports, "until he painted the Last Judgment in the chapel, by refreshing himself in the evening after he had finished the day's work, even though very frugally" (*pur parchissimamente*; 423, 121).[12]

Now to say that Michelangelo was something of an "eccentric"—to borrow the terms of Rudolph and Margot Wittkower—when it came to food is also to say something about the eccentricities of visual artists in the Italian Renaissance generally. For the great Michelangelo was not entirely unlike a number of other artists of the late fifteenth and sixteenth century in this regard. As the Wittkowers disclosed in *Born Under Saturn*, an historical study that traces the development of the character and conduct of artists from roughly the fifteenth century to the French Revolution, the Italian Renaissance witnessed sweeping changes in the "collective personality" of artists. Artists of various stripes now began to view themselves, and in turn sought to be viewed, as downright bizarre, particularly beginning in Florence at the turn of the fifteenth century, precisely, that is, during the period when Michelangelo was both working as an artist in Florence and forging his own personality as something of a man of professional improprieties in his terribilità.

The eccentricities displayed and fostered by these artists varied widely, and they found different forms of expression. Some artists could be just silly, absent-minded (not a few staring off into space), difficult, unpredictable, irascible, thin-skinned, bad-mannered (even to the point of appearing barbaric), pigheaded to the extreme, neurasthenic in their hypochondria, readily given to outbursts of excessive fury or hilarity, paranoid, and often overly concerned with seeking and ensuring their solitude. Along with this, they could reveal from time to time eccentricities regarding their intake (or lack) of food. The Tuscan painter Piero di Cosimo (1461–1521), for instance, ate only boiled eggs, cooking them by the bucketload and then consuming them one by one as he worked. The inveterate oddball Jacopo Pontormo (1494–1556), whose obsession with solitude Vasari rendered legendary (among other things he would purportedly lift up a ladder so no one could access his room),[13] detailed with unparalleled precision the quantity of food he ate during specific periods of his life.[14] The obscure artist Graffione Fiorentino (1455–1527) refused to "eat off a table laid with any other cloth save his own cartoons," as the Wittkowers have observed, and the inimitable Leonardo da Vinci (1452–1519), known for his unprecedented "aloofness," declared that he was a vegetarian in a world that, unlike our own today, rarely knew of their existence, thereby rendering him all the more "eccentric" in the eyes of others.[15] In this regard what distinguished Michelangelo was, as always, the order of magnitude. He went one step further: he could actually go without food, he repeatedly suggests, or scarcely any food at all. It is as if he sustained himself and nourished himself on air alone, which is really to say, his art. And this was not all. He ate so little, if in fact nothing at all, while working on superhuman projects, as so many of them were. There is always something larger-than-life about Michelangelo, and this is true when it comes to his habit of being exceedingly abstemious.[16]

Fact and fiction nevertheless begin to fuse here, and we would do well to try to separate them out for the moment. After all, characters don't need to eat food, Forster reminds us; people do. And as a number of scholars have argued over the years,[17] we should think of Michelangelo, who did in fact eat, as both a character *and* a person, as someone who was the subject of much mythologizing (and self-mythologizing) and as someone who had distinct bodily needs. It would certainly be difficult, for instance, to disavow completely Michelangelo's abstemiousness. Third-party witnesses record his abstemiousness when he was engaged in major, time-consuming projects, and we would have to be overly skeptical not to take what they reported seriously to some degree as reliable, ocular proof. Michelangelo's anxieties, he insists, also led him to refrain from eating at times: "Commend me to Michele Guicciardini," he writes in a letter of May 1545, "and tell him that I'm well, but have many worries—so many that I haven't time to eat" (2.53).[18] Worries kept him busy, in a state of constant, restless work, which is entirely believable given the colossal tasks he set up for himself and the kinds of exact accounting records he needed to keep as an inveterate micromanager. At the same time, we should certainly not hesitate to view his professed habit of not eating during moments of intense creative labor as partly the product of self-mythologizing, in which Michelangelo becomes a character within his own field of vision, performing for us and others in letters that were certainly not meant for publication but nevertheless seem to draw on fairly familiar commonplaces in Renaissance Italian literature about artists and their obsessive devotion to their work.

In this context, one reason Michelangelo presented himself as a person who didn't eat, or who ate very poorly, was that he was actively involved throughout his life, even in informal letters dashed off to friends and family, in presenting himself as a man so captivated by his work, so thoroughly caught up in what the psychologist Mihaly Csikszentmihalyi has called the creative process of "flow," that he simply did not bother to consume food.[19] The underlying notion is that the absorption of creativity, in which an artist's powers are fully engaged, feeds on itself to the point at which the organism forgets to fulfill its natural biological necessities and consume food, even to the point where the organism consequently begins to break down.[20] A colossal man facing colossal undertakings can do colossal, superhuman feats. He lives and breathes off nothing but his art, his tasks. His absorption in his work, which keeps him from eating, signals his absolute intensity and devotion in a manner that exceeds even that of three towering figures representing the arts of sculpture, painting, and architecture of the previous generation: Donatello, Masaccio, and Brunelleschi, all of whom occasionally did not eat, according to Vasari, when thoroughly engaged in their work.

If all of this has the trappings of a romantic myth, with Michelangelo playing out the role of the consumptive hunger artist, it would be better, and more historically appropriate, to frame it in terms of familiar communal rituals of the Renaissance, namely, the rituals of carnival and Lent. For if Aretino, as I argued in the previous chapter, can be viewed as a complex figure of carnival, that period of the year when all bets are off and cornucopian consumption becomes the model for transgressive public behavior enacted in celebrations of unbridled leisure within the marketplace, Michelangelo should be viewed as a figure of Lent, that period of the year when a thin slice of dried-up cod epitomized the most one might get to eat over the course of a meal, when work was the order of the day, and when denial of the flesh became an accepted, ritualized, communal practice.[21] Think of Aretino and you are likely to imagine a table set with a plethora of food, so much food that it tumbles onto the floor amid the boisterous, communal revelry. Think of Michelangelo and you're lucky to imagine a somewhat frugal meal consumed privately in the intervals between intense periods of work, if not during them. We can do better than that, in fact. Michelangelo inadvertently left us, as it so happens, a picture of three separate meals eaten while he was working in 1518 on the daunting project of the façade for San Lorenzo. Compared to Aretino's feasts, there is not much to these meals: some rolls, wine, herring, tortellini, spinach, anchovies, and soup. We have a concrete picture, then, both visual and verbal, of a Michelangelo meal in a period of intense *negotium* (Figure 6). And it is the very opposite of a

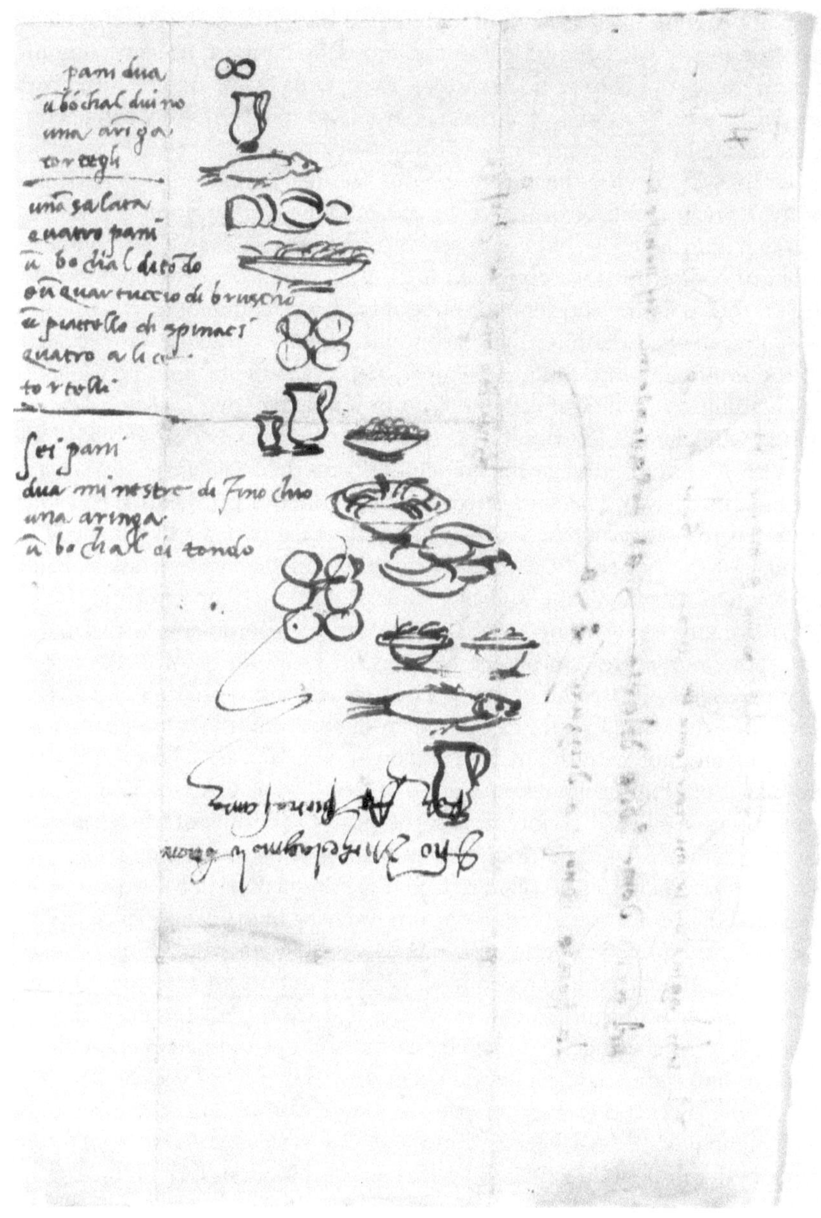

FIGURE 6. Michelangelo (1475–1564). *Michelangelo List and Sketch of Three Meals.* Casa Buonarroti, Florence. Photo courtesy Scala/Ministero per i Beni e le Attività Culturali/Art Resource, New York.

leisurely Aretino meal as Aretino represented his dining habits: not opulent, overflowing, or sumptuous. It is conspicuous, by contrast, in its parsimonious attention to his basic bodily needs. Even visually we are given the bare essentials in order to grasp the concept. A line or two furnish us with a concrete image of what the biology of his body demanded.

Unlike the previous chapter, then, this one focuses not on a professional writer's presentation of his habits of conspicuous consumption in times of self-aggrandizing *otium*, but conversely on a professional artist's self-conscious habits of conspicuous absorption during times of intense negotium. In focusing on this topic, my aim is not to understand how central food was to a man of unprecedented brashness within his culture, but to disclose how creative absorption figures into this great temperamental artist's life, first and foremost by focusing on themes of consumption in his *Bacchus*, which Michelangelo started when he was just twenty-one years old, and then by examining briefly themes of consumption in his meticulously finished *Children's Bacchanal*, a presentation drawing he completed in his late fifties or early sixties. For what mattered to Michelangelo, I will argue with these two works primarily in mind, was the ability to concentrate intensely on the creative task at hand, both when he was young and old. And all the letters he wrote in which he is haggling or working out nagging details and problems with anxiety and sometimes regret can be construed as the by-products of or the necessary preconditions for the hours spent in intense concentration and artistic devotion—or what I prefer to call a state of absorption.[22] "One paints with the head and not with the hands," he contended, "and he who cannot keep his wits about him brings disgrace upon himself" (2.26, C 4.150). Unimpeded concentration can lead to intense absorption, as Dante, one of Michelangelo's favorite authors, described eloquently in his *Vita nuova* and *Divina commedia.*[23] This is what Michelangelo often rendered so conspicuous in his artwork as he designed figures that seem removed from ordinary human experience and, in the process, explored the one topic that passionately interested him throughout his life: the naked human body in various positions of arresting, affective movement. It is in this context, moreover, that we might consider the story about how Michelangelo's proclivity to use a chisel and become a sculptor came to him early on, when he was fed by a wetnurse, who "was the daughter of a stonemason and was also married to a stonemason" amid the quarries of Settignano (Cv 6).[24] Michelangelo, we are led to believe, consumed his future passion, absorbing it directly into his own body as food, and all this took place arguably in a state of total rapt concentration and intense sensuous gratification. Thereafter, within the narrative of his life, it hardly matters if Michelangelo eats food once he sets to work. Work becomes his food, and the bodies he throws himself into as he represents them become, by extension as he nourishes himself through his labors in a state of absorption, his body as well.

The Bacchus *and the Absorption of Creativity*

In 1494 Michelangelo sculpted in Florence the *Sleeping Cupid*, a work that so stunningly captured the idiom of classical art that Lorenzo di Pierfrancesco de' Medici, dazzled by the artifact, suggested it would fetch a much higher price if it were made to appear an authentic antique recently unearthed from the ground. Michelangelo accomplished this feat with little effort. He was already a master of forgery, having allegedly weathered drawings he made to render them identical in appearance to the originals he had copied. And the life-size *Sleeping Cupid* was in fact sold for a goodly sum through Baldassare del Milanese, a middleman in Rome, though Michelangelo reaped little benefit from the sale.[25] The buyer turned out to be Cardinal Raffaele Riario, one of the most powerful men in Rome, who was not at all pleased when he became aware of the nature of the deception.[26] Irked that he had been fooled, Riario refused to keep the *Sleeping Cupid*, despite its beauty, and demanded return of payment after sending the artifact back to its seller—a fact that later stuck in Michelangelo's craw.[27] "Some were critical of the cardinal of S. Giorgio in this affair," Condivi writes, no doubt with Michelangelo's supervision and express approval, "because, if the work was seen by all the artists in Rome and by them all equally it was judged very beautiful, it did not seem that he should be so offended by its being modern as to deprive himself of it for the sake of two hundred *scudi* when he was an affluent and very wealthy man" (Cv 21).[28] Vasari was no kinder in his estimation: "This affair did not come about without damage to Cardinal San Giorgio, who did not recognize the value of the work, which consists in its perfection, for modern works are just as good as ancient ones when they are excellent, and it is greater vanity to pursue things more for their reputation than for what they really are, but these kinds of men can be found in any age; men who pay more attention to appearances than to realities" (423).[29] A great work of art, we are led to believe, is simply a great work of art and should therefore be appreciated as such aesthetically, even if the patron has been duped, receiving a clever fabrication as opposed to the anticipated real deal.

Though the *Sleeping Cupid* was rejected as a fake, and though Michelangelo "suffered" more than anyone else in this shady dealing (he never regained the statue nor his share of the money owed him), all was not lost (Cv 21).[30] Soon enough Michelangelo made good on the debacle of this failed sale. For Riario had been so impressed with the young sculptor's ability that, once Michelangelo arrived in Rome at his bidding, Riario invited him to view his collection of antiquities in his palace, which Michelangelo promptly deemed "beautiful things" (*belle chose*; 1.3, C 1.1).[31] Riario then asked Michelangelo, who had arrived in Rome armed with a letter of introduction from Lorenzo di Pierfrancesco, if he "had courage [*animo*] enough"—by which Riario meant also guts, spirit, initiative, stamina, and strength of mind—to attempt some work of art of [his] own" (1.3, C 1.1).[32] Michelangelo recorded this invitation to be engaged in a commission for Riario in his earliest letter sent from Rome, and the implication to be drawn from the letter is clear. Having mastered the art of both copying the ancients and the vocabulary of classical sculpture, Michelangelo was now being put to the test by the very person he had inadvertently deceived. He was being asked to make a sculpture that would not only stand up against those of the ancients, potentially to be displayed amid a host of antiquities in Riario's garden full of "beautiful things," but also to carve a sculpture that would stand on (and ideally stand out on) its own. This was not a moment to shy away from. It would take, as Michelangelo put it in his letter, "animo." The letter sent to Lorenzo di Pierfrancesco was dated July 2, 1496, a week after Michelangelo's arrival in the ancient holy city. The sculpture, which he would begin to carve the next Monday with "a piece of marble" bought for a "life-sized figure" (1.3), would turn out to be the *Bacchus* (Figures 7, 8, and 9).[33] In the end the commission would take Michelangelo approximately a year to complete (the last recorded payment for it is for August 1497), and in all probability Michelangelo made the sculpture not in Riario's house, which was then under construction (the future magnificent Cancelleria, the first great Renaissance palace in Rome), but in the house of Riario's neighbor, Jacopo Gallo, where the sculpture eventually resided amid a host of other artifacts (Figure 10).

It is easy to lose sight of the nature of Riario's challenge and how Michelangelo might have experienced it, as well as the sort of animo that he was expected to muster to fashion a sculpture worthy of this patron and the site in which it was in all likelihood to be ensconced. We have grown so accustomed, that is, to thinking of Michelangelo as "divine" (an epithet that was attributed to him by Ariosto only in 1516, by which time Michelangelo was truly renowned) that we may forget he was not exactly destined to become arguably the greatest sculptor who ever lived. Certainly we have been conditioned to think of him this way—and not least by Michelangelo himself, who worked hard to foster the image of his own predestined greatness. Vasari's narrative of his life, which culminates the first edition, casts Michelangelo as a sort of demigod who descended to earth in order to lead the way out of the darkness into light (all the stars had to be properly aligned for the coming of this miraculous savior of art), and as the height of perfection in all the major arts of painting, sculpture, and architecture (providence again played a role in this by bringing the overall achievement in the arts to a fullness of time, with many artists in the three major arts of painting, sculpture, and architecture having prepared the way for Michelangelo's advent). Similarly, Condivi's narrative extols Michelangelo as a natural genius, overflowing with fantasia and untainted by the limiting practices inculcated

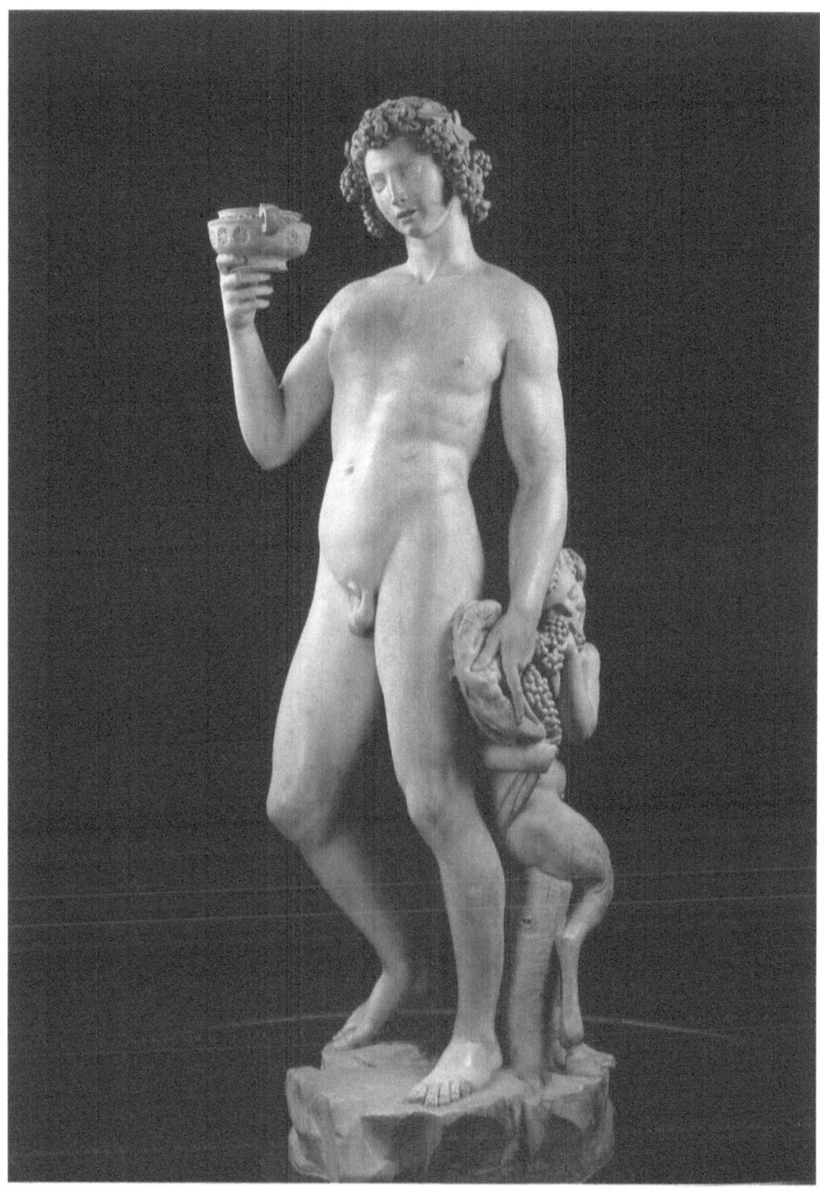

FIGURE 7. Michelangelo (1475–1564). *Bacchus*, 1496–1497. Museo Nazionale del Bargello, Florence. Photo courtesy Alinari/Art Resource, New York.

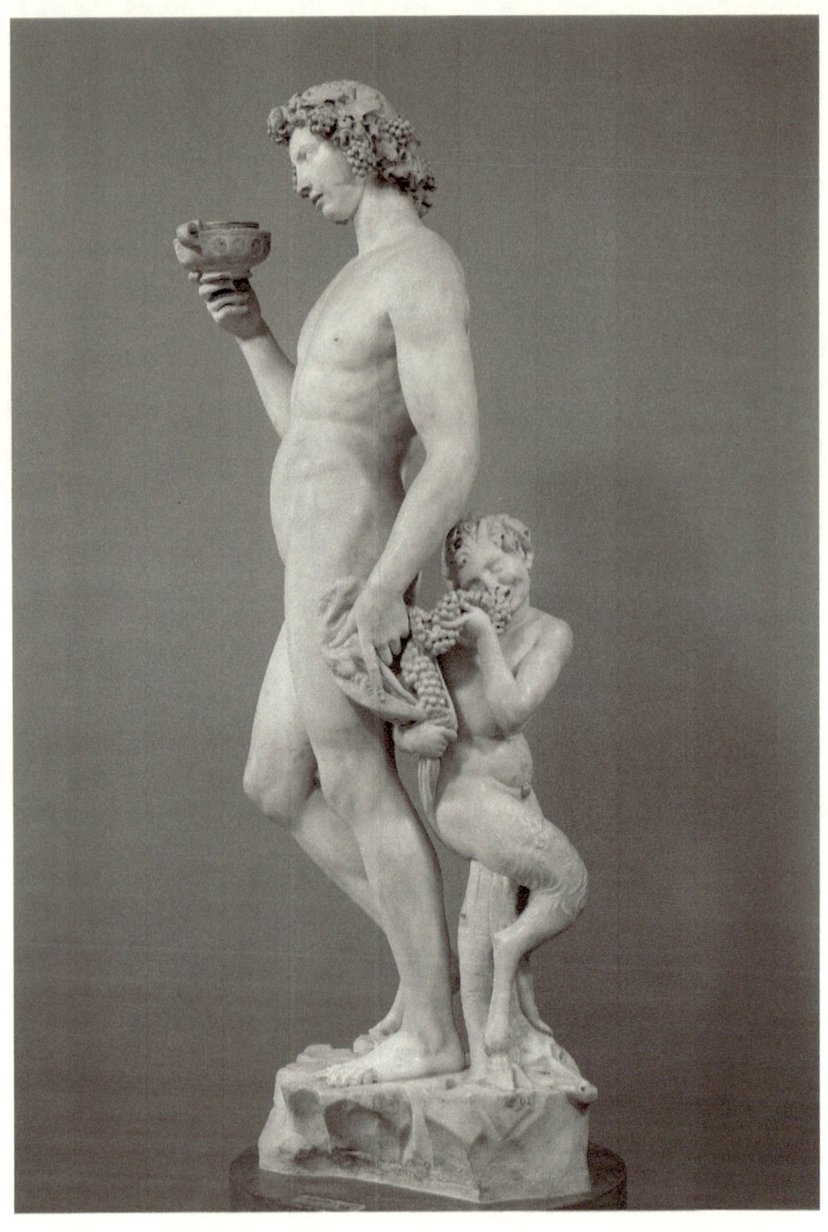

FIGURE 8. Michelangelo (1475–1564). *Bacchus*, 1496–1497. Museo Nazionale del Bargello, Florence. Photo courtesy Scala/Art Resource, New York.

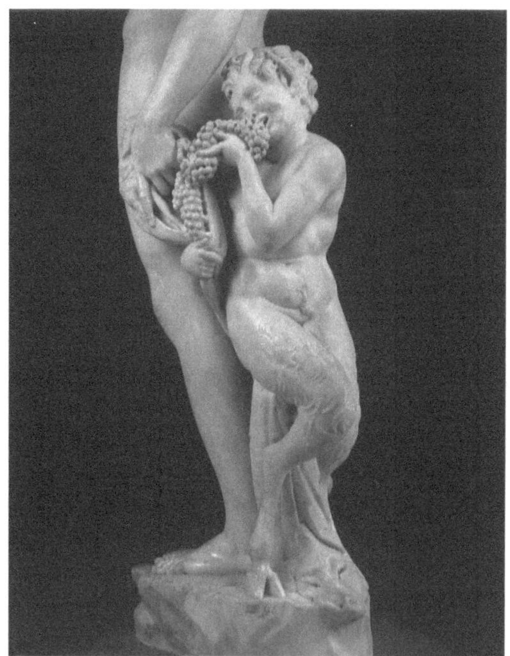

FIGURE 9. Michelangelo (1475–1564). *Bacchus* (detail of little satyr), 1496–1497. Museo Nazionale del Bargello, Florence. Photo courtesy Scala/Art Resource, New York.

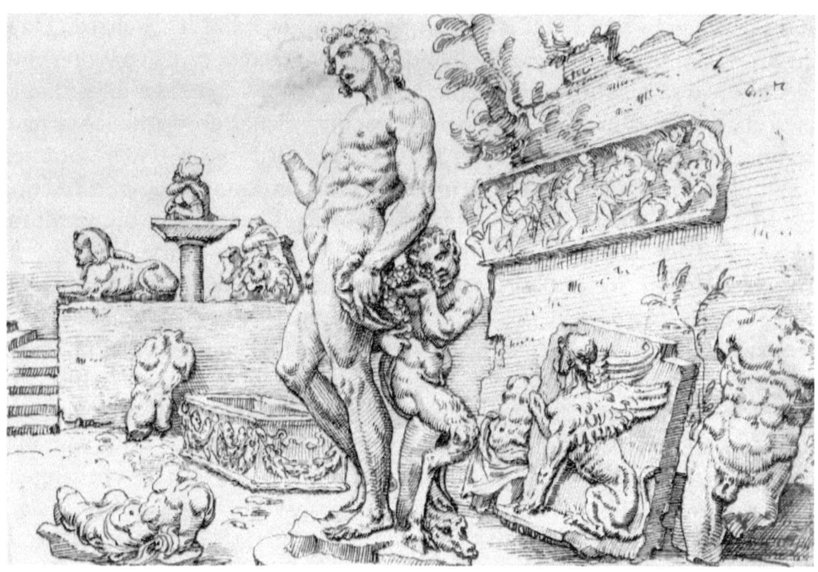

FIGURE 10. Maarten van Heemskerck (1498–1574). *The Garden in the Casa Galli, with Michelangelo's Statue of Bacchus*, ca. 1532–1536. Staatliche Museen zu Berlin, Berlin. Photo courtesy Bildarchiv Preussischer Kulturbesitz/Art Resource, New York.

through years of apprenticeship in a master's shop. He learned his art directly from Nature, much as he imbibed his absorbing passion for the profession of sculpture directly from a wetnurse who lived among the stonemasons in an area famous for its sculptors.[34] Michelangelo comes to us through Condivi as an autodidact, a man who never even learned the art of fresco painting from Domenico Ghirlandaio, which, as we know, was certainly not the case. The learned Florentine Benedetto Varchi makes virtually the same claim in his funeral oration, though he also acknowledges that Michelangelo had been apprenticed to Ghirlandaio with a "salary": "Michelangelo was very capricious, and did not deign to learn from others except from Nature. . . . He painted without having had, I do not say, anyone before him, having had God, the Heavens and Nature . . . as example and as Masters, but without anyone having told him either the rules or lessons."[35]

Both Vasari's and Condivi's narratives, not to mention Varchi's hagiographic eulogy, were composed long after Michelangelo achieved European renown. They therefore benefit from hindsight and, needless to say, a highly receptive audience in a thriving patronage system in which men and women were eager to buy a work of art by Michelangelo. Their judgment of Michelangelo, like our judgment, is likewise informed by his monumental achievements: the Sistine Chapel vault, the *Last Judgment*, the *David*, the *Pietà*, the *Moses*, the *Slaves*, and the sculptures within the sacristy of San Lorenzo, not to mention his architectural masterpieces. But in 1496, as Riario offered the young Florentine sculptor his first Roman commission and purportedly asked him if he had the animo to fulfill it, Michelangelo's greatness was not something he could take for granted, or that anyone else did. He had allegedly produced the marble head of a faun as a direct copy of a classical antiquity in Lorenzo de' Medici's sculpture garden. He had crafted for himself a battle relief in a manner that was patently antique, inspired in the choice of subject matter by the humanist Angelo Poliziano. He had completed another relief, this one of the Madonna, in the virtuoso *rilievo schiacciato* technique perfected by Donatello. He had carved a statue of Hercules, which eventually passed into the hands of the Strozzi family and was probably based on an antique in Lorenzo de' Medici's sculpture garden. He had carved a crucifix for the prior of Santo Spirito, in thanks and recompense for the opportunity to dissect cadavers at their hospital, which he did in order to perfect his understanding of human anatomy and thus the forms he displayed in his art. And in Bologna he had made for Gianfrancesco Aldovrandi three statuettes, which did not seem to have challenged him, as Howard Hibbard observes, perhaps because Michelangelo felt somewhat constrained by having to fit his still masterful designs into an existing unfinished tomb decoration originally conceptualized and begun by Giovanni Pisano and Niccolò dell'Arca (in fact, he did not complete the fourth statue of the commission).[36] Michelangelo had also produced a *St. John the Baptist*, which is lost, and of course the *Sleeping Cupid* (also lost), which had fooled many as a veritable work of antiquity. The largest of these works, the *Hercules*, may not have been commissioned in the first place (there is some debate about this); nor were many of the others, with the notable exception of the statuettes.[37] In short, Michelangelo had yet to prove himself fully on the grand scale, with a commission from a major patron. He had established himself, then, as an astonishingly adept imitator of the classics, a man with significant Florentine connections, and a most remarkable sculptor with exceptional promise to do magnificent things.

If Michelangelo's early career began, as the story has it, with his producing a copy of antiquity in the form of a marble faun in Lorenzo de' Medici's sculpture garden of San Marco, his career as a full-fledged sculptor in manhood began by producing a work that was meant to rival antiquity in yet another sculpture garden, this one located in the heart of the greatest Italian city of antiquity, whose ruins must have deeply influenced Michelangelo when he first arrived there in 1496. Unlike Lorenzo de' Medici, moreover, Riario, who had invited Michelangelo into his house, did not intend to pose as a benevolent patron, a substitute father figure who might be delighted at the precocity and subtlety of a witty boy ready to please his master.[38] We need to understand the animo allegedly required of Michelangelo, then, in terms of a rite of passage for a man who had finally arrived at the hallowed site of antiquity and was being asked to make a sculpture there for a major patron in a major court. The making of the *Bacchus* has all the elements of a public performance, in which Michelangelo takes on in a closed space—indeed, in a theatrical space, as Roman gardens and courtyards such as Riario's in his new courtly palace were designed to be[39]—the best of the ancients in patent, unabashed rivalry. The animo purportedly asked of Michelangelo should thus be viewed in terms of Renaissance emulation wherein the contestants aggressively imagine themselves in a sort of skirmish, agonistically combating in a paragone (competition) that pits them against one another and against those—in Stephen Spender's phrase—"who were truly great."[40] If Michelangelo failed, it would therefore be a form of humiliation on the grand scale, undermining not only his public persona, which he was forging through sculpture at this particular moment, but also his own standing within the professional community as a sculptor of enormous (though as yet fully unharnessed) potential. The animo asked of Michelangelo, then, is the courage, stamina, spirit, and guts of professional self-knowledge at a critical stage of his development.

Michelangelo had faced this sort of challenge earlier in his career, specifically on the occasion of his receiving the commission to construct the four statuettes in Bologna for Aldovrandi, the gentleman who had befriended him, taken him into his house, and saved him from some embarrassment with the local authorities. As Vasari relates the story, Aldovrandi candidly asked Michelangelo "if he had the courage to do them" (*gli domandò se gli bastasse l'animo di fargli*; 1206, 422). Now, however, much more was being requested of Michelangelo at the behest of Riario. Michelangelo's new commission took place in an entirely different, and certainly far grander, setting than Bologna. Rome was then becoming a privileged site of major patronage for Tuscan, as well as Umbrian, artists wishing to prove their mettle. It therefore offered Michelangelo, as Condivi puts it in his narrative, "a very wide field for everyone to demonstrate his ability [*virtù*]" (Cv 21).[41] And Michelangelo could never turn down an opportunity of that nature. Ever the performer, he was eager to put his prodigious talents to the test. The animo asked of Michelangelo, then, relates directly to his ability to know how to handle a major patron with an important court, in this case the cardinal-protector of the Augustinian order, the nephew of the defunct pope Sixtus IV, and the chief financial officer for the papal state. "Do not be surprised at my not returning," he wrote to his father in July 1497, in the process revealing some of his caution in dealing with Riario, "because I've not yet been able to settle up my affairs with the Cardinal and I do not want to leave without first receiving satisfaction and being remunerated for my pains. With these grand masters [*questi gra' maestri*] one has to go slowly, because they cannot be coerced/pushed" (1.4, C 1.3). With this letter, the second extant one written from Rome, we are still far from the days when Michelangelo, later known for his professional improprieties in his terribilità, would face down Julius II with intractable stubbornness, matching his own indomitable fierceness and *furia* to a headstrong pope. "Never before had an artist dared to turn his back on a pope," the Wittkowers have observed of Michelangelo's unusual and unprecedented behavior later in his life, when he had achieved fame and could freely indulge his aggressive drives, "and never had a patron shown so much understanding for the 'humors of such men.'"[42]

At this moment in his life, however, as he dealt with Riario in an effort to get paid for the work done, Michelangelo, at the fledgling age of twenty-one, evinced a temperament that was measured and circumspect even as he proved himself daring in the conception and execution of the *Bacchus*. He stood as an example, if not a paragon, of professional propriety. The great Michelangelo at the outset of his career was not very terrible in his dealings with one of "these grand masters." He controlled his aggressive instincts, tamed his performative self. And for good reason. Prudence was the order of the day, restraint the better strategy for present and future success. He was not yet willing, that is, to fly off the handle. This would come in time, to be sure. In the meantime, Michelangelo had the *Bacchus* to produce, a commission to get paid for, and above all a reputation to make at a pivotal moment in his career. Significantly, he also fulfilled this commission in a manner that helped define his identity in artistic form as someone eager to adhere to and upset artistic decorum, as well as engage both the unclassical and the classical, the ridiculous and the sublime. This is a work that was daring in the very moment that Michelangelo was challenged to produce something that could sit with, if not surpass, the ancients.

A word of caution and qualification, however, regarding what might seem to be an unlikely choice for the centerpiece of this chapter. Before creating the *Bacchus*, the youthful Michelangelo had been under the patronage of Lorenzo de' Medici and apparently interacted with his gentle circle, which included, among others, one of the greatest humanists of the late fifteenth century, the refined, erudite author and poet Angelo Poliziano, who had given Michelangelo the subject matter for his *Battle of Lapiths and Centaurs*. The Michelangelo persona associated with terribilità and capricious behavior in negotiations with patrons and public controversy does not, in fact, emerge fully until a decade after the construction of the *Bacchus*. In this regard, the Sistine Ceiling or the *Last Judgment*, it can be said, might have been more appropriate, if not certainly obvious, works to present in the context of a study of Michelangelo's untoward comportment. In the Sistine Ceiling or the *Last Judgment* we have not only direct evidence of Michelangelo's belligerent, difficult persona during the execution of the works but also concrete evidence of critical responses to the frescoes that demonstrate how Michelangelo was perceived to have transgressed the boundaries of decorum within the context of the commissions. Equally appropriate in such a context would have been the later two *Pietàs*, which Michelangelo intended for his own tomb. Both of these highly personal, late *Pietàs* dramatize and thematize the reflexive position of the "artist as God-like animator." Above all they constitute works with which Michelangelo had a tempestuous relationship, smashing one with a hammer and incessantly carving away into the other.

By contrast, one can readily normalize the *Bacchus* within the context of the late-fifteenth-century Roman interests in classical subjects and the variety of humanism practiced by intellectuals in Northern Italy, both churchmen and laypersons, as a number of scholars have elegantly done, from Edgar Wind to Linda Koch. And the *Bacchus* has as a pendant the exquisite, emotionally contained, and technically polished, Roman *Pietà* made at virtually the same time for another cardinal patron. To this effect, the artistic sensibility that made the *Bacchus* arguably sustained and underpinned the *Pietà*. Both were conceived as virtuoso performances meant to impress viewers and establish the sculptor as a master in his preferred area of expertise. Yet unlike the artist of the early *Pietà* of 1499, Michelangelo in the *Bacchus*, I maintain, was exploring critical issues related to artistic imagination and sensuous corporeality that were to cause him trouble later on, in other commissions, particularly in the *Last Judgment*, a fresco that shares affinities, as Stephen Campbell has demonstrated, with some obstreperous sensibilities of the time. In the *Bacchus* one finds, alongside the suavity of its sprezzatura and grazia, an intrepidness in its form of expression that renders it, according to the reading presented here, a harbinger of the sort of work that Michelangelo would produce later on, when he would incur the wrath of many, exert his influence as a master of intransigence, and exploit fantasies of indecorous, sensuous corporeality in novel, obtrusive ways. In this way the *Bacchus* has a proleptic function in this chapter, anticipating a brashness of the later years, particularly in the daring and unexpected way in which the young, ambitious Michelangelo tackles the classical subject of the inebriated wine god and relates it reflexively to his longstanding interests in fantasia, the human body, heroicism, and the frenzied, absorptive engagement of artistic production. Where all these issues come together, we shall see, is in Michelangelo's concern in the *Bacchus* for the conspicuous consumption of food.

Now housed in the Bargello museum in Florence, the *Bacchus*, which is 1.82 meters high, marks a bold statement in Michelangelo's career as his first major commission, his first undisputed masterpiece, and his first extant egregious attempt to outdo the ancients on the grand scale. The boldness—indeed, I would argue, the unsettling "in-your-faceness"—of the *Bacchus* derives in large measure from the formal tensions it embodies, as well as the overall interpretive problems it poses. At first glance, so much about the *Bacchus* deliberately evokes classicism. Ancient classical art defined for Michelangelo, as it did for so many others, the apex of artistic achievement in history. It thus represented a style of art that was in vogue and obviously desired by Riario, who had originally bought the *Sleeping Cupid* on the false pretense that it was a true classical antique, and who was well known as a discerning patron with a vested interest in collecting and promoting the study of antiquities. To this effect, the *Bacchus* bears familiar attributes of the pagan god of classical antiquity (the ivy and grapes, the cup bearing wine, the coy satyr nibbling at the grapes), and the main figure of the wine god stands before the spectator in what at first glance may seem to be a naturalistic pose, with the weight unevenly distributed from one side of the body to another so as to express life, energy, and potential spontaneous movement. In its execution, the sculpture exhibits, as Hibbard has argued, "grace," the "roundness and fullness derived from good judgment and design," which was praised by Vasari as hallmarks of great art—hallmarks, of course, that have since been identified as salient features of High Renaissance Italian art generally. The highly polished gleam of the surface further lends the sculpture, as Hibbard observes, "the newly-discovered 'appeal and vigor of living flesh,'" as if the wine god and satyr were animate, breathing creatures.[43] Additionally, the highly polished gleam of the surface lends the sculpture the overall appearance of effortlessness in execution, which is so typical of the sprezzatura exhibited in Michelangelo's completed early works in Rome, such as the *Pietà*. Furthermore, as Condivi asserted, the "form and appearance" of the *Bacchus* corresponded "in every particular to the intention of the writers of antiquity" (Cv 24), even though no distinct classical model exists for Michelangelo's rendition of the pagan god.[44] To use the artistic vocabulary of Michelangelo's own time, the *Bacchus* has the "aria" of a classical antique as a modern construction.[45]

Yet so much about the *Bacchus* also seems deliberately unclassical in form and intent, calculatingly unidealized, ludic, and subversive, so that it could easily provoke, as it did over time, vehemently hostile reactions.[46] If traditionally, for instance, the classical *contrapposto* pose served to convey a sense of natural balance, since the body automatically shifts weight from one leg to another to find its equilibrium in space, the pose of Michelangelo's Bacchus, with his left foot planted firmly on the ground and the right lifted high to a pointed toe, displays the opposite: the wine god here is not in a state of balance but complete imbalance. While Michelangelo's execution in his disegno exhibits grazia and sprezzatura, the wine god himself reveals affettazione in his exaggerated behavior as he is rendered in the round. He teeters in his unabashed intoxication, leaning backwards in the very moment that the placement of the legs suggests a possible contrary movement forward, with the pelvis thrust out as if to strain to hold the tottering body up and keep it—and consequently the wine cup, which is perhaps the most precious item that the inebriated wine god can imagine holding at that particular moment—from falling to the ground. Viewed from the front, which was Michelangelo's preferred vantage point for his earlier sculptures, Bacchus once more appears to be swaying, with perhaps his right leg buckling out from under him as he potentially lurches forward. The weight of the body, which is meant in a contrapposto pose to find a center of gravity, here shifts back and forth, with the head (and a rather comically undersized head at that!) tilted in one direction, the shoulders another, the pelvis yet another, and the legs ready to tumble out from under the staggering, inebriated god. This is a god who is standing up but is more probably about to fall down, a fact that is even structurally and formally incorporated into the entire sculptural ensemble: the wine god would, in fact, fall down if the figure were not buttressed by the presence of the little satyr behind, whose serpentine pose only emphasizes in its torsion the elements of suppressed movement contained within Bacchus himself.[47] In its blend of opposing elements, seriousness and wit, balance and imbalance, the overall sculptural ensemble is decidedly original, at once classical and unclassical, antique and brashly modern in conception.[48]

In this respect, if Michelangelo is getting in our face with this sculpture, he is doing so by crafting a Bacchus unlike any produced before—one that was calculated to outdo the ancients, defy classical models, and, in its apparent effrontery, perhaps outwit contemporary viewers of it and the discerning, powerful patron who had commissioned it in the first place. Indeed, as Luba Freedman has demonstrated, "no ancient statues," such as those figured on Roman sarcophagi, "ever showed Bacchus actually inebriated when presented as a lone figure."[49] The *Bacchus*, then, does not get in our face because it is so scary, mean, treacherous, or outwardly aggressive, but instead, as Ralph Lieberman has perceptively observed, because it is a "radical work" that upsets visual classical models and, as a consequence, was destined to upset the expectations of a patron interested in a familiar classical representation of the wine god based on those privileged, established models of antiquity. The *Bacchus*, Lieberman observes,

> is entirely unprecedented. In most free-standing classical portrayals of him there is usually nothing that suggests drunkenness or dissipation; he is identified only by his attributes—a drinking cup, grapes and leaves in his hair—and without the references to wine that he carries, most antique examples could be mistaken for Antinous, Doryphoros, or any other sober male figure. In Michelangelo's treatment, on the other hand, we understand from the figure's reeling pose that he is experiencing the effects of wine, and the stunning conjunction of character and behavior weds form to content at a level unknown in earlier Renaissance sculpture. Michelangelo's profound exploration of the nature and personality of his subject led him to create a figure difficult to accept by someone anticipating a more traditional representation, and Cardinal Riario was not prepared for a Bacchus who behaves in a drunken, indecorous way and who, in brief . . . is not the image of a god.

This is a sculpture, in sum, that was in a number of ways "revolutionary," cleverly designed, as a matter of expressing the artist's bravura and daring, to break noticeably with conventional expectations of what constituted classicism.[50] In this regard, if Riario challenged Michelangelo to see if he had the animo to produce a work of sculpture worthy of being placed in the great patron's collection of "beautiful things" of classical antiquity, Michelangelo seems to have upped the ante by challenging his viewer in return. Characteristically, Michelangelo always knew better than his patron what his patron should possess to view.

Furthermore, the tension between opposing formal elements embodied in the sculpture of Bacchus may have also served Michelangelo to evoke Donatello's *David*, a work of art that he had seen day after day as a boy lodged in the Medici household, that he had no doubt studied closely over his years of "apprenticeship" in the Medici gardens, and that Riario, his current patron, admired as a particularly accomplished work of a modern, even if Riario's tastes veered toward antiquities (Figure 11). The two sculptures

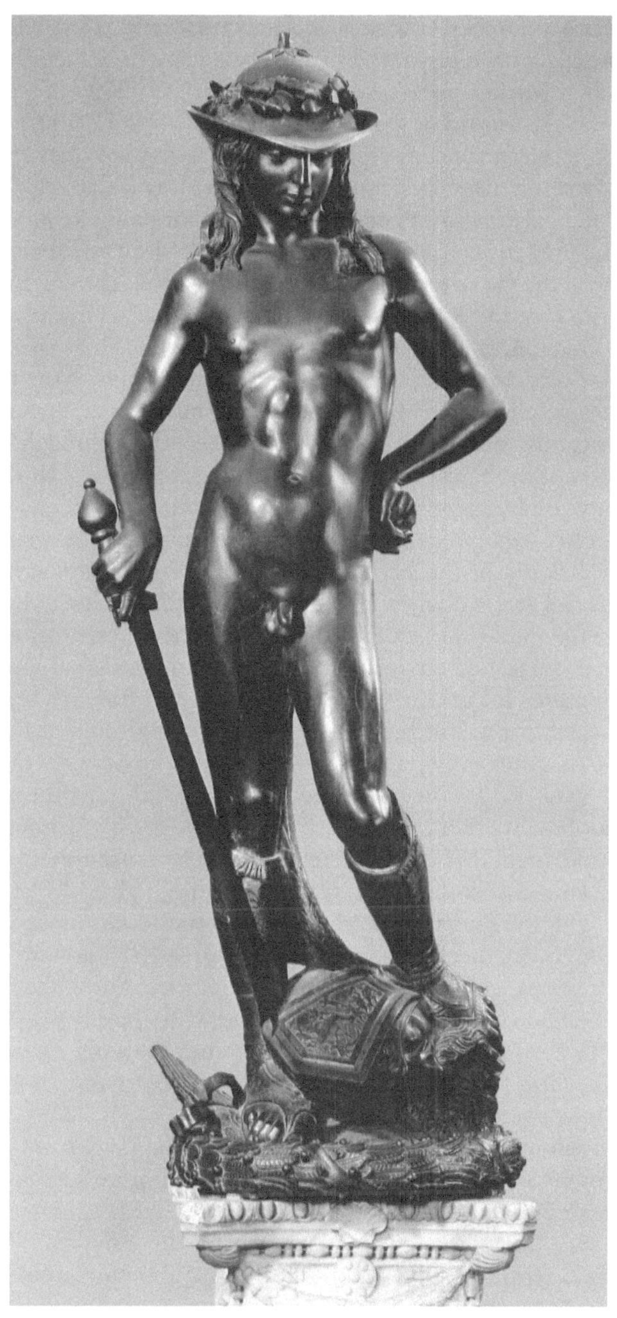

FIGURE 11. Donatello (ca. 1386–1466). *David*, 1440s. Museo Nazionale del Bargello, Florence. Photo courtesy Erich Lessing/Art Resource, New York.

certainly share a number of formal and structural traits. Donatello's *David*, for instance, was set in a privileged spot in the courtyard of the palace on via Larga, much as Michelangelo's *Bacchus* was to be set ideally in a privileged spot in Riario's courtyard or garden. Like the *Bacchus*, the *David*, a classically styled work of the Praxitelean type, stands in a contrapposto pose. However, in keeping with the late classicism of Praxiteles, David strikingly lacks the articulated musculature of Michelangelo's *David*, for example, and he has his right foot uplifted to such an extent that it seems, at least when viewed from below, to pitch the statue forward in a state of precarious balance, though obviously in this case to configure movement rather than, as in the case of the *Bacchus*, inebriation. Both figures bear wreathes around their heads, though Donatello's *David* does so as an adornment in the design of the shepherd's hat, Michelangelo's *Bacchus* about a helmetlike mass of grapes clustered on the drooping, tipsy head. Like Bacchus, David—perhaps through deliberate appropriation of the Praxitelean model of late classicism—is also markedly androgynous, combining masculine and feminine elements, at once lithe and seductive, even to the point where the two sculptures can be seen to evoke the mythical figure of the hermaphrodite.[51] Like the *Bacchus*, the *David*, which is the first freestanding sculpture since antiquity, invites us to view the sculpture in the round, thus creating a multiview perspective that constitutes yet another novel feature embedded within the earlier original composition: classical sculptures, for instance, were typically viewed from the front, not in the round (such is the standard model, moreover, regarding virtually all of Michelangelo's other early sculptures, which uniformly respect the classical precedent). Like the *Bacchus*, then, the *David* demands physical movement on the part of the spectator, a truly active, dynamic form of participation.

If it is true, then, that Michelangelo purposely evoked the *David* with his *Bacchus* (and it seems entirely likely and fitting, given Michelangelo's familiarity with the sculpture and his deep interest in Donatello's works as models for his own), then Michelangelo stands in open rivalry not only with the ancients in this sculpture, but with the greatest sculptor in the Florentine tradition of art—indeed, with the one sculptor who in time gave Michelangelo so many formal solutions to his works, from the early *Madonna of the Stairs* to the *Pietà* to the mature *Moses*. Though Vasari does not mention Donatello outright as the primary model and rival for Michelangelo among the artists of his own time when he was sculpting the *Bacchus*, it is clear that in Vasari's own assessment Michelangelo had once more surpassed all the moderns with this sculpture, both those living and dead.[52] Surely Donatello must have been one of the sculptors that Vasari had in mind.[53]

The formal tensions embedded in the *Bacchus* also raise problems of interpretation. They extend, that is, to a conceptual tension within the complex work itself, for it is difficult to understand what Michelangelo wished to convey with this enigmatic sculpture of the wine god and the accompanying mischievous satyr. On the one hand, in the Neoplatonic tradition that Michelangelo knew so well (beginning with his acquaintance with the circle of Marsilio Ficino from his days in the Medici household), the wine god had come to acquire a positive role as a figure of transcendence in his alcohol-induced ecstasy.[54] As a result, through Neoplatonic allegories, he became a symbol of a soul searching for spirit and God. Accordingly, as Bacchus holds aloft the cup of wine, he holds out the possibility of spiritual renewal and ascent. Inversely, the satyr to the god's left, which we are invited to view through a series of formal adjustments that force us to move to the right into a visual descent, represents the bestial side of human nature. That bestial side of nature grips us if we descend into our bodies and give ourselves over completely to our appetites, as surely seems to be the case with the "merry" satyr, who is placed to the "sinister" left side of the god and shows himself completely taken with the act of material consumption.[55] The reverse is true, moreover, as we are invited to move back around the free-standing sculpture in the opposite direction, retracing our steps. Beginning with the lowest order of nature (rock and tree stump), we pass, as Linda A. Koch has observed, to the bestial realm of the satyr's obsession with his appetites, then to the flayed skin (of a tiger? a panther?) sloughed off by the god as a symbol of renewal and inner growth,[56] and then, finally, to Bacchus as a Neoplatonic figure of divine frenzy, with the wine cup held aloft as if it were a sort of heavenly offering—the gift of transcendence toward an uplifting state of spiritual ecstasy.[57]

Depending on how we walk about the sculpture, then, we see and experience different forms and are indoctrinated into different stages of spiritual and moral growth. "In that the *Bacchus* engages the spectator in the dialectical process of knowing God through both active and arrested movement," Koch contends, with the weight of longstanding Neoplatonizing allegories to back up her fine argument, "it seems certain that Michelangelo conceived his sculpture as a challenge to its viewers to determine their own form of existence."[58] The entire sculptural complex, which includes rock, tree, flayed skin, satyr, and wine god, in this manner furnishes complementary backward and forward journeys in a harmoniously ordered and highly stratified universe wherein man, as in Pico della Mirandola's vision, is the one mobile, protean agent who, as he walks about the sculpture, must learn through action and contemplation to find his proper place in the cosmos. Thus, just as the wine god and the satyr are structurally related (the wine god cannot stand without the support of the satyr), so the wine god and satyr are symbolically related in a ladder of spiritual and moral movement that relates directly to the viewer's spiritual and moral movement. We can grow or not grow, rise or fall. The choice is ours to make.

On the other hand, for a god entrusted with the job of lifting us up into a state of divine furor and madness, the Bacchus designed by Michelangelo appears to be on the verge of ludicrously tumbling down. And for one so visibly invested in "divine furor" and the sloughing off of the bodily appearance for the spiritual essence and interior, which the stripped off animal skin putatively symbolizes, the inebriated god appears to be reeling from a physical plunge into bodily appetites, his stomach bulging, presumably with as yet undigested wine, and his head cocked to the side in an intoxicated trance of bibulous delight. Far from lifting us out of our bodies, the wine god, like the satyr with his tiny, swirling, tumescent erection, seems to make us all the more conscious of our material physical weight, leading us back into our bodies, not away from them into a state of upward spiritual transcendence. Similarly, the wine god's tentative smile, if viewed as a figuration of the sublime, could be taken to register the state of someone potentially seduced toward spiritual ecstasy and thus God; but it could also be taken as the barely suppressed expression of deep bodily satisfaction, the sort of satisfaction that also seems evident in the satyr's open-mouthed grimace of joy as he consumes the grapes that spill over into both his hands. There is much, in fact, that is ridiculous in this sculptural ensemble, in the sense of literally worthy of inviting laughter.

Hence, even a viewer thoroughly indoctrinated into searching for esoteric pagan mysteries would be hard pressed to see in the two figures an unambiguously clear illustration of Neoplatonic thought dramatized in material form. Both the wine god and the satyr seem too joyously immersed in their bodies, too pleased with the process of jubilant conspicuous consumption. To invert E. M. Forster's observation about the habits of consumption on the part of characters in realist novels, both Michelangelo's Bacchus and satyr, who are here presented in a high realistic mode, desperately *need* to eat. Their passion for the food they have either thoroughly imbibed, are about to drink, or are in the process of amorously consuming is as evident as the stone itself from which they are wrought. This is a sculpture, in short, that would have spoken as much to the melancholic Ficino, if read as an allegory of divine furor and madness, as it would have to Aretino, if read as a very material, sensuous expression of physical delights—particularly the delights in food, which, in good Aretino-like fashion, arouse the lascivious satyr in his appetites. Michelangelo's Neoplatonism, I would therefore urge, should be treated with some caution when viewing this work, as with so many others.[59] Michelangelo was as attached to the sensual matter of the body inhabiting his sculptures as he was to the possibilities of spiritual transcendence. In the words of Petrarca, a vernacular poet who, along with Dante, profoundly influenced Michelangelo's visual and verbal art: "et veggio 'l meglio et al peggior m'appiglio" (and I see the better, and I lay hold on the worse; *Rime*, 264.136).[60]

The wine god and satyr are structurally related, then, in a number of ways. They are related in their evident juxtaposition: spirit and divine furor stand in opposition to bestial desire, even as they are connected in a ladder of moral ascent and descent. They are related in their evident symmetry of purpose: the wine god and satyr are both avid consumers as they admire, cherish, or caress the food they hold on to and absorb directly into their bodies. And the two figures are related in their evident states of physical balance and imbalance: the wine god seems to stand on his own as he staggers in his precarious, classical contrapposto pose, but the same god is in fact held up by the serpentine-shaped satyr who furnishes him with the much-needed support.

Furthermore, the wine god and satyr are structurally related, I would like to posit, in the ways they inhabit and construct their own intense, self-enclosed spaces. These figures, intended to be placed in a theatrical space and perhaps become the subject there of collaborative discussion, seem entirely indifferent to the fact that they occupy highly dramatic poses and are being viewed in the round. They are simply too conspicuously absorbed in their states of either staggering inebriation (a state that compels the wine god to fix his gaze intensely on the cup he bears) or amorous consumption (a state that seems to intoxicate the satyr, twisting him into a position of flamelike serpentine furia that almost doubles for the contorted bunch of grapes that he nibbles on with such abandon and that arouses his erection in his unrepressed appetites). Neither the wine god nor the satyr—as tightly linked as they are, with the one fit into the backside of the other and an animal's skin held between them—even seems to acknowledge the other's presence, much less the presence of potential viewers, who may or may not respond with favor to their performances. Their world is not our world, their existence not our existence. This carefully conceived ontological divide between the hermetically sealed world of the sculpture and the engaged world of the audience, which is so typical of Michelangelo's works, is perhaps rendered all the more evident by the skull of the dead animal at the satyr's feet. The skull lies at the edge of the sculpture as if to mark off the world of the inert forms we view, even as the marble seems to come alive in its own world, so finely polished and full of movement and sensuous vitality.

Finally, if the *Bacchus* should be viewed within the context of autobiography, as Koch contends, it should be taken not only in terms of Michelangelo's ongoing project of "self-formation,"[61] which makes him resemble all the more Petrarca in his habit of continuously rewriting the narrative of his development in a sleight-of-hand of revisionary self-fashioning, but also in terms of Michelangelo's ongoing passion for presenting himself as inhabiting states of complete, impassioned absorption—the kind of state of absorption that has him cast by the Frenchman Blaise de Vigenère as a demiurge, not just carving the stone but attacking it, oblivious, it would seem, to anyone else who might be observing the enactment of his creative energy in process. "I have seen Michelangelo," the French visitor observed in astonishment,

> although more than sixty years old and no longer among the most robust, knock off more chips of a very hard marble in a quarter of an hour than three young stone carvers could have done in three or four, an almost incredible thing to one who has not seen it; and I thought the whole work would fall to pieces because he moved with such impetuosity and fury, knocking to the floor large chunks three or four fingers thick with a single blow so precisely aimed that if he had gone even minimally further than necessary, he risked losing it all.[62]

In one sense, as Michelangelo throws himself into the stone with "fury," he is transported into a state of divine madness, a heightened form of spiritual absorption in creativity, we are led to imagine. In another sense, as Michelangelo attacks a piece of marble and unleashes all his intense energy on it, inevitably sullying himself in the process with dust and dirt, as Leonardo would have insisted, he is arguably transported into a state of physical engagement with a hard yet still malleable block of matter.

This is relevant, I believe, to how we may choose to view the *Bacchus*. The enchanted state of the Bacchus, be it viewed as a state of Neoplatonic divine furor or simply a deep physical intoxication of all the senses, potentially mirrors the state of absorption of Michelangelo in his most intense moments of creative activity and devotion, when all his powers were fully engaged and he disappeared into his work, inhabiting his own space, potentially oblivious of surrounding spectators.[63] The story of Bacchus and the satyr in this way invites us to experience, in our own state of detached contemplation, elements of the great Michelangelo's most intense creative drives. Put differently, if Aretino's aesthetics of consumption leads us back into the body and the consumerism of his prolific self-fashioning, Michelangelo's aesthetics of consumption leads us into the body *and* the spirit through the transformative power of his art. Both artists are self-reflexive and aggressively performative within the context of their art as they reflect on appetites; but they exhibit these aspects of their characters through their representations in different ways and with differing degrees of emphasis. With Aretino we are drawn into a state of bodily leisure, fantasy, and pleasure alone. With Michelangelo we are invited to experience through the *Bacchus* not only a state of bodily leisure, fantasy, and pleasure (a drunken stupor, an aroused form of consumption, a cup held high as if in invitation for others to drink) but also the origins of Michelangelo's own originality as an artist bound to both the spirit and the body, transcendence and inviting sensuous matter.

The *Bacchus* embodies, then, a deep tension, which makes it, as Michelangelo's first great commission and his first undisputed masterpiece, a most telling one. It encapsulates a number of salient features of Michelangelo's visual art. It embodies his stubborn attraction to the sensual body placed often in such unusual poses of affective movement that they demand a viewer's keen, active engagement. It addresses his attention to classical forms and major works of contemporary masters that he deliberately echoes and pits himself against as he seeks to surpass—in Edmund Spenser's term, "overgo"—the very sources that present him with the origins for his aggressive, rivalrous originality. It dramatizes his self-reflexive fascination with the activity of creativity as a sort of intoxicating state of heightened, transporting absorption and physical pleasure. Similarly, it discloses his deep interest in the state of absorption that characterizes both divine frenzy and intoxicating sensual delights. At the same time, it renders evident his ability to fashion worlds of intense absorption that are at once removed from and contiguous to our own, so that the figures defined within those spaces, in all their theatricality and performative play within the viewer's gaze, appear sublimely oblivious to their surroundings and the spectators who are expected to view them, ideally in a state of equally intense, reflective absorption. Along with this, the *Bacchus* exhibits Michelangelo's concern for connecting himself to the works he creates, self-reflexively forging his own identity as he fashions figures that command all his formidable energies. Last but not least, the *Bacchus* gives concrete form, with all its internal ambiguities, to Michelangelo's desire to take on ever more challenging commissions in which he seeks to demonstrate his courage, his spirit, his animo. By so doing he renders the tasks he sets up for himself within the biography of his self-consciously mythicized life to appear to be all the more the product of an heroic endeavor, yet one more tangible piece of evidence of his predestined greatness and daring. The *Bacchus* in this way is the product of an artist with not just a self, and not just a self constantly under construction, but also an aggressively performative self capable of embracing in a single work both the unclassical and the classical, the ridiculous and the sublime.

On the face of it, Michelangelo's first great challenge and commission in Rome, it is finally important to point out, proved something of a failure, even if the sculpture is now viewed as a startling success. He had mustered the courage to produce a stunning work of art for a major patron in a powerful cardinal's court, a work that echoed classicism as it rivaled the antique and Donatello. But as Michael Hirst has persuasively argued, Riario rejected the *Bacchus* for his own courtyard or garden, much as he had rejected Michelangelo's earlier life-size *Sleeping Cupid*, though this time ostensibly not because the statue was fobbed off on him as a true antique when it was, as he well knew, modern in conception and execution. Indeed, "it is a striking case of a Renaissance work of art being rejected by the patron," Hirst has cogently observed in a discussion of the young Michelangelo: "Such episodes are relatively rare in the period. But it must also have constituted something of a crisis for the young artist."[64]

We will, of course, never know why Riario rejected the sculpture for his own garden or courtyard, if that was indeed the case. Perhaps Riario simply failed to grasp how the *Bacchus* engaged both the classical and the unclassical, the spiritual and the physical, sprezzatura and affettazione, decorous and indecorous behavior, the ridiculous and the sublime, each in equal measure and in an unresolved tension.[65] Perhaps, like Aretino, who chided Michelangelo later in his career for asking too much of his viewers by combining contradictory elements into his *Last Judgment* (indecorously mixing esoteric theological allegories with patent figures of sensuous, voluptuous nakedness), Riario was something of a purist when it came to the works he collected and appreciated. He may well have been unable to stomach all the ambiguities of the sculpture. Michelangelo, as Vasari first observed, was anything but unambiguous. In the end, perhaps Riario just liked his messages in the visual arts delivered plainly, his paganism and religion dished up alone and separately, without all the Neoplatonic obscurantism mixed into it. Like Aretino, he was perhaps just not one to combine matters.[66]

In any event, whatever the reason for Riario's refusal to keep the *Bacchus*, Michelangelo seems to have held something of a grudge against him. Indeed, later in life, Michelangelo—by then no great advocate or exemplar of professional propriety—had Condivi, whose biography he had such a hand in fashioning, observe: "The fact that the cardinal of S. Giorgio had little understanding or enjoyment of sculpture is made abundantly clear to us because in the whole time that [Michelangelo] stayed with him, which was about a year, he never worked on any commission whatever from the cardinal" (Cv 21–23).[67] Through the mouthpiece of Condivi, Michelangelo not only retroactively denounced Riario as a man of exceedingly bad taste (perhaps a worse crime among the elite seeking distinction in Renaissance Italy than anything else imaginable), but he also wrote Riario out of the narrative of his exemplary life as the patron who commissioned the work in the first place and paid for it to boot.[68] The erudite Jacopo Gallo, "a Roman gentleman of fine intellect," instead becomes the discriminating patron of the *Bacchus* in Condivi's narrative.[69] For, as it turns out, Gallo—Riario's neighbor and banker—did acquire the sculpture, and he placed it in his garden, where it remained for a long time, displayed among a host of antiquities, with the wine god's right arm (perhaps in time purposely) broken off, so that it now appeared all the more a veritable work of art unearthed from the past.[70] No doubt Michelangelo's *Bacchus*, given all the ambiguities it embodies, became the object of some refined conversation among the elite who gathered there to discuss topics of absorbing, classicizing interest in their staged celebrations and theatrical convivia.[71]

In time, Michelangelo's behavior also changed after his first commission in Rome, especially after producing the *Pietà*, the sculpture whose commission he received through Gallo not long after he completed the *Bacchus*, and that first won him widespread fame. Where Michelangelo appeared cautious with Riario, at least as he described his comportment in his letters, he soon became far more impatient and impertinent, not only with patrons in particular, but also, just as important, with all sorts of people in general. Eventually he became known for being hypersensitive and irascible, quick to fly off the handle—thin-skinned, we might say today. He became a lasting model figure of professional impropriety. Once, according to an anecdote of the time, Leonardo da Vinci was questioned over a disputed passage of the *Divina commedia* and referred the judgment to Michelangelo, who was passing by; Michelangelo, misunderstanding Leonardo's intention and thinking he had been made fun of, flew into a rage: "You made a design of a horse to be cast in bronze, and you were not able to cast it and for shame you abandoned it." Whether or not the story is true, it identifies a characteristic associated with Michelangelo once he became famous: his temper easily flared, and it could exhibit itself in distinctly antisocial, and professionally inappropriate, ways. His biting response to the rival artist Leonardo putatively took place in the company of other men, making it all the more an aggressive public act fueled by his unrepressed "ire."[72] Michelangelo's famed terribilità had to do not only with his style and artistic conceptions but also, as is well known, his antisocial, curmudgeonly character. Working with Michelangelo could be an exercise in strained patience. "Michelangelo's inapproachability," the biographer George Bull has observed, "or terribleness may have been one reason for Leo [X] using him at a distance from Rome."[73] Patrons might desperately want Michelangelo as their prized artist, but they often didn't want to have to deal with him. Kings found it difficult to handle him, Vasari asserts.

However, Michelangelo was not, it is important to stress, a violent man. In point of fact, he often fled violence, such as when he escaped Florence for fear of reprisals in 1494 or 1495, hid out in Florence until calm prevailed and he could once more take up his commissions in safety after the siege in 1530, or left Rome in the late 1550s for fear of the army of the Spanish viceroy in Naples, which had entered the Papal States. He got his nose permanently busted, it is worth remembering; he didn't bust Torrigiano's. In this respect he was very unlike Cellini, yet another artist of professional impropriety, whom we will discuss in the next chapter. But like Cellini, Michelangelo exhibited time and again an odd, difficult, antisocial behavior. The Renaissance historian Paolo Giovio tried to capture this aspect of Michelangelo's character when he observed that the great artist was unquestionably a man of genius but "his nature was so rough and uncouth that his domestic habits were incredibly squalid" and, as a result, "deprived posterity of any pupils who might have succeeded him."[74] The implication is that Michelangelo's strange habits of professional impropriety (which included, we learn from Vasari, his never even taking off his boots when he slept) alienated pupils, much as his fierceness, arrogance, and terribilità alienated potential patrons.

For his part, the courtly Vasari, who was by no means a lover of artists exhibiting professional improprieties, accounts for Michelangelo's habits of comportment as best he could, especially Michelangelo's habit of seeking solitude and his need for excessive secrecy. For Michelangelo, according to Vasari, "was sent by God into the world to the men of our craft/profession/art, so that one might learn from his life manners/habits/behavior [*costumi*] and from his works how to become true and splendid artisans" (482).[75] No one, to be sure, doubted Michelangelo's accomplishments as an artist, but his behavior, certainly when measured against the sprezzatura of the gracious, courteous, and delightful Leonardo or Raphael, was an entirely different matter altogether. Michelangelo often lacked tact. He could rile all sorts of people. He could, in brief, be crass. And with a model of comportment such as this, it is hardly surprising that all sorts of professional improprieties on the part of visual artists flourished among Michelangelo's ardent admirers, rivals, and imitators, both in his lifetime and in the period that followed.

The Children's Bacchanal *and the Absorption of Love*

Most drawings from the Italian High Renaissance had a utilitarian function. Typically they served as preparatory sketches for other finished works, be it for a painting, sculpture, or building. However, some artists occasionally made drawings as finished products to be given as gifts. This is certainly the case with Michelangelo's *Children's Bacchanal* (Figure 12), another work in Michelangelo's oeuvre (one of the few, in fact) that openly addresses the topic of consumption, though, unlike the *Bacchus*, this particular work was produced in Michelangelo's old age, in his late fifties or early sixties, rather than his early twenties.[76] The *Children's Bacchanal* is also among the most obsessively detailed of all of Michelangelo's finished presentation drawings.[77] Those drawings include the three additional extant ones sent to Tommaso Cavalieri, the handsome young Roman nobleman whom Michelangelo wrote love lyrics to and adored with such passion in his old age. In any event, the *Children's Bacchanal* is not just a well-worked design but also, one might say, an overworked design. For this reason the *Children's Bacchanal* can hardly be seen as just a study in technique, as a part of a larger lesson plan for Cavalieri, who had expressed interest in learning the art of disegno and would therefore have benefited, if we adopt Vasari's understanding of the genesis of the designs bestowed on Cavalieri, from viewing and handling such an accomplished drawing as this one.[78] Had Michelangelo's aim been merely to teach a close friend, there would have surely been easier ways for him to transmit the lesson to someone, not least through a sort of pattern book. The drawing of the *Children's Bacchanal*, like some of Michelangelo's other finished mythological drawings given to Cavalieri (the *Rape of Ganymede*, the *Punishment of Tytus*, and the *Fall of Phaethon*), is too much a labor of love to be viewed as just a lesson in form and function.

Michelangelo must have dedicated a significant amount of time to working out the composition to the *Children's Bacchanal*. Among his presentation drawings, this one is unprecedented in its complexity and *difficoltà*. He must have surely spent hours bent over the paper, drawing his hand back and forth again and again over the surface, making a plethora of varied marks with devotional energy as an act of intense, creative absorption.[79] There were, after all, swifter ways to make shading, if the overall aim was simply to furnish the viewer with a sense of volume through a calculated deception. Michelangelo engaged multiple techniques in this drawing, from time-consuming wedge-shaped marks of different intensities and gradations through painstakingly articulated soft and hard-edged lines to carefully rubbed and prepared surfaces. Similarly, if he had intended to demonstrate once more how he explored the human body in movement in an exceedingly broad range

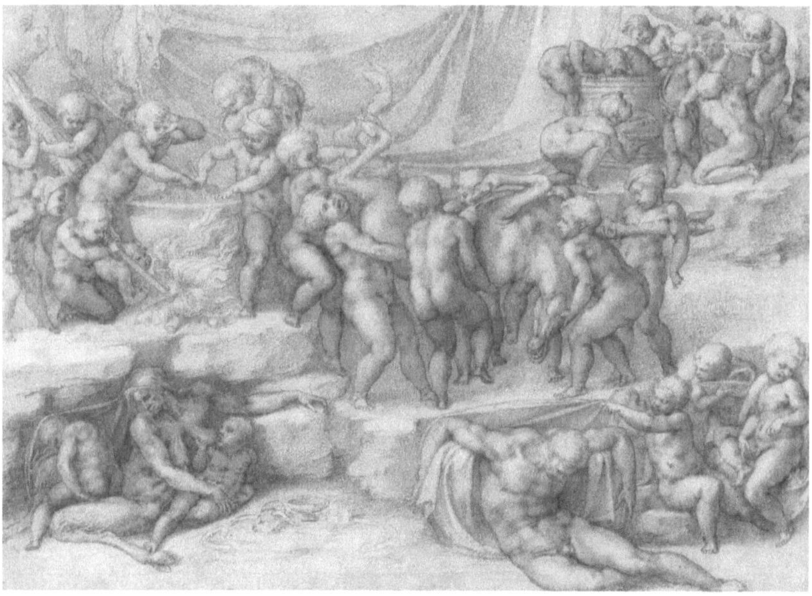

FIGURE 12 Michelangelo (1475–1564). *Children's Bacchanal*, ca. 1533. Courtesy The Royal Collection © 2008 Her Majesty Queen Elizabeth II.

of poses without ever repeating himself in the process, as Condivi observed in another context,[80] he could have found a far easier way of accomplishing this impressive feat than distributing thirty small naked children, an upside-down deer, a man stretched out on the ground like a classical river god, and a nursing satyr with withered breasts, all in a complex choreographed dance of poses onto a small sheet of paper with perfect compositional balance. In short, the drawing, which is as impressive for its range of techniques as it is for its range of poses, must have absorbed his creative energies. Everything about it marks it as a *tour de force*. And everything about it marks it as a work of absorption for a man thoroughly absorbed, as his lyrics make plain, by love. For if love is a state of absorption, as lyric poets in the Renaissance repeatedly attested, then Michelangelo, a lyric poet of some quality himself, has transferred that state into the material matter of the drawing, working and reworking it to a state of perfection worthy of the person on whom it was affectionately bestowed. Beauty and desire in the lyric mode and visual art of sixteenth-century Italy are once more self-reflexively conjoined with this presentation drawing.[81]

No text seems to underpin the overall story dramatized in the enigmatic drawing, as scholars have for a long time observed. But one important visual precedent exists for the central portion, which immediately captures the eye in its difficoltà with the zigzagging shape of the contorted deer being borne aloft in sacrifice.[82] The grouping of the children carrying a deer distinctly recalls Raphael's *Deposition*, with the naked child to the left of center leaning back and bracing himself with all his weight against the ground exactly as the figure positioned to the left does in Raphael's altarpiece painting (Figure 13).[83] In this light, the secular theme of consumption in revelry among the boisterous children carrying a slaughtered deer in a Bacchic-styled rite can be linked to the religious theme of lamentation for a god who gave up his body in charitable love for our sins. As the deer is sacrificed and then consumed, so, too, Christ was sacrificed and thereafter consumed through the sacrament of Mass. If we ask, then, what all this might have to do with Cavalieri, to whom the drawing was presented as a gift of love, we might tentatively posit the following, assuming, of course, that Michelangelo was not just trying to be indecorously irreverent through this visual echo but also intended to convey a deeper personal mystery through the religious model underpinning a distinctly pagan action. Arguably, Michelangelo, consumed by carnal love for Cavalieri as he makes this drawing as an old man, presents himself as a sacrifice: he sacrifices himself in spiritual love through his art, and the gift he bears to the beautiful and youthful Cavalieri is an extension of the artist, a sacramental part of his body—a material piece of the corpus of his work, which he shares in a communion of sublimated love.[84]

The theme of consumption in this drawing can also be read indirectly in relation to the very love that seems to have inversely fed Michelangelo by fulfilling him in such a profound way during his periods of intense infatuation with Cavalieri. "I know well that I can forget your name in the same hour when I forget the food I live on," Michelangelo claims in a letter to his beloved Cavalieri, "rather, I can sooner forget the food I live on, which only nourishes my body unhappily, than your name" (C 4.26). Much as when Michelangelo spoke about his inability to eat because he was so busy with his tasks that he could not find the time for it, so too, ever earnest in his lovesickness in his passionate letters to Cavalieri, he makes outrageous rhetorical claims about his powers of being able to go on in life without

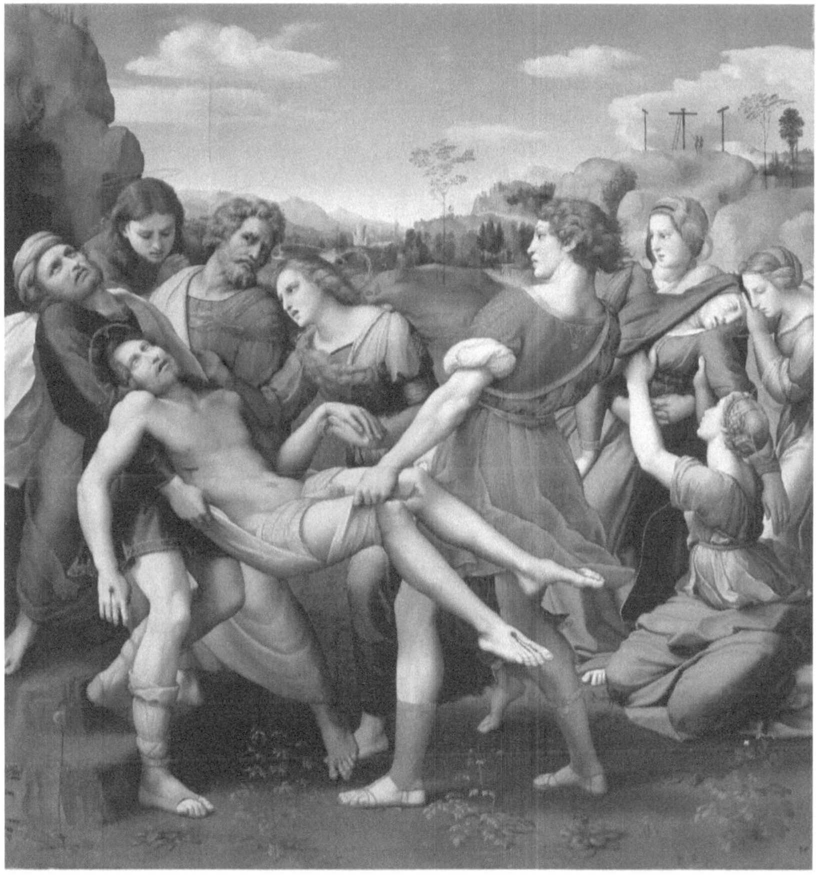

FIGURE 13. Raphael (1483–1520). *Deposition*, 1507. Galleria Borghese, Rome. Photo courtesy Scala/Ministero per i Beni e le Attività Culturali/Art Resource, New York.

any need for food. The language here is again not that of a person, to adopt Forster's terms, but of a character—a character who can somehow live without eating. Like many Petrarchan writers of his time, Michelangelo has here adopted the stylized tone of much love lyric of the Italian Renaissance, in which the lover, narcissistically consumed by his own passion, either wastes away in his pining or alternatively is nourished by his own self-sustaining sighs. Such is the stuff of love, both *in bono* and *in malo*, as Michelangelo gives us to understand in one of his own lyric poems:

> I' piango, i' ardo, i' mi consumo, e 'l core
> di questo si nutrisce. O dolce sorte![85]
>
> [I weep, I burn, I waste away, and my heart
> is fed by all this. O sweet fortune/chance!] (74.1–2)

Others may consume, but Michelangelo, in his poetry (as in his drawing to Cavalieri), is both absorbed and metaphorically consumed as he gives himself over to another in a gesture of love. Significantly, the very same theme of love and consumption is echoed in yet another finished presentation drawing for Cavalieri, his *Punishment of Tityus* (Figure 14), whose "dreadful" penalty for his transgressive lust, as Frederick Hartt observed, "was Michelangelo's metaphor for the torments of his own presumptuous love for Cavalieri."[86]

Michelangelo's absorption in the *Children's Bacchanal*, as powerful as it must have been, was on a small scale. More often than not, Michelangelo was absorbed in large-scale works and ongoing onerous projects that were

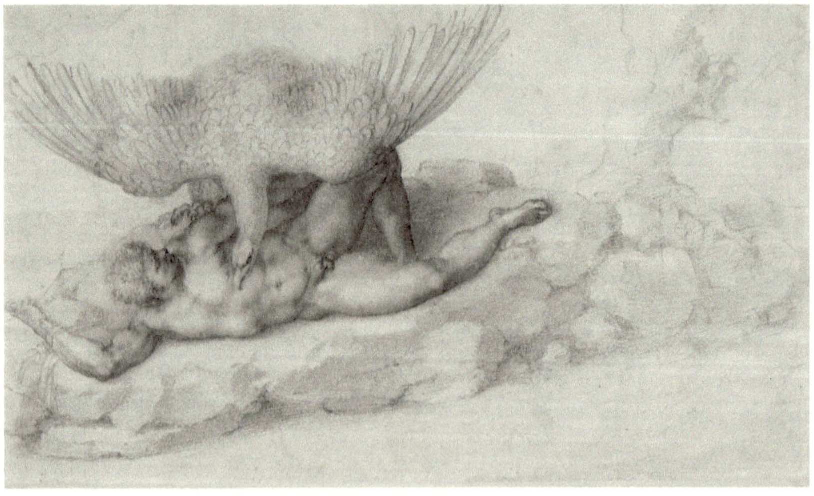

FIGURE 14. Michelangelo (1475–1564). *Punishment of Tityus*, 1532. Courtesy The Royal Collection © 2008 Her Majesty Queen Elizabeth II.

enormous in dimension and complexity and that occupied his talents not just for weeks, as was presumably the case with some of his more involved drawings,[87] or even for several months, as was the case with his *Bacchus*. Sometimes the projects Michelangelo worked on took several years to complete, if they were ever completed. Indeed, many of Michelangelo's projects, as is well known, were colossal in scale and inventive complexity, and his powers of concentration must have been prodigious when he was thoroughly engaged on them.

Here was a man, after all, who painted the entire vault of the Sistine Chapel, a project whose overall complexity in invention and conception (which Michelangelo surely had a hand in) still remains something of an interpretive puzzle. As far as the execution of the Sistine Chapel is concerned, the work involved was daunting to say the least. Though Michelangelo did not paint the ceiling absolutely by himself, as he liked to claim (even to the point where he insisted that he mixed his own colors),[88] and though he did not paint it lying down (as his first biographer, Giovio, indicated),[89] he certainly painted it at enormous physical strain. "I work harder than anyone who has ever lived," he asserts in one instance, "I'm not well and worn out with this stupendous labor [*chon grandissima faticha*] and yet I'm patient in order to achieve the desired end" (1.70, C 1.133). Michelangelo's most memorable account of the excruciating pain he endured while working on the chapel vault occurs in poetic form, with a picture of himself rapidly sketched on the side of the manuscript, with his head bent back and one arm akimbo, in a sort of strained classical pose (Figure 15).

Everything about Michelangelo, as he casts himself in the role of a demiurge in other instances, makes him heroic, his monumental achievements the product of much derring-do. With the *David* he even likened himself to the hero who saved a nation with a mere sling. The artist with the drill maneuvered by a bow is as absorbed by his works as the young hero is as he gazes out into the open space of the Piazza della Signoria. Both are presumably removed from reality and ordinary experience, living on a higher plane of self-enclosed intensity. Both are demonstrably performative selves constructed as heroic, the one with the deadly sling, the other with the life-giving bow. And both are intensely absorbed in their heroic, daring activities. "I'm here in the greatest discomfort and in a state of extreme fatigue, and not doing anything but work day and night, and I have endured and am enduring such fatigue," he observed on another occasion, this time with enormous pride in the nature of his undertaking the colossal bronze statue of Julius II in Bologna, "so that if I had to do the work over again I do not believe my life would be enough for me [to do it, or survive it], because it has been a tremendous undertaking and had it been in anyone else's hands it would have been a disaster" (40, C 1.55).

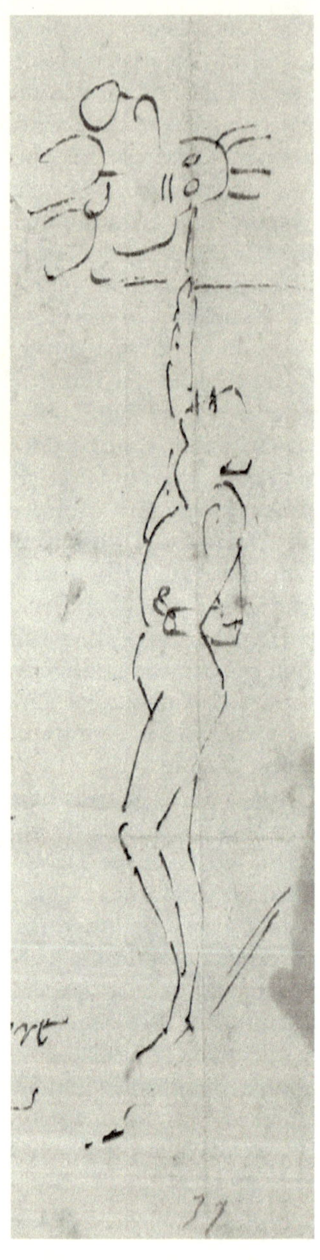

FIGURE 15. Michelangelo (1475–1564). Self-portrait while painting the ceiling frescoes in the Sistine chapel (from autograph sonnet), XIII fol. III. Casa Buonarroti, Florence. Photo courtesy Scala/Art Resource, New York.

Michelangelo's prodigious powers of creative absorption arguably never did in the end leave him, even though he feared their waning in time. One story, which we have already seen, has him in old age attacking marble with the furor of three stonemasons, and he does this with far greater technical precision than any of them could have ever possibly mustered. Another story, this one recounted by Vasari, tells of Michelangelo being so absorbed in his creative work in old age that he didn't even bother to sleep, just as he didn't even bother to eat food, we are led to believe, when deeply engaged in projects that occupied all his thoughts and energies. "Being unable to sleep," Vasari observes, he would set "to work with his chisel, having fashioned a helmet made of pasteboard holding a burning candle over the middle of his head, which in this manner shed light where he was working without tying up his hands" (475).[90] He produced with lightning speed, as men of such virtuosity and talent sometimes are when possessed with "furies [*furori*]," Benvenuto Cellini likewise reports, yet again enhancing the mythology of this larger-than-life man as a way of bolstering his own.[91] Well into old age, with his hands free and inventive powers restlessly flowing, the indefatigable Michelangelo still managed to produce some of the crowning glories of his career, not the least being the *Last Judgment*.

But over time he did, in truth, leave more and more commissions unfinished, not always purposely, as some scholars have contended, as they gesture toward the aesthetics of Auguste Rodin and the poetics of the *non finito*. Instead Michelangelo could not find the opportunity to bring so many of his works to the state of polished perfection that he would have sought had he possessed the time and the continued support of patrons.[92] When the opportunity arose and where the occasion warranted it, Michelangelo did in fact complete many of his works. However, the very myth of his greatness, which he had worked so hard to foster, now, in a sense, potentially contributed to undermining his ability to complete his colossal undertakings. He was so sought out that he simply had too much to do, too many massive projects to complete. This may account for some of his irritability, one might surmise, with the tragedy of the tomb for Julius II, eventually so diminished in size and conception, being a notable case in point. Not that Michelangelo needed much of an occasion to be irritable. By nature he was fairly irritable as it was, though perhaps in moments of absorption, it is worth imagining, his irritability diminished as he transferred himself with all his terribilità into his tasks, in youth and old age, as a "character" acting on the stage of life, to borrow Forster's terms, or as a person who doesn't even need to bother to consume any food.

PART THREE

Objects

CHAPTER 4

Benvenuto Cellini and the Art of Conspicuous Production

Things

In an essay on the habits and practices of conspicuous consumption in Renaissance Italy, Richard Goldthwaite, taking his cue from Henry James and the elite culture of the industrial revolution in late-nineteenth-century England, argued that Italians, particularly Florentines, were obsessed with the things—or, more precisely, "the empire of things"—that they placed at their command through the accumulation of enormous wealth.[1] Though Goldthwaite argues for a changed relationship in the period between the possessor and the object possessed, it is nevertheless important to emphasize that "things" did not exist unto themselves in Renaissance Italy, as would sometimes seem to be the case when objects are isolated for discussion in much contemporary "thing theory." Everything, which is to say every single thing in this putative empire of things, was mediated through a complex network of exchanges, a point Michael Baxandall made years ago when he insisted that every art object was first and foremost in Renaissance Italy a locus of social relations. Lauro Martines forcefully reiterates this point in a review essay of Goldthwaite's seminal book *Wealth and the Demand for Art in Italy, 1300–1600*.[2] A "thing"—a painting, a building, a block of marble from Carrara—had meaning by being constructed, viewed, and transmitted through social transactions—that is, through some process of human-centered exchange, interested or disinterested as it may be, some sort of unarrested "flow within the circuits of production and distribution, consumption and exhibition," to borrow the words of the contemporary thing theorist Bill Brown.[3] No one in Renaissance Italy had the sort of closed, intimate relationship with a thing that Michelangelo Antonioni's protagonists have, for instance, in his modernist Italian films of escape, numbness, isolation, and alienation.

Things were sites of conversation in Renaissance Italy, especially within the realm of nascent museum building and in the context of a collector's cabinets of curiosities or "studio."[4] Finally, the constant close interactions everyone had with one another daily throughout Renaissance Italy made it virtually impossible to have an unfettered relationship with a thing. Anonymity did not exist in Renaissance Italy as it did in the late nineteenth century or as it does today. Everything, it bears repeating, was mediated in Renaissance Italy. Everything formed, or was formed by, social relations. Nothing was, or could ever be thought of as being, just a thing that offered up its intractable, opaque thingness.[5]

No visual artist in Renaissance Italy better captures the notion that things are embedded in social relations and processes of exchange in which a person's identity is always at stake and on the stage than Benvenuto Cellini (Figure 16).[6] Not even Giorgio Vasari, the author of the celebrated *Le vite*, perhaps displays such a powerful understanding of the social life of things in sixteenth-century Italian culture. A goldsmith and sculptor by profession (first the former, then the latter), Cellini was not just a maker of things but, belatedly, after being humiliated through a conviction of sodomy, a writer about them. His activities in the world also brought him into contact with a host of people in very different places centered on things. Examining his works as an artist and author will thus allow us to see how a man's identity was constructed in relation to things produced and bought within his particular society in the context not only of art objects but also of words.[7] Moreover, Cellini's *Vita* articulates a concrete, gendered understanding of what constitutes social relations in sixteenth-century Italy as men constructed their identities through the production and consumption of things.[8] From the outset, Cellini's autobiography offers a male-dominated notion of social merit and productivity, in which all men, "tutti gli uomini," who have ever done anything of value should write about their lives. However, men should write about their lives only after they have turned forty, by which time, at what was then considered old age, they would have revealed their manhood and have hopefully accomplished something memorable. "It is true," Cellini opines, "that men who have labored with some show of excellence, have already given knowledge of themselves to the world; and this alone ought to suffice them; I mean the fact that they have proved their manhood and achieved renown" (*vedutosi essere uomo e conosciuto*; 3–4, 1.2). Additionally, what is so striking about Cellini's narrative from the outset and marks it so openly as a male-centered text is that the narrator makes a point of deliberately indicating in the opening pages how exceptional it is that he is, in fact, male. Everyone, we are told, expected a girl at his birth. Within a narrative that unfolds in a straightforward manner but is far more formally thought out than has always been acknowledged,[9]

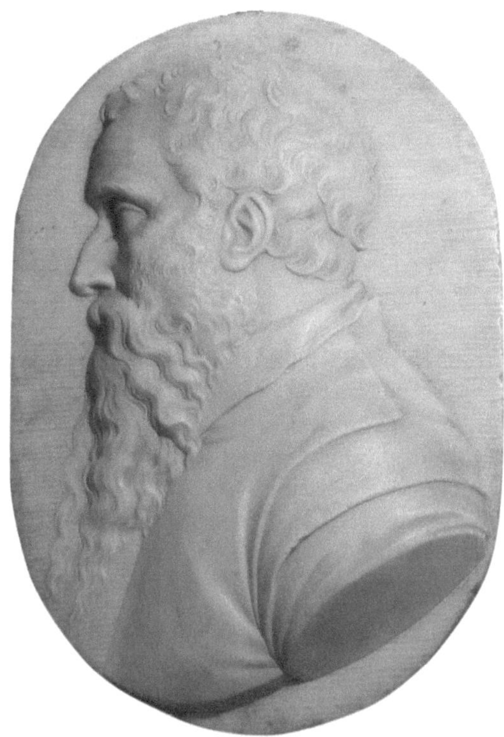

FIGURE 16. Francesco Ferrucci del Tadda (1497–1585), probably after a design by Cellini. *Portrait of Benvenuto Cellini*, ca. 1555–1570. Museo Nazionale del Bargello, Florence. By concession of the Ministero per i Beni e le Attività Culturali. Photo courtesy Louis A. Waldman.

the stage has thus been set for a baby girl being born, a baby girl who, once she has grown, could have perhaps given voice to a broader notion of what constitutes tutti gli uomini, perhaps even to include "tutti gli esseri umani." Instead, what we get is a "guy." To be sure, no one is disappointed within the text. The appreciative father is instead overjoyed when, much to his surprise, the infant growing inside his wife's womb finds itself externalized in material form as a baby boy.

Furthermore, though the focus throughout Cellini's life is his life, centered as it is on his activities as a maker of things, community also mattered deeply to him, and he participated in that community, he liked to proclaim in his *Vita*, both selfishly and selflessly. When a friend in Rome falls ill, for instance, Cellini is there for him, and he will hear nothing about receiving a reward for the service done: "To this I replied that I had not done for him as much as I would have desired, but only what I could, and that it was the duty of human beings to be mutually serviceable" (*il dovere delle creature umane si era sovvenire l'una l'altra*; 67, 1.32). In the best of circumstances, then, people in sixteenth-century Italy, we are led to believe from Cellini's narrative, can be mutually serviceable in a completely selfless way, by assisting others who are ill or in need, as Cellini does in this case by succoring another and bringing him back to life. In other circumstances people are mutually serviceable in giving each other company, as Cellini and his male companions do so often as they fight together, travel together, joke together after the plague, and work together as men bound together in life that is, to borrow Hobbes's terms, "nasty, brutish, and short." Then again, people are mutually serviceable in producing things that others of substantial social standing and financial means desire. The king of France, for instance, acknowledges within Cellini's self-glorifying narrative how he and Cellini are mutually serviceable to one another, the one as a doer of great deeds, the other as a maker of great things:

> Next, he patted me on the shoulder, saying: "*Mon ami* (which is the same as *my friend*), I know not whether the pleasure be greater for the prince who finds a man after his own heart, or for the great artist who finds a prince willing to furnish him with means for carrying out his great ideas." I answered that, if I was really the man his Majesty described, my good fortune was by far the greater. He answered, laughingly: "Let us agree, then, that our luck is equal!" [325, 2.22]

In yet other circumstances in his life, Cellini reveals how people are mutually serviceable to one another in a world of monetary exchange, especially when those people further the processes of communal interaction whereby one commission fluidly flows into another. Furthermore, people are mutually serviceable in writing about their experiences and in offering information about their lives as makers of things for other people to learn from and marvel over. To "sovvenire," after all, means not just to succor and assist but also, as the French *souvenir* more openly registers, to "remember," to "recall." Finally, *all* these aspects of serviceability make up Cellini's life as he recounts it, often with the tacit aim of highlighting his honor and status. And what we learn over and over again in reading Cellini's *Vita* is that the possibilities of making oneself serviceable to another in late sixteenth-century Italy are manifold for men of extraordinary talent such as Cellini, as he fashions a lasting image of himself in his autobiography as the consummate maker of things in a world of both interested and disinterested processes of exchange.

Cellini, the Astonishing Maker of Things

Cellini is certainly a bold and impetuous man, and he proves himself to be so in a number of ways not long after returning home to Florence from Rome in 1522, when he is a mere twenty-two years old, the age when Michelangelo, the artist he most admired and sought to surpass, completed his *Bacchus* more than two decades earlier. Most noticeably, Cellini stands up for himself and clobbers a number of people. He has just been treated harshly at the hands of the magistrates of the "Otto di Guardia," the Florentine criminal court housed in the Bargello and entrusted with seeing to the order of the city, specifically with overlooking both petty and major crimes. Infuriated by their behavior and slighted by Maestro Annibale, a relative who did not come to post bail and assist him in his time of need, Cellini returns to the house of his offenders, wild with rage. This is how Cellini then tells his story in his own inimitable way, presenting himself as a man who is not just slapped in the face but, much as he appears throughout the *Vita*, as a man capable of aggressively getting back at others and who is thus in their—as well as, I would claim, *our*—faces:

> Having left the palace, I ran to my shop, seized a dagger, and rushed to the house of my enemies, who were at home and shop together. I found them at table; and Gherardo [Guasconti], who had been the cause of the quarrel, flung himself upon me. I stabbed him in the breast, piercing the doublet and jerkin through and through to the shirt, without however grazing his flesh or doing him the least harm in the world. When I felt my hand go in, and heard the clothes tear, I thought that I had harmed him; and seeing him fall terror-struck to earth, I cried: "Traitors, this day is the day on which I mean to murder you all" [32, 1.17].[10]

In taking down Gherardo with ruthless efficiency and then bludgeoning so many others, directly after he has pounced on his prey while "raging like a mad bull" (32, 1.17), Cellini, always eager to assert his honor, not only proves himself a fierce, proud, impetuous man capable of getting in other people's faces, even though he claims, with obvious false modesty, that what he did when he stabbed Gherardo wasn't even enough to inflict a scratch. In attacking these men, who have cautiously grouped together to secure their own protection, Cellini, alone against them all, also reveals himself to fit well within his family line, chock full as it is with so many men who loved to fight, from his own brother, Cecchino, who chose to take on the "profession of arms" and is slain in Rome in a quarrel, to more distant relatives, whom Cellini lists at the beginning of his *Vita* in order to lay claim to the honor of his heritage, the sort of pasta from which he was made. "I glory," he asserts, "in tracing my descent from men of valor" (5, 1.2). Those men included Luca Cellini, "a beardless youth," who fought, Cellini tells us, "with such bravery and stoutness that he moved the folk to wonder" (*fé maravigliare il mondo*; 5, 1.2).

Benvenuto Cellini resembles his forbearer Luca Cellini, a "wonder," especially in two ways. Like Luca Cellini, Benvenuto elicits admiration for his ability to take down so many men, despite the terrible odds against him. Earlier, in fact, in the incident that provoked Cellini's wrath and that led him to stand in judgment before the Otto di Guardia, he had exhibited the same ardent desire to fight. When Gherardo, a rival Florentine goldsmith and ruffian, pushed him into a load of bricks, Cellini instinctively responded to the offense by smacking Gherardo directly in the face. Not long after, Cellini openly admitted as much in court when he asserted he had given the ruffian a *ceffata*, a slap. On the one hand, this admission of guilt placed Benvenuto in the positive light of having been honest, but on the other hand it placed him in the unfortunate position of being fined even more than if he had only admitted to having delivered a "punch" in the face. "It was a slap," he grumbles, as he is sent away by the Otto di Guardia, "not a punch" (*ceffata fu e non pugno*; 31, 1.17). Like Luca Cellini, Benvenuto is therefore strong and capable and to be admired for his audacity and firmness of position. Alone, he pitted himself against one of the most powerful goldsmith families in Florence, and he refused to back down in court, come what may.

At the same time, the narrator of this autobiography is even more like Luca Cellini in yet another way. He reveals his determination to fight and stand up for himself in his youth, thereby demonstrating his manhood at an early age. For instance, not long after he has fled from the authorities, who condemned him to death and thus issued against Cellini on November 13, 1523, "one of the most dreadful bans which were ever heard of" (33, 1.18), the impetuous Cellini reveals his manhood through a telling physical detail. He prepares to be led out of his hideout in the Franciscan church of Santa Maria Novella, where the friar Alessio Strozzi had kindly kept him in his cell. To disguise himself, Cellini asks a friend who has come to help him to "remove a few hairs from [his] chin, which were the first down [of his manhood]" (34, 1.18). Then, once he has achieved his escape from Florence disguised as a Dominican friar, Cellini takes off his cloak and reveals himself to be, once more, "a man." More to the point, Cellini insists that he has "ritornato uomo," literally "turned back into a man" (34, 1.18), as if the uncloaking had brought about a magical transformation in his maturation. Within the narrative Cellini has been symbolically reborn, reconstituted into the man he was destined to become as he leaves Florence to make his way in the world alone at the age of twenty-three.

In this episode, just before he sets off into the world, Cellini labors to show that he is a free man, capable of controlling his own destiny and saving others. And he does the same in many other episodes in his *Vita*. Indeed, in one instance he presents himself as the man who saved the day during the

Sack of Rome, keeping the invaders at bay as the Imperial army assaulted Castel Sant'Angelo, where the pope and his entourage had secured themselves. "In my enthusiasm," Cellini observes with characteristic immodesty, "I pushed myself to do what I could not: let it suffice that it was I who saved the castle that morning, and brought the other bombardiers to their duty" (76, 1.34).[11] But even as Cellini makes these assertions, it is also true that he is never as free as he declares himself to be—and not just because he lands in prison (toward the end of the first section of the book and, as we know from extant documents, just before he began composing his autobiography). Everywhere we turn we discover that what enables Cellini's freedom, the agency that he has in the world, is the economic demand for the things he has so conspicuously and ably produced—or, at the very least, the plethora of things he would like us to believe he produced in abundance throughout his life. Without that network of production and consumption of things, the "empire of things" Goldthwaite describes, Cellini could not have flourished so effectively. He would have lost his clients, each of which passed him on to another in a series of monetary transactions and valuable gift exchanges that materially bestow honor on Cellini. The king of France makes this painfully evident to Cellini when, in the course of scolding him for his overambitious attempt to accomplish too much at one time, he warns within the narrative: "There is one most important matter, Benvenuto, which men of your sort, though full of talent, ought always to bear in mind; it is that you cannot bring your great gifts to light by your own strength alone; you show your greatness only through the opportunities we give you" (362, 2.44). Dependency typically breeds resentment, and there is, practically speaking, little Cellini can do about it when he is facing the all-powerful king of France. The word Cellini has to describe his reaction to the king's observation is *stizza*, the indignation of the subordinate who would probably like to strike back but cannot (364, 2.46).

If the network of production and consumption of things that makes up the "demand for art" in Renaissance Italy were to fall apart, if the system of brokerage and clientage and conspicuous consumption were to break down, then Cellini, as a maker of things, would lose his power base and thus his manhood. He would lose, in truth, the very essence of what keeps him going, what fully gives him his identity, furnishes him with much of his sense of status, and feeds his ego, thus allowing him to make all sorts of outrageous claims about his greatness, even to the point where he insists that he would have fared better as a man of arms than as a man engaged in his current profession as a visual artist (1.34). For according to Cellini, he is, exactly as he thinks of Michelangelo, one of those "men of worth" who, as he puts it in an effort to diminish at one point the "vainglorious" Jacopo Sansovino, can make good and beautiful things of value (167, 1.78). To be sure, not every single thing Cellini makes is artistically of great importance to him, but everything he makes (and he would like us to think that he has made an enormous quantity of things) has importance as a means of assuring him some measure of independence and agency in the world. Consider, for instance, the importance of things to him when he returns to Rome in book 1. Cellini quickly meets up with his usual friends and gets straight back to his shop, overwhelmed, he states, by all sorts of commissions. No time was lost before he sets himself to work at things that brought him profit, he asserts, but remained unworthy of being described (*non da nome da descrivere;* 95, 1.43). "Since I did not produce things [*cose*] of importance at that period," Cellini observes in another occasion, "I need not waste time in talking about them" (73, 1.34). In one instance, having things to work on while in prison gives Cellini some degree of consolation, absorbing his mind, engaging his hands, and allowing him to keep his shop open and running, even while he is absent: "Ascanio, my apprentice, came to the castle and brought me things [cose] to work at. Though I could not do much, feeling myself being imprisoned so unjustly, nevertheless I made a virtue of necessity, and bore my adverse fortune with as light a heart as I was able" (227, 1.104).[12]

Things always lie at the center of Cellini's attention. No sooner has he returned to Rome after his second, and far more debilitating, imprisonment than he focuses his concerns on the things in his shop, "molta quantità di altre cose di molto valore" (with a great quantity of other things of great value; 283, 2.1). In Machiavellian terms, these cose produced in apparent abundance allow Cellini to exercise his *virtù* in the face of adverse *fortuna*, shaping if not his destiny then at least his own value. By making things over and over again, as he vaunts he does, he retains and asserts his identity. What is more, throughout his narrative Cellini makes a point of conspicuously showing us how many things he makes. He aims to overwhelm us, whether or not he was such a prolific producer of them. And he probably even means for us to imagine that he is making things while, in the fiction of the construction of the tale,[13] he dictates his autobiography to a young boy in his shop: "I began to have him do the writing, and *while I was working*, I dictated the story of my life to him; and since I actually took some pleasure in it, *I worked much more diligently and produced many more works of art*" (my emphasis).[14] It is essential for Cellini that we envision him this way: always busy, making things, whether it be just to keep his hands occupied or to exercise enormous *fatica* in the production of, on a rare occasion, a massive work of art. As the king of France puts it: "He ought never to stop working!" (312, 2.16)

A host of things, we are given to understand, are just made to feed the demand for art within a society of consumption that loved all sorts of objects,[15] from medals to vases, to seals, to belt buckles, to perfume burners, to rings, to bridal bits, to candelabras, to water vessels called "acquereccia, which are used for ornaments to place on sideboards" (40, 1.22), to jewels of all sorts, to saltcellars, to dies, to medals placed in caps with a device engraved in them ("of these I made very many," he comments, 65, 1.31), to the elaborate, detailed, bejeweled "morse" for the pope's priest's coat (97, 1.43). Needless to say, Cellini is in on this appetite for art. He is in on it, moreover, not just for the honor and reputation that it brings him but also for the monetary reward, which gains him substantial "profit," as he candidly puts it in various instances.[16] He understands, then, not only the ideal nature of value as it is transmitted within the court through symbolic exchanges that confer honor—many of which leave him disillusioned in Florence under Duke Cosimo I (1519–1574), a parsimonious, "mercantile"-minded patron if there ever was one, according to Cellini—but also gratified under the aegis of Francis I in Paris, where he is regaled with gifts and showered with opportunities for advancing his career. Cellini also understands from the very beginning of his adult life, even as he sets out to make his way in the world with only the hint of a beard on his face, the nature of value as it is transmitted within a vigorous workshop and patronage system, just as he understands the cultural significance of monetary and gift exchanges for the acquisition of things *and* their compensatory value in terms of honor in a courtly world of conduct. "Though I was very badly paid," he remarks when describing the completion of a commission for Raffaello Lapaccini in Florence, "it was such the honor that I received from doing it that it was worth more than the reward that I rightly could have gotten from making it" (29, 1.15). There are the great things he makes and the small ones, and both sustain him, allowing him some measure of income and independence, along with, at times, great honor. Moreover, how much Cellini gets paid for a commission allows him to assert vigorously his prideful manhood as he mocks a rival, for instance, and enrages him at one and the same time: "The bystanders openly declared against him [his rival, Lucagnolo], holding him for a lout, as indeed he was, and me for a man [*e me in concetto di uomo*], as I had proved myself to be" (40, 1.21).

Self-worth, monetary gain, honor, mobility, status: all these elements make up Cellini's life as a man who is above all a conspicuous maker of things. But what also distinguishes Cellini's approach to the things he makes is that he often conceives of them in relation to some sort of shocking event that has an impact on his memory, and by extension our memory as he relates them to us in his *Vita*. To see how this is so, we need to turn briefly to the opening pages of the *Vita*, for in them we catch a glimpse of how shocking events will symbolically have an impact on Cellini's memory and how, at the same time, he learns that a shocking event can have an effect on people's memories generally.

It is significant, for instance, that in the very first paragraph of the autobiography, as Cellini looks back over his life, he views his survival through fifty-eight years of personal hardship and historical upheaval with wonder, "meraviglia" (1.1). He is stunned, and so should we be, that he could have made it thus far alive and unscathed, especially when we later learn how he even dueled with so many men, fought the Imperial troops attacking Castel Sant'Angelo, and was sentenced to death. The first image we have of Cellini as a child, interestingly enough, is of him playing nonchalantly with a scorpion, which is about to sting the boy before the father, gripped by "wonder," leaps to his son's rescue—yet another "augury" (9, 1.4), Cellini vaingloriously assures us, that his life was destined for great things. Soon after describing this incident, Cellini then tells us how his father struck him on the cheek one day so that he would recall later in life a truly memorable event. The father's strategy seems to have been successful, for Cellini has indeed remembered the event, and now he relates it to us so that we too may be shocked by it and consequently remember it well. "When I was about five years old," he reports,

> my father happened to be in a basement-chamber of our house, where they had been washing, and where a good fire of oak-logs was still burning; he had a viol in his hand, and was playing and singing alone beside the fire. The weather was cold. Happening to look into the fire, he spied in the middle of those most burning flames a little creature like a lizard, which was sporting in the core of the most intense coals. Becoming instantly aware of what the thing was, he had my sister and me called, and pointing it out to us children, gave me a great box in the ears [*una gran ceffata*], which caused me to howl and weep with all my might. Then he pacified me good-humouredly, and spoke as follows: "My dear little boy, I am not striking you for any wrong that you have done, but only to make you remember [*perché tu ti ricordi*] that that lizard which you see in the fire is a salamander, a creature which has never been seen before by any one of whom we have credible information." So saying, he kissed me and gave me some pieces of money [9, 1.4].

Noticeably, just the boy receives the box on the ear and then gets rewarded. This is important within the highly male-oriented, gendered relationships that define Cellini's autobiography and sixteenth-century culture in general. For already, as a very young boy Cellini learns from his father a succinct lesson here that instructs him on how to recall memorable moments, and as a result how to render them memorable in return. There will be many such shocking moments in his life worth remembering as he proves himself to be a man who constantly gets in other people's faces and then, significantly, is rewarded often enough in the process. Indeed, the appearance of the salamander, which was the "emblem of the French King," as John Pope-Hennessy observed, anticipates Cellini's "later career at the French court," a career that marks one of the high points of his professional life and brought him many honors.[17]

As Cellini describes his life in a world that functions often enough as a school of hard knocks, in which he receives blow after blow and delivers memorable ones in return, we are invited time and again to feel a kind of astonishment that inspires suspended wonder before something so different, like the salamander living in the midst of the flames.[18] Part of the astonishment in the *Vita* also serves to focus our attention on Cellini as a man whose life was invested completely in the making of things, even to the point where he sometimes becomes one with the thing made, so that the two—the man and material shaped by the man—seem fused within the narrative. This is certainly the case when it comes time for Cellini to produce his most magnificent work of art described in the autobiography, the famous *Perseus* (Figure 17).[19] His investment in the making of this statue is total, even to the point where he begins to throw into the fire his own material investments ("pewter platters, porringers, and dishes, to the number of some two hundred pieces"; 418, 2.77) to make sure the bronze will melt properly and the molding take. He uses, as he puts it, "*all* the forces of my body and my purse, employing *all* of the little money that still remained to me" (412–13, 2.75). He aims to give it everything, go for broke, not just monetarily but physically as he pushes himself to the edge (*Io mi sforzavo*; 2.75), "exerting [himself] in his exhausting labor beyond the measure of [his] powerful constitution" (414, 2.75).

The conspicuous producer of things makes himself over in this emblematic moment as one who is willing to gamble it all. He thinks, as he so often does in the autobiography, in absolute terms. And his determination as a maker of the *Perseus* shocks everyone, even before he begins working on it and has to retire to his room because he has fallen ill, partly from exhaustion, but also partly, he observes, from a debilitating fever. No one, to be sure, thinks the casting can be achieved, since a bronze of this magnitude and complexity has never been done before in modern times. Cosimo I, who has commissioned the sculpture, even challenges Cellini on this matter when the duke questions the artist's method of metallurgy. As Cellini explains his method of casting bronze in this instance, he observes that, given the enormousness of the statue, his method necessarily differed from that of the other masters in the trade. Yet, to everyone's astonishment, Cellini does manage to make the sculpture in one pouring, he claims, though in telling the story in this self-ingratiating manner Cellini noticeably fudges with the facts. Later the duke expresses wonder that Cellini had the requisite foresight to see how the casting of such a complex statue would actually take place, right down to his realization that the Medusa head held aloft would come out perfectly, while the foot at the very base would have suffered, because, according to Cellini, heat rises: "When I arrived at the foot of *Perseus*, and said it had not come out perfect, just as I previously warned his Excellency, I saw

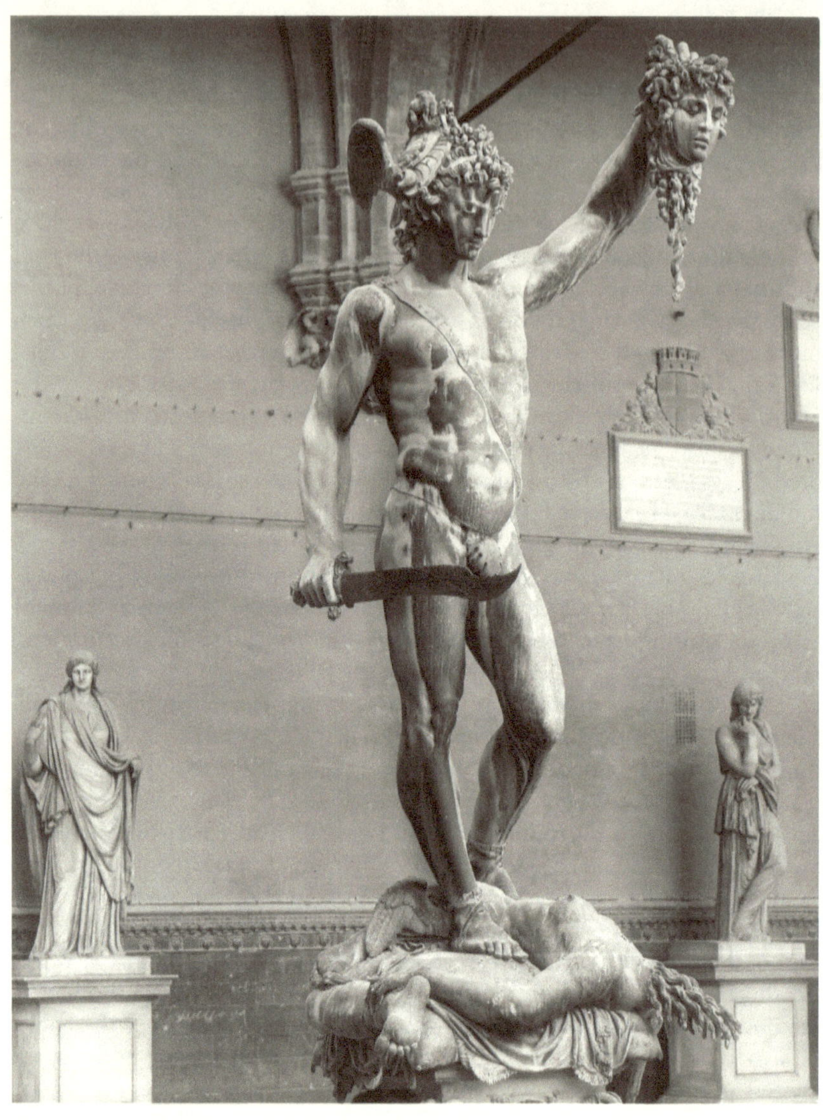

FIGURE 17. Benvenuto Cellini (1500–1571). *Perseus with the Head of Medusa*, 1545–1553. Loggia dei Lanzi, Florence. Photo courtesy Alinari/Art Resource, New York.

an expression of wonder pass over his face, while he related to the Duchess how I had predicted this beforehand" (420, 2.78). So, too, Cellini's workers tell an embellished story full of amazement, making it sound as if Cellini had otherworldly powers that allowed him to produce miracles. In turn, the story told by Cellini's workers is then even more embellished, so that it becomes, as Cosimo I's majordomo relates it to the duke within Cellini's narrative, "far more terrifying/awesome" (*terribilmente*)—a term, to be sure, closely associated with Michelangelo—"and full of greater wonder than what they had narrated" (419, 2.77).

At the heart of Cellini's tale about his construction of the *Perseus* is intense energy in a narrative that is repeatedly filled with expressions of wonder. All night long, Cellini, who has been playing the role of Vulcan laboring in the demonic depths of Aetna, has been exploding—or so he gives us to believe through the voice of one his workers within his narrative. "I think the blows and kicks you dealt us last night," the worker assures Cellini, "when you were so enraged with the diabolical fury that you showed, must have forced your enormous fever to take flight, fearful that you would have delivered the same blows and kicks to it" (418, 2.77). Then, at one point, the boiling mass in the cauldron bursts:

> All of a sudden an explosion took place, attended by a tremendous flash of flame [*con un lampo di fuoco grandissimo*], as though a thunderbolt [*saetta*] had formed and been discharged amongst us. Unwonted and appalling terror astounded every one, and me more than the rest. When the din was over and the dazzling light extinguished, we began to look each other in the face. Then I discovered that the cap of the furnace had blown up, and the bronze was bubbling over from its source beneath [417–18, 2.77].

Giving shape to an energy that explodes like thunder requires bursts of energy itself, a sort of creative counterforce. And this strategically staged dialectic between life and death—between dynamic, explosive energy transmitted through a near bursting furnace and the reification of that energy into solid, impermeable form through Cellini's creative forces and "blows"—is coded into the statue being created. Medusa would try to transform people into things, robbing them of life and turning them into stone through her gorgonizing gaze; Perseus, by decapitating Medusa, would try to liberate people from the threat of reification, armed as he is with a helmet and a sword. The two together—Perseus and Medusa—thus self-reflexively describe within the autobiography Cellini's wonder-eliciting act of creation as a near divine, conspicuous maker of things. Indeed, the fluid bronze needed to make the statue almost dies, caked into a solid mass, but it is revived thanks to the strength, perseverance, and vital force, we are told, of Cellini. "I had brought the dead to life again," he affirms (417, 2.77).[20] He has made the dead living, as one writer observed in a poem of praise attached to the base of the *Perseus* once the sculpture was finished and displayed in the central city square:

> Quod stupeant homines viso occisore Medusae
> Non est vipereum, quod gerat ille caput,
> Sed manus artificis, quae tot iam secula nobis,
> Mortua, quae fuerant corpora, viva facit[21] [S ii, v].

> [What people are [or should be] astounded at when they see the slain head of Medusa is not the snaky head that he [Perseus] carries, but the hand of the artist, which makes bodies, which have been dead for so many centuries, living for us.]

Finally, it is important for our understanding of Cellini's presentation of himself as a conspicuous and indefatigable maker of things that he talks at some length in his *Vita* about how he nearly botched the job. As a self-conscious narrator, he wants us to see, that is, the other narrative possibilities for his life's story as a maker of things in a society with an impressive appetite for art. In this regard, the story of the execution of the *Perseus* is *almost* the story of how an object was turned into a shapeless thing, a blob of churned bronze and a busted mold buried in a trench in a make-shift shop with a blazing furnace bursting at its seams. No one, particularly Cosimo I, we are led to believe in the narrative, expected that Cellini could accomplish the task of fusing the entire sculpture as one seamless piece of bronze (a feat that Cellini, in fact, did *not* achieve, but nonetheless feels justified in boasting about as if he had). Casting such a bronze was an accomplishment unheard of in the modern age. Cellini even has to come back from the brink of death, as he tells the story, to bring the material for the sculpture back to life as a liquid ready to be poured into the mold. Keeping the bronze from turning into just a shapeless mass—and then, what is more, creatively using that bronze, once it has properly liquefied, to make a thing of lasting beauty—takes a man of astounding, life-enhancing force, someone with Michelangelo-like terribilità. It requires a man capable of delivering blows of creative energy to keep his workers in line, at their post, doing their job. In many ways we are supposed to see Cellini as the absolute center of it all, yelling, feeling, testing, rebuking, chiding, infusing the mold with molten bronze, praying to God for its success and revivification. And yet, even so, we always need to bear in mind that bringing the *Perseus* back to life, Cellini makes clear, also requires a host of people. It also requires a host of people afterwards to admire the sculpture, so that Cellini can feel truly fulfilled and vindicated as the great heir of Michelangelo, whom he aims, like his archrival Bandinelli, to surpass.[22]

The *Perseus* Cellini constructs within his narrative therefore exists ultimately not in and of itself as a thing but within a network of social relations, both in its casting and in the publicly staged unveiling and reception of the statue in the central piazza of Florence on April 27, 1554 (Figure 17). Not even the duke, who has commissioned the sculpture and approved the design, can properly value the *Perseus*, we learn, until the sculpture has been claimed and appraised by the community at large, replete with sonnets affixed to its base. It is only then, once the *Perseus* has been viewed in a truly conspicuous way, "exposed to view from all sides" (440, 2.91), that Cellini can finally enjoy his hard-won success:

> Now as it pleased my glorious Lord and immortal God, at last I brought the whole work to completion: and on a certain Thursday morning I exposed it to the public gaze. Immediately, before the sun was fully in the heavens, there assembled such a multitude of people that no words could describe them. All with one voice contended which should praise it most. The duke was stationed at a window low upon the first floor of the palace, just above the entrance; there, half hidden, he heard everything the folk was saying of my statue. After listening through several hours, he rose so proud and happy in his heart that he turned to his attendant, Messer Sforza, and exclaimed: "Sforza, go and seek out Benvenuto; tell him from me that he has delighted me far more than I expected: say too that I shall reward him in a way which will astonish; so bid him be of good courage" [441–42, 2.92].

Cellini will be astonished by the duke's rewards, he asserts in his narrative, for Cellini has astonished others with his *Perseus*. But, more important, in his narrative it is Cellini, as we have seen, who has indeed astonished us as the man with the incomparable *manus artificis*. For Cellini, we learn, is something worth staring at in the center of Florence as the man who has dedicated his life to making things such as the *Perseus*. "They meanwhile continued loading me with compliments," he observes, "until at last I prayed them, for kindness' sake, to leave the piazza in my company, because the folk were stopping and staring at me more than at my *Perseus*" (442, 2.92). Like the salamander, Cellini is a person to look at with astonishment, "as something wondrous and strange" (442, 2.92). And he means to shock us with the blows of his demonic energy, so that we will take notice and remember him, just as, to compare big things to small, he was taught to remember things worth remembering when his father unexpectedly gave him a great box on the ear as he stared into the blazing fire as a young boy.

More Things: The Master's Stupefying Hand at Work

Toward the end of his career, Cellini, the consummate maker of things, turned to writing even more directly about things in his treatises on goldsmithing and sculpting, his *Trattato dell'oreficeria* and *Trattato della scultura*. These two treatises, published in 1568 with a number of sonnets praising his *Perseus* printed in the back, should be read, Margaret Gallucci and Paolo L. Rossi have observed, within the context of the proliferation of how-to books in midsixteenth-century Italy, from those on perfuming and childrearing and marriage and housekeeping to those on secretarial, ambassadorial, and courtly work, including, as we have seen, even satires on the flourishing genre, such as Pietro Aretino's dialogues on how to become a winning prostitute.[23] Needless to say, Cellini's twin treatises, like those composed by a host of authors of how-to books, presupposed the existence of a community of interested people eager to learn more about a wealth of topics; a print culture that had the means to produce and sell such books; a history of commendable artists or artisans who had once labored in the field, thereby creating a respected tradition for others to admire and wish to become a part of; and a consumption society of buyers with an appetite to spend some money on books about goldsmithing and sculpting—a society not only enchanted by things but also, in this instance, interested in learning how to make them or to know how they are made in some detail. In this light, if the *Vita* focused on Cellini as a conspicuous maker of things, the treatises, we can reasonably expect, were supposed to focus objectively on how to make things themselves, without placing Cellini at the absolute center of attention. But that is not the case. Like so many how-to books in the period, as well as books of secrets, Cellini's treatises on goldsmithing and sculpting are filled with information about the author's own life. They therefore can, and should, be read as marginal forms of autobiography.[24]

In both treaties, Cellini spends a lot of time talking about practical matters of strictly professional concern. But he also talks at length about how *he* specifically learned these things, in what conditions *he* learned them, and how good *he* was at doing what he had been trained to do. Indeed, Cellini was so good at what he did that on one occasion Michelangelo, who consistently stands for Cellini as the supreme model of imitation and emulation, comments on the unsurpassed beauty of Cellini's work and craftsmanship. In chapter 12 of the treatise on goldsmithing, for instance, Cellini places us once more in the general mode of autobiographical narrative, repeating for his readers an event that he had already developed in his *Vita* (1.41):

> I once fashioned a medal for a certain Girolamo Marretta, a Sienese; and on this medal was a Hercules rending the jaws of the lion. I made both Hercules and the lion in such high relief that they only just touched the background by means of the tiniest attachments [since they were so real they almost seem to jump off the medal and live on their own]. The whole work had been done in the abovementioned method, that is to say without the bronze models; now working from in front, now from the reverse, and brought to such an end and design that our great Michelangelo himself came to my very workshop to see it, and when he had looked at it for a bit, he, in order to encourage me, said: "If this work were large, whether of marble or of bronze, and fashioned with an exquisite design like this, it

would astonish the world; and even in its present size it seems to me so beautiful that I do not think a goldsmith of the ancient world ever fashioned anything that could come up to it!" These words stiffened me up just, and gave me the greatest longing to work, not only on the smaller things [*cose piccole*], but to try larger things [*cose grande*, sic; 48, 1017].[25]

Just as the author of the *Vita* concentrated on the central theme of his professional activity as a maker of things, of cose piccole and cose grande, thereby rendering everything else mentioned in his narrative something of a digression (as colorful and as exciting and, above all, as shocking and novel as that "everything else" might be), so too the author of these two treatises on professional expertise cannot help but constantly weave his own life's tale into the fabric of technical discussions that should, at least in theory, be strictly and objectively about only goldsmithing and sculpting.

Why does Cellini do this? Why does he constantly call attention to himself? Why not just cut to the chase and tell us what we need to know in an objective and detached manner? Why do we need to know in these two treatises that he worked in France, was showered with gifts and honors in France, adored Paris as a city without equals, and was in turn adored by the Parisians as a great artist? In one sense, we might say that Cellini includes all this information because he is a vainglorious self-promoter, a person who cannot resist putting into the foreground his identity at every turn and assert his status. He is an inveterate show-off, a man who desperately needs to make himself not just conspicuous but aggressively conspicuous as he transforms himself, we might say, before our eyes from an adept artisan to a sort of celebrity artist.

But in another sense, Cellini, who here writes about matters of professional concern, is also attempting to build *ethos*, a credible, persuasive character, so that a public interested in the topics covered in his two treatises (which, unlike the *Vita*, were printed in his lifetime) will take him seriously as a person thoroughly informed about the material he treats at length. This rhetorical strategy is important, particularly within the tradition of how-to books in sixteenth-century Italy. Torquato Tasso, for instance, felt perfectly comfortable writing about secretarial work even though he had never been a secretary and knew very little about it (worse, a century earlier, Leon Battista Alberti had written about family life without ever having had a family himself—or, what is more, much felt part of one). Moreover, a number of how-to books, such as books of secrets, were compilations. They offered readers not so much a systematic approach to a topic (such as goldsmithing) as they did a range of possibilities associated with the topic at hand presented in an unstructured way. They certainly did not offer the reader a coherent beginning, middle, or end in a fluid narrative form. A book on perfumes by Giovanventura Rosetti, for instance, published roughly a decade before Cellini's treatises, presents us with numerous ways of making soap, but it is not an in-depth book on soap, and there is only incidental information contained within it that might alert us to the fact that the author had in fact ever witnessed soap being made.[26]

By contrast, Cellini aims to show over and over again that he has experience, practical, first-hand, professional knowledge of what it means to do the things that he teaches us to do. He has been in France, Rome, and Florence working with his hands, governing shops, commanding respect, acquiring one commission after another from men of distinction, authority, and power. He is a recognized master, and he would have us appreciate and recognize him as such. Hence, if you want to learn how to be a goldsmith, he would have us know, you must learn from Cellini. In this regard, all these autobiographical references within the treatise can be construed as self-authenticating devices whereby Cellini, in the absence of a diploma to pin on the wall and a résumé full of reliable and readily available references, makes claim to the community's universal recognition of him as an authority. In order to be able to "talk well" about the topic at hand, to "ben dire," as he puts it in the preface, one must be able to "do well" ("ben fare") all the things he claims he can in fact fashion with his hands.[27]

But there is also another element to Cellini's professional self-representation that is important in these treatises. We are meant to appreciate not only the work that went into making the small and big things of wonder. We are also meant to appreciate the baffling "hand" of the individual artist at work. The treatise on goldsmithery, for instance, is full of instances when Cellini stresses how his "way" of doing something matters: the "*modo*," the method, is everything. The maniera is distinct and strong, not bland and general. Thus, when Cellini received a commission we are reminded over and over again that he received it because of his handiwork, which is grounded not in some easily transmitted schooled technique. When you get Cellini, you get, as it were, Cellini's hand in his handiwork, the stupefying manus artificis, as we have seen one poet describe it in lauding the *Perseus*. And this is essential to Cellini. You can learn the lessons he teaches over and over again. You can memorize all the rules of goldsmithing and try to copy his art of sculpting. But something makes him inimitable as a professional, much as Michelangelo, his longstanding admired rival, was typically viewed. That something, that special quality, is his modo, his unsurpassed method, his "sa fare," embodied in "gli esempli fatti con le mie mani." And the stress here should always be placed on Cellini's hands, which shape these things stylishly, both big and small, in a direct and tangible way (1044). In this respect, Cellini, at one level, demystifies his technique by showing us all how he can detect any flaw in a modo and immediately disclose the nature of a modo put into practice. But at another level he actually remystifies the art of goldsmithing by indicating that his modo always wins praise and renders both him and the things he makes a marvel.[28] "The pope would scarce let three days pass without sending for me," Cellini vaunts in his *Trattato dell'oreficeria*,

> and each time would he see first one, then another of those beautiful putti peep forth, and this made him marvel greatly, and each time he asked me about the manner [modo] that I had used: and what made him marvel all the more was that he considered that I could bring so difficult a piece of work about in so short a time, and all without a single rent in any place, so that, being an intelligent person, this made him marvel yet more, saying: "I have seen some works of Caradosso which were full of holes and solder long before they had got as far as this." And thus he gave me encouragement always and the occasion of doing/working well [*al ben fare*; 56, 1026].

There is not only a burning intensity to Cellini as a man, as we saw in his *Vita*, ablaze with his own energy like the salamander in the fire, but also an originality that is bound to his specific time and place as he presents himself in his narratives. No one is quite like him. Professionally he remains like Michelangelo, he would have us believe, inimitable in his making of things, both big and small.

In a society of conspicuous consumption, then, Cellini is not portraying himself as a consumer with an enormous appetite, as Aretino did, but a conspicuous maker of things to be consumed. For all that he presents himself as a free agent, he is dependent both on patronage and the workshop in order to have a profession and a career, which is the real topic of his *Vita* (with all its digressions and memorable stories of shocks and blows) and the critical underlying feature in his treatises on goldsmithing and sculpting (with their overt focus on craft and technique). But in a society of conspicuous consumption, Cellini also aims to show that his work cannot be reproduced. His words can be printed and reproduced in an age of mechanical reproduction, but not the things he makes directly and tangibly with his hands and, as he puts it in his treatise, with "extreme effort" (*estreme fatiche*). If you want him, you have to pay for him. He's unique, inimitable, a wonder. And there is nothing Cellini wants so much as to appear to everyone as the true, unique, and worthy heir of a great artistic tradition, as he makes evident over and over again in his *Vita*. Along with that, he wants nothing so much as to be seen as the fountainhead of originality for a community of great-minded men. For this reason, he assures us in a poem, a person's habit of talking about things must finally stop when we see beautiful things done well:

> Se l'opera è buona, si conoscie a un tratto;
> né importa aver del mastro prima indizio.
> Sculpite, or voi.[29]
>
> [If the work is good, one recognizes it in an instant;
> it is not important to have information about the master artist.
> So now sculpt, you all.]
>
> [*Rime*, 969]

A noticeably loquacious man, whose unfinished life story goes on (with some noticeable gaps in time) for copious manuscript pages, which makes it far longer than any single "life" in Vasari's monumental narrative of artists, Cellini may talk at length (if not endlessly) about all the things he does, shaping the way we look at both him and the things he's made. But, as he repeatedly distinguishes between *il fare* and *il dire*, we are ultimately meant to leave his words behind and silently admire those things made by him.

With this in mind, we may consider for a moment the notion of thing theory espoused by the contemporary scholar Bill Brown, which was addressed in passing at the beginning of this chapter. Thing theory often privileges the possibility of establishing a new relationship between the subject and the object by recognizing—or rather, by being forced to recognize spontaneously—the thingness of a thing. The astonishment emphasized by such thing theorists as Brown occurs, it would seem, primarily when things come to our awareness because they no longer function as they are expected to within familiar networks of economic or social exchanges. A slide projector momentarily makes itself evident in a dark room, for example, only when the slide jams, the hypnotic hum becomes a screech, and the damned thing doesn't work. In that moment of aggravation and frustration, when the machine breaks down and thus fails to make itself invisible, our prior blindness to the presence of the slide projector, as we face the bright blank screen in the darkened room, momentarily becomes insight into its intractable thingness. In that very moment we are ideally silenced by the opaque presence of the slide projector's astonishing thingness. By contrast, the astonishment described throughout Cellini's *Vita* is astonishment at the thing *made*, not the thing falling apart or failing to function or upsetting currents of market and social flow. As Cellini describes those things that he so conspicuously made with his hand, we are meant to be silent in astonishment at the workmanship that went into making those things so that they could come to light in the presence of others. For Cellini's hand, as we have seen, is like no one else's. His modo is irreducibly his.

This, in essence, encapsulates Cellini's brand of manierismo, which materializes above all in his *Vita* in such sculptures as the *Perseus*.[30] His specific modo of doing things, his maniera, is unveiled in his writings time and again. We can see how he does it in his treatises and his autobiography. He gives us the origins of his own originality as he accounts for so many things he made. But we cannot, for the life of us, imitate him with the same success. We cannot, as he does in the *Perseus*, make mixed metals, the vital sources of the earth (copper, tin, and zinc) function in hardened form so fluidly as human blood, the vital source of human life.[31] And the fact that Cellini tells us how he makes those complex things, which people in their turn repeatedly marvel over, constitutes a poker-faced upping of the ante in a game of professional showmanship. Cellini boldly, confidently, and aggressively aims to outdo everyone else in order to make himself appear all the more conspicuously a wonder. In this respect, the relationship between the subject and the object in sixteenth-century Italy—a relationship that is grounded in continuous and fluid processes of exchange—is not so much altered by the thing witnessed with wonder as Cellini creates things and fashions himself in his narrative as a conspicuous maker of them. The relationship between the subject and the object in an economy of exchange is instead forged and reaffirmed as things openly figure, to adopt Brown's terms again, into "the circuits of production and distribution, consumption and exhibition." Indeed, Cellini's underlying concern toward the end of his life as he began his autobiography—stuck at home, charged with sodomy, weary, neglected, and without commissions from the court to which he felt so bound—is that he isn't in circulation any more, making, as he had made before, cose piccole and cose grande. He wants to get back in the game, even if he has to do so with a stingy patron. Because by getting back in the game he can once again experience his identity as a goldsmith and a sculptor and thus have something memorable to say as he continues to age. He still wants to be able to shock people. This man who has been shunned by Cosimo, perhaps for his glaring professional improprieties, labors to serve his patron in the court. He longs to baffle, to acquire honor, to impress.

If Cellini's *Vita* ends without a conclusion, quite literally in midparagraph, it is, I maintain, perhaps because his life as a maker of things had virtually ended as well. He was losing the great commissions to the likes of Baccio Bandinelli and Bartolomeo Ammannati, both of whom he disdained.[32] So there was plausibly nothing left for him to do but reminisce about his originality and account for its origins. And therein lies in part the strangeness of Cellini's life, both the life he lived, as we can ascertain from surviving documents, and the life he artistically fashioned, as he described it in his *Vita*. On the one hand, Cellini's life as he tells it was invested in conspicuously making things, both big and small, and he kept close track of accounts owed and paid, as is evident in his *Vita* and in surviving account books. He shared with mercantile Florentines a love of calculating the value of his own production. Though in a risky act of impetuosity he chides Cosimo I in his *Vita* for being too mercantile in his desire to know the precise monetary value of an object of art, much of Cellini's life, especially during his lengthy stay in Florence, was equally calculating and mundane. He repeatedly wanted to know what he would get for what he did, down to the last nickel and dime. As Pope-Hennessy has pointed out, Cellini was something of an "accountant," obsessed with calculating every penny of his material existence, much as Renaissance Florentines of financial means typically were. In this respect, Cellini's identity was once more grounded in things as he filled "volume after volume with details of his life, income, and expenditures" (14). Significantly, though we have only a portion of Cellini's *Vita* in his "hand," an autograph copy in the precise meaning of the term, we do have page after page of his monetary transactions that he copied out precisely.

As he aged and his career collapsed, the great and conspicuous maker of things became more of a talker about how he had once been a maker of things for the courts of Francis I and Cosimo I (perhaps even the talk of the town as a famous convicted sodomite partly driven to expiate his sins through narrating the story of his life). During these years, Cellini turned to writing his treatises and his *Vita* and also to composing poetry. Once again, as in his *Vita* and *Trattati*, he makes it clear that experience constitutes the source of all authority, though this time no one, not even patrons or buyers, should be allowed to determine what is good and bad. According to Cellini, the maker alone knows for certain what is and is not of true, lasting value.[33] Nevertheless, given his excellence as a sculptor, an excellence confirmed by so many in the community through poetic exchanges, Cellini cannot for the life of him understand why he has fallen out of the grace of his patron and is shunned by the court. He was once showered with praise for his *Perseus* and now lacks commissions. A great demiurgic maker of things in this world, Cellini can explain his fall from grace only by imagining that the envy of others has robbed him of his rightful place in the pantheon of the truly great artists of his time. It never seems to occur to him that it was perhaps because of his obvious professional improprieties, because he simply behaved the way he did with a duke of a major court, with obstinance, impetuosity, and arrogance. Instead, is it possible, he wonders, to be *too* good? Could it be that he invited reproach because he was so successful at doing well, "ben fare"?

> Fé Perseo Benvento, e Cristo in crocie;
> e perché ei ben mostrava la scultura,
> gli han tolto 'l pane e dato in su la vocie.
> [. . .]
> Dunque troppo ben far cotanto nuocie?
> Dunque 'l falso operar il bene oscura?
> Dalle lutezie mura
> sol venne per far bene, e 'n tanti affanni,
> povero, afflitto, vecchio sventurato,
> chiede 'l promesso, e quel che ha guadagniato
> con servir venti de' suoi migliori anni.

> [Benvenuto made Perseus, and Christ on the cross;
> and because he honored sculpture so much with his work,
> they took from him bread (sustenance) and scolded him.
> [. . .]
> Does doing things so well [or doing too much good] thus bring so much harm?

Do the false dealings [of others] so obscure the good work done?
From the Parisian walls
alone he came [returned to Florence] to do well, and in so much anxiety,
poor, downcast, an unfortunate old man,
he asks what has been promised him [from the duke], and what he earned
in the twenty of his best years in service.]

[*Rime*, 894–95]

Cellini's voice as an elegiac poet perhaps best comes through in poems such as these, when he speaks with great pathos about himself as a maker of things who has been unjustly punished and who desperately wishes to reclaim his status with his patrons.[34] In his fall from grace, he can only reflect on all the great and "beautiful things" (cose belle) he has made, things that have landed him, despite all his labor as a goldsmith and a sculptor, whiling away his time, without commissions of any important kind:

Son Benvenuto, il qual diverse pruove
d'arte subblime ho fatto; e l'aspre stelle
con tutto il lor poter m'han misso al basso.
In Roma e 'n Francia il trionfante Giove,
Perseo a Fiorenze, e altre cose belle
mi paga un carcer: or son stanco e lasso.

[I am Benvenuto, who has made many
demonstrations of sublime art; and [yet] the harsh stars
with all their power have cast me down.
[For having created] in Rome and in France the triumphant Jove,
Perseus in Florence, and other beautiful things—
I am paid with a prison cell: I am tired and weary now.]

[*Rime*, 905]

Tired and weary, Cellini can only hope to retrieve the recognition due him by making more things, more cose belle, not by talking about them. He will never get the recognition he craves by filling out page after page in a manuscript that renders him conspicuous only in verbal form, however well crafted the manuscript happens to be, and however much it might accrue to his benefit to be known, like Michelangelo, as a highly literate, verbal artist. For sculpture, Cellini asserts in one letter, has to do with the "thing" (cosa), the actual embodied matter that "casts a shadow" (*che fa l'ombra*; 1005). And this is what ultimately mattered to Cellini professionally.

The term *ombra*, which is here drawn from a letter of 1546 to Benedetto Varchi, is significant, especially when placed within the context of Neoplatonizing traditions of thinking about art in Renaissance Italy. For in Platonic terms, the shadows of things, like those on the cave described in the *Republic*, pertain to the world of appearances. Shadows are mere signs, *simulacra* that have come to replace the originals. But sculpture for Cellini had a special solidity to it, which required us to experience it firsthand in the round; indeed, we are invited and expected to view it from all sides, much as one would a piece of jewelry, albeit on a far grander scale. In the case of the *Perseus*, for instance, we have to see the sculpture from the back, from which vantage point one can make out a portrait in the mask created by the helmet and hair. We must also see the sculpture from below, which best allows one to see the blood gruesomely yet elegantly bursting out of Medusa's shorn neck. And then again, we should see the *Perseus* especially from above, which was the privileged vantage point that Cosimo I occupied from the window of the Palazzo Vecchio when the sculpture was first unveiled to the public in Piazza della Signoria. Indeed, from this elevated and privileged vantage point Cosimo I, the slayer of evil and corrupt republics, could witness, as Cellini surely intended him to witness, not only how everyone looked at the sculpture with astonishment but also how Cellini brilliantly twisted onto the altar of his base, beneath the feet of the proud Perseus, the languorous, decapitated body of the bare-breasted Medusa with stylized blood gushing out of her severed head.[35]

Moreover, and more important I would insist in conclusion, it is to those three-dimensional, material things such as the *Perseus* that Cellini always returned to define himself as a conspicuous fabricator in a world of conspicuous consumption and in a society with an enormous appetite for art. For through those things Cellini externalized his manhood, rooted himself in the world, and made himself serviceable to the community at large so that he would have something memorable to say, even if he lost commissions in the end through his professional improprieties. As a result, the *Vita* in our own time has cast a shadow across literary history as one of the first full-blown autobiographies of the early modern era, telling the story of a male artistic self constructing its identity through conspicuous and prodigious production of things. But for Cellini it would have ultimately been the things themselves—the multifarious things that he would have us believe he forcefully and artfully made with his own hand, delivering blows to them so that they would come alive thanks to his manus artificis—that were really meant to cast a shadow in the world. It is therefore to those things that he would always have us turn, for they—not his treatises, his poetry, or his *Vita*—bear the true imprint of his hand and retain it for posterity. Those material things, not words, embody his genius, his mystifying ingenium. And in the end, Cellini would have those things leave us, as we examine them today in a piazza or a museum or a palace, dazzled, in a state of admiring bewilderment, especially when we think about how someone could have ever made them, and actually did make them, with his own incomparable and inimitable hands.

CHAPTER 5

Anton Francesco Doni and the Art of Conspicuous Reproduction

Prologue: Books as Objects

Art historians of Renaissance Italy have to face a problem that literary scholars typically manage to steer clear of, if not completely ignore. At some point they have to come to terms with the fact that they are dealing with an object, a material "thing" that is tangible, three-dimensional (even if literally paper thin), and often unique, whether the object has survived the ravages of time, as Cellini's *Perseus* managed to do, or has failed to make it through the centuries, as was the case with much of Cellini's jewelry and thus virtually all the things that allowed him to prosper early on in his career. Paleographers, bibliographers, and specialized philologists bent on producing critical editions certainly have to take into consideration the book as an object, and like art historians they must think about its physical make-up, provenance, and setting. But literary scholars of Renaissance Italy, at least in the Anglo-American tradition over the past several decades, have tended to examine books not so much as objects of study in and of themselves as objects allowing them to study linguistic utterances, formal relationships, rhetorical and narrative strategies, philosophical positions, and political, social, and cultural practices. Books perceived in this way often turn into battlegrounds for competing critical interests. Moreover, as a society we are conditioned to think that it is essential to see the "real" objects of works of art, and we are willing to travel long distances and at some expense to see them. We are also willing to wait in long lines, pay sometimes exorbitant fees (even to enter churches in Florence and Venice currently), and endure a host of nuisances, from bad lighting to crowds standing in front of the works of art we would ideally like to see with an unobstructed view. We are not, however, conditioned as a culture to think that it is essential to see the original manuscript of Castiglione in the Biblioteca Laurenziana in Florence in order to appreciate Castiglione, much less handle a manuscript or a printed book of the period in order to have a deeper and more direct appreciation of the period. In this regard, just try to enter the manuscript room of the Biblioteca Nazionale of Florence with the claim that you want to witness and handle a Renaissance holograph for personal pleasure, simply because you're casually curious about what it looks and feels like, its special character as a "thing." Fat chance. You will be firmly sent away. These are places for scholars whose job it is to get the necessary accreditation to enter the privileged domain, and who sometimes have to endure a battery of tests, a sort of professional rite of passage, in order to enter it, if they can.

Literary scholars who do focus on the book as an object are often viewed in our own time as having carved out for themselves a subfield within the broad (and by now unabashedly amorphous) discipline of what gets dubbed, for the lack of a better term, "literary studies," though it is important to recognize that historically these scholars, insofar as they create critical editions, represent the backbone of the field. Although nowadays they are not exactly viewed as typical literary scholars—in the sense that they do not necessarily examine the narrative or poetic strategies of the text, for example—they are certainly literary scholars, in the sense that they do indeed closely examine literary texts. They are, in the root sense of the term, philologists, who can arguably trace their origins as professionals in the modern period back to humanists such as Lorenzo Valla and Angelo Poliziano who helped make the Italian Renaissance so famous. These scholars can also tell you, for instance, a lot about a book just by looking at its cover—and at the paper, typeface, binding, nature of the glue, stitching, and the like. Currently, however, because of our focus on material culture, there is a surge of interest in the book as an object, particularly in the burgeoning fields of textual studies, history of the book, and collecting and editing practices. Now scholars in America who never used to care about whether a book was printed in Venice or Florence or Ferrara are suddenly getting curious about all sorts of things, from the professional habits of the printer to the quality of the binding.

Much of this interest in the book among American literary scholars dovetails with, or more likely derives from, a rise of interest in the book among historians, from medical to intellectual to cultural to art historians, who focus on everything from the painted illuminations and woodcut illustrations to the penned marginalia contained within books and their connections to local cultures. We now know a lot more about the relationship between words and images thanks to these scholars' interests, and we also know a lot more now about not only the production of meaning in the Renaissance, but also the reception of it through studies dedicated to the reading practices that individuals engaged in when they confronted books in private and public spaces—what we might call in its broadest contours not just a history of the book but a history of perception and reception.[1]

This chapter examines the writings of a man who had a lot to do with the making of books and who was interested in books, as well as words, as visual objects. He was also a peculiar and extremely difficult, cantankerous man, it was generally felt, who managed to take on successfully even Pietro Aretino, the great scourge of princes, in an explosive diatribe titled, appropriately enough, *Terremoto*, which we can translate as "Earthquake."[2] His name was Anton Francesco Doni (Figure 18) and, like Aretino, he was a man who liked to get in your face.

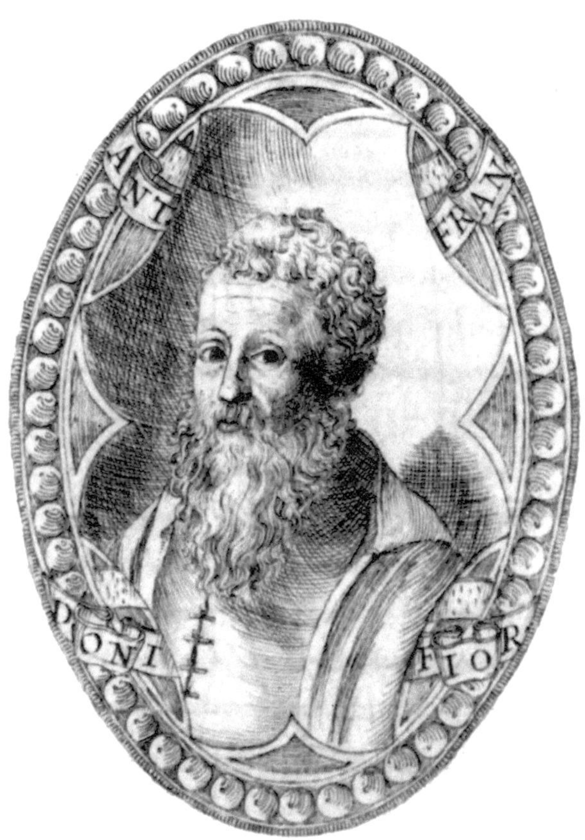

FIGURE 18. Anton Francesco Doni (1513–1574). *Self-Portrait*, 1573. In *Le ville del Doni*. Archivio Storico Civico Biblioteca Trivulziana di Milano, Castello Sforzesco, ms. Triv. 15. © Comune di Milano, all rights reserved. Photo courtesy Fabio Saporetti.

He was born in Florence but lived in various places throughout Northern Italy, including Piacenza, Mantua, Bologna, Genoa, Pavia, Milan, Alessandria, and Monselice.[3] Like Cellini, he also managed to make enemies wherever he traveled. He was, I think it is also safe to say, a conspicuous, incorrigible, inflammatory man with a vicious, irascible side to him and an appetite for revenge that was as durable as he claimed print itself was, despite his disingenuous, self-serving assertion in a letter that he was always accommodating and "discreet."[4] My aim in concentrating on Doni—apart from the fact that he represents yet another upstart of professional impropriety from the period under consideration—is to bring together different discourses centered on the books he produced and the books he wrote and designed.

First, in focusing on Doni, we shall take into consideration the discourse of printing, the art of mechanical reproduction that allowed a host of writers and workers in the midsixteenth century to make a living largely outside of court culture in Italy. This discourse is closely bound up with the emergence of the polygraphs, the professional adventurers of the pen, who thrived for roughly three decades after the Sack of Rome. They found their center of gravity in commercial republican Venice, though some also traveled widely and exhibited an incessant restlessness, a wanderlust spirit that gave them little time to pause.

Second, we shall consider the discourse of authorship, or more precisely the questionable nature of authorship when one passes off what is someone else's as one's own through the art of *riscrittura*, the accepted literary strategy of assemblage and calculated collage. Today we would customarily call that strategy not an "art" but plagiarism, the intellectual theft that constitutes reproducing someone's arguments or writings and then fobbing them off as one's own. In Doni's period, however—which was a period lacking an effective legal means of protecting intellectual property—it was more accepted as a practice than it is now. Strikingly, Doni both criticized others for plagiarizing (accusations of this sort always swirled) and freely engaged in it himself over and over again as one of the major exponents of the art of riscrittura of midsixteenth-century Italy.[5]

Third, we shall examine the discourse of conspicuous enmity, the art of aggressively attacking others—the practice of abrasively getting in someone else's face, that is—in order to acquire recognition and perhaps status through acts of professional impropriety. What unites these discourses in Doni's case, we shall see, is the act of reproduction: the conspicuous reproduction of words in material form through printing for a public interested in works widely accessible in the vernacular; the conspicuous reproduction of ideas and language through the egregious copying of them; and the conspicuous reproduction—in the sense of aggressive, relentless recreation and reinvention—of one's own identity through a professional rivalry made public for all to witness and arguably enjoy in print.

Doni's Libraria

Typically, though not always, reflexive books make us self-conscious that we are reading a book. In our own time, Italo Calvino's *If on a Winter's Night a Traveler*, a postmodern novel wedded to the interlaced structure of Ariostan romance, represents the most explicit, sustained, and imaginative reflection on this narrative strategy in the Italian literary tradition. But there is one book written in the vernacular in the late Italian Renaissance that manifestly makes us all too aware that we are reading a book, for the book we read, and that palpably rests in our hands with its worn paper in extant sixteenth-century editions, is nothing other than Doni's book about books. The title of his book remained fundamentally the same in its varied editions and enlargements, though it changed dramatically in its reincarnations over a seven-year period. As Roger Chartier has summarily observed, Doni's two *Librarie* (that is, the first and second treatises)

> form a complex book. Their bibliographic definition ("they were not only the first Italian national bibliographies; they were also the first bibliographies in a vulgar tongue") fails to do justice to their multiple significance. They proclaim the excellence and the dignity achieved by the vulgar language; they constitute a repertory of contemporary authors; they dismantle, in a parodic key, the recipes for literary invention.[6]

When the *Libraria* first appeared it contained only one treatise and was dedicated exclusively to books in print composed in the vernacular.[7] Initially it was titled *La libraria del Doni Fiorentino* and was published by the Giolito press in two versions in 1550. Then, just a year later, in 1551, *La seconda libraria del Doni* appeared in print, this time from the Marcolini press, in which version Doni made fundamental changes. He wrote an entirely new treatise, this one dedicated only to books in the vernacular still in manuscript form. These are manuscripts that Doni, in all his wisdom as a purveyor of writings, deems worthy of being brought out in print for consumption. Just as important, in the *Seconda libraria*, which presumes but does not absolutely require extensive prior knowledge of the first *Libraria* to succeed as a project on its own right, Doni finds an even wittier and more whimsical voice. He severs his ties, in both a literary and ideological manner, with the more understated, sober works he had composed before this one and that were appropriate, as Giorgio Masi has observed, to the "traditional technical, treatise styled and 'serious' genres" of the Giolito press, though it is important to stress that the first *Libraria* was, as Jonathan David Bradbury has emphasized, also playful, witty, and odd on its own.[8] The Marcolini press reissued the *Seconda libraria* in 1555, with only minor revisions.[9] Finally, a much-revised *Libraria* came out in print in 1557 and then, in the same format, in 1558. The Giolito press printed the last version of this book; it appeared with the elongated title of *La libraria del Doni Fiorentino divisa in tre trattati*. This final version of the *Libraria* now contained numerous additions and emendations, as well as a third treatise along with the earlier two, precisely as Doni makes clear in the new title. With this final edition Doni also brought the three treatises together to form a single volume. (Unless otherwise noted, this will be the edition referred to throughout this chapter.)

Finally, from beginning to end, from 1550 to 1557, Doni's book about books was written, it is essential to recall, by a man who maintained close working relationships with his editors. He had learned his trade in part as a printer, first in Florence, where he failed as a printer after a year or two of effort in the highly competitive business, and then in Venice, the great center of European book making, where Doni worked his way up the Giolito and Marcolini presses, beginning as a copyeditor, translator, and jack-of-all-trades hack writer. Eventually, however, Doni became successful enough as a writer in Venice, thanks in part to the success of his *Libraria* and his congenial working relationship—at least for a period—with the Marcolini and Giolito presses, that he no longer needed to make or assist in making books and could just write them.[10] In this respect, Doni's writing about books indirectly enabled him to separate himself gradually from parts of the industry that produced them.

When Doni composed the first edition of the *Libraria* in 1550, however, he was still down and out in Venice, an apprentice living in crowded quarters, with four people to a bed, he maintains, and vermin crawling about the house. In a colorful letter contained in the first version of the *Libraria* and then later attached to the end of the last, he complains of throngs of hungry lice, armies of bedbugs the size of coins, spiders swarming all over the place below him, and a veritable ecclesiastical college of mice thriving in the attic. He lived across from a putrescent canal, he moans, and he can be found, if one were to look for him ever in his cramped apartment, engaged in any number of activities in the very same room: writing, sitting at a table, lying in bed, or squatting, as he crudely puts it, on "the crapper" (*cacatoio*).[11] True, Doni had already accomplished quite a lot for a man who struck out on his own. He published books of his letters (two at his own press in Florence in 1546 and 1547), as well as his *Dialoghi della musica* (1544), *Gli spiriti folletti* (under a pseudonym, 1546), and the *Prose antiche di Dante, Petrarca e Boccaccio e di molti altri nobili e virtuosi ingegni* (1547). He had written the introductory preface to Ortensio Lando's translation of Thomas More's *Utopia*, titled *Repubblica nuovamente ritrovata* and published for Aurelio Pincio in 1548. And he had written for the Giolito press *Il disegno* (1549), a Platonizing treatise on the comparative merits of painting and sculpture, as well as a translation (a plagiarized one, which he had freely passed off as his own) of the letters of Seneca, which was also published by Pincio.[12] In 1550 he produced *Le medaglie*, *L'effegie di Cesare*, and *La fortuna di Cesare*, which were by and large composed in a restrained, temperate style.

Nevertheless, despite his productivity, Doni was still not faring well financially during his first years in Venice. His real break came between 1551 and 1553, a period marked by a flurry of literary activity unmatched by any other in Doni's life, beginning with the *Seconda libraria* in 1551 and extending on to *La zucca* (1551–52, Marcolini press), *La moral filosofia* (1552, Marcolini press), *I pistolotti amorosi* (1552, Giolito press), the *Tre libri di lettere* (1552, Marcolini press), and three of his most well-known works today, *I marmi* (1552, Marcolini press) and *I mondi* and *Inferni* (1552–53, Marcolini press).[13] In just two years, Doni's output and creativity had increased markedly. By the time Doni published the last version of his *Libraria* in 1557/1558,[14] which combined the earlier two treatises into a single revised volume with the addition of a third treatise on academies (something about which Doni, who had been a member of certainly two, and perhaps even three, academies, knew a great deal),[15] he could count himself one of the more popular writers in Italy. He could also present himself as a man able to afford his own living quarters in Venice, however modest those quarters probably were, and even consider investing in a farm.[16] In less than a decade living in Venice, this impoverished son of a Florentine scissors maker had worked his way out of the printer's bookshop and his overcrowded quarters, where he struggled to seclude himself to find a bit of privacy. However, no sooner had Doni achieved some measure of success through the print marketplace of commercial Venice than he was off again, moving about. Why he left Venice is not entirely clear, though various practical considerations should be taken into account when trying to explain his departure, among them the breaking up of his collaboration with Marcolini in 1554/1555, the financial problems associated with this loss of editorial backing within the Venetian print industry, and his conflict with Aretino and Aretino's withdrawal of support. Whatever occasioned Doni's departure, however, it is clear that in 1555 Venice was no longer a good base for gaining the success he longed for, and his position there had weakened considerably.

Forced perhaps by circumstances, Doni turned to some other creative activities after leaving Venice. Significantly, much of Doni's literary activity after 1557 was devoted not only to producing new editions of his own books but also to producing manuscripts of newly conceived books copied out in his own hand, designed and often painstakingly drawn by him, and dedicated to illustrious persons, perhaps with the hope of receiving either patronage or assistance from them in bringing these potentially costly books out in print. Strikingly, a number of these manuscripts owe their format to the "look" of midsixteenth-century print, including the designs contained within them. Doni's self-portrait (Figure 18), which is a copy of a previously printed design by Enea Vico (1523–1567),[17] is a case in point, though one could adduce a host of similar examples from a number of his surviving manuscripts. Print, as a developing medium of expression with its own visual and verbal conventions in midsixteenth-century Italy, permeated much of Doni's imagination and had a formative influence on his career long after he left Venice as a polygraph. If after living in Venice the apparent "uniqueness" of manuscripts as singular works fashioned by his own hand appealed to Doni, so too did the look, along with the mechanical reproducibility, of print as an underlying model for self-expression. In this respect, in his later years Doni was positioning himself squarely within a culture, as Brian Richardson has shown, that still very much valued the scribal "publication," dissemination, and circulation of writing throughout the sixteenth century, and in which print production and scribal production evolved, influenced one another, and pursued separate though often interconnected paths.[18] The best of Doni's manuscripts, then, which come off as highly original, expressive works by this multitalented verbal and visual author, implicitly entail a critique of the new technology of the print industry and the impact that industry had on the position of letterati in an age of mechanical reproduction, but they are also very much indebted to and recall the look of print.

Before Doni was a writer, he was by profession a member of the printing industry, first in Florence and then for a few years in Venice. We would therefore do well to bear in mind what it must have been like for Doni, a man who made his living from books for so many years, to have worked in the environment of the busy and competitive sixteenth-century Italian printing industry. This is especially significant since the *Libraria* addresses the importance of books being in print, as well as the manuscripts Doni thinks should be in print for public consumption. To begin with, Doni's Florentine press, which he operated from 1546 to 1547,[19] was located in the neighborhood of Santa Croce, near the parish church of San Pier Maggiore, and not far, he tells us, from the corner of the then "via Nuova."[20] It was a small typographer's shop with only one typeface at its disposal, and it produced about twenty books, beginning with Doni's own edition of his *Lettere*.[21] The books Doni made, which drew on the writings of the Accademia Fiorentina of which he was a part, were not of extremely good quality by most standards of the time, as Claudia di Filippo Bareggi observes,[22] and Doni himself thought they were not up to snuff. He acknowledged this in a letter to the Florentine Filippo Strozzi, though in doing so Doni blames the typographer, Bartolomeo Zanetti, whom he describes as an incompetent "idiot, namely a beast, that is, an ox," who appeared bent on making Doni waste tremendous sums of money on refurbishing his shop so that in the end "everything," Doni laments with characteristic sarcasm, "was done backwards."[23]

By contrast, the Giolito and Marcolini presses in Venice, though fundamentally different in the types of books they printed, were large, successful editorial houses located in the center of the city, and they boasted a good-sized staff, along with an already developed marketplace niche and bookstores in other cities.[24] Despite these differences, however, in both instances what one must have witnessed on entering Doni's, Giolito's, or Marcolini's presses in Florence and Venice must have been more or less the same. There would have been pullers, the *tiratori*, who had the taxing job of printing the sheets beneath the square-shaped presses, and the inkers, the *battitori*, who prepared the type in the *forme* and inked it with ink balls (*mazzi*). Printed sheets might have been hanging to dry on cords underneath the ceiling or, once dry, placed in stacks. Copyeditors probably labored in poorly lit, and surely noisy, rooms, though there was generally no need for these editors in the production of popular books, such as Doni's. Typesetters toiled at large slanted desks for twelve to fourteen hours a day, sometimes laboring by candlelight. There might be a hack writer composing prose or verse at a table; Doni himself is characterized as working "amid the noise of the presses."[25] At the same time, people might have been milling about, exchanging ideas in Doni's press in Florence and the ones he worked in early on when living in Venice, for these presses could have certainly functioned as centers of social interaction and intellectual conversation. Consequently, the things that would have no doubt distinguished the Giolito and Marcolini presses from Doni's own in Florence included (1) volume (there were more books being produced in the Venetian presses), (2) ambience (there would have been more hustle and bustle in them, with more workers), and (3) environment (there would have been more people entering and exiting the shop in a thriving city with the largest print industry in Europe).

By the time Doni wrote the *Libraria*, then, he had real firsthand experience in the making of books. He understood their texture and shape. And so should we, as we approach this novel book on books, which is the first of its kind as an annotated bibliography in Italian literature. The *Libraria*, which can be conceived as a sort of expanded version of the printer's list, is a conventional book in shape and form composed by the polygraphs, those professional writers who could often be so unconventional in their books. The first and last editions of the *Libraria* were printed by Giolito, and the second by Marcolini, the privileged press of Aretino for a long stretch of time.[26] The various editions of the *Libraria* are (for those unfamiliar with the terms of the printing industry even today) octavos or duodecimos. This simply means that the individual printed sheet, which could vary in size, was folded three times to create an octavo, a leaflet about the size of a modern paperback, to create sixteen pages; four folds produced a duodecimo, a leaflet roughly the size of a miniature prayer book today. The folded pages, or gatherings (*fascicoli*), may or may not have been numbered on both sides. The stitching together of these gatherings to form the desired complete volume took place elsewhere; the binding of a finished book could cost a substantial amount of money and depended highly on an individual person's taste, as is evident, for instance, in Castiglione's insistence that the bindings of his *Cortegiano* intended for certain people of repute appear exactly as he desired. Typeface varied, but the preferred format for the Giolito and Marcolini presses producing books such as Doni's was a combination of Roman and italic type, and those typefaces indeed appear in the *Libraria*.[27]

Like a number of books by polygraphs, the *Libraria* in the third edition includes a number of images, in this case profiles of some of the more famous authors contained within the book. A number of engravers worked for the Giolito and Marcolini presses, but Doni often used preexisting images, such as those in Francesco Marcolini's *Le sorti* (1540), which gave Doni the conceptual blueprint, it has been argued, for his own inventions in a number of his books.[28] In the end, the overall aim of the Giolito and Marcolini presses was to make good-quality books, yet in doing so the presses also surely wanted to get these books (which could reach a print run of about two thousand copies but were more likely on the order of a thousand) onto the shelf and then off the shelf so as to keep the press operating smoothly and in the black.[29] This is the case with Doni's *Libraria*. It must have sold fairly well, for it needed to come out in various enlarged editions, each time with substantial revisions and emendations. A viable market, then, existed for this sort of work of popular literature, though many books of this type still lingered, it should be said, in a bookseller's inventory well into the end of the century.[30] And Doni aimed to be part of the market as a writer, which proved modestly lucrative. He also aimed to cash in on this market as a printer, an effort that proved, by contrast, unsuccessful.[31] All things considered, making a living as the owner of a press was not an easy thing to do in sixteenth-century Italy, even if one had, as has been argued in the case of Doni, the support of a duke. Running a shop as a printer was expensive, requiring a substantial investment of capital.

If in its physical shape the *Libraria* presents itself as a typical book of the polygraphs, once you open it up everything starts to change after the obligatory, prefatory letter, in which Doni seeks to ingratiate himself, much as he will do *ad nauseam* throughout the book.[32] For the *Libraria*, beginning with the very first version and treatise, is perhaps one of the stranger books written in the Italian Renaissance, as Doni's contemporary Ortensio Lando (another polygraph) seemed to have intuited when he compared it to Konrad Gesner's massive, erudite *Bibliotheca universalis* (1545–55).[33] The *Libraria*, as we have said, is a book about books, but the way it is arranged, albeit conventional in many respects, is still peculiar, and not everything in it is as clear-cut as it seems to be. The *Libraria*, for instance, lists the books Doni has chosen to include in it by author alphabetically, though for readers today that listing appears in an unusual format: in Doni's *Libraria* we access the list of books compiled by the author's first name, rather than the last (as is the custom in modern editorial practices), so a search for Ariosto will turn up under "Ludovico." There is, however, not only a practical but solid professional reason for employing this familiar alpha system of organization. As Doni tells us in his opening letter to the "readers" in the final version, he has adopted in particular the alpha organization in order to avoid the slightest appearance of bias: "I would not want to make an enemy of anyone." At all costs he does not want to incur the wrath of other writers, whose ire, no doubt, he will inevitably stoke for one reason or another: "I will begin, then, in this first part to place the authors in alphabetical order to flee from this other noise that one could make from the start, with writers telling me: 'You put me above and below this one and that author who is better or worse than I,' whereas by placing everyone according to the letter of their name, they will be quiet" (63–64).

Doni thus wants to come off as impartial, and the alpha organization, admittedly a familiar format, preserves at least the appearance of professional propriety and the absence of bias. Doni, it would seem, is worried—though we can suspect he protests too much—about how other writers perceive him as he goes about listing their works in public. In the process, he gives us, with all these precautionary measures, some idea of the touchy world in which he lives. Writers got upset quickly, then as they do now. Tempers flared. Woe to you if you should fail to place Pinco Pallino before Pinco Pallone.

But organization does not address the problem of inclusion, of who is "in" and who is "out." Doni's list may be "impartially" organized, but it is also incomplete. Indeed, even in the final, enlarged edition, there are some curious omissions,[34] such as the fellow Florentine Anton Francesco Grazzini's recently published *La gelosia* (1551). Does the absence of Grazzini cast doubt on Doni's assertion that he really had no axe to grind, especially since Doni insists scornfully that he has excluded an "infinity of hideous things" (*cosacce*; 64) from his collection? Perhaps. Yet Doni, who is far too clever to let things just rest like that without a comment, has given this matter some thought—not specifically about Grazzini (a man who shared with Doni an interest in Il Burchiello and burlesque poetry) but about the absence or presence of an individual author within his collection. Anticipating any possible objection with a preemptive strike against his potential detractors, Doni shows he has thought about a critic faulting him for missing an author or two. In an effort to excuse himself, he observes disingenuously, "I tell you that there are many books, good and bad, that have remained out [of this one] because I didn't know of them, and for this reason one leaves some space in the printing of books, whereby whoever will possess the book can write down whatever he wants on it and, if he likes, can still provide me with information, because in the reprinting of it, always in the hope of making it more perfect, one can add the authors who should be brought to light" (64). Good ex-printer that he is, Doni takes into consideration not just the type on the page but also, significantly, the blank space on the page, the negative space, as artists would formally describe it today. And Doni has taken into consideration the adaptable usefulness of that space for the purposes of including marginalia—that familiar practice of adding all sorts of information around and about the words on the page.

For Doni, then, this book is eminently expansive and elastic, capable of emendation and additions. Doni himself did add to the book as it came out in future editions, including yet more works of printed books by the authors he has listed, and adding other writers he neglected to include in the first 1550 edition—including Francesco Petrarca, the privileged poet of the sixteenth century, who, believe it or not, was somehow missing from the very first edition.[35] Anyone still left out of Doni's *Libraria* simply had to be penned in the margins of an individual's personal copy, if indeed the individual owning the copy possessed the requisite insight to detect the lacuna and then the memory to make the emendation by putting it in by hand.[36] But how, we might ask, would this ever make a difference to a writer who finds himself or herself absent in a printed edition of Doni's impressive, novel compendium of books available in the vernacular? If a writer is not actually *in* the book, who cares if someone individually, in the privacy of his or her home, scribbles in the name of the writer on the margins of the page? Surely writers interested in inclusion in this book about books would want their names (and their books) made public, in every edition of Doni's *Libraria*, beginning with the first. After all, the writer not included in Doni's *Libraria* will never know if he or she has been placed in the margins of someone's personal copy. Nor will anyone else know, unless the book circulates widely as it is passed from hand to hand. It is therefore essential to be in print, for books in print, like Doni's own published letters, bear witness "to the entire world" (146).[37]

Print culture broadcasts an identity boldly and loudly, and as Doni points out it is not always fair how the process plays itself out. Print, for instance, brings fame in an almost aleatory manner, serendipitously lifting up those who should be denigrated, while debasing those who should be elevated. "The printing press," Doni writes in his *Libraria*, "which is an honored art and worthy of the highest fame, sometimes has been the cause to anger many men who died thinking they would live on, and many who are living witness the death of their writings for various reasons" (127). This power of print in its turn gives Doni awesome authority. He possesses the ability to conserve, as well as the power to bring some authors "to light" (68). To be cut from a list in Doni's book therefore means that one is deprived of a life transcending the humidity that fosters the accumulated rot on the back of a dusty shelf where so many books, as he puts it, have "gathered mold" (68). It is therefore imperative, one would presume, for writers of all ages, genders, and stripes that Doni accumulate their names and place them in the ranks of the worthy. Every book is another item in his book on books, an incremental growth of a reputation that could last, ideally, for all eternity. And "Eternity," Doni observes, as he personifies the concept, "once having become aware [of everyone's desire for fame], found the medium of print, which, with all the astonishment of those who have come after the invention, has brought back to life and in an integral, complete form the images of those who will never be now without fame" (85).[38]

Doni knows the power of print, then, its capacity to immortalize, and he ends up awarding fame to some while potentially casting others to oblivion through *accidental* omission in at least some occasions, he claims. It seems strange, then, that Doni protests so much about being impartial when it is likely that he is not. But what is far stranger is that this book about books contains so many extraneous asides in which Doni does precisely what he said he would *not* do. No sooner do we pass from the introductory note to the reader and to predictably yet another obligatory dedicatory note to a person than Doni begins to describe the books he has listed and pass critical judgment on them. He does, that is, exactly what he said he had intended to avoid doing in order to appear an impartial author of professional propriety. Some writers, for instance, get lengthy asides, while some have nothing mentioned beneath their names except the title of the book or books they wrote. If Doni had hoped to avoid the suspicion of subtly planting in our minds his own prejudices as an author claiming authority over his personal, choice selection of books, he has already failed miserably by the time we've reached the second page. Alpha listing aside, Acarisio da Cento and Achille Marozzo come off a lot better than Agostino Giustiniano, given that the first two authors have a paragraph of information beneath their names (each of those paragraphs full of glowing accolades), while poor Giustiniano, remembered today as a pioneering Biblical humanist from Genoa, has the mere listing of a single book. Indeed, some descriptions accompanying the names are so dazzling with praise that we might be tempted to think that Doni, the vitriolic antipedant, might in fact be trying his hand in that well-established humanist rhetorical practice of composing encomia. More to the point, some of the asides are just absurdly digressive. Doni, a garrulous man, sometimes talks about everything other than the author in question, as if the real purpose behind his glosses were to allow Doni to showcase his talents, or maddening foibles. To be sure, in the *Libraria*, and especially in the second treatise, Doni includes stories, vignettes, facetiae, all of which have absolutely nothing to do with the author whose works he is purportedly intending to gloss at that particular moment.

But there is more. For what makes this book so strange, beyond its many extraneous asides, is that a host of the books mentioned in the second treatise are not real: they are inventions all his own. Doni is a deliberate, incorrigible tease *and* liar.[39] He holds out the possibility, for instance, that a book by Ariosto that no one has ever read, the *Rinaldo ardito, dodici canti*, lurks somewhere in manuscript form. By the time Doni has created the final version of his *Libraria*, then, he has sent his readers out in pursuit of false books that we might wish existed—indeed, we may even believe they do exist as we travel about the globe in search of those elusive manuscripts out of a self-deluded yearning for a new inviting text to read. Needless to say, these manuscripts, such as Machiavelli's comedy called *Il secretario* or Boccaccio's *Corona napolitana*, can never be found as we move from library to library searching for them. In this way, Doni, with playful irony, has worked fantasy into the serious business of bibliography, mingling fact, the sort of hard facts one finds in Gesner's exhaustive *Bibliotheca universalis*, with fiction. Indeed, some lovers of books, those incurable pedants and book hunters whom Doni deplored and mocked with malicious glee, may even fall for his trick. In this respect, Doni, a hater of pedants, has fabricated a book just for them. It is a book that will potentially keep pedants running and hunting about in their search to uncover yet more alluring manuscripts that will elude their grasp for generations to come. As a result, lovers of Boccaccio, Ariosto, and Machiavelli may still hope one day to discover the manuscripts that Doni claims he has seen and feels should be printed for public consumption, but they will never find those books—at least not until some cunning author like Umberto Eco incorporates tidbits of the putative lost manuscript into one of his novels, as he did the lost notes of Aristotle's observations on comedy into *The Name of the Rose*.[40] Not to be outdone, Doni even includes a book or two that he claims he has written but were in all likelihood self-authenticating products of his own fertile and playful imagination.[41]

Why, we might ask, did Doni write a book of this sort? For one, Doni is demonstrating his knowledge about books in many ways, so that he can justifiably claim that he is offering something not only pleasurable but also, as he announces at the outset, "profitable [*utile*] to all those who have need of knowledge of the language and want to know, write, or reason about all the authors, books, and works" (55). Rhetorically, Doni is building his professional ethos, much as Cellini was building his in the treatises on goldsmithing and sculpture. Indeed, at the most fundamental level Doni is showing us that he understands how books are made and what goes into making them. He has been there from the ground up. He understands orthography, for instance, which perhaps accounts for his interest in books on that topic. He reminds us that printers furnish margins not only for the ease of reading but also for editorial glossing. Along with that, he lets us know that he can tell the difference between a good and bad woodcut maker, the *intagliatore*, who would have received a steady stream of work from such presses as the ones Doni wrote and worked for in Venice. In one instance, for example, Doni chides an editor, Pietro Perna, for having once sent him an intagliatore lacking in talent when he had a press of his own in Florence. He kept this woodcut maker on his payroll even though he was a good-for-nothing. Moreover, a bookseller tellingly comes into play as a witty and engaging person in the *Libraria*. In this instance the bookseller is rendered capable of putting a translator and three pedants into their places (71–72), the very sorts of people who haunted bookshops, since bookshops offered the literate wonderful places to read, converse, study, and discover new books. Furthermore, along with understanding who prints books and works in the print industry, Doni understands *why* people print books to begin with. Professionally, he grasps their motivation, which can be local or broad-minded, selfish or selfless: "those who print," he proclaims, "do it for many and different reasons: for the glory, for utility, for ambition, out of presumptuousness, to feed themselves, for the honor of the nation [a "nazione" here understood as the local group of people sharing a common language and origins], for the honor of the family, or out of a debt to their profession, for a whim to wile away leisure time, or to sharpen their minds and abilities and become better" (151).

Additionally, just as Doni understands why all sorts of people print books, he understands that all sorts of books exist for all sorts of readers, "because all types of people," he summarily observes, "read" (*ogni sorte di gente legge*; 249). Noticeably, we become aware as we move through his *Libraria* that the books selected for inclusion are also by no means all literary. The selection is indeed catholic, though not complete, and Doni has fashioned it for the broadest possible public.[42] In this light, we can certainly say that the effect of an expansive list like Doni's *Libraria* serves to flatten out cultural hierarchies. At the same time, however, as Doni breaks down established hierarchies by including in his *Libraria* so many types of books arranged in an alpha list, he is also engaged in upsetting what scholars today would term a highly selective "canon formation" by offering us, as Vanni Bramanti observed, "a panorama of a culture and its people."[43] In this first book on books in Italian, Doni is defining parameters, showing us up front, in plain, reader-friendly and paper-printed view, what he chooses to place before the eyes of potential consumers, as if his readers had just entered his shop and were browsing for a book to read, or were in need of assistance in putting together a private library.

This strategy of "showcasing" books, to be sure, is not unfamiliar to us today. Entering a bookstore gives us instantaneously a real, material understanding of what a culture has available for consumption in print. Much the same can be said of how revealing a personal collection of books can be. A household book collection, like a bookstore, is not at all like a public library, as Calvino observes in *If on a Winter's Night*. It tells us what people consume in print, or, as F. Scott Fitzgerald dramatized in *The Great Gatsby*, what they would like us to believe they consume in print.[44] And Doni is telling us up front with his *Libraria* what Italians read, should read, and have available for them to read in print and in manuscript form in the vernacular. He is presenting himself, in sum, as an arbiter of taste, even though he pretends at the outset that he is not going to occupy that position. Put differently, were this a small private bookstore and Doni the owner of it today, or if this were his actual home with a well-stocked study, he would be ushering us around the stacks or shelves.[45] "Try this one, try that." He is helping readers, instructing them, as Lando observed, to build their own library. And all this takes place as Doni laments the loss of books from our shelves (144). As a professional writer tied to the marketplace of print, he is arguably trying to stimulate our appetites for consumption of a host of works of familiar and unfamiliar literature in—and *only* in, it is worth stressing—the vernacular.

Amid all these descriptions of varied books, discussed in both serious and playful ways, Doni includes himself as an author of books, not once but twice. He also uses the occasion to tell us a story or two. In some instances he tells someone else's story, as he does often in Part II, in which he recounts—which is to say, he literally reproduces—the essence of Machiavelli's "Belfagor" (374–88). Doni's curious book, then, involves a great deal of professional self-promotion, the kind of conspicuous self-promotion for which outspoken authors such as Aretino were so famous. Doni is advertising himself in the process of advertising the books he thinks should be read or should be printed for public consumption.[46] In this light, we should hardly be surprised that what Doni has to say about himself in the first treatise, beginning with the first printing of the *Libraria* and extending to the last, is a great set piece of conspicuous self-promotion. And we should hardly be surprised that the lengthy list of Doni's books that follows the description of him as an apologetic, penitent, and rehabilitated writer is far longer than anyone else's in the last edition of the *Libraria*. By the time Doni began to acquire recognition and reached, at least for a brief period, a level of modest economic comfort, he could boast no fewer than twenty books in print (some of which cannot be found to this day). Add to this impressive list the additional nineteen books he has suppressed from the final edition (which appeared in the second edition of 1550), as well as the two books he includes in the second treatise under the list of those that should be printed,[47] and Doni's list of completed books (those in print and not in print) proves even more impressive, arriving at just under forty.[48] In this regard, even though Doni tries to level out cultural and literary hierarchies by ordering the authors alphabetically, his self-presentation in his *Libraria* stands as a high-water mark in his book on books. From the 1550 edition on, we even find the book we're holding in our hands self-reflexively listed among the books Doni has written and completed. To this effect, if Dante envisioned himself among the greatest poets of antiquity in the fourth canto of the *Inferno*; if Petrarca placed himself among the most worthy classical authors in his letters to pagan authors and posterity; if Ariosto has himself welcomed back home in the final canto of his *Orlando furioso* with ringing applause by everyone worth knowing in the early sixteenth century; Doni, midway into the sixteenth century, places himself within his own book on books in plain view and prominently shows off that his own impressive list of books is larger than anyone else's. He emerges as the real "gigante" (giant; 80) among those he's talked about in his description about his prior activities as a professional writer in the marketplace of print.

Finally, it should be said that Doni wrote this book not only to promote and elevate himself in the most conspicuous of ways, so that he could constantly reproduce yet more vainglorious versions of himself as a prolific writer. Doni also wrote this book, vindictive man that he was, to get even and taunt others—to get in their face, to put it bluntly. In the opening letter, as we have seen, he claims with tactful professional propriety that he did not want to elicit anger by prejudicing anyone's opinion of another author. In truth, that was precisely what Doni wanted to do in select cases. Throughout his life he established friendships wherever he went, often professing faith and effusive love, but just as often he made enemies. The most famous case of Doni proving himself cantankerous and vengeful has to do with his abrupt about-face in regard to Aretino, the most powerful and feared professional writer in the vernacular during the period, and the man to whom Doni declared his love early on and who, it would seem, assisted Doni in beginning his career as a writer in the marketplace of print. In an early letter, sent from Piacenza on April 28, 1548, for instance, when Doni hoped to arrive in Venice and make his way as a writer (or perhaps one day become a courtier),[49] Aretino is deemed the great arbiter of taste, the final literary judge, "the flaying tooth for the skin of vice," the "sharp knife of justice," a powerful, influential man without whose positive appraisal Doni cannot imagine pursuing a career as a writer.[50] If his letters do not please Aretino, Doni indicates, then he would prefer Aretino to hurl them into the water, leaving them submerged forever under the waves of the canals of Venice where all the other "garbage" (*spazzatura*) goes to waste and disappears.[51] Eight years later, however, in a decisive break in their relationship (a break occasioned, it seems, because Aretino refused to recommend Doni for a position with Guidobaldo della Rovere, the duke of Urbino), the tables turned. Aretino, Doni claims in his vitriolic *Terremoto*, was the anti-Christ, a libertine, sodomite, and drunkard. Doni, in short, certainly didn't fail to pull punches in this all-out savage attack in which he predicted, no less, that Aretino would die in 1556. If Doni's vituperation doesn't find its way into the *Libraria* directly, it did so by its noticeable absence. The most famous writer of works in the vernacular, the "scourge of princes" and "secretary to the world," whose very name denoted fame in sixteenth-century Italy, doesn't even get his name included in the final version of Doni's book.

In this respect, the *Libraria* unmistakably bears traces of the fight between Doni and Aretino as we move from the first to the last edition. In the first edition, Aretino is well represented with a narrative accompanying his name full of praise and a quantity of books that surpasses everyone else's. By the last edition, however, Aretino has quietly disappeared; Doni takes over and tries to position himself as a sharp-tongued, witty, pugnacious author worthy of universal recognition within the marketplace of print. Now Doni, not the sodomitical anti-Christ Aretino, deserves to be conspicuous and recognized as a man of exceptional status.

Furthermore, Doni's exclusion of Aretino from this book on books tells us something else about the professional habits of the polygraphs in general (and about Doni in particular) when it came to composing their works. They needed to act quickly, with the kind of speed (prestezza) that allowed them to beat everyone else to the punch.[52] They had to get books out before another person grabbed the idea and thus, as it were, the headline, much as competitive journalists do today. As Tom Nichols has demonstrated, theirs was an aesthetic that, like Tintoretto's with his loose brushwork in the visual arts and his calculated rapidity of production, privileged through prestezza at least the appearance of spontaneity, improvisation, and versatility.[53] In comparison, consider Castiglione, the author with whom we began in the first chapter, and who epitomizes the idealized, understated, courtly savoir faire of the previous generation. In the preface to his *Cortegiano*, Castiglione claims that he finally felt compelled to rush his book into print because he feared a pirated edition might come out in the meantime. The unsuspecting but always gracious Vittoria Colonna, whom Castiglione hastens to excuse for any slight lapse of judgment on her part, had allowed his manuscript to wander into perhaps pilfering hands, so Castiglione needs to set the record straight and get his words out in the public domain in print before his book appears in a potentially mangled, pirated form. Castiglione's rush to print, however, has little to do with income within the market, or even with plagiarism, at least as he elucidates the matter. He is not particularly worried, it would seem, that some unscrupulous person might take his work and pass it off as his own. He is anxious that the words attributed to him might not appear exactly as he had written them. They might lack the final polish that allowed a man of erudition to work away slowly and meticulously over sometimes long stretches of time the little ruinous bristles or barbs that rendered it less than perfect. The verb typically employed by Renaissance Italian writers to express their desire to perfect a work until it was just right was *limare*, "to file or polish." Courtly authors aspiring to be remembered through their works within the court culture of sixteenth-century Italy wanted to file away and polish a poem, drama, or narrative to create a smooth literary corpus of perfected form. Time, in terms of production, was not of the essence.

Such was not the case for polygraphs such as Doni. He was not interested in the niceties of Bembian diction, the aulic turn of phrase, the well-polished periodic prose that might appear to have been nimbly dashed off but potentially took ages to complete to exhibit the proper legerdemain. Professionally, he cared about getting the stuff out fast to the public within the marketplace of print, he maintained. "I had no sooner churned out [literally shat out] a page or a tale," he confesses in the *Libraria*, as he casts his glance back over his earlier writings, "than I slipped it under a press to be printed [*non sì tosto avevo scacazzato un foglio o una leggenda, che io la ficcavo sotto le stampe*], so that they came out as they did" (80). Moreover, Doni was not so concerned with someone attributing certain words to him, despite what he says in his *Libraria* about how he was tricked by certain "treacherous" men who included their words into his facile and quickly produced "tittle tattle" (80). The underlying fear for Doni, as he reproduces himself figuratively in this book about books, is that other people will beat him to the punch and produce something in printed form for public consumption before he has a chance to do so. We can find support for the notion that Doni felt the need to act quickly in getting his works out in print in part by looking directly at what he says in his letters. "I know full well," he self-mockingly admits, "that I am at fault in bringing to light my poems and my prose before I've let them go gather mold in the cupboard of revisions, and allow them to be picked at and pecked at by men of judgment, but I don't have the patience for that: beyond which, many steal these things from me in order to better piss me off."[54] We can also indirectly test the notion that Doni was anxious to get stuff into print within the marketplace by observing what he had to say in his life in regard to even the appearance of plagiarism, that familiar practice in the second half of the sixteenth century in Italy of riscrittura, of artfully creating literary patchworks of other people's writings, both classical and modern.

In the *Libraria*, for instance, Doni observes in one entry that the greatness of the storyteller Masuccio Salernitano in part has to do with the fact that he invented stories of his own, despite the monumental and unavoidable authority of Boccaccio as a model: "I will put to the side now those who steal the tale of others, or who take the complete words of another in order to avoid effort. Blessed be Salernitano, who at least never even stole a word from Boccaccio; rather, he wrote a book that is all his, and it is called *Cinquanta novelle*" (140). The greatness of Salernitano lies in both his powers of invention and his ability not to have to resort to being a literary thief.

Doni's former friend Lodovico Domenichi (1515–1564), by contrast, whom Doni accused of intellectual theft, comes off as an out-and-out dunce, whose name finds itself mangled in anagram form in the second treatise into ECHIMENEDO COVIDOLO, with a host of sarcastic observations placed below it. Perhaps Doni mangles Domenichi's name out of a desire to protect himself against accusations of slander, but he also does it, just as likely, out of spite, in a vindictive effort to get in someone else's face.[55] In any event, part of Domenichi's fame in the *Libraria* rests on his representing the worst that any writer can aspire to be, which only makes it stranger that Doni includes at the very beginning of the 1551 and 1555 editions of the *Seconda libraria* two of Domenichi's sonnets—sonnets presumably composed earlier in praise of Doni before the squabble between the two commenced.[56] Domenichi, in essence, is viewed as an intellectual and unimaginative thief in his rush to get into print, an accusation that smacked of outrageous, beat-'em-to-the-punch chutzpah since Doni in the meantime had been stealing wholesale from Domenichi's *Dialogo della stampa* in the ostensibly hasty composition of his very own *I marmi*—and, what is more, parts of the *Libraria*.[57] "Some others," such as Domenichi, we are given to understand in a diatribe that lasts over two pages,

> have sent translations already printed and done by others to the press to be printed, and they have attributed to themselves both the book and the work [involved in composing the book], using the fruit of their arrogant ignorance [in doing this], dedicating the work in their own name[58] in an effort to cling to the pocketbook of some gentleman, colonel, or captain, hoping to steal some ducats from them. How many are there still in the world that, being scoundrels, men of little value, insolent fellows, and rascals, have not felt shame in having stuck their hands in the works of the learned, with the desire—without the slightest embarrassment—to fix [those works], correct, enlarge and reduce them, putting modern names in place of ancient ones [within the books themselves], as much for the cities as for the people mentioned? [307–8]

Domenichi, we are led to believe, also stole and copied from other writers in putting together his book on witticisms and on illustrious women, his *Facezie* and *Donne illustri* respectively. "And whoever is not satisfied with these works," Doni assures us, as his irony escalates into outright sarcasm at the end of his diatribe, "go ahead and read his poetry, which will put to rest the marveling of those people who had marveled at [in the sense of also "doubted"] the substance of such an important character" (*le quali faranno fine alla maraviglia di chi si maravigliasse della sufficienza d'un tanto sì fatto personaggio*; 309).[59] Getting things out quickly into the marketplace of print obviously led some—including, especially, Doni!—to copy the works of others and fob that work off as their own. Prestezza could make these kinds of practical professional writers resort to all sorts of hurried tactics of composition and presentation.

Given Doni's attack here on Domenichi, which is part and parcel of so many other vicious charges of foul play leveled against Domenichi in the second treatise of the *Libraria* (charges, incidentally, presented under the subterfuge of the names of yet more fictitious authors),[60] it is hard not to think of Doni as a particularly vindictive man who would never allow a grudge to subside. In the end he perhaps punished Domenichi far more than his former friend and companion probably ever deserved, whatever he happened to have done to offend Doni so severely.[61] And Doni, uncompromising and unwilling to be mollified, continued to pursue Domenichi with fury long after the attack could have been put to rest.[62] He publicly attacks Domenichi, for instance, also in his *Disegno*, *Mondi*, *Marmi*, *Lettere*, and *Zucca*, as well as here and there in his commentary on the poems of Il Burchiello and in his tirades against Aretino.[63] In the *Libraria* itself, where the accusation of plagiarism is blithely aired, Doni, who was certainly not immune to reproducing other people's writings word for word, aims to wipe Domenichi out of the cultural memory, beginning with a book that not only undermines him but also fails to acknowledge overtly his identity. Domenichi's name is turned inside-out, twisted around, placed backwards.[64] In terms of literary pugnacity, this is aggression indeed. Nevertheless, we can still understand and appreciate the ferocity of Doni's attack, if not exactly admire him for it, much as we can understand and appreciate Domenichi's belated retaliatory stabs at Doni in his *Dialogo della stampa*.[65] For Doni, as for Aretino before him, the aim was not to be nice and liked but, in Machiavellian terms, to be feared. If a professional popularizing writer climbs into the ring to play the game, these are the tacit rules, the bellicose Doni would have us know. To be forewarned is to be forearmed. You can get knocked out, bloodied, turned inside out, with your literary weaknesses displayed for everyone to view. The world of the opportunistic polygraphs was not for the squeamish or faint of heart. It was, at least for Doni, for the writers who were willing to get out in the open, truly make themselves conspicuous, and then see where the punches fell and how well they could dodge or parry them. Professional propriety, for all that they might advocate it, was certainly not their principal concern.

Coda: Doni's Designed Manuscripts and His Marmi

Doni was not a professional visual artist, though he did engage in the paragone over the relative merits of painting and sculpture with his *Disegno*, one of the early such paragoni of the Renaissance, and though he did define himself in one instance as not only a writer and a musician but also as a "painter."[66] Needless to say, if he did paint there is no record of his work. Doni, who befriended a number of visual artists, including Tintoretto, also claimed he was a "draftsman" (perhaps Baccio Bandinelli's father, the goldsmith Michelangelo di Viviano, trained him in the art?),[67] and he was a gifted artist, as is evidenced by some of the designs for his manuscripts, including *I numeri*, *Le pitture*, and, in a number of stunning instances, his *Ville*. In one case, for instance, in the version of the *Ville* contained in the Bayerische Staatsbibliothek of Munich, he depicts a group traveling down a crowded road along the shore (Figure 19). In the manuscript of the *Ville* housed in the Biblioteca Trivulziana in Milan, he furnishes us not only with a self-portrait (Figure 18, based on Enea Vico's engraving) but also with a number of elaborate images of villas and their rustic settings. He also proved adept at designing borders around manuscripts and at the end or beginning of sections, especially early on with his comedy *Lo stufaiuolo*. Above all, he produced a number of magnificently designed books on emblems, in particular his *Le dimostrationi de gli animi degli huomini del Doni*, dedicated to Duke Alfonso II d'Este, which is among his finest designed presentation manuscripts (see, for instance, Figure 20).[68] But the place to find Doni, that obnoxious, irreverent, conspicuously self-promoting man lacking often enough professional propriety and full of irrepressible gall, is not in the images he produced in the manuscripts he designed and then gave as gifts intended to win him favor. Instead, he is found in the words he composed with lightning speed, almost on demand amid the clamor of the presses, and with a spontaneity and caustic irony all his own—at least, to be sure, when he was not filching someone of his or her words through the midsixteenth-century art of riscrittura.

Unlike Cellini, who was concerned with describing things with words, Doni—though also concerned with the representation of visual reality through verbal forms—was obsessed with words as things in and of themselves. For Doni, as a professional writer with direct experience in the print industry, words had a sort of material quality to them, and they were to be appreciated not only in manuscript form, where he penned them with a beautiful script, but also when they were mechanically reproduced. In fact, words in printed form acquired even more meaning for him, he contends at least in his printed books, precisely because they were reproduced. Doni drives the concept home in his *Libraria*; he also did so in another book composed about the same time, his *Marmi*, where he dedicates an entire section to the important social and cultural power of the reproduction of things through print. In the process of rehearsing much of the ongoing debate over the merits and demerits of print publication, in the *Marmi* he all the more strikingly plagiarizes from Domenichi's *Dialogo della stampa*, literally reproducing it word for word, probably from a manuscript that Doni had in possession from 1547–1548, before the friendship between the two men turned

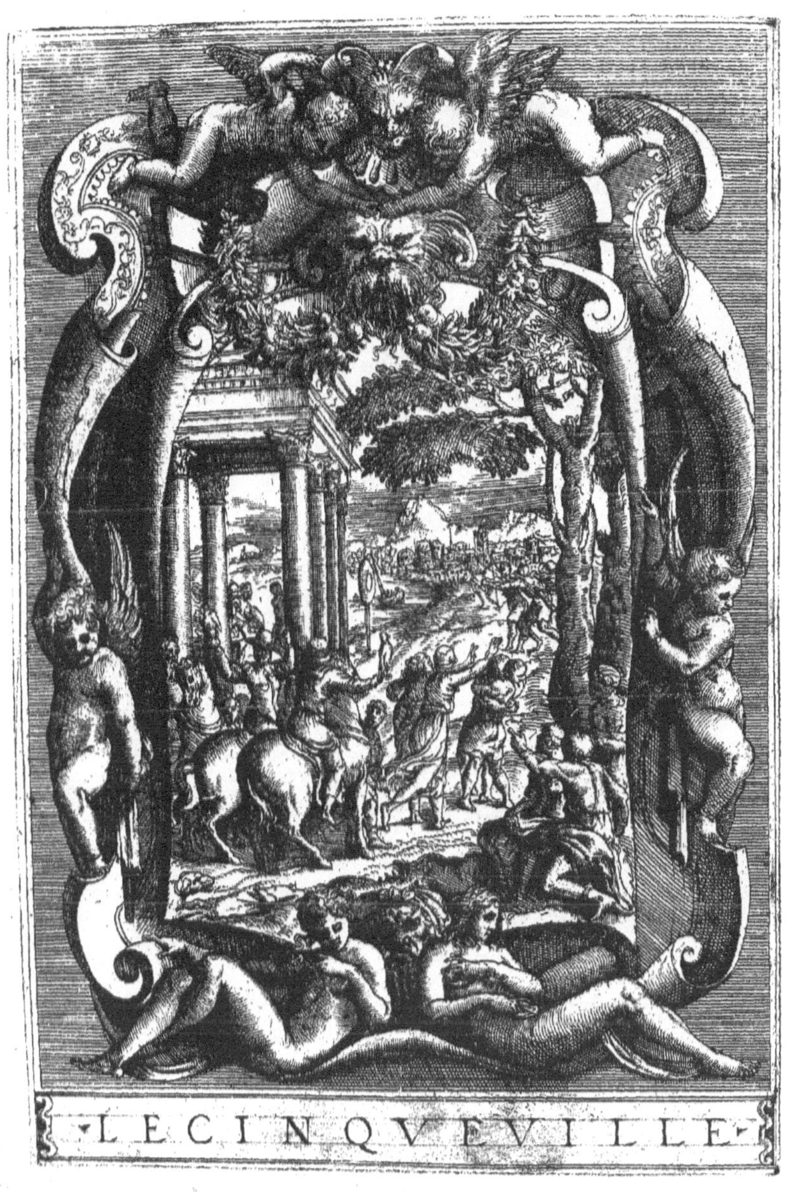

FIGURE 19. Francesco Doni (1513–1574). Design from *La villa Fucchera, libro primo delle Ville del Doni*, 1559. Shelfmark: Cod.ital. 36. Courtesy Bayerische Staatsbibliothek of München.

Il mostro di marmo adunque udito questo fece una Impresa
et se la appiccò al collo: nō disse della materia risibile, ne
circa all'humore stravagante, ma dipinse cosa alla vita et
governo loro apropriata. E fece un Pesce grosso che uomi=

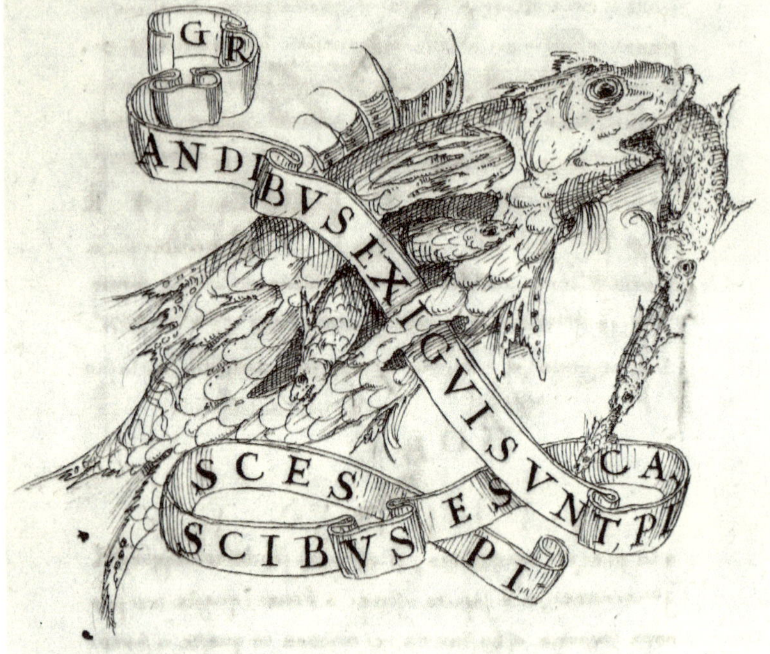

tava de gli altri pesci, o mangiava: manco di lui grossi, et que=
gli de minori di mano in mano, cō il suo motto: ——
In somma voleva mostrare che pesci grossi mangiavano i pic=
cinini: così faceva il Papa Caraffa: un dire che accade alle=
var gente che mangino pesci crudi. Qual più nuovo pesce
et crudo huomo di voi Barba Crich.' voi bisognerebbe man=
giare, che mangiate, come pesce grosso tutto il mondo de pic=
coli pesci. Dietro a la pietra che ha messa il Brevio a=

FIGURE 20. Anton Francesco Doni (1513–1574). Design from *Le dimostrationi de gli animi degli huomini*, 1561. Florence, BNF, Fondo Palatino, ms. E.B.10.8, str. 1392, c. 33v. By concession of the Ministero per i Beni e le Attività Culturali della Repubblica Italiana/Biblioteca Nazionale Centrale di Firenze. Photo courtesy GAP srl.

forever sour.[69] At the same time that Doni in the *Marmi* fobs off Domenichi's writing as his own, he is concerned not only with the productive uses of reproduction but also with its abuses. Hacks lurk out there, Doni warns (or rather, we might say, "Domenichi" warns), and they will take advantage of printing to reproduce their thoughts in order to elevate themselves and acquire momentary recognition, perhaps even lasting recognition. "Every last pedant," he has one interlocutor remark,

> seems bent on printing a tale that has been shat out, patched together, filched, and torn from thousands of clumsy tales; he then gads about all puffed up on account of a couple of meager sheets of paper, as though he'd just sipped dragons' blood or stuffed himself on chameleons! The minute he sees one of his fables in the marketplace, he sticks up his tail and calls out: "Out of my way! I yield not to Bembo! Ariosto is but a dream, Sannazaro and Molza are unworthy to drag behind me Petrarca!" Thus, thinking he's stealing others' thunder, in fact he heaps shame upon himself [1.186, 34].[70]

Print brings about a loss in value—or so the familiar argument goes, as Doni rehearses a standard topic of debate in the period. Poets used to be rare, but now they are a dime a dozen thanks to the proliferation of books through the power of mechanical reproduction in the fast-paced marketplace of print. But that is not the fault of print, we learn, or the printers themselves, but of the people who abuse print. Nevertheless, for Doni the upside to printing is far more compelling. Had the art of printing existed in the past, we are told, we would still have works that are now lost to us. Print, we consequently learn, is a medium, exactly as Doni had insisted earlier in his *Libraria*, as enduring in its own way as sculpture and stone:

> Crivello: If the custom of printing books had existed when the Latin tongue was flourishing and the sciences and the arts were at their apogee, we would not now hanker after and vainly regret the loss of so many beautiful objects, buried in the countless pillages of Rome and Italy.
>
> Lollio: Messer Paolo speaks the truth.
>
> Crivello: What disaster can be compared to the loss of Cicero's *Republic*, of the *Economics* of Xenophon translated by Cicero into Latin, of thirty-five books of Polybius's *History*, of Livy's *Decades*, of Ovid's tragedy, *Medea*, and six books of his *Fasti*, of the greater part of Terence's comedies, which were forgotten, as were many other lost masterpieces, along with any reverence for their name? [1.175–76, 15–16].[71]

Print, we learn, would have allowed the truly great to have endured, so that all those lost classical books "would have been preserved in spite of the barbarians destroying them with fire or carrying them off to their lands along with other booty from wretched Italy" (1.176, 16).[72] Somewhere, tucked away in the recesses of a house or monastery or church, one of those volumes would surely have fallen into our hands, if only it had it been printed. Then the author would have survived, and our understanding of the past would have been more complete. Reproduction equals conservation and, best of all, immortality. "But I am all the more certain," Doni likewise insists in his *Pitture*, which he composed toward the end of his life, "the written word through the means of the press will last more centuries [than other art forms, such as paintings]."[73] For Doni, as for Domenichi, then, reproduction of ideas in print was always more of a blessing than a curse.

With this in mind, we might consider in conclusion how the power of print as Doni fantasizes about it, with all its imagined capacity to confer honor and preserve authority, relates to Doni's search for uniqueness through his presentation manuscripts composed in significant numbers beginning with the late 1550s.[74] As a printer versed in the appearance of mechanically reproduced books, and as a polygraph who worked closely with printers in Venice for a number of years, Doni often labored, as Giorgio Masi has observed, to make his calligraphic letters in his manuscripts resemble "the standard of the characters used in typography," much in keeping with how he imagined such manuscripts should appear when he discusses the function of printing in his *Marmi* and compares printed books to manuscripts in the course of both critiquing and defending the art of printing.[75] But Doni also aimed in general for his manuscripts to stand out as special works made by his hand alone, even as they often borrowed from midsixteenth-century standards of print culture in their overall format and appearance. His manuscripts were also purposely directed toward a specific destinee to whose tastes he meant to appeal through a variety of visual and verbal means, right down to the handwriting. In an age of mechanical reproduction, the manuscripts Doni created were intended to strike readers and viewers as unique works of art grounded in a specific time and place and directed by a specific author-artist to a particular patron-collector.[76]

Indeed, "the notable formal care" of his manuscripts, as Masi synthetically observes, "testifies to the full knowledge on his part of the need to emphasize in the manuscript as a work [*opera*] those characteristics of external value and distinction, as a *unicum* that distinguished it, in an epoch devoted to the affirmation of the book as a means of communication and a type of consumption at the ready grasp of the always more vast swaths of the public."[77] Moreover, it is clear that Doni's interest in composing manuscripts for specific individuals began in earnest in about 1557, though he also drafted manuscripts as early as 1546–1547, 1550, and 1554, none of which, however, are richly illustrated (see appendix). It is also clear that by 1557, with the designing of his *Stufaiuolo*, and then later with the same comedy in 1559, Doni began to feel he could enhance his manuscripts with his drawings. Consequently, he devoted attention to these drawings after 1557 and increasingly lavished attention on their design and how they should appear in his manuscripts. As such, by the time he left Venice in 1555 and set out on his own once more, roughly around the time he lambasted Aretino in his blistering attack, the *Terremoto*, Doni is presenting himself with these manuscripts not only as a professional writer of talent—a writer, that is, who could meet a plethora of public interests with his variety of printed books and with his full grasp of disegno—but also as a draftsman of some dexterity who could produce manuscripts as collectable works of art. He is presenting those manuscripts, in short, as original, creative objects, perhaps even new forms of expression for someone as multitalented in the visual and verbal arts as he.

Needless to say, in putting together his manuscripts to be presented as gifts, Doni must have felt that a book drafted in his own hand, as well as a book designed by him, might just have appealed more to potential patrons, and thus perhaps more readily win him their favor and a longed-for position at court, patronage, or at least financial assistance in bringing some of his more elaborately designed manuscripts into print.[78] Doni lavished attention on a number of these delightful and elegant manuscripts, and he sought to refine some of them over time, adjusting the ideas expressed in them to meet the tastes and interests of the designated recipient. Doni was a gifted illustrator who sometimes aimed to dazzle the eye in his manuscripts, as well as a gifted writer who aimed to delight the ear. Furthermore, we should note that he sometimes liked to reveal his dexterous calligraphic hand within the body of his manuscripts as a particularly speedy one. At one point in his manuscripts on emblems he presented his hand, in fact, as capable of vying with the rapidity and productivity of a printing press that mechanically fashioned books by the hundreds. Yet it is also important to point out that for all his love of prestezza he obviously took the time to craft slowly, painstakingly, and meticulously a number of his manuscripts. Put differently, though Doni labors in his manuscripts to come off as supremely cavalier when he flaunts the fact that he is churning out one copy after another with the speed of a printing press, he is no doubt striking a pose as he makes this audacious claim. He aims through this posturing to maximize his sprezzatura, even if, all things considered, his nonchalance as a fast-paced writer and visual artist comes off professionally through hyperbole as affettazione rather than Castiglione-like coolness and suave, courtly bravura. Indeed, in an address to Duke Alfonso II d'Este within the fabric of the *Le dimostrationi de gli animi degli huomini* (1561), Doni announces that a second book on emblems (of which we have no physical record) should come out in print in Lyons and that, even if this book presented to the duke does not appear then or afterwards in print, he has nevertheless produced (he claims with characteristic fustian boastfulness) so many versions of the book in his own hand that it would matter little, in the end, if it actually finds its way into print.[79] This is Doni at his best: aggressive, bold, overly self-confident, full of bluster. Far from just competing with other professional writers, such as Domenichi, whose writing about the merits and demerits of print he freely plagiarized, Doni is now ludicrously competing, it can only be said, with a machine.

Though Doni eventually turned to producing manuscripts in his career as a professional writer, and though he boasted in his manuscripts on emblems that he could match the speed of the printing press with his agile, fast-paced hand, in the earlier years of his career as a polygraph in Venice it is clear, as we have seen, that print production had certain advantages over manuscript production for Doni. Print simply permeated his consciousness. Even his manuscripts, in format and in the designs themselves, often borrowed from the image and look of print. For in the end, printing is indeed magical, he exclaims in the *Marmi*, precisely because it can be reproduced. Moreover, printing, at least in the minds of many, is according to Doni closer to alchemy than any other "art." "La stampa," he candidly observes in the *Libraria*, "poi è uno essercizio alchimistico" (printing, then, is an alchemistic exercise, 67).[80] From a mass of pulp transformed into paper, some ink, and the turn of a wheel on a press, one gets—lo and behold!—magically a book. And the creative, alchemical process marveled over by fools, who mistakenly think it such an easy job to transform paper and ink into real monetary gain, is not only physical as the printer takes varying materials and transforms them into something distinctive of marketable value.[81] The creative, alchemical process of producing printed books even extends to the conceptual and the imaginary as writers take a multitude of books, together with a veritable deluge of words contained within them, and construct yet one more book to print and read through the midsixteenth-century art of riscrittura: "We put before ourselves a pile of books, in which there is inside a flood of words, and with that mixing of them together we make others, so that from so many we are able to extract one more" (*di tanti libri ne caviamo uno*; 247). One book leads to another, just as one book assimilates others. The process of re-creation endlessly reproduces itself, "whence," as Doni puts it in his *I mondi*, "our discovery of the printing press is like the Hydra [the mythical serpent slain by Hercules], which, once its head has been cut off, gives birth to seven in its place." Books in print organically and miraculously give birth to other books in print, one by one, so that, he exults, "it seems to me that one book gives birth to thousands."[82]

It is through this process of renewal—through the imaginative process of reproducing those books (and, we might add, through the imaginative process of reproducing other people's books circulating in manuscript and printed form)—that Doni, perhaps taking his cue from the reproducibility of print itself, aimed throughout his career as a professional writer in Venice to renew himself by reproducing yet more versions of himself in verbal form for us to appreciate and take note of. To be sure, no one did this more aggressively than Doni in sixteenth-century Italy, not even the inveterate performer Aretino. And no one more than Doni championed the importance of books as objects to collect and consume, for each and every one of them contains and preserves within it the indelible presence, if not the unique voice, of an author, thanks to the enduring capacity of print.

In this regard, we might let the last words in this chapter go to Doni, that incorrigible man of professional impropriety, whose words about the reading and writing of books in his own time are used as the framing epigraph to *this* book; whose works produced with such velocity and verve are only recently beginning to come out in critical editions[83]; and whose sense of selfhood was so influenced by the "magical" press in the age of mechanical reproduction of midsixteenth-century Italy, even when he blithely reproduced the writings of another and passed them off, word for word, as his own:

> The eternity of one's name is something that can be preserved in more substantial matter than paper. Yet surely you cannot deny that some people have been made more famous by paper and writings than by metal and marble. And you could have well understood what I just said with regard to statues and other works of antiquity. Because the latter were preserved only for a short period or else have come down to our times marred or broken, so I cannot see how they have attained their purpose. But the former, to the marvel of whoever has come after, have made appear alive and whole the likenesses
>
> of those who will not be without fame
> if the universe itself does not first dissolve.
> [*di tai che non saranno senza fama,*
> *se l'universo pria non si dissolve.* 1.175, 14][84]

Epilogue

THE COURT IN SIXTEENTH-CENTURY ITALY was a complex socioeconomic and political system—admittedly more complex than what this book, under some pressure for compression, could possibly give shape to in a fully nuanced way. Far from being static, monolithic, and one-dimensional, much less oppressively and eerily panoptic in its ability to peer into every participant's life, the court in sixteenth-century Italy, scholars have increasingly come to realize, changed over time. It varied from place to place. It did not constitute the only locus for people to demonstrate and enact sociability. And in the visual arts it involved the coexistence of other forms of socioeconomic exchange and interaction, such as guilds, gift giving, friendship, literary and artistic academies, associations formed through epistolary and sonnet exchange, on-spec and export "markets," and the like. The primary visual artists discussed in the core chapters of this book, Benvenuto Cellini and Michelangelo Buonarroti, are in fact quite exceptional among the larger group of practitioners in the period. These two artists were able to create a demand for their products that was extraregional and associated with their particular virtuosity and expertise. They were also able to play different patronage and homosocial environments off one another in a manner that gave them greater mobility and choice in determining their working environments: Florence, Rome, and the French court, for Cellini, and chiefly Florence and Rome for Michelangelo. Both artists also had literary pretensions, which was not the norm in the period and only conferred greater status on them—the Florentine mannerist painter Agnolo Bronzino being another exception in this regard.[1] In sum, there were many artists who still operated within the guild system, or who worked for corporations and individuals whom we would not necessarily associate with court culture (confraternities, guilds, monasteries, abbots and abbesses, and the like). The artist-courtier discussed in this book, including those examined in the Introduction (Giorgio Vasari and Baccio Bandinelli, for instance), constituted a model that would have been exceptional rather than normative for practitioners in the visual arts of the period, and it was a model full of difficulties for visual artists to aspire to on account of their social status, social connections, level of education, and knowledge of the appropriate behavioral conventions.

This is therefore a book, all things considered, that is fundamentally about the elite. It focuses on men who labored during a period when most practitioners of the visual arts operated within the artisanal sector of the economy and social hierarchy. It examines how certain members aspiring to be a part of the elite, to be engaged by the elite in some manner, or to be recognized by the elite, were represented as having purposely and somewhat astonishingly deviated from accepted habits of proper comportment.

Now humanists in particular, as is well known, contributed significantly to the formation of professional identity in the Italian Renaissance as they exercised or wrote about professions. This contribution took place at a time when there was, more generally, an increased concern for, and arguably more developed and variegated discourse about, professional choice and experience in both high and low culture. As George McClure has argued, Italy experienced a profound shift in a "rhetoric of profession" from the midfifteenth century to the end of the sixteenth, with rhetoric here understood not just as the formal art of persuasion (though McClure does consistently focus throughout his study on an epideictic rhetoric of praise and rebuke) but as a discourse that is bounded with traceable commonplaces (*topoi*) and historically and culturally determined. This shift in a rhetoric of profession involved, among other things, a marked attention to professional self-definition; a truly broad-based cultural exploration, leveling, and secularization of professions; an increased attention to the value of vocational choice and work as a source of happiness and self-worth; a popularizing of these issues through the commercial press and in the vulgar tongue; an astonishing proliferation of the topic of professions in a variety of less learned cultural forms, from encyclopedic compendiums to chronicles, to jokes, to civic rituals, to carnival songs, to parlor games; and an extraordinary increase in—as well as cultural acceptance of and resistance toward—different professions *as* professions. The contribution of humanists was therefore one among many, all of which culminated in Tomaso Garzoni's cornucopian *La piazza universale di tutte le professioni del mondo*, a quirky encyclopedic book that was composed and printed at the end of the sixteenth century and that, in all its exuberant cornucopia, covered virtually every profession under the sun, from that of lofty lawyers to lowly latrine cleaners.[2]

At the heart of this broad-based discourse about professional formation and self-definition was, as is also well known, a major ideological concern of the period: propriety. As Norbert Elias observed in his classic *The Civilizing Process*, new "thresholds of embarrassment and shame" emerged within court culture in the Renaissance, especially, as Jacob Burckhardt intuited, in the Italian Renaissance. More recently, Rudolph Bell has demonstrated how an impressive production of printed how-to books in Renaissance Italy meticulously detailed every aspect of proper behavior, from infant nursing to child rearing.[3] Boundary violations began to be processed in all sorts of ways in a period that policed behavior with a vengeance, whether those boundaries had to do with the body, confined domestic spaces, walled urban environments, or broad public regions. Cleanliness, civility, court culture, and centralized authority were tightly bound together. Language needed to be purged of infelicities of speech, crude barbarisms, and awkward spellings, much as a servant might vigorously apply scented soap (an increasingly important product of the period) to a worn shirt to scour it clean of the filth that would otherwise mar the appearance of a decorous gentleman standing elegantly about in court, dining at a well-stocked table, or conversing in the midst of a sort of fashionable salon. One had to appear in the right manner, with elegant slivers of white peeking out about hems and collars, just as one had to speak and write in precisely the right way, whether it be in the form of the resuscitated classicizing Latin favored by humanists or the highly instrumentalized medium of the vernacular then in vogue. To phrase it crudely, one not only had to spell very well in Renaissance Italy to succeed among the cultural elite but also—as Gaston Godin in Vladimir Nabokov's *Lolita* would have no doubt quipped—smell very well. Decorum ruled. Etiquette typically affected position. Propriety lent distinction, much as it helped confer (but did not necessarily guarantee) status.

All in all, then, as interest in professional self-definition intensified and as competition within the verbal and visual arts increased markedly,[4] writers in sixteenth-century Italy concerned themselves not just with professional know-how but also professional comportment. Overall their concern was practical *and* behavioral as they policed professional performance. Castiglione, for instance, is not just explaining and describing through examples elegantly ensconced in Ciceronian dialogue form what to do within the court and, conversely, what not to do. He is also demonstrating through those examples and his own deft performance as a writer *how* to perform. He aims to come off as a model type of person, which he always sought to exemplify in his own work as a courtier and ambassador. Similarly, Vasari is interested in not just what artwork was constructed and for whom and when, but the character of the person who did the work and why certain types of people with certain personalities (such as the temperate and moderate Vasari himself) were better suited to do specific forms of work and would therefore prosper in the courtly world within which Vasari played such a vital and versatile part. And certain types of personalities, we may tacitly assume, are in the end simply better adapted for certain forms of work in certain environments at certain periods. Hence, when Castiglione, Vasari, and others urged collectively that what one needed to survive and thrive in the courtly world of sixteenth-century Italy was moderation, sociability, prudence, discretion, gentility, grace, affability, sweetness, and temperance, among other qualities of character deemed laudable at the time, one would have probably been well advised to heed their counsel.

For the most part, despite their occasional disappointments, these men succeeded professionally. Others who ostensibly exhibited these behavioral traits and who exercised these virtues of polish and decorous restraint, from Raphael to Bembo to Titian, seemed to have succeeded too, sometimes brilliantly. And so it was as well for men in other fields of professional expertise, such as the mathematician, scientist, and astronomer Galileo Galilei, who, as Mario Biagioli has demonstrated, succeeded in court culture not just because he was exceptionally good at what he did but also because he behaved the way he did with the requisite politia.[5] He had the acumen, but he also had the polish. Proper comportment matched with excellence in professional expertise did not guarantee success, but arguably it helped pave the way for it. It was to everyone's advantage to behave appropriately. Good manners mattered professionally; it was better, for instance, to be inconspicuously conspicuous, as Castiglione maintained, than aggressively so.

But then again there were others, men of egregious professional impropriety, such as the incomparable and intransigent "superstar" Michelangelo,[6] whom the Venetian painter Sebastiano del Piombo confirmed terrified his very superiors: "you frighten everyone," he observed with some astonishment, "including popes" (*ma facte paura a ognuno, insino a' papi*).[7] Michelangelo's off-putting, contumacious, immoderate, and sometimes fearsome and curmudgeonly behavior marks him as representing not just a change in degree—the "divine" Michelangelo, of course, happens to be more terrifying for Sebastiano, we may presume, than other visual artists before him—but also a change in *kind*, as an unparalleled figure of intensity and terribilità worthy of eliciting awe. Historically Michelangelo's comportment, as it is represented by Vasari and Condivi and in Michelangelo's own letters, marks a significant change in behavior on the part of a sculptor, painter, and architect seeking recognition in Renaissance Italy in the visual arts as he repeatedly, consciously, and aggressively violated accepted codes of conduct in a truly grand manner. We are dealing here with an entirely new economy of scale, aptly enough, we might say, in a period so invested in the sublimity of the colossal, from Julius II's massive planned imperial reconstruction of the Vatican to the sort of magnificent palaces sprouting in major urban centers. In the same way, Aretino's behavior, as he stages himself aggressively and conspicuously in print as the sometimes intimidating, larger-than-life "scourge of princes," stands out as new within the verbal arts in Italy. Aretino was unrestrained and aggressive in an unprecedented way and on an unprecedented scale, lending him a sort of celebrity status, in great measure thanks to his ability to capitalize, as Erasmus in another context and manner did,[8] on the commercialization of language through the medium of print. In terms of comportment, a different breed of professional writer and visual artist seems to have emerged on the grand scale in such figures as Michelangelo and Aretino in the first half of sixteenth-century Italy. And these men then stood as viable models for others later in the century, paving the way through their behavioral excesses for the immoderate comportment of such bellicose visual artists and writers as Cellini and Doni in the generation succeeding them.

In many ways the sometimes unbridled comportment of these men, at least as it finds itself represented in a variety of venues, resonates with that of some of the abrasive, aggressive, off-putting, and fearsome figures of power of the previous generation and their own time, from Cesare Borgia, the brilliant yet menacing condottiere, to Julius II, the indomitable, terrifying, and mercurial warrior pope. Indeed, within their culture men such as Aretino, Michelangelo, Cellini, and Doni occasionally presented themselves and were represented *as if* they had self-evident power and authority—as if, that is to say, they were men of such stature and clout and virility within their professions as writers and visual artists that they could permit themselves the luxury of acting sometimes with unrestrained aggressivity in a courtly world that would not normally condone their ill-mannered, immoderate behavior. Perhaps most stunningly, they appeared as if they were entitled to behave the way they did.

Why they felt so entitled is especially intriguing and worth a word in conclusion. In many instances they were undoubtedly asserting their honor, their own sense of self-respect grounded often enough, though not exclusively, in their uncompromising belief in their professional excellence, so that their violations of accepted codes of conduct, rather than diminishing their honor, paradoxically allowed them to garner more of it. (Indeed, some of the men discussed in this book received substantial material proof of the honor bestowed on them over time, physical and demonstrable evidence, that is, of their distinction, status, and virtù, such as the gold chain hung around Aretino's neck and prominently displayed in portraits of him.) In many instances they engaged in professional rivalries with uninhibited vehemence in a highly competitive world, as they contended for coveted commissions in the visual arts and for widespread, sometimes pan-European exposure through the highly instrumentalized medium of print, hoping, as always, that they would prove victorious through an agon that was at once fierce and self-aggrandizing. In many instances they no doubt sought to attract attention to themselves on the grand scale, to heighten and broaden their own fame, and to feed a competitive yearning to earn recognition—indeed, to *demand* recognition—as men of unsurpassed ingegno, with an inimitable talent, maniera, and fantasia worthy of placing them among the truly great. At the very least they were expressing themselves in the moment that they publicized themselves, perhaps not as socially unfettered "free" men harboring a "social message," to borrow Peter Burke's terms,[9] since these artists and writers were so keenly conscious of the constraints placed on them and the roles they sometimes had to play in an increasingly stratified world, but certainly as men who felt free enough to present themselves as they saw fit, and in the end as conspicuously and aggressively as they did.

These men, with their highly aggressive performative selves, thus helped redefine not just what it meant to do *something* in a profession in sixteenth-century Italy, but indeed what it meant behaviorally to be *someone* in a profession. And in the process they invested themselves, as I have argued in the core chapters of this book, in often novel and exciting ways in their visual and verbal art.

APPENDIX

Extant Manuscripts with Designs by Doni, in Rough Order

1. "Musical Manuscripts," Biblioteca Nazionale di Firenze [BNF], II.III.437–40. Date: ca. 1546–47.
   Dedicated to Cosimo I.

2. *Humori del Doni*, Biblioteca del Museo Civico Correr, ms. misc. Correr LI/2187. Date: ca. 1550.

3. *Discorsi del Doni*, BNF, Fondo Landau Finaly, ms. 257. Date: ca. 1554.
   Dedicated to Aluigi d'Este.
   There is a modern edition: *Umori e sentenze*, eds. Vincenza Giri and Giorgio Masi, with a presentation by Renzo Bragantini (Rome: Salerno, 1988).

4. *Lo stufaiuolo*, Houghton Library, Harvard University, ms. Typ 853.
   No date, but certainly after 1551.
   Dedicated to Ottavio Farnese, duke of Parma.

5. *Lo stufaiuolo*, Biblioteca Valentiniana di Camerino, ms. 2. Date: 1557.
   Dedicated to Pietro Cesis, president of Romagna.

6. *Lo stufaiuolo*, Biblioteca Riccardiana, ms. 1184. Date: 1559.
   Dedicated to Jacopo Piccolomini.
   There is a modern edition: *Tutte le novelle, Lo stufaiuolo* (Milan: G. Daelli, 1863).

The dating of the Doni manuscripts is a complex task and has finally been worked out by Giorgio Masi. See his article, with Carlo Alberto Girotto, "Le carte di Anton Francesco Doni," *L'Ellisse* 3 (2008): 1–51.

7. *La villa Fucchera, libro primo delle Ville del Doni*, Bayerische Staatsbibliothek of Munich, codices italici 36. Date: November 13, 1559.
Dedicated to Jacob Fuegger.

8. *Attavanta: Villa del Doni*, Biblioteca del Museo Civico Correr, ms. Correr 1433. Date: ca. 1559–60.
Dedicated to Pandolfo Attavanti.

9. *Le nuove pitture*, Città del Vaticano, Biblioteca Apostolica Vaticana (BAV), codice Patetta, ms. 364. Date: 1560.
Dedicated to Luigi d'Este.
See the comments (as well as the illustrations) in the modern edition: *Pitture del Doni*, ed. Sonia Maffei (Naples: Arte Tipografico, 2004), with a number of reproductions of Doni's images in it, and especially *Le nuove pitture del Doni fiorentino: Libro primo consacrato al mirabil Signor Donno Aloise da Este, illustrissimo et reverendissimo*, eds. Sonia Maffei, Virgilio Bernardoni, and Carlo Alberto Girotto (Naples: La Stanza delle Scritture, 2006). There are no such designs in the printed version of the *Pitture del Doni* (Padua: Perchacino, 1564).

10. *Le dimostrationi de gli animi degli huomini*, BNF, Fondo Palatino, ms. E.B.10.8. Date: 1561 (after April).
Dedicated to Duke Alfonso II d'Este.
One of Doni's finest and most elegantly designed manuscripts, far more finely worked than the one designed the same year, *Una nuova opinione*, which was a fair copy.

11. *Una nuova opinione del Doni circa all'imprese amorose et militari*, BNF, Nuovi Acquisti, ms. 267. Date: 1561.
Dedicated to Davit Otto.
This manuscript is the "fair copy" for the Museo Correr 1387, also dedicated to Otto but not designed by Doni.
Le dimostrationi contains fifty-eight images and *Una nuova opinione* fifty-nine. There is obvious overlap between the two manuscripts, with some reordering, compression, and minor rewording. The two manuscripts share fifty-two images, counting compression of images. A few images, however, are not shared: seven in *Le dimostrationi* do not appear in *Una nuova opinione*, and six in *Una nuova opinione* do not appear in *Le dimostrationi*. We should also note that it is clear that Doni substantially revised the book of emblems as he first began to conceive it in 1552. The book in manuscript form presented as a gift in its various guises to a number of men is not the same one Doni had first projected in his two letters to Marcolini of 1552: in fact, very few of the emblems outlined in the letter to Marcolini actually

appear in the manuscripts of his books of emblems. See Anton Francesco Doni, *Tre libri di lettere* (Venice: Marcolini, 1552), 310, but also 310–13 and 372–81.

12. *I numeri*, Vienna, Nationalbibliothek, Codex Vindobon, Palatinus, ms. 10892. Date: February 11, 1562.
Dedicated to Georg Fuegger.
There is a modern facsimile copy, ed. Alessandra del Fante, *I numeri* (Rome: Bulzoni, 1981).

13. *Primo libro delle sentenze*, Biblioteca Estense di Modena, ms. γS.I.63. Date: March 1, 1562.
Dedicated to Francesco de' Medici.
There is a modern edition: *Umori e sentenze.*

14. *Imprese reali*, Wellesley College Library, Frances Taylor Pearsons Plimpton Collection, ms. 897. Date: January 27, 1563.
This manuscript shares some designs with the other two manuscripts on emblems in Doni's hand but is largely different, with no accompanying text; it is more narrowly dedicated, as the title indicates, to emblems of royal and influential families and illustrious persons. It is also less finely worked.

15. *Le ville del Doni libro V*, Biblioteca Municipale di Reggio Emilia, ms. Regg. F. 536. Date: November 3, 1565.
Dedicated to Count Orazio Malaguzzi.
On the *Ville*, see the modern edition edited by Ugo Bellocchi (Modena: Aedes Muratoriana, 1969).

16. *La lumiera*, British Library, ms. Add 33790. Date: September 3, 1567.
Dedicated to Gianvincenzo Gonzaga.
There is a modern edition: Fredi Chiappelli, "Un poema inedito e sconosciuto di Anton Francesco Doni," *La rassegna della letteratura italiana* 58 (1954): 561–68.

17. *Le ville del Doni*, Biblioteca Trivulziana di Milano, ms. Triv. 15. Date: April 1, 1573.
Dedicated to Paolo Calvini.

18. *La guerra di Cipro*, Biblioteca Universitaria di Padova, ms. 4. Date: ca. 1574.
In July 1574 Doni traveled to Venice to give the poem to the King of France, Henry III.
There is a modern edition: *La guerra di Cipro*, ed. Vincenzo Jacomuzzi (Turin: Tirrenia Stampatori, 2001).

Notes

Notes to Introduction

1. I should stress that I am speaking of visual artists and writers. There were women, of course, who acted in untoward and aggressive ways in sixteenth-century Italy, but they were not, to my knowledge, visual artists and writers. See, for instance, the observations about gender with respect to insults and aggressive behavior in Renaissance Venice and Rome in Elizabeth Horodowich, *Language and Statecraft in Early Modern Venice* (Cambridge: Cambridge University Press, 2008); and Thomas V. Cohen and Elizabeth S. Cohen, *Words and Deeds in Renaissance Rome: Trials Before the Papal Magistrates* (Toronto: University of Toronto Press, 1993), 45–64, 85–95, and *passim*.

2. On polygraphs, the major studies are Giovanni Aquilecchia, "Pietro Aretino e altri poligrafi a Venezia," in *Storia della cultura veneta*, eds. Girolamo Arnaldi e Manlio Pastore Stocchi, vol. 3, pt. 2 (Vicenza: Neri Pozza, 1980), 61–98; Claudia di Filippo Bareggi, *Il mestiere di scrivere: Lavoro intellettuale e mercato librario a Venezia nel Cinquecento* (Rome: Bulzoni, 1988); Renzo Bragantini, "Poligrafi e umanisti volgari," in *Storia della letteratura italiana*, ed. Enrico Malato, vol. 4, *Il primo Cinquecento* (Rome: Salerno, 1996), 681–754; and Paul F. Grendler, *Critics of the Italian World, 1530–1560: Anton Francesco Doni, Nicolò Franco and Ortensio Lando* (Madison: University of Wisconsin Press, 1969).

3. At the same time, it is important to point out that the dependence of artists on the patronage system in sixteenth-century Italy did prove to be as much a boon as a bane when it came to securing commissions and maintaining a steady flow of work. On visual artists and the courts generally in Europe, see Martin Warnke, *The Court Artist: On the Ancestry of the Modern Artist*, trans. David McLintock (Cambridge: Cambridge University Press, 1993), who also argues on pp. 249–52 for the centrality of court culture in the creation of "artistic eccentricity" and "recalcitrance." As the artist within the court positioned himself as irreplaceable, so, according to Warnke, he adopted new habits of comportment to present himself as such—and as a "genius." For an overview of the professionalization of the painter in the Renaissance and the role of the court, see Bram Kempers, *Painting, Power, and Patronage: The Rise of the Professional Artist in Renaissance Italy*, trans. Beverley Jackson (London: Penguin, 1987), 219–309. For reassessments of Warnke, with thoughts on eccentric artists of the period as "vertical invaders," see Stephen J. Campbell, "Introduction," *Artists at*

Court: Image-Making and Identity, 1300–1500, ed. Stephen J. Campbell (Boston: Isabella Stewart Gardner Museum, 2004), 9–18; and Evelyn Welch, "Painting as Performance in the Italian Renaissance Court," ibid., 19–32, who argues, as she has elsewhere, for the problematics associated with the term *court artist*.

4. A solid overview of this enormous topic with respect to the papacy and the role of cardinals as patrons in Rome remains the magisterial synthesis by Charles L. Stinger, *The Renaissance in Rome* (Bloomington: Indiana University Press, 1985).

5. The courts patronized much more in the arts, such as music, in the sixteenth century, but this book focuses strictly on visual and verbal art. According to Rab Hatfield, for instance, "The High End: Michelangelo's Earnings," 195 and *passim*, in *The Art Market in Italy: 15th–17th Centuries*, eds. Marcello Fantoni, Louisa C. Matthew, and Sara F. Matthews-Grieco (Modena: F. C. Panini, 2003), 195–201, Michelangelo was the first "superstar" in an emergent "'star system' in the arts," which paved the way for such successful and wealthy artists as Rubens and Bernini.

6. On Vasari, see in general Patricia Lee Rubin, *Giorgio Vasari: Art and History* (New Haven, Conn.: Yale University Press, 1995). I have also found of value Leon George Satkowski, *Giorgio Vasari: Architect and Courtier* (Princeton: Princeton University Press, 1993); and Mario Pozzi and Enrico Mattioda, *Giorgio Vasari: Storico e critico* (Florence: Olschki, 2006). I cite from the 1568 edition throughout, unless otherwise indicated, and from Giorgio Vasari, *Le vite dei più eccellenti pittori, scultori e architetti* (Florence: Newton, 1991).

7. On which see also, more generally, Douglas Biow, *The Culture of Cleanliness in Renaissance Italy* (Ithaca, N.Y.: Cornell University Press, 2006), 54.

8. Patricia Fortini Brown, *Private Lives in Renaissance Venice: Art, Architecture, and the Family* (New Haven, Conn.: Yale University Press, 2004), vii, but see also 3–5: "The term *politia* had two distinct, if related, meanings in the sixteenth century. One usage derived from the Greek *politeia* and connoted good government, the political life, and civil comportment. Another came from the Latin *politus*, meaning refinement in fashion, politeness of behavior, or the display of luxury. The word is related, as well, to the Italian *pulita* or *polita*: a gleaming cleanliness and orderliness." For a broad treatment of the topic in primarily verbal form, see Biow, *The Culture of Cleanliness*.

9. Martin Kemp, ed., *Leonardo on Painting: An Anthology of Writings by Leonardo da Vinci with a Selection of Documents Relating to His Career as an Artist*, trans. Martin Kemp and Margaret Walker (New Haven, Conn.: Yale University Press, 1989), 38–39; Paola Barocchi, ed., *Scritti d'arte del Cinquecento*, vol. 1 (Milan: Ricciardi Editore, 1971), 475. Paolo Pino, *Dialogo di pittura* in *Trattati d'arte del Cinquecento*, vol. 1, ed. Paola Barocchi (Bari: Laterza, 1960), 137, voices similar concerns about cleanliness, though he is concerned with the potentially sullying work of painters, whom Leonardo instead deemed to be professionally clean.

10. Benvenuto Cellini, *Vita*, ed. Ettore Camesasca (Milan: BUR, 1985), 298.

11. Rubin, *Giorgio Vasari*, 154, succinctly characterizes the Vasarian project regarding manners and style in the context of established humanist history writing in the period.

12. Vasari is naturally more emphatic about the role of Medicean patronage in the flowering of the arts in Florence in the 1568 version, on which see the concise observations of Rubin, *Giorgio Vasari*, 200–203.

13. More generally, see Pozzi and Mattioda, *Giorgio Vasari*, the section "Il perfetto artista," 309–92.

14. On Vasari's Raphael, see the synthetic observations of Rubin, *Giorgio Vasari*, the chapter "Raphael, the New Apelles," 357–401, esp. 374–79 on his grazia, courtly manners, and art.

15. For a balanced account of Piero di Cosimo's life in Vasari's *Vite*, see the concise remarks of Louis A. Waldman, "Fact, Fiction, Hearsay: Notes on Vasari's Life of Piero di Cosimo," *Art Bulletin* 82 (2000): 171–79; and more generally Dennis Geronimus, *Piero di Cosimo: Visions Beautiful and Strange* (New Haven, Conn.: Yale University Press, 2006), 1–33. On Vasari's purposive use of Piero's life as part of an overall rhetorical strategy, see Sharon Fermor, *Piero di Cosimo: Fiction, Invention and "Fantasìa"* (London: Reaktion Books, 1993), 13–40. As Stephen J. Campbell (in private communication) observed, one crucial issue for Vasari is that Piero di Cosimo, in addition to being an eccentric, worked for a series of anti-Medicean patrons during the Republic. This would have colored Vasari's view of Piero di Cosimo.

16. I borrow the term *conversable space* from Jay Tribby, "Cooking (with) Clio and Cleo: Eloquence and Experiment in Seventeenth-Century Florence," *Journal of the History of Ideas* 52 (1991): 417–39; Tribby, "Body/Building: Living the Museum Life in Early Modern Europe," *Rhetorica* 10 (1992): 139–63; and Tribby, "Of Conversational Dispositions and the *Saggi*'s Proem," in *Documentary Culture: Florence and Rome from Grand-Duke Ferdinand I to Pope Alexander VII*, eds. Elizabeth Cropper, Giovanna Perini, and Francesco Solinas (Bologna: Nuova Alfa Editoriale, 1992), 379–90.

17. Arguing for the unreliability of Vasari's narrative, Elizabeth Pilliod, *Pontormo, Bronzino, Allori: A Genealogy of Florentine Art* (New Haven, Conn.: Yale University Press, 2001), 5, points out that "Vasari used his criticism of Pontormo to undermine not only Pontormo's legacy, but also the strength of the independent *bottega* system" in order to promote instead the "new institutional and state-oriented Accademia del Disegno."

18. On Piero di Cosimo in Vasari's *Vite* and fantasia, see also Fermor, *Piero di Cosimo*, 29–37.

19. On fantasia, see David Summers, *Michelangelo and the Language of Art* (Princeton: Princeton University Press, 1981), 103–43; and Martin Kemp, "From 'Mimesis' to 'Fantasia': The Quattrocento Vocabulary of Creation, Inspiration, and Genius in the Visual Arts," *Viator* 8 (1977): 347–98, esp. 361–98. I borrow the first quotation from Charles Dempsey, "Review of Michelangelo and the Language of Art by David Summers," *Burlington Magazine* 125 (1983): 625, who cautions against equating fantasia with imagination; and the second from Harry Berger, Jr., *Second World and Green World: Studies in Renaissance Fiction-Making*, ed. John Patrick Lynch (Berkeley: University of California Press, 1988), esp. 3–62. See also Fermor, *Piero di Cosimo*, 29–37.

20. On competition in Vasari, see James Clifton, "Vasari on Competition," *Sixteenth Century Journal* 27 (1996): 23–41.

21. Kemp, "From 'Mimesis' to 'Fantasia,'" 367.

22. On the topic of genius generally in the Italian Renaissance, see Noel L. Brann, *The Debate over the Origin of Genius During the Italian Renaissance: The Theories of Supernatural Frenzy and Natural Melancholy in Accord and in Conflict on the Threshold of the Scientific* (Leiden: Brill, 2002). See also Kemp, "From 'Mimesis' to 'Fantasia.'"

23. On Salviati's structural function in *Le vite*, see the concise observations in Rubin, *Giorgio Vasari*, 28–30.

24. On the problematics of Michelangelo's fantasia, see Stephen J. Campbell, "'Fare una Cosa Morta Parer Viva': Michelangelo, Rosso, and the (Un)Divinity of Art," *Art Bulletin* 84 (2002): 596–620.

25. Ibid.

26. A point made by the polygraph Lodovico Domenichi in his dedicatory letter to Francesco Salviati in his translation of Leon Battista Alberti, *La pittura* (Venice: Gabriel Giolito, 1547; rpt, Bologna: Forni, 1988), 3r–v.

27. On Bandinelli, see Louis A. Waldman, *Baccio Bandinelli and Art at the Medici Court: A Corpus of Early Modern Sources* (Philadelphia: American Philosophical Society, 2004); Rona Goffen, *Renaissance Rivals: Michelangelo, Leonardo, Raphael, Titian* (New Haven, Conn.: Yale University Press, 2002), 341–85; Kathleen Weil-Garris, "Bandinelli and Michelangelo: A Problem of Artistic Identity," in *Art, the Ape of Nature: Studies in Honor of H. W. Janson*, eds. Moshe Barasch, Lucy Freeman Sandler, and Patricia Egan (New York: Abrams, 1981), 223–51; and Leonard Barkan, *Unearthing the Past: Archaeology and Aesthetics in the Making of Renaissance Culture* (New Haven, Conn.: Yale University Press, 1999), 271–338. Louis A. Waldman has cautioned (in private correspondence) that we know so little about Bandinelli's own style as a painter that it is hard to guess who really executed it. We know from Vasari and from documents that after around 1530 the artist generally commissioned executants to carry out his various paintings. The style of the Gardner painting, according to Waldman, looks a lot like one of his hired brushes, Andrea del Minga. Still, the painting would have been to Bandinelli's design and should thus be counted as a self-portrait; the idea—disegno—was undoubtedly Bandinelli's.

28. Barkan, *Unearthing*, 271.

29. Brief but valuable observations on this self-portrait can be found in Goffen, *Renaissance Rivals*, 363–64.

30. Ibid., 362.

31. *Le vite*, 986–87.

32. Bandinelli's artistry has deservedly been the subject of much positive reevaluation over the past decade; see Waldman, Goffen, and Barkan.

33. Vasari is adamant in defending Michelangelo in this regard; *Le vite*, 1256.

34. It is difficult to characterize this group socially in global, unifying terms, even if di Filippo Bareggi, *Il mestiere*, 121 and *passim*, views them as constituting a "homogeneous" group; as Grendler, *Critics*, 65–69, observes, some came from undistinguished backgrounds, and others, such as Ludovico Dolce and Francesco Sansovino, from more respectable ones. For the purpose of this study, I have included Aretino among the polygraphs, as Grendler does, even if Aretino did not have the sort of direct experience with printing presses that characterizes the work of the polygraphs, and even though he enjoyed a much more fruitful and remunerative relationship with court culture. He nevertheless stood as the model for the polygraphs, over and against which they defined themselves both positively and negatively, with respect and hostility.

35. Vanni Bramanti, "Introduzione" to *La libraria*, ed. V. Bramanti (Milan: Longanesi & C., 1972), 16–17.

36. Noteworthy in this regard is the fierce squabble between George of Trebizond and Poggio Bracciolini, the two fifteenth-century humanists who, in the privacy of the Roman Curia, on May 4, 1452, allowed provocative words spoken in private to turn into an actual physical fight as they pummeled each other, with one humanist, Poggio, trying to poke out the eyes of the other in a state of maddening rage, while the other, George, restrained himself, as he later claimed in a letter, from using both his hands to firmly squeeze Poggio's testicles. John Monfasani, *George of Trebizond: A Biography and a Study of His Rhetoric and Logic* (Leiden: Brill, 1976), 109–11.

37. I am not counting here the physical attack against Nicolò Franco, since it did not come directly from Aretino, on which see Grendler, *Critics*, 42.

38. Grendler, *Critics*, 37–38 on Lando; 39–45 on Franco, whose poems against Aretino can be consulted in Franco, *Rime di Nicolò Franco contro Pietro Aretino* (Lanciano: Carabba, 1916). See also Roberto L. Bruni, "Polemiche cinquecentesche: Franco, Aretino, Domenichi," *Italian Studies* 32 (1977): 52–67.

39. As did Dolce also with Franco. See di Filippo Bareggi, *Il mestiere*, 294–301.

40. On Franco, see Margaret T. Rosenthal, *The Honest Courtesan: Veronica Franco, Citizen and Writer in Sixteenth-Century Venice* (Chicago: University of Chicago Press, 1992). We find the same strategy in place among a number of women writers of the Italian sixteenth century, including, for instance, Tullia d'Aragona, on which see Julia L. Hairston, "'Di sangue illustre & pellegrino': Eclipsing the Body in the Lyric of Tullia d'Aragona," in *The Body in Early Modern Italy*, eds. Julia L. Hairston and Walter Stephens (Baltimore: Johns Hopkins University Press, 2010).

41. Women could be and were indeed conspicuous, but they were not aggressively, relentlessly, and sometimes obnoxiously conspicuous as were the polygraphs. Arguably, they even lacked the capacity to strut and rebel as these men did within the realm of the imaginary, which only reminds us of how unfree women were to strike out as assertive oddballs in elitist culture. On this, see Deanna Shemek, *Ladies Errant: Wayward Women and Social Order in Early Modern Italy* (Durham, N.C.: Duke University Press, 1998), where half of the "errant" or "wayward" women in her book are imaginary and—with the exception of de Luna and perhaps the whores of chapter 1—tame, however threatening they may have been perceived to be. For a broad view, which takes into consideration social propriety from time to time, see Virginia Cox, *Women's Writing in Italy 1400–1650* (Baltimore: Johns Hopkins University Press, 2008), esp. 28, 36, 58, 79, 89, 92, 100–102, 136–37, 152, 154–55, 164; amid the plethora of women writers surveyed by Cox, none in the period covered in this book (roughly 1500–1575) can claim the sort of reputations of an Aretino or Doni. One has to wait until well into the seventeenth century and the period of the baroque to find Italian women writers who were so assertive and self-styled as "bizarre," on which see Cox, op. cit., 208–12.

42. Georg Lukács, *Realism in Our Time: Literature and the Class Struggle*, trans. John and Necke Mander (New York: Harper & Row, 1964), 93–135.

43. Di Filippo Bareggi, *Il mestiere*, 121–22, 143, and *passim*; only Dolce comes from Venice, though one could argue that Francesco Sansovino does as well.

44. On Aretino, indispensible is Paul Larivaille, *Pietro Aretino* (Rome: Salerno, 1997), who gives Aretino's estimates of his impressive income on p. 242. For his

relationship with court culture, see Giulio Ferroni, "Pietro Aretino e le corti," in *Pietro Aretino nel cinquecentario della nascita*, vol. 1 (Rome: Salerno, 1995), 23–48.

45. Aretino, to be sure, presents himself as distinct in this sense, advocating instead the familiar practice of polishing writing over time. For a compelling reading connecting Tintoretto's early artistry to the work of the polygraphs, and Aretino's distancing from Tintoretto's practice and the speed with which certain polygraphs produced their works and aligned themselves too closely with the mechanical arts of printing, see Tom Nichols, *Tintoretto: Tradition and Identity* (London: Reaktion Books, 1999), 69–99.

46. David Quint, "Courtier, Prince, Lady: The Design of the *Book of the Courtier*," *Italian Quarterly* 37 (2000): 185–95, reviews the scholarship on the topic and adds his own observations about how Castiglione's text is complicitous in this gender conflict. Of particular importance are the studies by Valeria Finucci, *The Lady Vanishes: Subjectivity and Representation in Castiglione and Ariosto* (Stanford: Stanford University Press, 1992); and Finucci, "In the Name of the Brother: Male Rivalry and Social Order in B. Castiglione's *Il libro del cortegiano*," *Exemplaria* 9 (1997): 91–116. See as well the most recent historical treatment of the topic in Horodowich, *Language*, 165–206.

47. Valuable in this context are, by contrast, the observations of Deanna Shemek, "'Mi mostrano a dito tutti quanti': Disease, Deixis, and Disfiguration in the *Lamento di una cortigiana ferrarese*," in *Medusa's Gaze: Essays on Gender, Literature, and Aesthetics in the Italian Renaissance, in Honor of Robert J. Rodini*, eds. Paul A. Ferrara, Eugenio Giusti, and Jane Tylus (Lafayette, Ind.: Bordighera Press, 2004), 49–64. See also Horodowich, *Language*, 191. For the case of Aretino, see the concise, excellent observations of Raymond B. Waddington, *Aretino's Satyr: Sexuality, Satire, and Self-Projection in Sixteenth-Century Literature and Art* (Toronto: University of Toronto Press, 2004), 41–46.

48. Lisa Pon, *Raphael, Dürer, and Marcantonio Raimondi: Copying and the Italian Renaissance Print* (New Haven, Conn.: Yale University Press, 2004).

49. Nothing in the art market (to the extent that we can call it such) matched the economy of scale of the print market, though the art market was evolving in the late sixteenth century and had a multiple character, with a complexity of relationships, a variety of producers, and a far different shape from place to place. On aspects of this evolution, see the concise observations of Richard A. Goldthwaite, "Economic Parameters of the Italian Art Market (15th–17th Centuries)," esp. 431–38, in Fantoni, Matthew, and Matthews-Grieco (eds.), *Art Market in Italy*, 423–44. An important qualification, however, needs to be made regarding artists who used print to their advantage to circulate their ideas and visual vocabulary. On aspects of the emergence and evolution of the profession, see Evelyn Lincoln, *The Invention of the Renaissance Printmaker* (New Haven, Conn.: Yale University Press, 2000).

50. Waddington, *Aretino's Satyr*, 34–55; he also observes, however, that it took some time for Aretino to "see the full possibilities of the new medium" of print (p. 34), on which, see Larivaille, *Aretino*, both for Aretino's strategies for receiving significant, sustaining financial gifts from patrons and his gradual instrumentalizing of the press. For the latter, see also Fabio Massimo Bertolo, *Aretino e la stampa: Strategie di autopromozione a Venezia nel Cinquecento* (Rome: Salerno, 2003).

51. Di Filippo Bareggio, *Il mestiere*, 254.

52. Harald Hendrix is currently working on the material conditions of Doni's

living spaces, as well as those of Aretino and other polygraphs, in a monograph tentatively titled *The Italian Writer's House: A Cultural History from Petrarch to Pasolini.*

53. On polygraphs and their relationships to courts, see di Filippo Bareggi, *Il mestiere*, 242–318. It is important to emphasize, as she does, that many felt the need, given the difficulty of making a living in the print market of Venice, to attach themselves to courts. Many may have written against court culture, but many needed it, since living by the pen as a polygraph did not make for an easy or stable career. As di Filippo Bareggi also points out, given the precariousness of living off the print marketplace, a number had to supplement their income as teachers or secretaries. Moreover, none made anywhere near the significant sum Aretino earned largely through patronage gifts, which Bertolo, *Aretino e la stampa*, 29, calculates at around 1,600 scudi annually—an amount that dwarfs the 100 scudi annually that Domenichi earned at his best during about the same period as the official historian for Cosimo I, beginning in 1552 (see di Filippo Bareggi, *Il mestiere*, 246). I am not aware of a comparative economic analysis of the wages of the polygraphs, who were not, I think it is safe to say, big earners. For wages in the period and the buying power of earnings, see Brian S. Pullan, "Wage-Earners and the Venetian Economy, 1550–1630," in *Crisis and Change in the Venetian Economy in the Sixteenth and Seventeenth Centuries*, ed. Brian Pullan (London: Methuen, 1968), 146–74. There are good accessible summaries about wages and buying power in the period in Venice in Iain Fenlon, *The Ceremonial City: History, Memory and Myth in Renaissance Venice* (New Haven, Conn.: Yale University Press, 2007), 252, and Brown, *Private Lives*, 86.

54. On Fioravanti in the ambit of polygraphs, see William Eamon, *Science and the Secrets of Nature: Books of Secrets in Medieval and Early Modern Culture* (Princeton: Princeton University Press, 1994), 168–93. More generally see Piero Camporesi, *Camminare il mondo: Vita e avventure di Leonardo Fioravanti, medico del Cinquecento* (Milan: Garzanti, 1997).

55. *Le vite*, 1162.

56. See Douglas Biow, *Mirabile Dictu: Representations of the Marvelous in Medieval and Renaissance Epic* (Ann Arbor: University of Michigan Press, 1996) for Italian literature; and James Biester, *Lyric Wonder: Rhetoric and Wit in Renaissance English Poetry* (Ithaca, N.Y.: Cornell University Press, 1997) for literature in England. More generally, in Italian criticism of the sixteenth century see Baxter Hathaway, *Marvels and Commonplaces: Renaissance Literary Criticism* (New York: Random House, 1968).

57. I borrow the term *unclassical* from Goffen, *Renaissance Rivals*, 102.

58. Fundamental here is the seminal work of Richard A. Goldthwaite, *Wealth and the Demand for Art in Italy, 1300–1600* (Baltimore: Johns Hopkins University Press, 1993). See as well adaptations of his position in Lisa Jardine, *Worldly Goods: A New History of the Renaissance* (New York: Norton, 1996); Paula Findlen, "Possessing the Past: The Material World of the Italian Renaissance," *American Historical Review* 103 (1998): 83–114; Brown, *Private Lives*; Evelyn S. Welch, *Shopping in the Renaissance: Consumer Cultures in Italy 1400–1600* (New Haven, Conn.: Yale University Press, 2005); and Dora Thornton, *The Scholar in His Study: Ownership and Experience in Renaissance Italy* (New Haven, Conn.: Yale University Press, 1997). See also the thoughts in Stephen J. Campbell, *The Cabinet of Eros: Renaissance Mythological Painting and the "Studiolo" of Isabella d'Este* (New Haven, Conn.: Yale University Press, 2004), 29–57.

59. Goldthwaite, *Wealth and the Demand*, 5.

60. On palaces and the construction industry, see Richard A. Goldthwaite, *The Building of Renaissance Florence: An Economic and Social History* (Baltimore: Johns Hopkins University Press, 1980); and, more generally, Goldthwaite, *Wealth and the Demand*.

61. Randolph Starn, "The European Renaissance," in *A Companion to the Worlds of the Renaissance*, ed. Guido Ruggiero (Malden, Mass.: Blackwell, 2002), 49.

62. Foremost in my mind here is the important article by John Jeffries Martin, "Inventing Sincerity, Refashioning Prudence: The Discovery of the Individual in Renaissance Europe," *American Historical Review* 102 (1997): 1309–42, which takes on, while still recognizing the value of, New Historicism. See as well more generally his *Myths of Renaissance Individualism* (New York: Palgrave Macmillan, 2004), and the studies by Natalie Zemon Davis, "Boundaries and the Sense of Self in Sixteenth-Century France," in *Reconstructing Individualism: Autonomy, Individuality, and the Self in Western Thought*, eds. Thomas C. Heller et al. (Stanford: Stanford University Press, 1986), 53–63; Ronald F. E. Weissman, "The Importance of Being Ambiguous: Social Relations, Individualism, and Identity in Renaissance Florence," in *Urban Life in the Renaissance*, eds. Susan Zimmerman and Ronald Weissman (Newark: Delaware University Press, 1989), 269–80; Thomas V. Cohen, *Love and Death in Renaissance Italy* (Chicago: University of Chicago Press, 2004); Horodowich, *Language*; Peter Burke, *The Italian Renaissance: Culture and Society in Italy* (Princeton: Princeton University Press, 1986); and Lauro Martines, *Strong Words: Writing and Social Strain in the Italian Renaissance* (Baltimore: Johns Hopkins University Press, 2001). I cite from Guido Ruggiero, *Machiavelli in Love: Sex, Self, and Society in the Italian Renaissance* (Baltimore: Johns Hopkins University Press, 2007), 8 and 112; but see also 21 and *passim*. Greene's term comes from Thomas Greene, "The Flexibility of the Self," in *The Disciplines of Criticism: Essays in Literary Theory, Interpretation, and History*, eds. Peter Demetz, Thomas Greene, and Lowry Nelson, Jr. (New Haven, Conn.: Yale University Press, 1968), 241–64. For an intellectual history of the development of the concept of the self over a *longue durée*, with only brief attention to the Renaissance in the early chapters, see Jerrold E. Seigel, *The Idea of the Self: Thought and Experience in Western Europe Since the Seventeenth Century* (Cambridge: Cambridge University Press, 2005).

63. The phrase *free, unfettered subjectivity* derives, of course, from Stephen Greenblatt, *Renaissance Self-Fashioning: From More to Shakespeare* (Chicago: University of Chicago Press, 1980), 256. I have explored issues related to the mystification of know-how in Douglas Biow, "Reflections on Professions and Humanism in Renaissance Italy and the Humanities Today," *Rinascimento* 43 (2003): 333–53.

64. Albert R. Ascoli, *Dante and the Making of a Modern Author* (Cambridge: Cambridge University Press, 2008).

65. I have in mind the famous letter in which Machiavelli discusses how he "transfers himself" into the past after a day of multiple activities. See Niccolò Machiavelli, *Tutte le opere*, ed. Mario Martelli (Florence: Sansoni, 1992), 1558–1560, letter 216. On Machiavelli and the many roles he played and strategies he deployed, consider in English, for instance, the studies of John M. Najemy, *Between Friends: Discourses of Power and Desire in the Machiavelli-Vettori Letters of 1513–1515* (Princeton: Princeton University Press, 1993); and Wayne A. Rebhorn, *Foxes and Lions: Machiavelli's Confidence Men* (Ithaca, N.Y.: Cornell University Press, 1988).

66. Ronald Witt, *In the Footsteps of the Ancients: The Origins of Humanism from Lovato to Bruni* (Leiden: Brill, 2000).

67. Tasso's life has been nicely summarized in Charles P. Brand, *Torquato Tasso: A Study of the Poet and of His Contributions to English Literature* (Cambridge: Cambridge University Press, 1965), 3–37; but for an in-depth biography, see Angelo Solerti, *Vita di Torquato Tasso*, 2 vols. (Rome: Loescher, 1895).

68. Solerti, *Vita di Torquato Tasso*, 306–495, discusses the events of Tasso's imprisonment.

69. Sergio Zatti, *L'uniforme cristiano e il multiforme pagano: Saggio sulla "Gerusalemme liberata"* (Milan: Saggiatore, 1983), still offers the best reading of these inversions as they take place throughout the epic.

70. The terms I employ, *differences within* and *differences without*, were suggested to me from Barbara Johnson, *The Critical Difference: Essays in the Contemporary Rhetoric of Reading* (Baltimore: Johns Hopkins University Press, 1980), x.

71. Helpful readings of the *Malpiglio* include Dain A. Trafton, "Tasso's Dialogue on the Court," *English Literary Renaissance Supplements* 2 (1973): 1–13; and Virginia Cox, "Tasso's *Malpiglio overo de la corte*: *The Courtier* Revisited," *Modern Language Review* 90 (1995): 897–918. For the *Malpiglio* in the context of secretarial treatises and Tasso's own secretarial treatise, see Biow, *Doctors, Ambassadors, Secretaries*, 191–93. For the *Malpiglio* I cite from *Tasso's Dialogues: A Selection, with the "Discourse on the Art of the Dialogue,"* trans. Carnes Lord and Dain A. Trafton (Berkeley: University of California Press, 1982).

Notes to Chapter 1

1. The *editio princeps* is *Il libro del Cortegiano del Conte Baldesar Castiglione* (Venice: Aldine Press, 1528). Even though he was abroad in Spain, Castiglione took great care in the printing of this book so that it would appear exactly as he wished it when bound and finally sent as a gift to designated persons of stature. I have used throughout the edition of *Il cortegiano* edited by Vittorio Cian, 3rd ed. (Florence: Sansoni, 1929) and the translation, modified on occasion, by Charles S. Singleton, *The Book of the Courtier* (New York: Anchor Books, 1959), cited by page number, first English translation, then original version. For his letters, I have drawn from *Lettere*, ed. Pierantonio Serassi, 2 vols. (Padua: G. Comino, 1769–1771), indicated as P, cited by volume and page number; and *Le lettere: Tomo primo (1497–marzo 1521)*, ed. Guido la Rocca (Verona: Mondadori, 1978), indicated as R, cited by page number.

2. In a letter written early on in his residency to the pope, Castiglione acknowledges at the outset the importance of his position; see P 2.19. In the letter in which he announces to the Marquis of Mantua, Federico Gonzaga (in whose service he was then retained), that he has been asked by the pope to be the *nuncius apostolicus* to Spain, Castiglione once more acknowledges the central importance of the office, this time even more emphatically (P 1.133).

3. This comes through time and again in his letters, but perhaps never so well as in P 2.93, from Granada on September 26, 1526.

4. The self-references occur in the first and last book, thus framing the *Cortegiano* with Castiglione's subtle presence even in his absence (12, 14; 322, 456).

5. For the notion that the hierarchical structures are momentarily leveled out during the games of the *Cortegiano*, I am indebted to Wayne A. Rebhorn, *Courtly Performances: Masking and Festivity in Castiglione's "Book of the Courtier"* (Detroit: Wayne State University Press, 1978), 151–76. The point, to be sure, is not that all these people are equals, but that the game, for it to work as a game, enforces for its duration the semblance of equality, even as participants take both subtle and not-so-subtle jabs at one another. For a more aggressively pessimistic view of Castiglione's reasons for staging the dialogue in his absence, in which "the worldly diplomat commemorates the figure of loss they [the courtiers] are an escape from, namely, the figure of Duke Guidobaldo and what the author makes it mean," see the incisive remarks of Harry Berger, Jr., *The Absence of Grace: Sprezzatura and Suspicion in Two Renaissance Courtesy Books* (Stanford: Stanford University Press, 2000), chap. 6, esp. 163–65. My reading does not discount Rebhorn's assertion that Castiglione exempts himself "to avoid the indiscretion of participating in his own dialogue" (*Courtly Performances*, 54), any more than it does Berger's reading of loss. It asserts only that Castiglione's absence is both formally and structurally motivated at another level: as a matter of professional concern.

6. For an understanding of Castiglione's life, I am indebted, both here and throughout this chapter, to Julia Mary Cartwright, *Baldassare Castiglione: The Perfect Courtier*, 2 vols. (New York: Dutton, 1908), identified hereafter as C; and Vittorio Cian, *Un illustre nunzio pontificio del Rinascimento: Baldassar Castiglione* (Città del Vaticano: Biblioteca Apostolica Vaticana, 1951). There is a good overview of his life in John R. Woodhouse, *Baldesar Castiglione: A Reassessment of "The Courtier"* (Edinburgh: Edinburgh University Press, 1978), 6–37.

7. On the revisions of Castiglione's *Cortegiano*, see Ghino Ghinassi, "Fasi dell'elaborazione del *Cortegiano*," *Studi di filologia italiana* 25 (1967): 155–96.

8. Peter Burke, *The Fortunes of the Courtier: The European Reception of Castiglione's "Cortegiano"* (Cambridge: Polity Press, 1995).

9. On the Aristotelian underpinnings to Castiglione's *Cortegiano*, with a particular focus on the fourth book, see Eduardo Saccone, "*Grazia, sprezzatura, affettazione* in the *Courtier*," in *Castiglione: The Ideal and the Real in Renaissance Culture*, eds. Robert W. Hanning and David Rosand (New Haven, Conn.: Yale University Press, 1983), 45–67; Saccone, "The Portrait of the Courtier in Castiglione," *Italica* 64 (1987): 1–18; Alfred D. Menut, "Castiglione and the Nichomachean Ethics," *Publications of the Modern Language Association* 58 (1943): 309–21; Lawrence V. Ryan, "Book IV of Castiglione's *Courtier*: Climax or Afterthought," *Studies in the Renaissance* 19 (1972): 156–79; and Woodhouse, *Baldesar Castiglione*. James Hankins, "Renaissance Philosophy and Book IV of *Il Cortegiano*," in *The Book of the Courtier*, ed. Daniel Javitch (New York: Norton, 2002), 377–88, does not see Castiglione as the "partisan of any one school or doctrine," which is correct if we are to say that Castiglione was not a philosopher strictly making use of philosophical positions to make a philosophical point, but Castiglione does reveal throughout the *Cortegiano*, despite the Platonic ending with Bembo's description of the Courtier's love, a marked preference to think in overarching Aristotelian terms when it comes to discussing aims and ends.

10. Rebhorn, *Courtly Performances*, 32.

11. Rebhorn has best defined *sprezzatura* in this manner in *Courtly Performances*, 38.

12. Castiglione in this instance is discussing "character," but it holds for virtually every other notion of what is visible to others. What we see is only what is ideally presented for us to see, and we must fill in the gaps to construct the overarching whole—the complete picture.

13. Baldness in the *Cortegiano*: it is joked about on 110, and mentioned in terms of Caesar on 139.

14. A good example appears in *Cortegiano*, 120, as well as 273, for someone being pointed and laughed at—the most humiliating form of being conspicuous.

15. As recorded in Cian, *Il cortegiano*, 9, n.16, from a letter dated September 20, 1524.

16. On Castiglione's designation of the courtier as being both a "professione" and "new," see Douglas Biow, *Doctors, Ambassadors, Secretaries: Humanism and Professions in Renaissance Italy* (Chicago: University of Chicago Press, 2002), 6–11.

17. Occasionally it could backfire, on which see Cartwright, *The Perfect Courtier*, 1.292–93.

18. I have in mind here Saccone, "*Grazia, sprezzatura, affettazione*," as well as his "Trattato e ritratto: L'introduzione del *Cortegiano*," *Modern Language Notes* 93 (1978): 1–21; José Guidi, "Baldassar Castiglione et le pouvoir politique: Du gentilhomme de cour au nonce pontifical," in *Les écrivains et le pouvoir en Italie à l'époque de la Renaissance*, ed. André Rochon (Paris: Université de la Sorbonne Nouvelle, 1973), 243–78; and Frank Whigham, *Ambition and Privilege: The Social Tropes of Elizabethan Courtesy Theory* (Berkeley: University of California Press, 1984).

19. Scholars have argued for some time now over the nature of the fourth book—not *if* the fourth book fits into the overall *Cortegiano* but *how* it fits in. Some argue that a noticeable shift takes place in book 4 and thus look for change, even contradictions, as we pass from book 3 to book 4. Some argue that the shift occurs only with Bembo's speech and that the themes are consistent; they thus look for continuity. My own position—at the risk of adopting a typically American pragmatic stance—is that these scholars are both right in their own way. On the fourth book, see Biow, *Doctors, Ambassadors, Secretaries*, 6–11; Saccone, "The Portrait of the Courtier"; Rebhorn, *Courtly Performances*, 177–204; Ryan, "Book IV of Castiglione's *Courtier*"; Amedeo Quondam, "On the Genesis of the *Book of the Courtier*," in *The Book of the Courtier*, ed. Daniel Javitch (New York: Norton, 2002), 283–95, which synthesizes the extended argument in *"Questo povero Cortegiano": Castiglione, il libro, la storia* (Rome: Bulzoni, 2000); and Lawrence Lipking, "The Dialectic of *Il cortegiano*," *Publications of the Modern Language Association* 81 (1966): 355–62.

20. "Thus we might perhaps say that to become the prince's instructor was the goal of the Courtier" (47).

21. See the concise observations of Quondam, "On the Genesis."

22. March 2, 1505, R 54.

23. Hankins, "Renaissance Philosophy," 377. I would take issue only with Hankins's notion that a humanistic education constituted a "training" to be an ambassador. Humanistic education had, from what I can tell, no particular professional bent to it, though it was deemed good preparation toward different sorts of professions: secretarial, pedagogical, and to be sure ambassadorial. See Biow, both *Doctors, Ambassadors, Secretaries* and "Reflections on Professions and Humanism in Renaissance

Italy and the Humanities Today," *Rinascimento* 43 (2003): 333–53. Woodhouse, *Baldesar Castiglione*, 60, discusses in chapter 2 the humanist training of Castiglione and his ideal courtier and then acknowledges in chapter 3 that "the best courtiers were invariably used by their patrons as diplomatic representatives" (60), but he does not discuss that work of diplomacy in his analysis of the separate books of the *Cortegiano*, other than to assert in a very general way that the *Cortegiano* would have served courtiers to understand themselves better, as well as the world they worked in, and therefore would have putatively served ambassadors well as a treatise for diplomatic work (60–62, 79).

24. See the still-unsurpassed Garrett Mattingly, *Renaissance Diplomacy* (Mineola, N.Y.: Dover, 1988, reprint).

25. For an excellent reading of this, see Rebhorn, *Courtly Performances*, 117–50, which also examines closely the dialogic nature of Castiglione's text, a point later developed by Virginia Cox, *The Renaissance Dialogue: Literary Dialogue in Its Social and Political Contexts, Castiglione to Galileo* (Cambridge: Cambridge University Press, 1992).

26. Consider as well that the courtier must surround the prince with the right people with whom he can discuss matters freely and who can, in their turn, feel they can freely discuss important matters with the prince in order to edify him and lead him on the right path (315, 442–43).

27. This is certainly evident in a number of places. To cite just two: 1. 11, in which it is inappropriate for the courtier to dress up as a prince in a masquerade, though the prince can act as an equal of the courtier, and that behavior accrues to his credit; and 2.18, in which Castiglione qualifies the notion of conversation as a term ("conversation" suggests equality among the individuals conversing, but equality does not exist between the prince and courtier).

28. I argue about the *Cortegiano* being descriptive rather than prescriptive in *Doctors, Ambassadors, Secretaries*, 6–11; see bibliography there on that topic. All this can take place, however, only if the prince himself is absent, so that these courtiers can talk freely (and indirectly) about matters important to them, on which see Javitch, "*Il Cortegiano* and the Constraints of Despotism."

29. See also P 2.60.

30. On this, see Biow, *Doctors, Ambassadors, Secretaries*, 108–20.

31. As he points out to the pope himself, most of the rumors about the intentions of the pope come from the French, who are not to be trusted as conduits of information, given their obvious partisanship. Still, Castiglione wants clarification; see, for instance, P 2.19–20.

32. Elizabeth Horodowich, "The Gossiping Tongue: Oral Networks, Public Life, and Political Culture in Early Modern Venice," *Renaissance Studies* 19 (2005): 22–45.

33. Mattingly, *Renaissance Diplomacy*.

34. A point reiterated in one of his letters sent home from Rome (P 2.101).

35. He wins the emperor's faith, but arguably this places him at risk of being tricked or beginning to see things from the emperor's viewpoint. This comes through, I would imagine, in P 2.42, 64, 88–89, 101.

36. On Guicciardini's ambassadorial work and how it plays into his writings, see Biow, *Doctors, Ambassadors, Secretaries*, 128–52, and relevant bibliography.

37. C 2.342.

38. P 2.148.

39. His self-dignity comes through in a number of letters, such as P 2.112.

40. See also 2.149.

41. See Cian, *Il cortegiano*, 529. On Castiglione choosing Don Michel da Silva, see also Saccone, "Trattato e ritratto," 8–9; Quondam, "*Questo povero Cortegiano*," 504 and 512; and especially Sylvie Deswarte, *Il "perfetto cortegiano" D. Miguel da Silva* (Rome: Bulzoni, 1989).

42. Kenneth Gouwens, *Remembering the Renaissance: Humanist Narratives of the Sack of Rome* (Leiden: Brill, 1998). I do not mean to imply that the sack in any way caused all the historical changes outlined in this paragraph, and Rome does seem to have continued to thrive afterward, but it seems to have facilitated a number of changes that were already well in motion. Historians have certainly viewed the event, which was traumatic for many, as a convenient historiographical marker of great social, cultural, and political changes that took place in Italy. See, for instance, Ingrid D. Rowland, *The Culture of the High Renaissance: Ancients and Moderns in Sixteenth-Century Rome* (Cambridge: Cambridge University Press, 1998); and Charles L. Stinger, *The Renaissance in Rome* (Bloomington: Indiana University Press, 1985).

43. See his letter, for instance, of November 27, 1537, to Messer Francesco Alunno.

44. Castiglione's defense of the church, along with the letter by Valdès, can be accessed in P 2.169–202.

Notes to Chapter 2

1. All references to Aretino's plays in the Italian, with the exception of *La cortigiana*, are taken from *Tutte le commedie*, ed. G. B. De Sanctis (Milan: Mursia, 1968) and are cited by act and scene; all references to his letters in Italian are taken from *Lettere: Edizione nazionale delle opere di Pietro Aretino*, eds. Giovanni Aquilecchia and Angelo Romano, vols. 1–6 (Rome: Salerno, 1997–2002), and they are cited by volume followed by page number. Where possible I have used the translations of his letters by George Bull, *Aretino: Selected Letters* (Harmondsworth: Penguin, 1976) and Thomas Caldecot Chubb, *The Letters of Pietro Aretino* (Hamden, Conn.: Archon Books, 1967), both modified for accuracy, and identified in my text as B and C and cited by page number.

2. Guardabasso also becomes upset when Liseo tells him to prepare the "table" for Ipocrito, who will be a house guest, because this will cut into Guardabasso's share of the food (1.4).

3. Piero Camporesi, *The Land of Hunger*, trans. Tania Croft-Murray (Cambridge: Polity Press, 1996), 120.

4. Paul F. Grendler, *Critics of the Italian World, 1530–1560: Anton Francesco Doni, Nicolò Franco and Ortensio Lando* (Madison: University of Wisconsin Press, 1969), 72. The literature on famine and hunger in the period is vast. For an overview of Europe generally, see Mary Lindemann, "Plague, Disease, Hunger," in *A Companion to the Worlds of the Renaissance*, ed. Guido Ruggiero (Malden, Mass.: Blackwell, 2002), 438–41.

5. Richard A. Goldthwaite, *The Building of Renaissance Florence: An Economic and Social History* (Baltimore: Johns Hopkins University Press, 1980).

6. Brian S. Pullan, "Wage-Earners and the Venetian Economy, 1550–1630," in *Crisis and Change in the Venetian Economy in the Sixteenth and Seventeenth Centuries*, ed. Brian Pullan (London: Methuen, 1968), 146–74. Massimo Montanari has written extensively about food, but see, for the purposes of this study, *The Culture of Food*, trans. Carl Ipsen (Oxford: Blackwell, 1994), 68–97, especially with regard to the rise in meat consumption in Europe generally; more broadly on Italian food history, Alberto Capatti and Massimo Montanari, *Italian Cuisine: A Cultural History*, trans. Aine O'Healy (New York: Columbia University Press, 2003).

7. This is not a topos discussed at much length by Curtius in his monumental rhetorical reading and classification of literature in the Western tradition, but it does receive a brief treatment under the section "Alimentary Metaphors." See Robert Ernst Curtius, *European Literature and the Latin Middle Ages*, trans. Willard R. Trask (Princeton: Princeton University Press, 1953), 134–36.

8. Ken Albala, *Eating Right in the Renaissance* (Berkeley: University of California Press, 2002), 4 and 2. Albala identifies three periods in the European Renaissance regarding eating habits as they are defined in discourse: the first, from 1470–1530 (which is focused on courtly dietaries), the second from 1530–1570 (influenced by the revival of Galen), and the third from 1570–1650 (embracing a period when orthodoxies about food habits are both reinforced and vehemently challenged). In the second period, anxieties begin to rise about what foods one should or should not consume, and by the third period people are obsessing over it. Aretino bridges the first and second period. For a fine treatment of food in visual art of the late Italian Renaissance, corresponding nicely to the third period outlined by Albala and complementing his argument, see Sheila McTighe, "Foods and the Body in Italian Genre Paintings, ca. 1580: Campi, Passarotti, Carracci," *Art Bulletin* 86 (2004): 301–23.

9. Allen J. Grieco, "The Social Politics of Pre-Linnaean Botanical Classification," *I Tatti Studies: Essays in the Renaissance* 4 (1991): 131–49; and Albala, *Eating Right*.

10. Albala, *Eating Right*, 185; he discusses "food system" on 164–65 in terms that are relevant to our understanding of how food became one more way in which Aretino could conspicuously fashion his personhood. The entire chapter on "Food and Class" is particularly germane, as is Montanari, *The Culture of Food*, 82–94, on social class and food ideology for Europe generally in the period, and on Italy, Capatti and Montanari, *Italian Cuisine*, 36–37 and *passim*.

11. On Aretino and the polygraphs, see Introduction, n. 2.

12. See Raymond B. Waddington, *Aretino's Satyr: Sexuality, Satire, and Self-Projection in Sixteenth-Century Literature and Art* (Toronto: University of Toronto Press. 2004), 41.

13. Mikhail Bakhtin, *Rabelais and His World*, trans. Hélène Iswolsky (Bloomington: Indiana University Press, 1984).

14. According to Emily Gowers, *The Loaded Table: Representations of Food in Roman Literature* (Oxford: Clarendon Press, 1993), the more refined and elite the genre (epic, Platonic dialogue, tragedy, and so on), the less the attention will be on food and the more on conviviality, conversation (perhaps affable, perhaps not), and mutual edification; conversely, the less refined the genre (satire, comedy, familiar letters, and so on), the more likely food will come into play, even to the point where it becomes the

sole focus of the text, displacing spiritual and moral concerns for bodily ones. This hierarchy would seem to exist in the Italian Renaissance, a period that resuscitates classical models and hierarchies. Hence Castiglione, whose *Cortegiano* participates in the tradition of narratives about an edifying symposium (a tradition that extends back to Plato), hardly discusses food at all, whereas Aretino, whose *Dialogues* (as we shall see below) participate in the tradition of narratives about a symposium rooted in the senses (a tradition that extends back to Petronius's *Satyricon*), transforms verbal exchange into not only a discussion that takes place with food present but also one that constantly concentrates on food to the point where food itself can become *the* central topic. At the same time, we see that the focus on the materiality of food is concomitantly on the materiality of language.

15. Norbert Elias, *The Civilizing Process: The History of Manners*, 2 vols., trans. Edmund Jephcott (New York: Urizen Books, 1978); and Peter Burke, *Popular Culture in Early Modern Europe* (New York: Harper & Row, 1978).

16. *La cortigiana* has come down to us in two distinct forms, the 1525 version, which was drafted while Aretino was in Rome, and the later version of 1534, which was composed while he was in Venice. I cite here from the earlier version, *La cortigiana*, ed. Giuliano Innamorati (Turin: Einaudi, 1972), and use the English translation by J. Douglas Campbell and Leonard G. Sbrocchi (Ottawa: Dovehouse, 2003), which contains an excellent introduction to the play by Raymond B. Waddington. For a reading that closely compares the plays, see Paul Larivaille, *Pietro Aretino fra Rinascimento e manierismo* (Rome: Bulzoni, 1980), 123–37; for a synthetic overview of the plays and their placement in Renaissance comedy, see Richard Andrews, *Scripts and Scenarios: The Performance of Comedy in Renaissance Italy* (Cambridge: Cambridge University Press, 1993), 67–74 and *passim*. There is a helpful study of *La cortigiana* in Giulio Ferroni, "Il teatro di Roma: La prima *Cortigiana*," in *Le voci dell'istrione: Pietro Aretino e la dissoluzione del teatro* (Naples: Liguori, 1977), 35–70.

17. On food and carnival in Renaissance and early modern Europe, the classic work is Bakhtin, *Rabelais and His World*; see also Camporesi, *The Land of Hunger*. The Chigi household instead taught Aretino munificence, as he announces in one of his letters (2.321). On Chigi patronage, see Ingrid D. Rowland, "'Render unto Caesar the Things Which Are Caesar's: Humanism and the Arts in the Patronage of Agostino Chigi," *Renaissance Quarterly* 39 (1986): 673–730, and 687–88 for his habit of putting on sumptuous feasts. See also Roy Strong, *Feast: A History of Grand Eating* (London: Jonathan Cape, 2002), 128–209.

18. Paul Larivaille, *Pietro Aretino* (Rome: Salerno, 1997), 39–79. Giuliano Innamorati, "Aretino, Pietro," *Dizionario biografico degli italiani*, vol. 4 (Rome: Istituto della Enciclopedia Italiana, 1962), 91–93, gives a concise overview of Aretino as courtier in Rome. On Aretino's early life in Rome, see also Anne Reynolds, *Renaissance Humanism at the Court of Clement VII: Francesco Berni's "Dialogue Against Poets" in Context* (New York: Garland, 1997), 119–42; and Bette Talvacchia, *Taking Positions: On the Erotic in Renaissance Culture* (Princeton: Princeton University Press, 1999). For the period in Venice, after his stay in Mantua, see Christopher Cairns, *Pietro Aretino and the Republic of Venice: Researches on Aretino and His Circle in Venice, 1527–1556* (Florence: Olschki, 1985); and Larivaille, *Pietro Aretino*.

19. See additional comments in 1.98 as well.

20. See also C 40, 1.85, and especially C 98–99, 1.353.

21. 1.236. Aretino has nothing but praise for Chigi in his letters, imagining himself to have adopted Chigi's habits of munificence and style. See Larivaille, *Pietro Aretino*, 43–47.

22. Ken Albala, *The Banquet: Dining in the Great Courts of Late Renaissance Europe* (Urbana: University of Illinois Press, 2007), 140, and 139–58 generally on the role of the scalco.

23. See Luciano Chiappini, *La Corte Estense alla metà del Cinquencento: I compendi di Cristoforo di Messisbugo* (Ferrara: Belriguardo, 1984); and Cristoforo di Messisbugo, *Banchetti composizioni di vivande e apparecchio generale*, ed. Fernando Bandini (Venice: Neri Pozza, 1960). On the importance of food in classical Roman literature, see the fine, engaging study by Gowers, *The Loaded Table*.

24. Even the images accompanying Messisbugo's *Banchetti*, which were surely intended to display chivalric magnificence of the d'Este household, show us dogs chewing on bones about a table laden with food. Albala, *The Banquet*, 4 and 6 on banquets as competitions among courts.

25. Chiappini, *La corte Estense*, 183, for instance. See also Evelyn S. Welch, *Shopping in the Renaissance: Consumer Cultures in Italy 1400–1600* (New Haven, Conn.: Yale University Press, 2005), 246.

26. As in Renaissance humanist discussions on eating and conviviality, which merge the body and the mind and make us whole, as discussed in Michel Jeanneret, *A Feast of Words: Banquets and Table Talk in the Renaissance*, trans. Jeremy Whitely and Emma Hughes (Chicago: University of Chicago Press, 1991), 32ff.

27. Goldthwaite, *The Building of Renaissance Florence*.

28. Patricia Fortini Brown, *Private Lives in Renaissance Venice: Art, Architecture, and the Family* (New Haven, Conn.: Yale University Press, 2004), esp. 150–57, though the focus in Venice tended to be more on display, as Brown points out, than on the actual sumptuous consumption of food: "costume," fashion, took precedence over "comestibles."

29. Francesco Marcolini, *Lettere a Pietro Aretino*, eds. Gonaria Floris and Luisa Mulas, vol. 3 (Rome: Bulzoni, 1997), 434–35 (originally published by Marcolini press in 1552). It is perhaps not accidental that Ortensio Lando—a polygraph greatly influenced, as all polygraphs were, by Aretino's writings and the position he occupied so successfully in society—wrote extensively about the material culture of food in his *Commentario delle più notabili e mostruose cose d'Italia e d'altri luoghi di lingua aramea in italiana tradotto. Con un breve catalogo degli inventori delle cose che si mangiano* (Venice: Cesano, 1553), reprint, eds. Guido Salvatori and Paola Salvatori (Bologna: Pendragon, 1994); in his *Commentario* Lando reconstructs Italy and defines it for an outsider through a traveling geography of food, on which see Capatti and Montanari, *Italian Cuisine*, 18–21, as well as 235–36.

30. See Timothy Moore, "Who Is the Parasite: Giving and Taking in *Phormio*," in *Greek and Roman Comedy: Translations and Interpretations of Four Representative Plays*, ed. Shawn O'Bryhim (Austin: University of Texas Press, 2001) 253–64, esp. 254. More generally, see Cynthia Damon, *The Mask of the Parasite* (Ann Arbor: University of Michigan Press, 1998).

31. Camporesi, *The Land of Hunger*. On Giulio Cesare Croce, see Piero Campo-

resi, *La maschera di Bertoldo: G. C. Croce e la letteratura carnevalesca* (Turin: Einaudi, 1976); and Douglas Biow, *The Culture of Cleanliness in Renaissance Italy* (Ithaca, N.Y.: Cornell University Press, 2006), 95–143, and relevant bibliography cited there.

32. Baldassar Castiglione, *The Book of the Courtier*, trans. Charles S. Singleton (New York: Anchor Books, 1959), by page number in my text. There are few discussions about food in the *Cortegiano*. Consider the joke at Serafino's expense, 1.28; the brief, offhand mentioning of the duchess having eaten, 2.71; the lengthy comic, Boccaccesque story of a man stealing capons from a peasant, 2.89; and its use as a metaphor, 4.16.

33. The other central target of attack is the Platonizing dialogues about love, the most famous at the time being Pietro Bembo's *Asolani*.

34. I have used Aretino, *Dialogues*, trans. Raymond Rosenthal (New York: Ballantine Books, 1971) and *Ragionamento dialogo*, ed. Giorgio Barberi Squarotti (Milan: BUR, 1988), cited in that order in my text. The first set of dialogues, *Il ragionamento della Nanna e della Antonia* (1534), covers Nanna explaining to comare Antonia, over three days and in three separate parts, how she passed from being a nun to a wife to a prostitute, with the final judgment being that prostitution constitutes the best of all possible vocations/professions for a woman. The second set of dialogues, *Dialogo nel quale la Nanna insegna a Pippa* (1536), which also contains three parts and three separate dialogues, covers Nanna indoctrinating Pippa into the profession of prostitution (as well as a discussion of betrayals by men) and a discussion between a midwife and a wetnurse on how to become a pimp. For an extended analysis of the evolution of the composition, style, and themes of the dialogues, see Larivaille, *Pietro Aretino fra Rinascimento e manierismo*, 139–227. See also David O. Frantz, *Festum Voluptatis: A Study of Renaissance Erotica* (Columbus: Ohio State University Press, 1989), 43–90; and Paula Findlen, "Humanism, Politics and Pornography in Renaissance Italy," in *The Invention of Pornography: Obscenity and the Origins of Modernity, 1500–1800*, ed. Lynn Hunt (New York: Zone Books, 1993), 49–108. On the role of the court, see Margaret T. Rosenthal, *The Honest Courtesan: Veronica Franco, Citizen and Writer in Sixteenth-Century Venice* (Chicago: University of Chicago Press, 1992), 30–37 and *passim*.

35. On della Casa, see Biow, *The Culture of Cleanliness*, 17–29, as well as the bibliography.

36. On the importance of the buone maniere in the second set of dialogues, see Larivaille, *Pietro Aretino*, 197–99.

37. Castiglione's courtiers talk about sex—not the pleasures of it, to be sure, but the need to transcend it—in the third book of the *Cortegiano*.

38. Talvacchia, *Taking Positions*; see also Waddington, *Aretino's Satyr*.

39. On Aretino's verbal play, see Larivaille, *Pietro Aretino* and *Aretino fra Rinascimento e manierismo*; Cesare Segre, *Lingua, stile e società: Studi sulla storia della prosa italiana* (Milan: Feltrinelli, 1963); and Waddington, *Aretino's Satyr*. On talk about food lending itself to verbal play, see Jeanneret, *A Feast of Words*, *passim*.

40. See also 109, 197; 218, 337.

41. See, for instance, *Cortegiano*, 1.2. On Aretino's attitude toward the court, see Waddington, *Aretino's Satyr*; Innamorati, "Aretino, Pietro"; Amedeo Quondam, "La scena della menzogna: Corte e cortegiano nel 'Ragionamento' di Pietro Aretino,"

Psicon 8–9 (1978): 4–23; Rosenthal, *The Honest Courtesan*, 30–37; and Giulio Ferroni, "Pietro Aretino e le corti," in *Pietro Aretino nel cinquecentario della nascita*, vol. 1 (Rome: Salerno, 1995), 23–48.

42. Wayne A. Rebhorn, *Courtly Performances: Masking and Festivity in Castiglione's "Book of the Courtier"* (Detroit: Wayne State University Press, 1978), 117–50, first articulated this concept at length as he explored the underlying aggressive impulses and rivalry among the members of the dialogue; it has been subsequently developed by Carla Freccero, "Politics and Aesthetics in Castiglione's *Il Cortegiano*: Book III and the Discourse on Women," in *Creative Imitation: New Essays on Renaissance Literature in Honor of Thomas M. Greene*, eds. David Quint et al. (Binghamton, N.Y.: Medieval and Renaissance Texts and Studies, 1992), 259–79; and Valeria Finucci, *The Lady Vanishes: Subjectivity and Representation in Castiglione and Ariosto* (Stanford: Stanford University Press, 1992).

43. Interestingly, in the final edition Castiglione omits mention of the courtiers eating with Guidobaldo before the evening events commence, though he does discuss it in the *seconda redazione*. See Baldassar Castiglione, *La seconda redazione del "Cortegiano,"* ed. Ghino Ghinassi (Florence: Sansoni, 1968), 7.

44. Much has been written on the topic, but see Natalie Zemon Davis, *The Gift in Sixteenth-Century France* (Madison: University of Wisconsin Press, 2000).

45. On the letters generally, see Larivaille, *Pietro Aretino*, 220–68, esp. 227 on the topic of the gift.

46. See, for instance, McTighe, "Foods and the Body."

47. For comparisons between Petrarca and Aretino, see Waddington, *Aretino's Satyr*, 20–30, as well as the brief comment in Paul Barolsky, *Why Mona Lisa Smiles and Other Tales by Vasari* (University Park: Penn State University Press, 1991), 82–91.

48. Capatti and Montanari, *Italian Cuisine*, xix.

49. For the notion in the European Renaissance generally, see the apposite section "Eating the Text," in Jeanneret, *A Feast of Words*. For the widespread theme of digestion in literary and poetic invention in the Renaissance, along with the roots of the concept in classical literature and rhetoric as it was resuscitated by humanists, see, for instance, Thomas Greene, *The Light in Troy: Imitation and Discovery in Renaissance Poetry* (New Haven, Conn.: Yale University Press, 1982).

50. Jean Antheme Brillat-Savarin, *The Philosopher in the Kitchen*, trans. Anne Drayton (Harmondsworth: Penguin, 1970), aphorism 2. Albala, *Eating Right*, is particularly helpful here.

51. On the role of satire and satyrs in Aretino's art, see Waddington, *Aretino's Satyr*. It was conventionally believed in the Renaissance that a "satire" derived from the term *satyr*. Its correct derivation, from the term *satura*, meaning a dish offering up various foods, was not disclosed until Isaac Casaubon supplied the accurate definition in his *De Satyrica Graecorum poesi et Romanorum satira* (1605). The consumption of food and discussions about it are conventional in satire, from classical satires by Juvenal and Petronius to modern versions.

52. Waddington, *Aretino's Satyr*, 34–46.

Notes to Chapter 3

1. E. M. Forster, *Aspects of the Novel* (New York: Harcourt, Brace & World, 1955), 53.

2. For a discussion of some of these oddball interests of Dante scholars over the years, see John Kleiner, *Mismapping the Underworld: Daring and Error in Dante's "Comedy"* (Stanford: Stanford University Press, 1994).

3. Michelangelo Buonarroti, *Letters*, trans. E. H. Ramsden, 2 vols. (Stanford: Stanford University Press, 1963), cited by volume and page number; the Italian is taken from *Il carteggio di Michelangelo*, eds. Paola Barocchi and Renzo Ristori, 5 vols. (Florence: Sansoni, 1965–1983), 4.301, hereafter cited by volume and page number as C.

4. C 4.309.

5. C 4.309.

6. C 4.312.

7. C 4.299.

8. Michelangelo's terribilità is, of course, far more than his wrath and an eccentricity, but it also comprises those aspects of his character. Much has been written on Michelangelo's terribilità, but see the synthetic observations of David Summers, *Michelangelo and the Language of Art* (Princeton: Princeton University Press, 1981), 234–41. My argument about Michelangelo's behavior, I should stress, is not that it was *only* that of a difficult man (he did have friends, and he treated his workers well); my argument is that, in addition to having all sorts of laudable qualities, Michelangelo could be an extremely difficult man. On his character, much has been written in the modern period, but see, for instance, Robert J. Clements, *Michelangelo's Theory of Art* (New York: Gramercy, 1961); Robert S. Liebert, *Michelangelo: A Psychoanalytic Study of His Life and Images* (New Haven, Conn.: Yale University Press, 1983); George Bull, *Michelangelo: A Biography* (New York: St. Martin's Griffin, 1998); and John Addington Symonds, *The Life of Michelangelo Buonarroti*, 3rd ed. (New York: J. C. Nimmo and C. Scribner's Sons, 1911, rpt. Philadelphia: University of Pennsylvania Press, 2002), in particular 16, 30, 78.

9. A fact that is rendered fairly evident in other documentary sources. See, for instance, Michael Hirst, "The Young Michelangelo: The Artist in Rome 1496–1501," in Michael Hirst and Jill Dunkerton, *Making and Meaning: The Young Michelangelo* (London: National Gallery Publications, 1994), 74, n. 15; and Rab Hatfield, *The Wealth of Michelangelo* (Rome: Edizioni di Storia e Letteratura, 2002), 245, 249, 259, 261, 265, 267, 270.

10. Though they do certainly occur, as in May 1525, in a letter to Sebastiano del Piombo (1.160, C 3.156). That Michelangelo attended numerous dinner parties is well documented, and that he enjoyed the conversations is equally certain as well. See, for instance, Summers, *Michelangelo*, 12–13.

11. Ascanio Condivi, *The Life of Michelangelo*, trans. Alice Sedgwick Wohl, ed. Hellmut Wohl (Baton Rouge: Louisiana State University Press, 1976), hereafter cited as Cv in my text; the Italian is cited from the *Vita di Michelagnolo Buonarroti*, ed. Giovanni Nencioni, with essays by Michael Hirst and Caroline Elam (Florence: Studio per Edizioni Scelte, 1998), hereafter cited as Cdv. In her prefatory article to the Nencioni edition, Elam shows that Tiberio Calcagni recorded annotations directly from Michelangelo, who balked at some of the statements in Condivi's biography; nevertheless, it is clear that Michelangelo had a large hand in the making of it. For a contrasting reading, see Michael Hirst, "Michelangelo and His First Biographers," *Proceedings of the British Academy* 94 (1996): 63–84.

12. I cite by page number in my text from Giorgio Vasari, *Le vite dei più eccellenti pittori, scultori e architetti* (Rome: Newton, 2005); for translations of Michelangelo's life, I draw from *The Lives of the Artists*, trans. Julia Conaway Bondanella and Peter Bondanella (Oxford: Oxford University Press, 1991), modified for accuracy (1258).

13. Elizabeth Pilliod, *Pontormo, Bronzino, Allori: A Genealogy of Florentine Art* (New Haven, Conn.: Yale University Press, 2001), 67–77, has documented the unreliability of Vasari's narrative.

14. It has now been translated, with the facing original: *Pontormo's Diary*, trans. Rosemary Mayer (New York: Out of London Press, 1979).

15. Rudolf and Margot Wittkower, *Born Under Saturn: The Character and Conduct of Artists: A Documented History from Antiquity to the French Revolution* (New York: Random House, 1963), 67–78.

16. In their magnitude, Michelangelo's habits go well beyond those described by Vasari regarding his and Salviati's missing a meal on account of their working through the night (*Le vite*, 1359). Even Benedetto Varchi, in his encomiastic *Orazione funerale di M. Benedetto Varchi* (Florence: I Giunti, 1564), 37, reiterates the commonplace of Michelangelo being abstemious.

17. I have in mind the varied works by Paul Barolsky, such as *Michelangelo's Nose: A Myth and Its Mythmaker* (University Park: Penn State University Press, 1990); and Barolsky, *The Faun in the Garden: Michelangelo and the Poetic Origins of Italian Renaissance Art* (University Park: Penn State University Press, 1994). For a careful narrative that reconstructs Michelangelo's working habits during a specific period, see William E. Wallace, *San Lorenzo: The Genius as Entrepreneur* (New York: Cambridge University Press, 1994). A more popular version for the Sistine Chapel is Ross King, *Michelangelo and the Pope's Ceiling* (New York: Walker & Company, 2003).

18. C 4.212.

19. Mihaly Csikszentmihalyi, *Creativity: Flow and the Psychology of Discovery and Invention* (New York: HarperCollins, 1996).

20. I use the term *absorption* advisedly. The Latin *absorbeo* meant not only to be "engrossed" and therefore "to absorb" but, according to its primary sense, "to devour, to consume." However, I am not aware of it being used to signify the workings of the mind or soul in a state of intense concentration in Neoplatonic thought. Ficino's terms, for instance, tend to be *vacatio* or *contemplatio*.

21. On the characterization of Lent as lean, see Peter Burke, *Popular Culture in Early Modern Europe* (New York: Harper & Row, 1978), 188 and *passim*.

22. William E. Wallace, "A Week in the Life of Michelangelo," in *Looking at Italian Renaissance Sculpture*, ed. Sarah Blake McHam (Cambridge: Cambridge University Press, 1998), 203–22, neatly captures much of what I have in mind when he writes in his "imaginary" description of a week in the life of Michelangelo: "He had a busy week, although he had not carved much. He was really happy only when immersed in work" (218).

23. Dante expresses this experience synthetically in *Purgatorio* 4.1–15. For the philosophical and scholastic underpinnings to Dante's conception of the soul and how the intellect can be so absorbed that it loses a sense of time, see the commentary to that passage in Charles S. Singleton, *The Divine Comedy*, 6 vols. (Princeton:

Princeton University Press, 1970–1975), *ad locum*. See also *Dante's "Vita Nuova,"* trans. Mark Musa (Bloomington: Indiana University Press, 1973), 71–72.

24. Cdv 8–9. On the wetnurse in Renaissance Italy, see in particular Christiane Klapisch-Zuber, "Blood Parents and Milk Parents: Wet Nursing in Florence 1300–1530," in *Women, Family, and Ritual in Renaissance Italy*, trans. Lydia G. Cochrane (Chicago: University of Chicago Press, 1985), 132–64. For thoughts on the image of the virgin *lactans*, especially with regard to Michelangelo, see Rona Goffen, "Mary's Motherhood According to Leonardo and Michelangelo," *Artibus et historiae* 20 (1999): 35–69, esp. 43–45.

25. Martin Warnke, *The Court Artist: On the Ancestry of the Modern Artist*, trans. David McLintock (Cambridge: Cambridge University Press, 1993), 82–83, gives a synthesis of how merchants made off with much money, to the chagrin of visual artists.

26. On Riario as patron, see Ingrid D. Rowland, *The Culture of the High Renaissance: Ancients and Moderns in Sixteenth-Century Rome* (Cambridge: Cambridge University Press, 1998), 33–40.

27. The *Cupid* passed into the hands of Cesare Borgia, Guidobaldo of Urbino, and then Isabella d'Este; it is now lost.

28. Cdv 18.

29. *Le vite*, 1206–7.

30. Cdv 19.

31. On some of the surrounding sculptures, see Hirst, "The Young Michelangelo," 31.

32. C 1.1. On Riario's commission of the *Bacchus*, see Michael Hirst, "Michelangelo in Rome: An Altarpiece and the *Bacchus*," *The Burlington Magazine* 123 (1981): 581–93.

33. C 1.1.

34. Vasari presses the point that Michelangelo did have teachers, specifically and above all Domenico Ghirlandaio, from whom he learned the art of fresco mural painting; yet he also asserts over and over again that Michelangelo had a natural talent—Nature was ultimately his great teacher.

35. Varchi, *Orazione*, 13; translation from Rona Goffen, *Renaissance Rivals: Michelangelo, Leonardo, Raphael, Titian* (New Haven, Conn.: Yale University Press, 2002), 71.

36. Howard Hibbard, *Michelangelo*, 2nd edition (Boulder, Colo.: Westview Press, 1998), 34.

37. These are matters of debate by connoisseurs. Some have argued that Piero de' Medici commissioned the *Hercules*; see, for instance, Caroline Elam, "Lorenzo de' Medici's Sculpture Garden," *Mitteilungen des Kunsthistorischen Institutes in Florenz* 36 (1992): 41–83.

38. Edgar Wind, *Pagan Mysteries in the Renaissance* (New York: Norton, 1968), 177. Michelangelo, it is generally believed now, was lodged in Gallo's, rather than Riario's, house. Gallo, who acquired the *Bacchus*, was Riario's neighbor. See Hirst, "The Young Michelangelo," 31–32.

39. See Christoph L. Frommel, "Raffaele Riario, la Cancelleria, il teatro, e il *Bacco* di Michelangelo," in *Giovinezza di Michelangelo*, exh. cat., eds. Kathleen Weil-Garris Brandt et al. (Florence: Artificio Skira, 1999), 143–48, on the courtyard of the

Cancelleria in the context of discussing Michelangelo's *Bacchus* and Riario's patronage. See also Linda A. Koch, "Michelangelo's *Bacchus* and the Art of Self-Formation," *Art History* 29 (2006), 346 and 366–67. As will become evident in the course of this chapter, I am indebted to Koch's fine discussion of the *Bacchus*.

40. On the rivalry among artists in Renaissance Italy, with Michelangelo functioning as the defining protagonist, see Goffen, *Renaissance Rivals*.

41. Cdv 18.

42. Wittkowers, *Born Under Saturn*, 40.

43. Hibbard, *Michelangelo*, 41.

44. Ibid., 41. Charles H. Carman, "Michelangelo's *Bacchus* and Divine Frenzy," *Source* 2 (1983): 6–13, explores the lack of a precise visual classical precedent for Michelangelo's version of a specifically drunken Bacchus. Hirst, "The Young Michelangelo," 32, posits ancient versions of the Silenus. The source may have been as much verbal as it was visual for Michelangelo and his patron. Goffen, *Renaissance Rivals*, 102, and Summers, *Michelangelo*, 165–68, emphasize the verbal precedents over visual ones. For a broad analysis of the problem, see Luba Freedman, "Michelangelo's Reflections on Bacchus," *Artibus et historiae* 24 (2003): 121–35.

45. Summers, *Michelangelo*, 56–59, on "aria."

46. As Wind, *Pagan Mysteries*, 178, observes, the *Bacchus* has not met with much favor from critics. See also Giorgio Vasari, *La vita di Michelangelo*, ed. Paola Barocchi, vol. 2 (Milan: Ricciardi Editore, 1962), 162–67. Also Hirst, "The Young Michelangelo," 33. I borrow the term *unclassical* from Goffen, *Renaissance Rivals*, 102.

47. Many have noted that the satyr embodies the figura serpentinata, the privileged form for Michelangelo and, eventually, for the mannerists. See, for instance, Summers, *Michelangelo*, 60–70; and Ralph Lieberman, "Regarding Michelangelo's 'Bacchus'," *Artibus et historiae* 22 (2001): 65–74, 67.

48. On the classicism and anticlassicism of the *Bacchus*, see Freedman, "Michelangelo's Reflections," 124–30; Lieberman, "Regarding," 65–74; and Koch, "Michelangelo's *Bacchus*." Leonard Barkan, *Unearthing the Past: Archaeology and Aesthetics in the Making of Renaissance Culture* (New Haven, Conn.: Yale University Press, 1999), 201–4, observes that the *Bacchus* was deliberately constructed to fool viewers into thinking it an antique, though Hirst, "The Young Michelangelo," 33, certainly emphasizes, by contrast, the anticlassical features to this sculpture, to the point where he envisions it defying in a variety of ways the classical canons of art, as does Goffen, *Renaissance Rivals*, 101–2. On Michelangelo's wit, see the remarks of Paul Barolsky, *Infinite Jest: Wit and Humor in Italian Renaissance Art* (Columbia: University of Missouri Press, 1978), 52–54.

49. "Michelangelo's Reflections," 125–26. Freedman overemphasizes the femininity of Michelangelo's *Bacchus* when stating that "in no known ancient image is the deity's feminine character so visually accentuated as in this statue," with its "soft abdomen" and "slightly swelling breasts." In Jonathan Richardson's *An Account of Some of the Statues, Bas-reliefs, Drawings and Pictures in Italy* (London: J. Knapton, 1722), 44–45, we read the precise opposite as Michelangelo's sculpture is compared to a classical version in the Medici gallery. At the time Michelangelo's *Bacchus* was stationed right next to an ancient statue of Bacchus, which is also holding a cup and is accompanied by a faun, and Richardson makes a number of interesting observa-

tions in the course of comparing the two. In sum, Michelangelo's is "of very excellent Gout," he writes, but it does not have the "delicacy" that a Bacchus "ought" to have, and, being a work of Michelangelo, it is more masculine than a Bacchus ought to be. The ancient statue, on the other hand, he finds similar to the Medici Venus in "delicacy" and Bacchus-appropriate femininity. He says that the two sculptures differ "as Masculine does from Feminine." The ancient Bacchus referred to can be viewed in Anton Francesco Gori, *Museum florentinum exhibens insigniora vetustatis monumenta quae Florentiae sunt*, vol. 3, *Statuae antiquae deorum et virorum illustrium* (Florence: ex typographia Michaelis Nestenus et Francisci Moücke, 1731), plate XLVII (pp. 52–53); Michelangelo's *Bacchus* can be found on plates LI–LIII (pp. 55–56), while the Medici Venus, to which Richardson compares the ancient Bacchus, is on plates XXVI–XXIX (pp. 34–36). Vasari perhaps has it correct when he observes that Michelangelo worked for a fusion of the two, the feminine and the masculine: "In this figure it is clear that Michelangelo wanted to attain a marvelous combination of various parts of the body and, most particularly, to give it both the slenderness of the young male figure and the fleshiness and roundness of the female" (424, 1207).

50. Lieberman, "Regarding," 66–67.

51. For a compelling reading of such gender ambiguities in sixteenth-century Italian art, see Fredrika H. Jacobs, "Aretino and Michelangelo, Dolce and Titian: *Femmina, Masculo, Grazia*," *Art Bulletin* 82 (2000): 51–67.

52. "It was such an astonishing work that it showed Michelangelo to be more skilled than any other modern sculptor who had ever worked up to that time" (424, 1207).

53. On Vasari's calculated and structured staging of Michelangelo's rivalry with Donatello, see Barbara J. Watts, "Giorgio Vasari's *Vita di Michelangelo Buonarroti* and the Shade of Donatello," in *The Rhetorics of Life-Writing in Early Modern Europe: Forms of Biography from Cassandra Fedele to Louis XIV*, eds. Thomas F. Mayer and D. R. Woolf (Ann Arbor: University of Michigan Press, 1995), 63–96.

54. Carman, "Michelangelo's *Bacchus*," 6–13 in particular; Koch, "Michelangelo's *Bacchus*," 354; and Wind, "A Bacchic Mystery," 177–90.

55. Koch, "Michelangelo's *Bacchus*," 356–57. See also Wind, "A Bacchic Mystery," 178. Lieberman, "Regarding," 65–74, explores with great sensitivity the effect of moving around the sculpture. Hibbard's argument and that of others (namely, that we are invited to turn to the right, rather than the left) is predicated on the notion in part that the arm holding the cup aloft disturbs the natural movement of the viewer to be guided to the left; but, if as Wind, "A Bacchic Mystery," 178–80, argues, the cup and top of the arm are "clumsy" restorations, the original design by Michelangelo may have included a more fluid arrangement that would have guided us around to the left. Either way, even if we are invited to the left as we are to the right, the argument still holds about the duplication of the moral and spiritual development of the viewer in his or her movement about the sculpture in relation to the moral and spiritual development inherent in the sculptural ensemble itself.

56. This is certainly a familiar theme, from Dante on. For a compelling reading of the role of skin and flaying in Renaissance (as well as Michelangelo's art and self-portraiture in the *Last Judgment*), see Daniela Bohde, "Skin and the Search for the Interior: The Representation of Flaying in the Art and Anatomy of the

Cinquecento," in *Bodily Extremities: Preoccupations with the Human Body in Early Modern European Culture*, eds. Florike Egmond and Robert Zwijnenberg (Aldershot: Ashgate, 2003), 10–47. As for the identity of the animal, this has been up for debate. Condivi saw a tiger, Goffen a panther, Wind the Plinian "leopardus" as a cross between a lion and a panther, Freedman a wolf.

57. Again, Koch, "Michelangelo's *Bacchus*," 362–63.

58. Ibid, 365.

59. For a reading of how Michelangelo constructed his own divinity and often scandalously undermined it, as well as how Michelangelo fits into the careers of a number of eccentric visual artists of his time, see Stephen J. Campbell, "'Fare una Cosa Morta Parer Viva': Michelangelo, Rosso, and the (Un)Divinity of Art," *Art Bulletin* 84 (2002): 596–620.

60. I cite from Francesco Petrarca, *Petrarch's Lyric Poems*, trans. Robert M. Durling (Cambridge, Mass.: Harvard University Press, 1976).

61. This is Koch's argument, built in part on the works of John T. Paoletti, "Michelangelo's Masks," *Art Bulletin* 74 (1992): 423–40; Laura C. Agoston, "Sonnet, Sculpture, Death: The Mediums of Michelangelo's Self-Imagining," *Art History* 20 (1997): 534–55; Barolsky, *Michelangelo's Nose*; and Barolsky, *The Faun in the Garden.*

62. Quoted in Wallace, "A Week in the Life of Michelangelo," 216; see also R. J. Clements, "Michelangelo on Effort and Rapidity in Art," *Journal of the Warburg and Courtauld Institutes* 17 (1954): 301–10.

63. It is well known that Michelangelo invited viewers to see his own identification in his sculptures. Most famously is the *David.* See Charles Seymour, *Michelangelo's David: A Search for Identity* (New York: Norton, 1967), 8–9; and Irving Lavin, "David's Sling and Michelangelo's Bow," in *Past-Present: Essays on Historicism in Art from Donatello to Picasso* (Berkeley: University of California Press, 1993), 29ff.

64. Hirst, "The Young Michelangelo," 31.

65. Michelangelo was everything but unambiguous, as we read from Vasari in the first edition of the *Lives*, of 1550; see Giorgio Vasari, *Le vite de' piú eccellenti architetti, pittori, et scultori italiani*, 2 vols., eds. Luciano Bellosi and Aldo Rossi (Turin: Einaudi, 1986), 2.912. On Michelangelo's love of paradox and ambiguity, in which he was able to entertain alternative positions in the same work, see the synthetic observations of Summers, *Michelangelo*, 10. See Campbell, "'Fare una Cosa Morta Parer Viva,'" for his ability to engage both the lofty and the base—or what sixteenth-century literary theorists might have termed the sublime and the ridiculous—in the same work of art.

66. See, for instance, Aretino's letter to Michelangelo, in C 4.215–17; see also Mark W. Roskill, *Dolce's Aretino and Venetian Art Theory of the Cinquecento* (Toronto: University of Toronto Press, 2000), 161–67.

67. Cdv 19.

68. It is clear that Riario both commissioned the work and, what is more, paid for it; see Hirst, "Michelangelo in Rome," 590–93, appendix C.

69. Cdv 19.

70. Regarding the fragmentary quality of the *Bacchus*, with its lopped-off arm and penis, some have postulated that it was intended to be viewed that way: see the observations of Koch, "Michelangelo's *Bacchus*," 351; Lieberman, "Regarding," 73,

n. 13; and Freedman, "Michelangelo's Reflections," 122. It was sometimes mistaken for a work unearthed from the ground. See Koch, "Michelangelo's *Bacchus*," 372–73; Wind, *Pagan Mysteries*, 180–81; Barkan, *Unearthing*, 382, n. 170; and Freedman, "Michelangelo's Reflections," 122–23, 133, n. 9.

71. Koch, "Michelangelo's *Bacchus*," 366, posits that in creating a sculpture that, in its deliberate obscurantism, veiled "Christianized moral truths in the guise of pagan sensuality, overindulgence and animal sacrifice" (365–66), Michelangelo "may well have conceived the Bacchus as an intellectual and thematic counterpart to the activities of the Accademia Pomponiana" (366). As she also suggests, he could have constructed it with the idea that it would have been the object of their contemplation, not just a clever analogue to it in the visual arts. See Phyllis Pray Bober, "The *Coryciana* and the Nymph Corycia," *Journal of the Warburg and Courtauld Institutes* 44 (1977): 223–39; and Bober, "Appropriation Contexts: Décor, Furor Bacchicus Convivium," *Antiquity and Its Interpreters*, eds. Alina Payne, Ann Kuttner, and Rebekah Smick (Cambridge: Cambridge University Press, 2000), 229–43. Rowland, *The Culture*, 42–67. On the conversational function of much Italian Renaissance art, see John Shearman, *Only Connect: Art and the Spectator in the Italian Renaissance* (Princeton: Princeton University Press, 1992).

72. Carl Frey, ed., *Il codice Magliabechiano cl. XVII. 17, contenente notizie sopra l'arte degli antichi e quella de' Fiorentini da Cimabue a Michelangelo Buonarroti, scritte da Anonimo Fiorentino* (Berlin: G. Grotesche Verlagsbuchhandlung, 1892), 115.

73. Bull, *Michelangelo*, 143.

74. In *Scritti d'arte del Cinquecento*, ed. Paola Barocchi, vol. 1 (Milan: Ricciardi Editore, 1971), 12.

75. *Le vite*, 1262. Francisco de Hollanda, *Four Dialogues on Painting*, trans. Aubrey F. G. Bell (Oxford: Oxford University Press, 1928), 11–12, is also quick to excuse Michelangelo and men like him.

76. The *Madonna of the Stairs* treats the familiar *Madonna lactans* image, though in Michelangelo's version the Christ child is not being nursed but asleep, as this prefigures Christ's later death and anticipates Mary's (visual) role in a Pietà-styled imagery. See also, however, Michelangelo's "Medici Madonna" sculpture and "Madonna and Child" drawing, along with related themes of nursing, in Goffen, "Mary's Motherhood," 59–64, as well as 44–45. Similarly, we can safely doubt, given the existing ancient models, if the topic of consumption would have ever been emphasized in the *Sleeping Cupid* (lost). To my knowledge, the only other major works that openly address the topic of consumption in Michelangelo's oeuvre are the *Bacchus*, the *Children's Bacchanal*, and the *Punishment of Tityus.*

77. See Michael Hirst, *Michelangelo and His Drawings* (New Haven, Conn.: Yale University Press, 1988), 101–18, for a discussion of these presentation drawings, as well as the precedents; he has provided a close analysis of the techniques, and argued convincingly that the *Children's Bacchanal* represented the most involved of all Michelangelo's presentation drawings, occupying more of his time than the others. On the *Children's Bacchanal*, see also James M. Saslow, *Ganymede in the Renaissance: Homosexuality in Art and Society* (New Haven, Conn.: Yale University Press, 1986), 44–45.

78. *Le vite*, 1256.

79. In thinking about these drawings, I have benefited indirectly from David

Rosand, *Drawing Acts: Studies in Graphic Expression and Representation* (Cambridge: Cambridge University Press, 2002), 208–19.

80. Cv 107, Cdv 64. Conversely, Dolce has "Aretino" wittily remark in his *Dialogo* that if you've seen one Michelangelo figure, you've seen them all—a comment that is very much in the character of the obstreperous Aretino; see Roskill, *Dolce's Aretino*, 172–73.

81. For complex reflections on how Petrarchan lyric and the nature of desire encoded in that form underpins sixteenth-century Italian reflections on "beauty," as well as how Michelangelo's *Bacchanal* and his other presentation drawings figure into the period aesthetics, see Elizabeth Cropper, "The Place of Beauty in the High Renaissance and Its Displacement in the History of Art," in *Place and Displacement in the Renaissance*, ed. Alvin Vos (Binghamton, N.Y.: Medieval and Renaissance Texts and Studies, 1995), 159–205, esp. 200–201.

82. There are other visual sources, of course, for the overall work, including sarcophagi and Michelangelo's own Sistine Chapel vault, which is echoed in numerous places: the children recall the architectural putti placed in pairs, the old man being covered recalls Noah, and so on.

83. Alexander Nagel, *Michelangelo and the Reform of Art* (Cambridge: Cambridge University Press, 2000), 158–68. Significantly, Michelangelo would seem to be quoting from a work that, according to Goffen, marked Raphael's first attempt at appropriating the style of Michelangelo and engaging in a rivalry with him; see Goffen, *Renaissance Rivals*, 206–10.

84. Consider the related thoughts of Rosand, *Drawing Acts*, 217: "Materiality of surface, a constant reminder of the operations of the drawing hand," Rosand observes in terms that are congenial to this reading of the *Children's Bacchanal*, "cannot but become a record of the physical presence of the draftsman."

85. Michelangelo, *The Poetry of Michelangelo: An Annotated Translation*, trans. James M. Saslow (New Haven, Conn.: Yale University Press, 1991). See Saslow, *Ganymede in the Renaissance*, chap. 1, 17–62, on Michelangelo's *Ganymede* drawing, his sexuality, and his relations with Tommaso de' Cavalieri.

86. Frederick Hartt, *Michelangelo Drawings* (New York: Abrams, 1970), 249. On the *Tityus*, see also Erwin Panofsky, *Studies in Iconology: Humanistic Themes in the Art of the Renaissance* (New York: Oxford University Press, 1939), 217–18; and Saslow, *Ganymede in the Renaissance*, 34–36.

87. Hirst, *Michelangelo and His Drawings*, 24.

88. William E. Wallace, "Michelangelo's Assistants in the Sistine Chapel," *Gazette des Beaux-Arts* 110 (1987): 203–16. Cv 57–58: "He finished this entire work in twenty months," Condivi claims, "without any help whatever, not even someone to grind his colors for him" (Cdv 34–35).

89. *Scritti d'arte*, 10.

90. *Le vite*, 1258.

91. I cite from *Opere di Baldassare Castiglione, Giovanni della Casa, Benvenuto Cellini*, ed. Carlo Cordié (Milan: Ricciardi Editore, 1960), 1107 (from "Sopra l'arte del disegno").

92. This is not to gainsay, however, the importance of sprezzatura in some instances of Michelangelo not finishing works, such as his play on the concept of

faciebat, and the importance, for instance, that Condivi ascribes to Michelangelo purposely not polishing the top of the *David* as a way of marking that he had used the entire marble block (Cv 28, Cdv 21). See as well in the same passage Michelangelo's criticism of Donatello for his roughness, the absence of complete polish.

Notes to Chapter 4

1. Richard A. Goldthwaite, "The Empire of Things: Consumer Demand in Renaissance Italy," in *Patronage, Art and Society in Renaissance Italy*, eds. F. W. Kent and Patricia Simons (Oxford: Oxford University Press, 1987), 153–75. See also his *Wealth and the Demand for Art in Italy, 1300–1600* (Baltimore: Johns Hopkins University Press, 1993) for a more developed treatment. All citations from Cellini's *Vita* come from *The Autobiography of Benvenuto Cellini*, trans. John Addington Symonds (New York: Modern Library, 1927), modified for accuracy; and *Vita*, ed. Ettore Camesasca (Milan: BUR, 1985).

2. Lauro Martines, "Review Essay: The Renaissance and the Birth of Consumer Society," *Renaissance Quarterly* 51 (1998): 202: "In sum, all early collecting, down at least to the eighteenth century, was a social affair, not a secluded, private business between the possessor and the possessed." Michael Baxandall, *Painting and Experience in Fifteenth-Century Italy: A Primer in the Social History of Pictorial Style* (Oxford: Oxford University Press, 1972).

3. See Bill Brown, ed., *Things* (Chicago: University of Chicago Press, 2004), 4.

4. On this see Paula Findlen, *Possessing Nature: Museums, Collecting and Scientific Culture in Early Modern Italy* (Berkeley: University of California Press, 1994). See also for the studio as a site for collecting and conversation, Dora Thornton, *The Scholar in His Study: Ownership and Experience in Renaissance Italy* (New Haven, Conn.: Yale University Press, 1997), 99–126; and for the visual arts in a particular city, Patricia Fortini Brown, *Private Lives in Renaissance Venice: Art, Architecture, and the Family* (New Haven, Conn.: Yale University Press, 2004), 217–51.

5. I should perhaps stress that I am not claiming here that thing theorists have got it right, or that things in the modern period have lives of their own. I would claim, however, that in sixteenth-century Italy no one, to my knowledge, would have ever imagined that (or strove for an aesthetic in which) things existed in the manner currently theorized by thing theorists.

6. I follow here the recent attribution and identification by Louis A. Waldman, "A Rediscovered Portrait of Benvenuto Cellini Attributed to Francesco Ferrucci del Tadda and Cellini," *Burlington Magazine* 2007 (149): 820–30.

7. On the fashioning of a male identity in Cellini's writings, his "masculinity," see now Margaret A. Gallucci, *Benvenuto Cellini: Sexuality, Masculinity, and Artistic Identity in Renaissance Italy* (New York: Palgrave Macmillan, 2003), *passim*. I have also benefited from Paolo L. Rossi, "The Writer and the Man: Real Crimes and Mitigating Circumstances—il caso Cellini," in *Crime, Society, and the Law in Renaissance Italy*, eds. K. Lowe and T. Dean (Cambridge: Cambridge University Press, 1994), 157–83; and Rossi, "*Sprezzatura*, Patronage and Fate: Benvenuto Cellini and the World of Words," in *Vasari's Florence*, ed. P. Jacks (Cambridge: Cambridge University Press, 1998), 55–72. On his life, see the synthetic discussion by Nino Borsellino, "Cellini,

Benvenuto," *Dizionario biografico degli italiani*, vol. 23 (Rome: Istituto della Enciclopedia Italiana, 1979), 440–51.

8. He began the *Vita* in about 1558 while in house arrest and in an effort to take charge of his immortal soul (and perhaps also to receive commissions or retaliate against his entrenched enemies). On this see Rossi, "Il caso Cellini," 180–81; and Margaret A. Gallucci, "Cellini's Trial for Sodomy: Power and Patronage at the Court of Cosimo I," in *The Cultural Politics of Duke Cosimo I de' Medici*, ed. Konrad Eisenbichler (Aldershot: Ashgate, 2001), 37–46.

9. Which a number of scholars have seen as highly structured, on the basis of a number of literary and art historical models, from Dante to Vasari. See, for instance, Gallucci, *Benvenuto Cellini*, 71–108; Victoria G. Gardner, "*Homines non nascuntur, sed figuntur:* Benvenuto Cellini's *Vita* and Self-Presentation of the Renaissance Artist," *Sixteenth Century Journal* 28 (1997): 447–65; Guido Davico Bonino, *Lo scrittore, il potere, la maschera: Tre studi sul Cinquecento* (Padua: Liviana, 1979); Dino Cervigni, *The "Vita" of Benvenuto Cellini: Literary Tradition and Genre* (Ravenna: Longo, 1979); the fine study of Cellini in Jane Tylus, *Writing and Vulnerability in the Late Renaissance* (Stanford: Stanford University Press, 1993), 31–53; Corinne Lucas, "L'artiste et l'écriture: *Il dire* et *il fare* dans les écrits de Cellini," in *Culture et professions en Italie (XVe–XVIIe siècles)*, ed. A. C. Fiorato (Paris: Publications de la Sorbonne, 1989), 67–96; Maria Galetta, "Tradizione ed innovazione nella *Vita* di Benvenuto Cellini," *Romance Review* 5 (1995): 65–72; Jonathan Goldberg, "Cellini's *Vita* and the Conventions of Early Autobiography," *Modern Language Notes* 89 (1974): 71–83; and Marziano Guglielminetti, *Memoria e scrittura: L'autobiografia da Dante a Cellini* (Turin: Einaudi, 1977), 292–383. For the complex reception of Cellini's manuscript and final publication in 1730 in Naples, see the forthcoming study of Thomas Willette, tentatively titled *Cellini Among the Freemasons: Language, Natural Science and Radical Politics in the Eighteenth Century*.

10. The legal procedures surrounding this event, and Cellini's ties professionally to Salvatore and Michele Guasconti, are discussed by Rossi, "Il caso Cellini," 161–64.

11. Again, see 76, 1.34.

12. John Wyndham Pope-Hennessy, *Cellini* (New York: Abbeville Press, 1985), 82–84, discusses the "things" made by Cellini while in prison.

13. As Rossi, "Sprezzatura," observes, it is improbable, if not impossible, that Cellini dashed off this tale while working.

14. I have adopted the Bondanella translation here: Benvenuto Cellini, *My Life*, trans. Julia Conaway Bondanella and Peter Bondanella (New York: Oxford University Press, 2002), 3.

15. See 1.31.

16. And Cellini is *not* going to back down when his pay isn't forthcoming. The profit is everything, from the outset. Consider the instance early on in his career when he has to stand up for himself against the Bishop of Salamanca (46–47, 1.24).

17. Pope-Hennessy, *Cellini*, 24. Cellini brings this to our attention as well, in a manner that once more indicates, as Rossi, "Sprezzatura," has argued, that this is a highly crafted autobiography in which one event foreshadows another (323, 2.21).

18. Consider, for instance: 38, 1.20; 101, 1.45; 102, 1.45; 106, 1.46; 195, 1.90; 127,

1.58; 348, 2.36. On the role of the marvelous in Cellini's autobiography, see Tylus, *Writing and Vulnerability*, 49. Rossi, "Il caso Cellini," also nicely discusses the importance of meraviglia in light of Cellini's desire to figure himself, like Michelangelo, as a person of terribilità.

19. The best study of the *Perseus* is the superb analysis by Michael Wayne Cole, *Cellini and the Principles of Sculpture* (Cambridge: Cambridge University Press, 2002), 43–78.

20. Admittedly the translation alters the original syntactically: "Or veduto di avere risuscitato un morto, contro al credere di tutti quegli ignioranti."

21. Cellini, *Due trattati: Uno intorno alle otto principali arti dell'oreficeria* (Florence: Per Valente Panizzij, & Marco Peri, 1568; New York: Broude International Editions, 1980), S ii.verso.

22. On the calculated role of spectatorship with regard to the *Perseus*, which transforms into stone through its gorgonizing gaze (in the sense of paralyzed astonishment) the viewers and the surrounding sculptures with which it playfully vies, see John Shearman, *Only Connect: Art and the Spectator in the Italian Renaissance* (Princeton: Princeton University Press, 1992), 48–58.

23. Gallucci, *Benvenuto Cellini*, 82. On how-to books in different areas of interest, see Rudolph Bell, *How to Do It: Guides to Good Living for Renaissance Italians* (Chicago: University of Chicago Press, 1999); Douglas Biow, *Doctors, Ambassadors, Secretaries: Humanism and Professions in Renaissance Italy* (Chicago: University of Chicago Press, 2003); and William Eamon, *Science and the Secrets of Nature: Books of Secrets in Medieval and Early Modern Culture* (Princeton: Princeton University Press, 1994). For a study of these treatises, see Paolo L. Rossi, "Parrem uno, e pur saremo dua: The Genesis and Fate of Benvenuto Cellini's *Trattati*," in Margaret A. Gallucci and Paolo L. Rossi, *Benvenuto Cellini: Sculptor, Goldsmith, Writer* (Cambridge: Cambridge University Press, 2004), 171–98.

24. Galucci, *Benvenuto Cellini*, 80.

25. I cite from *Opere di Baldassare Castiglione, Giovanni della Casa, Benvenuto Cellini*, ed. Carlo Cordié (Milan: Ricciardi Editore, 1960), by page number in my text; I have adopted, though with modifications, the serviceable translation *The Treatises of Benvenuto Cellini on Goldsmithing and Sculpture*, trans. C. R. Ashbee (New York: Dover, 1967), cited by page number before the Italian reference. The event is described in the *Vita* in less detail, but with the same self-aggrandizing effect.

26. Giovanventura Rosetti, *Notandissimi segreti de l'arte profumatoria, Venezia 1555*, eds. Franco Brunello and Franca Facchetti (Vicenza: Neri Pozza, 1973); for more on this topic, see Douglas Biow, *The Culture of Cleanliness in Renaissance Italy* (Ithaca, N.Y.: Cornell University Press, 2006), 13–14 and *passim*.

27. Tylus, *Writing and Vulnerability*, 42–43, has a good reading of this.

28. For other aspects of Cellini's efforts at presenting himself as inimitable, especially in comparison to Michelangelo, the artist of the period known for being so inimitable, see Jane Tylus, "Cellini, Michelangelo, and the Myth of Inimitability," in *Benvenuto Cellini: Sculptor, Goldsmith, Writer*, eds. Margaret A. Gallucci and Paolo L. Rossi (Cambridge: Cambridge University Press, 2004), 7–25.

29. Cellini, *Opere: Vita, trattati, rime, lettere*, ed. Bruno Maier (Milan: Rizzoli, 1968).

30. This has been, rightly so, a privileged locus of Cellini studies that focus on his autobiography. I found Tylus, *Writing and Vulnerability*, to be the most helpful.

31. On this, see the perceptive fine study by Cole, *Cellini*, 43–78.

32. Consider, for instance, 2.105.

33. Cellini, *Opere*, 891.

34. On Cellini as a poet, see Giulia dell'Aquila, "Benvenuto Cellini lirico," *Rivista di letteratura italiana* 18 (2000): 47–69; and Margaret A. Gallucci, "A New Look at Benvenuto Cellini's Poetry," *Forum Italicum* 34 (2000): 343–71.

35. From his treatise on the paragone between painting and sculpture, *Opere*, 866. By contrast, as Vasari argues, Giorgione—in disagreement with Andrea del Verrocchio's colleagues—maintained the opposite, on which see Goffen, *Renaissance Rivalries*, 61–64, especially for how painters and sculptors engaged this agon in their works regarding the privileging of one medium over another.

Notes to Chapter 5

1. The books on this topic in Renaissance studies are legion. To name a few from several disciplines, which have inspired me in writing this chapter and are either in English or have been translated into English: Anthony Grafton, *Commerce with the Classics: Ancient Books and Renaissance Readers* (Ann Arbor: University of Michigan Press, 1997); Grafton, "Renaissance Readers and Ancient Texts: Comments on Some Commentaries," *Renaissance Quarterly* 38 (1985): 615–49; Grafton, "Is the History of Reading a Marginal Enterprise? Guillaume Budé and His Books," *Papers of the Bibliographical Society of America* 91 (1997): 139–57; Anthony Grafton and Lisa Jardine, *From Humanism to the Humanities: Education and the Liberal Arts in Fifteenth- and Sixteenth-Century Europe* (London: Duckworth, 1986); Grafton and Jardine, "Studied for Action: How Gabriel Harvey Read His Livy," *Past & Present* 129 (1990): 30–78; Andrea Carlino, *Books of the Body: Anatomical Ritual and Renaissance Learning*, trans. John and Anne C. Tedeschi (Chicago: University of Chicago Press, 1999); Lina Bolzoni, *The Gallery of Memory: Literary and Iconographic Models in the Age of the Printing Press* (Toronto: University of Toronto Press, 2001); Craig Kallendorf, "Marginalia and the Rise of Early Modern Subjectivity," in *On Renaissance Commentaries*, ed. Marianne Pade (New York: Olms, 2005), 111–28; Kallendorf, *Virgil and the Myth of Venice: Books and Readers in the Italian Renaissance* (Oxford: Clarendon Press, 1999), 1–11, who gives an excellent overview of the change that took place in the academy roughly in the 1980s toward a "new literary history" of the sort described above; William H. Sherman, "What Did Renaissance Readers Write in Their Books?" in *Books and Readers in Early Modern England: Material Studies*, eds. Jennifer Anderson and Elizabeth Sauer (Philadelphia: University of Pennsylvania Press, 2002), 119–37; Sherman, *Used Books: Marking Readers in Renaissance England* (Philadelphia: University of Pennsylvania Press, 2007); Brian Richardson, "Inscribed Meanings: Authorial Self-Fashioning and Readers' Annotations in Sixteenth-Century Italian Printed Books," in *Reading and Literacy in the Middle Ages and Renaissance*, ed. Ian Frederick Moulton (Turnhout, Belgium: Brepols, 2004), 85–104; and Alison K. Frazier, *Possible Lives: Authors and Saints in Renaissance Italy* (New York: Columbia University Press, 2005). There is, of course, a venerable tradi-

tion in Italian studies of placing authors within their studies ("scrittoi"). A classic study in this vein is that of Giuseppe Billanovich, *Petrarca letterato: Lo scrittoio del Petrarca* (Rome: Edizioni di Storia e Letteratura, 1947).

2. On polygraphs, see the Introduction, n. 2. For Doni's attack, see Doni, *Contra Aretinum: "Teremoto," "Vita," "Oratione funerale": Con un'appendice di lettere*, ed. P. Procaccioli (Manziana: Vecchiarelli, 1998). Doni also wrote yet another anti-Aretino harangue, on which see Paolo Procaccioli, "Per il Doni antiaretiniano: *L'orazione funerale*," *Studi e problemi di critica testuale* 47 (1993): 119–34.

3. Doni studies are scattered and growing rapidly in volume, with some important scholarly insights contained in introductions to his reprinted books, which are only now being offered to the public in critical editions. On Doni, essential remains Cecilia Ricottini Marsili-Libelli, *Anton Francesco Doni scrittore e stampatore* (Florence: Sansoni, 1960). I have found particularly valuable for an understanding of his life and work, Salvatore Bongi, "Vita di Anton Francesco Doni fiorentino" and "Catalogo delle opere di Antonfrancesco Doni," in *I marmi*, ed. Pietro Fanfani, 2 vols. (Florence: Barberi, 1863), ix–lxiii and 277–309; Paul F. Grendler, *Critics of the Italian World, 1530–1560: Anton Francesco Doni, Nicolò Franco and Ortensio Lando* (Madison: University of Wisconsin Press, 1969); Vanni Bramanti, "Introduzione" to *La libraria*, ed. Vanni Bramanti (Milan: Longanesi & C., 1972), 10–43; Carlo Cordié, "Nota introduttiva" and "Nota bio-bibliografica," in *Folengo, Aretino, Doni*, ed. C. Cordiè, vol. 2 (Milan: Ricciardi Editore, 1976), 571–96; G. Romei, "Doni, Anton Francesco," *Dizionario biografico degli italiani*, vol. 41 (Rome: Istituto della Enciclopedia Italiana, 1992), 158–66; Giorgio Masi, "'Quelle discordanze sì perfette': Anton Francesco Doni 1551–1553," *Atti e memorie dell'Accademia toscana di scienze e lettere La Colombaria* 53 (1988): 11–112; Masi, "Appunti su Anton Francesco Doni e sull'edizione dei *Mondi* e degli *Inferni*," *Filologia e critica* 22 (1997): 264–93; Masi, "Coreografie doniane: L'Accademia Pellegrina," in *Cinquecento capriccioso e irregolare: Eresie letterarie nell'Italia del classicismo*, eds. Paolo Procaccioli e Angelo Romano (Rome: Vecchiarelli, 1999), 45–85; Sonia Maffei, "Introduzione" to *Pitture del Doni*, ed. S. Maffei (Naples: La Stanza delle Scritture, 2004), 11–128; and Patrizia Pellizzari, "Nota biografica," in Doni's *I mondi e gli inferni*, ed. P. Pellizzari with intro. Marziano Guglielminetti (Turin: Einaudi, 1994), lix lxxxiv. For a recent assessment of Doni scholarship, see Giorgio Masi, "Bibliografia: Anton Francesco Doni," http://www.nuovorinascimento.org/cinquecento/doni.pdf (accessed January 1, 2007). For editions and manuscripts, see Giorgio Masi, "Prospettive editoriali e questioni filologiche doniane," in *"Una soma di libri": L'edizione delle opere di Anton Francesco Doni*, ed. G. Masi (Florence: Olschki, 2008), 1–35; and Masi and Carlo Alberto Girotto, "Le carte di Anton Francesco Doni," *L'ellisse* 3 (2008): 1–51.

4. Anton Francesco Doni, *Tre libri di lettere* (Venice: Marcolini, 1552), 224. Doni, we shall see, fought with many, Aretino and Domenichi in particular, but Grendler, *Critics*, 54, calls attention also to a minor fight that nevertheless reveals why it was so difficult for this intemperate, anticourtly man to find a patron: "The reason for Doni's lack of success in finding a patron stemmed from his irascible temper and his dislike for the signori, both of which were becoming known. In 1545 Doni, in reply to some now unknown slight, wrote a vindictive letter about Giulio Albicante, a minor literary figure. Albicante was inclined to reply in kind, but a mutual acquaintance, Luca Contile, dissuaded him, and the quarrel was patched up. In the course of

his letters at the time, Contile evaluated Doni as a virtuoso of great ability, but with rabid and vengeful tendencies." See Luca Contile, *Il primo volume delle lettere* (Venice: [Comin da Trino], 1564), 95–97.

5. Accusations of plagiarism are common in the period. One of the famous ones among polygraphs concerns Aretino accusing Nicolò Franco of plagiarism in the break of their once exceedingly warm friendship, a break that took place by August 1538. See Grendler, *Critics*, 39. On plagiarism and the acceptance of it in sixteenth-century Italy, with the explosion of print, see the concise observations of Amedeo Quondam, "Note su imitazione e 'plagio' nel classicismo," in *Sondaggi sulla riscrittura del Cinquecento*, ed. Paolo Cherchi (Ravenna: Longo, 1998), 11–26; Paolo Cherchi, *Polimatia di riuso: Mezzo secolo di plagio (1539–1589)* (Rome: Bulzoni 1998), esp. 143–65 for Doni; and the collection *Furto e plagio nella letteratura del classicismo*, ed. R. Gigliucci (Rome: Bulzoni, 1998). The scholarly literature on the topic of the art of riscrittura is now immense. On Doni's plagiarism, and an up-to-date bibliography, see for a fine overview Maffei, "Plagi e riscritture: Doni, Camillo e Toscanella," in "Introduzione," *Le pitture*, 69–80; and in particular Paolo Cherchi, "Nell'officina di Anton Francesco Doni," *Forum Italicum* 21 (1987): 206–16; Cherchi, *Polimatia di riuso*, 143–65; Cherchi, "La 'selva' dei *Marmi* doniani," *Esperienze letterarie* 26 (2001): 3–40; Doni, *Mondi*, appendix 2, 417–31; Masi, "'Quelle discordanze'"; Masi "Interpolazioni editoriali e refusi d'autore: Il Doni e l'*Oratio de charitate* di Giovanni Nesi," *Studi italiani* 1 (1989): 43–90; Masi, "Appunti," 267–68; and Masi, "Postilla sull'*affaire* Doni-Nesi: La questione del *Dialogo della stampa*," *Studi italiani* 2 (1990): 41–54.

6. Roger Chartier, "Libraries Without Walls," *Representations* 42 (1993): 43. Chartier cites from Theodore Besterman, *The Beginnings of Systematic Bibliography* (Oxford: London, 1935), 23.

7. Doni, *Libraria* (Venice: Giolito, 1550); the second edition contains more books and authors, as is noted in the frontispiece.

8. Masi, "'Quelle discordanze,'" 12, n. 1. On this shift, consider the incisive observations of Masi, idem., 15–19, and more generally, Masi, "Appunti." On the Giolito press during this period, see Amedeo Quondam, "'Mercanzia d'onore,' 'mercanzia d'utile': Produzione libraria e lavoro intellettuale a Venezia nel Cinquecento," in *Libri, editori e pubblico nell'Europa moderna: Guida storica e critica*, ed. Armando Petrucci (Bari: Laterza, 1977), 51–104; and for Marcolini, Quondam, "Nel giardino del Marcolini: Un editore Veneziano tra Aretino e Doni," *Giornale storico della letteratura italiana* 157 (1980): 75–116. Doni, *La seconda libraria* (Venice: Marcolini, 1551 and 1555). For a compelling reading of the *Libraria*, which came to my attention as this book was going to press, see Jonathan David Bradbury, "Anton Francesco Doni and His *Librarie*: Bibliographical Friend or Fiend," *Forum for Modern Language Studies* 17 (2008): 91–107; Bradbury argues cogently against setting up the first and second *Librarie* in strict opposition, and he emphasizes correctly how playful and parodic the first *Libraria* in many ways is.

9. For instance, the 1555 version contains Anselmi Giusto (26), but the 1551 and 1557/1558 do not.

10. As Masi, "'Quelle discordanze,'" has meticulously demonstrated, much of this success can be attributed to the influence of Marcolini.

11. I draw from *Libraria*, 416–23. For a free lively translation of parts of this "let-

ter," see David Chambers and Brian Pullan, eds., *Venice: A Documentary History, 1450–1630* (Oxford: Blackwell, 1992), 181.

12. The translation is largely the same as Sebastiano Manilio's of 1494.

13. For this period, readers should carefully consult Masi, "'Quelle discordanze.'" *La zucca*: this version is the first part of large-scale, helter-skelter collection of anecdotes, maxims, commentaries on proverbial wisdom, letters, and tales, and it was immediately translated into Spanish. *La moral filosofia* is a collection of Eastern stories eventually translated into English by Sir Thomas North in 1570. *I pistolotti amorosi* is a series of fictional letters that stylistically make light of the popular Petrarchan amatory verse, letters, and prose of the period. The *Tre libri* represents Doni's complete collection of letters now reordered and reworked with emendations, additions, and exclusions. His most well-known works today are *I marmi* and *I mondi*. The first is a book about the varied conversations overheard during the dog days of summer when groups of people from all ranks of society chit-chat as they cool themselves on the refreshing marble steps of Santa Maria de' Fiori in Florence. The second is a quasi-philosophical yet satirical work that posited the existence of different spaces wherein moral judgments are sometimes cast on our own sublunary world.

14. There were two printings, exactly the same, from what I can tell, in 1557 and 1558.

15. In Piacenza Doni was a member of the Accademia Ortolana, in Florence of the Accademia Fiorentina (where he was first secretary), and in Venice of the Accademia Pellegrina (whose existence has been doubted and for which there is no reliable record); see Pellizzari, "Nota biografica," lxxix, n. 64, who argues for the existence of the Accademia Pellegrina, and Masi, "Coreografie doniane," who vigorously and persuasively voices reserve.

16. Grendler, *Critics*, 61. Doni, *Tre libri*, 313.

17. Enea Vico's portrait can be consulted in Adam von Bartsch, *The Illustrated Bartsch*, ed. Walter L. Strauss, vol. 30 (New York: Abaris Books, 1985), 161.

18. Brian Richardson, "Print or Pen? Modes of Written Publication in Sixteenth-Century Italy," *Italian Studies* 59 (2004): 39–64.

19. My understanding of printing (and bookselling) of sixteenth-century Italy is indebted to Angela Nuovo, *Il commercio librario nell'Italia del Rinascimento*, 3rd edition (Milan: Franco Angeli, 2003); Brian Richardson, *Printing, Writers, and Readers in Renaissance Italy* (Cambridge: Cambridge University Press, 1999); Martin Lowry, *The World of Aldus Manutius: Business and Scholarship in Renaissance Venice* (Ithaca, N.Y.: Cornell University Press, 1979); Claudia di Filippo Bareggi, *Il mestiere di scrivere: Lavoro intellettuale e mercato librario a Venezia nel Cinquecento* (Rome: Bulzoni, 1988); Paul F. Grendler, *The Roman Inquisition and the Venetian Press, 1540–1605* (Princeton: Princeton University Press, 1977); and Amedeo Quondam, "La letteratura in tipografia," *Letteratura italiana*, ed. Alberto Asor Rosa, vol. 2, *Produzione e consumo* (Turin: Einaudi, 1983), 555–686. For a recent, concise summary of the press in Venice, see Iain Fenlon, *The Ceremonial City: History, Memory and Myth in Renaissance Venice* (New Haven, Conn.: Yale University Press, 2007), 233–71. For Doni's habits in writing, see additionally Cherchi, "Nell'officina"; and Maffei, "Introduzione."

20. Romei, "Doni," 159. Claudia di Filippo Bareggi, "Giunta, Doni, Torrentino: Tre tipografie fiorentine," *Nuova rivista storica* 58 (1974): 318–48.

21. Marsili-Libelli, *Anton Francesco Doni*, 342–56.

22. Di Filippo Bareggi, "Giunta, Doni, Torrentino," 326.

23. Romei, "Doni," 159. Doni, *Tre libri*, 253. Virtually the same letter appears in the 1547 edition of letters, *Il secondo libro* (Florence: Doni, 1547), 5r–6v. Doni, hardly a level-headed businessman, bears much of the blame for the failure of the printshop, even though it was, as di Filippo Bareggi observes, not a good way for a writer to make a living and thus a project botched from the start as an economic venture. Doni overloaded the shop with too many workers, no fewer than seven, including even his friend (at the time) from Piacenza, Domenichi. See di Filippo Bareggi, "Giunta, Doni, Torrentino," 326–29. See also Masi, "Interpolazioni."

24. Grendler, *The Roman Inquisition*, 5.

25. Doni, *I mondi e gli inferni*, 255; see also 252–54 for observations of how Doni composed.

26. See in particular, Quondam, "Nel giardino del Marcolini"; and Masi, "'Quelle discordanze.'"

27. As Richardson, *Printing*, 142, observes, gothic and an old-fashioned Roman type tended to be used for "popular" works, such as chivalric romances. See also on popular books generally, and their appearance, Paul F. Grendler, "Form and Function in Italian Renaissance Popular Books," *Renaissance Quarterly* 46 (1993): 451–85.

28. On Marcolini, see Doni's praise of him in his *Libraria*, 106.

29. On costs, see the information and table in Grendler, *The Roman Inquisition*, 12–14.

30. Grendler, *Critics*, 184.

31. There is no evidence, as Pellizzari ("Nota biografica," lxxxii, n. 87) observes, that Doni tried to set up a press in Ancona, as some scholars have claimed he did.

32. Doni, it seems, was recognized in his own time as something of a sycophant when it came to dedications; see Richardson, *Printing*, 56–57.

33. Vanni, *La libraria*, 31–32; Ortensio Lando, *La sferza de' scrittori antichi e moderni*, ed. Paolo Procaccioli (Rome: B. Vignola, 1995), 63, first published in 1550. Bradbury, "Anton Francesco Doni," does a nice job of capturing the strangeness of the first *Libraria*.

34. Bradbury, "Anton Francesco Doni," calls attention to a number of these omissions.

35. At some point or other, from the first 1550 edition to the final one in 1557/1558, a host of varied authors—most of whom we would never deem canonical in modern Anglo-American and European scholarship today, but some of whom are well known (such as Vasari)—made their way at long last into Doni's expansive book on books. Many of them in the second *Libraria* were Doni's inventions; the same may hold true for some authors listed in the first.

36. For instances when this was in fact the case, see Masi, "Prospettive," 22 and 22 n.76.

37. Niccolò Machiavelli certainly brought this concept home when, in a moment of dejected, literary peevishness, he considered himself a "prick" for not being included in the list of contemporary writers welcoming home Ludovico Ariosto (the real prick here for Machiavelli) after the Ferrarese poet returns to port from his long literary voyage in the concluding, fortieth canto of his massive, sprawling

Orlando furioso (1516 version). Conversely, Andrea Calmo has only words of gratitude on finding himself placed in Doni's *Libraria*. See Andrea Calmo, *Le lettere*, ed. V. Rossi (Turin: Loescher, 1888), 210–11. For Niccolò Machiavelli, see *Tutte le opere*, ed. Mario Martelli (Florence: Sansoni, 1992), 1194–95, writing from Florence December 17, 1517, shortly after the printing of the first edition of Ariosto's romance.

38. See also 84–85.

39. One gets a sense of Doni's playful smugness early on in the second treatise, *Libraria*, 250.

40. Doni also includes titles of books that are now lost, among them the *Lavandaria* and the *Rosa*. I am more suspicious than Masi, "Prospettive," 4–5, that they ever existed. Bradbury, "Anton Francesco Doni," also voices suspicion, viewing Doni as something of a "fiend" from the outset, who toys with his readers even in his first *Libraria*.

41. Masi, "Prospettive," 6–7.

42. In this regard see his comments under "Giovan Sabadino":

> This book will be the Ark of Noah, or so it should be called rather than the *Libraria*, because there is in it every sort of rational animal, whence everybody will be able to find pleasure for an hour in reading it. Some will say that this writer is clumsy, that one a gabber, this one worthy, this other as wise as Solomon. Oh, what would I pay to hear what they say of Sabadino, who so exaggeratingly and affectedly wrote the *Settanta novelle*! [120]

43. Doni, *Libraria*, 38; a point made earlier by Giovanni Getto, *Storia delle storie letterarie* (Milan: Bompiani, 1942), 19–23.

44. F. Scott Fitzgerald captured the concept memorably in his classic *The Great Gatsby* when a drunken partygoer pulls off a book in Gatsby's mansion and admires the eponymous hero's talent for full deception. See F. Scott Fitzgerald, *The Great Gatsby* (New York: Charles Scribner's Sons, 1925), 50.

45. Doni does in fact fantasize about owning a bookstore, in such places as *Pistolotti amorosi* (Venice: Marcolini, 1554), in the opening address, "A color che leggono."

46. Under the lemma ANTON FRANCESCO DONI (capitalized as such), we find the following in the final version:

> Also I will put my pen to work to discuss my writings, and this is the reason: when I was several years younger than I am now, I had not so quickly churned out [literally shat out, *scacazzato*] a page or a tale than I slipped it under a press to be printed, so that they came out as they were. Some I handed over to others for proofing, and I trusted the judgment (I was new at it) of who, according to my opinion, knew more than I did. Sometimes I would write negatively about someone at the request of others, and it seemed to me that I was doing a good, kind deed. I have put up with two or three awful pieces for his own benefit and slipped them in among my tittle-tattle; in thinking that he [the corrector of my writings?] was a giant [*parendomi d'essere un gigante*], I let him do as he wanted with the consequence that he boasted he had also written the rest. I praised many because of the false words of others [on the basis of information given me from others] and vituperated some [without investigating the sources], whom some traitorous men got me to blame; for the former I have been reproached, and for the latter I castigated myself on my own. I thank above all God

who gave me the time and place so that I could almost rewrite, gather together, or patch together all my chattering [*cicalerie*]. And a day doesn't go by when, in the Accademia Peregrina, I find myself cleaning up my writings [that is, his "cicalerie"] of the unmerited, stained, filthy, venomous praises composed at pay, so that as soon as they are in order, I will publish them, so that they will finally appear as they should, another thing altogether, erasing in the process those who did not merit ever being mentioned and praising those who wrongly received blame from the pen of another [namely, the traitorous men who slipped writings into my books or tricked me with false information; 80–81].

47. The two added books supposedly in manuscript form are *Il giornale, de' debitori e creditori* and *Ritrattationi, libri tre* (the latter not in 1550 or 1555 editions).

48. Doni falls just short of Aretino in the second 1550 edition—not by many, given Aretino's prominence in the field. The first 1550 edition does not contain *Stanze alla villanesca, Cicalamento sopra il Burchiello, Vita de' poeti,* and *Spiriti folletti.*

49. Doni, *Tre libri,* 44.

50. Ibid., 42–43.

51. Ibid., 44.

52. On prestezza as a shared value of polygraphs and visual artists in the sixteenth century, see the observations of Una Roman d'Elia, "Tintoretto, Aretino, and the Speed of Creation," *Word & Image* 20 (2004): 206–18; Tom Nichols, "Tintoretto, *Prestezza* and the *Poligrafi*: A Study in the Literary and Visual Culture of Cinquecento Venice," *Renaissance Studies* 10 (1996): 72–100; and Nichols, *Tintoretto: Tradition and Identity* (London: Reaktion Books, 1999), 69–99. As D'Elia points out, speed was not necessarily associated only with the polygraphs. See, for instance, with regard to Michelangelo, Robert J. Clements, "Michelangelo on Effort and Rapidity in Art," *Journal of the Warburg and Courtauld Institutes* 17 (1954): 301–10. On prestezza within the ambit of court culture, which could be construed as the virtuosity (*facilitas*) of putting things together rapidly on an impromptu basis, see Martin Warnke, *The Court Artist: On the Ancestry of the Modern Artist,* trans. David McLintock (Cambridge: Cambridge University Press, 1993), 209–11.

53. Nichols, *Tintoretto,* 73.

54. *Tre libri,* 29–30. As Nichols observes in *Tintoretto,* 95, "His books are presented as swiftly executed improvisations and in his dedication to Tintoretto [the dedication to his new edition of the *Rime del Burchiello*] he refers to himself in self-mocking fashion as 'Il Negligente'. . . . Doni may thus have been referring to a common charge laid against the *poligrafi,* while at the same time assuming a parallel between his own rapid, unfinished literary manner and that of Tintoretto."

55. Bongi, "Vita," l.

56. It can be found in Bramanti's edition, 437–38. As Bongi, "Vita," li, observes, Doni nonetheless seems to have valued Domenichi's abilities.

57. On Domenichi's dialogue, which Doni plagiarized, see *Dialogo della stampa,* in *Dialoghi* (Venice: Gabriel Giolito, 1562), 367–99, which becomes part of the section "Ragionamento della stampa" in *I marmi* (discussed below). On Doni appropriating Domenichi's dialogue, see Masi, "Postilla." Doni boasts that he wrote the nearly contemporaneous *I mondi* in twenty days.

58. Literally "his name" (*suo nome*). The passage from the plural to the singular

is telling here—an indication that Doni really has one person in mind, Domenichi, who, we are to understand, has the habit of using his name in the place of others as he robs people of their work.

59. The language here is colorful and highly metaphoric, as well as ironic and sarcastic, so this translation, like all those others offered in this chapter, can only be at best an approximation:

> Behold now Mr. Doctor [*il signor dottore*; this is the term that Doni uses in his writings to signal Domenichi], the Signor chinimeDo covidoLo, no less excellent as a lawyer than as a writer, who in his works has always praised and honored all the people, for which reason he merits a mitre, a crown or some high honor: he extracted from the most secret, hidden parts [literally "boxrooms," *ripostigli*] a book of witticisms worthy of his knowledge and he composed a volume about illustrious women, taken from [*cavato da*, which is to say, extracted, copied from] all those who have written about them, and he didn't include in it anything other than most honorable women. And for this [work], and for the many translations brought to light in so very brief a time, one can understand the knowledge that he has; and whoever is not satisfied with these works, go read his poetry, which will bring to a halt the marveling of those people who had marveled at [in the sense of doubted] the substance of such an important character" [308–9].

Domenichi had, like Doni and others, plagiarized. On Domenichi's creative plagiarisms, see, for instance, Roberto Gigliucci, "Il dialogo *Della fortuna* di Lodovico Domenichi e Ulrich von Hutten," in *Furto e plagio*, 263–82; and Gigliucci, "Virtù e furti di Lodovico Domenichi," in *Cinquecento capriccioso e irregolare*, 87–97.

60. See 263–65, 319–24, 332–33, 334–38.

61. For some thoughts on this, see Enrico Garavelli, "Una scheda iconografica per la polemica Doni-Domenichi," *Neuphilologische Mitteilungen* 103 (2002): 133–45, esp. 136–39.

62. Bongi, "Vita," xlvi, in his letter to Ferrante Gonzaga. In the *Libraria* he mentions how he would have liked to see him hanged and laments that Domenichi managed to escape his fate.

63. Bongi, Ibid., l–li; Procaccioli, "Per il Doni antiaretiniano," 130. He accused Domenichi of everything from sodomy to treachery.

64. In the very same section of Echimenedo Covidolo, in fact, Doni expresses the following, probably as justification for his own actions in trying to erase Domenichi from our memory: "I will praise always those people who are offended that they rid from [all of us] the memory of the person who offended them, and [I will always praise those same people who] in reprinting their works where they once praised that person incorrectly, they with good reason erase him [from their works], for that is the true punishment of one who is among the number of the dead, to take away from him that bit of life that had been bestowed on him through the power of the pen of one who is of elevated genius/talent" (308).

65. Domenichi, *Dialogo*, 390–91.

66. Doni, *Tre libri*, 51. See also Ibid., 87. But in his letter on "Il disegno" to his friend, the sculptor Giovanni Angelo Montorsoli, which precedes and prepares for the treatise published later, Doni more accurately states that he is not a painter but a draftsman (*disegnatore*), in Doni, *Lettere* (Florence: Doni, 1547), 48.

67. Anton Francesco Doni, *Disegno*, ed. Mario Pepe (Milan: Electa, 1970). He could have also perhaps learned the art from Montorsoli. He boasts about his ability to design in a number of instances (see, for instance, *Tre libri*, 63; *Lettere*, 50r), and he counted Tintoretto as a friend (on which see Nichols, *Tintoretto*, 76–77 and his illuminating exposition of their shared sensibilities, 69–99).

68. Three of the four extant manuscripts of imprese with Doni's own designs in them are autographs, and two of the earliest ones drawn by him are located in the Biblioteca Nazionale di Firenzi: the Fondo Palatino ms. E.B.10.8, titled *Le dimostrationi de gli animi degli huomini del Doni*, which is dedicated to Duke Alfonso II d'Este and dated 1561, and the Fondo Nuovi Acquisti, ms. 267, titled *Una nuova opinione circa all'imprese amorose e militari*, which is dedicated to Davit Otto and is also dated 1561 (8v). *Una nuova opinione* was certainly the fair copy for the Museo Correr 1387 manuscript, *Nova opinione del Doni sopra le imprese amorose et militari*, which does not contain designs in Doni's hand, but was perhaps supervised by him (there are notable divergences in style); the designs in the Museo Correr 1387, which is likewise dedicated to Davit Otto, were penned by the artist Jo. Bellochio, whose name is recorded at the bottom of the frontispiece of the manuscript. The Museo Correr 1387 manuscript also follows by and large the order and emblems of *Una nuova opinione*, the fair copy. The *Imprese reali* at Wellesley College (Frances Taylor Pearsons Plimpton Collection ms. 897) was composed in 1563, two years after *Le dimostrationi*. It shares some emblems and designs with the other two but is largely different, with no accompanying text; it is more narrowly dedicated, as the title indicates, to emblems of royal and influential families and illustrious persons, beginning, for instance, with King Philip and the motto "illustrabit omnia."

Moreover, it is important to bear in mind that Doni, who loved to capitalize on trends, showed a keen interest in these sorts of books on emblems early in his career as a writer in Venice. This interest appears even before Paolo Giovio's popular *Dialogo dell'imprese militari e amorose* (1555) came into print. As is evident in a letter to the printer Francesco Marcolini (see *Tre libri*, 310, but also 310–13 and 372–81), Doni—inspired by Claude Paradin's *Devises heroiques* (1551)—had already begun to think out a book on emblems, if not, in fact, a series of books on emblems, as early as 1552, shortly before Giovio had completed his *Dialogo* and four years before Domenichi (by then Doni's archenemy) had brought out in print his own book of emblems (on this see Paolo Giovio, *Dialogo dell'imprese militari et amorose*, ed. Maria Luisa Doglio [Rome: Bulzoni, 1978], 9). Not to be outdone, Doni, who always wished to seize the limelight when he could, tried to get Marcolini interested in a project on emblems by submitting to him a kind of preliminary book proposal.

But Marcolini, a perspicacious editor who helped transform Doni's style, did not take up Doni's project, perhaps because this proposed book on emblems would have required multiple images designed by a professional engraver. It would also have been an immense, if not interminable, project, as well as an enormous and time-consuming undertaking for the publisher, who must, in the final analysis, always think about the bottom line. Doni, it turns out, is actually thinking in the hundreds, perhaps even thousands, when he speaks of images. As he informs Paolo Giovio, Doni also had in mind books on "medaglie," which would have surely been costly to reproduce with all the images in them; see *La prima parte de le medaglie del Doni* (Venice: Giolito, 1550), 36.

Needless to say, a book (or books) with several hundred images in it (or them) would be costly to produce, both then, in midsixteenth-century Italy, and now, in early twenty-first century America and Europe. Thus, we can hypothesize that the four surviving Doni manuscripts on emblems, which collectively contain numerous designs in them, may well have been dedicated to people who, given their position and means, might be willing to subsidize an expensive book of this sort and, consequently, be willing to assist financially in bringing it out in print. Marcolini was evidently ill disposed to do so, either because a book of this sort, as "wondrous" and "rare" as Doni insists it would be, would have cost Marcolini too much to reproduce, or because a book of this sort just did not fit Marcolini's interests in his market niche (that is to say, it would not have fit into what publishers today would call a press's editorial "list"). It is clear, in any event, that the book of emblems dedicated to Duke Alfonso II d'Este, which is a folio, required much more work, care, and attention than the other two in Doni's own hand. For a host of reasons, the book given to the duke represented a valuable gift. It was also a gift likely designed for ducal favor and perhaps a position at court, something Doni often sought throughout his adult life but never, to his dismay, obtained.

69. On which, see Brian Richardson, "The Debates on Printing in Renaissance Italy," *La bibliofilìa* 100 (1998): 135–55. Historically we should not, of course, overstate the differences, both ideological and formal, between print and scribal publication, thereby reproducing the rhetoric of the debate (the sort of rhetoric Doni engages in) as constituting actual differences in kind. Print and scribal publication developed together in sixteenth-century Italy, borrowing from each other, and the very same authors (as Richardson has observed in "Print or Pen?") could choose to use one or the other to meet specific aims.

70. Anton Francesco Doni, *I marmi*, ed. Ezio Chiòrboli (Bari: Laterza, 1928); and Anton Francesco Doni, *A Discussion About Printing Which Took Place at "I Marmi" in Florence*, trans. David Brancaleone (Turin: Alberto Tallone Editore, 2003), modified throughout for accuracy. Doni reproduces Domenichi, *Dialoghi*, 388–89 here.

71. Doni reproduces Domenichi, *Dialoghi*, 371, here. Cicero's *Republic* was in fact later discovered in a palimpsest in the eighteenth century.

72. A point also made earlier in the *Libraria*, 132, under the section on Ariosto, in virtually the same way. Again, Doni reproduces Domenichi, *Dialoghi*, 371, here.

73. Doni, *Le pitture*, 143–44.

74. On presentation manuscripts used to fashion authorial uniqueness within the still vibrant scribal mode of publication, see Richardson, "Print or Pen?" 44 and *passim*.

75. Giorgio Masi, "Introduzione" to *Sentenze* in *Umori e sentenze*, eds. Vincenza Giri and Giorgio Masi (Rome: Salerno, 1988), 113. Masi's primary example in this instance is Doni's *Primo libro delle sentenze dette da fiorentini*, which was dedicated to Francesco de' Medici and produced by hand just a year after Doni dedicated his book on emblems to the Duke Alfonso II d'Este. See also Masi, "Prospettive," 15.

76. In this respect, Doni is making use of scribal "publication" to forge what Richardson ("Print or Pen?" 43 and *passim*) has described as "in-groups."

77. Masi, "Introduzione," 113–14. Scholars have tended to devote their attention to Doni's reuse of existing engravings for books, rather than the drawings made and designed by him for his manuscripts, but a notable exception is the recent study by Maffei, "Introduzione," *passim*, which contains a number of reproductions of Doni's images in it. For the relationship between word and image in Doni, see Patrizia Pellizzari, "Riscrittura per immagini: La 'Moral filosofia' e i 'Trattati' di Anton Francesco Doni," *«Levia Gravia»: Quaderno annuale di letteratura italiana* 2 (2000): 97–127; Daniel Arasse, "*Ars memoriae* et symboles visuels: La critique de l'imagination et la fin de la Renaissance," in *Symboles de la Renaissance* (Paris: Presses de l'École Normale Supérieure, 1976), 57–73; Lina Bolzoni, *Il teatro della memoria: Studi su Giulio Camillo* (Padua: Liviana, 1984), 59–76; Bolzoni, "Riuso e riscrittura di immagini: Dal Palatino al della Porta, dal Doni a Federico Zuccari, al Toscanella," in *Scritture di scritture: Testi, generi, modelli nel Rinascimento*, eds. G. Mazzacurati and M. Plaisance (Rome: Bulzoni, 1987), 171–206; Nichols, "Tintoretto," 72–100; Masi, "'Quelle discordanze,'" 28–29 and 90–112; Anna Paola Mulinacci, "Quando 'le parole s'accordano con l'intaglio': Alcuni esempi di riuso e riscrittura di immagini in Anton Francesco Doni," in *Percorsi tra parole e immagini (1400–1600)*, eds. A. Giudotti and M. Rossi (Lucca: Lucini Fazzi, 2000), 111–40; and Michel Plaisance, "Il riuso delle immagine ne *I marmi* del Doni," in *Percorsi*, 9–18. It is worth mentioning that Doni, when he examines books, is clearly interested in the designs within them, as is evident in his *Libraria*, ed. Vanni Bramanti, 69 (Achille Marozzo), 106 (Francesco Marcolini), and 289 (Currado Adimari), 310 (Enea Vico); see also his familiarity with Enea Vico, 139 (and his *Sopra l'effigie di Cesare fatta per M. Enea Vico da Parma, Dichiaratione del Doni* [Venice: s.n., 1550], a1v, dedication).

78. This was certainly not uncommon, both among writers in general in the Renaissance and for Doni in particular. Consider, for instance, the dedication to Ottavio Farnese at the beginning of his manuscript on the *Stufaiuolo*, housed at Harvard University: *Lo stufaiuolo*, Houghton Library, Harvard University, MS Typ 853, 2r. In his manuscript "Ornamento della lingua Toscana del Doni Fiorentino," Biblioteca Nazionale di Firenze, Fondo Nuovi Acquisti, ms. 268, dedicated to Baccio Tolomei, Doni laments how he has received little remuneration typically for all his efforts—a lament that is not unfamiliar in the Italian Renaissance as writers sought some measure of compensation and recognition for their labors (4r).

79. *Dimostrationi*, 40r, and *Nuova opinione*, 59r–60v. The speed of printing was, of course, one of the characteristics attributed to it by its praisers, on which, see Richardson, "Print or Pen?" 137–39.

80. For others in the Italian Renaissance who saw printing as a transformative and exciting invention, and Doni's contribution, see Quondam, "La letteratura in tipografia," 566–72, esp. 623–31.

81. A point made in *I marmi*.

Lollio: I have often heard people in the trade claim this art is related to alchemy. What do you say to that?

Coccio: I can confirm what you say. Let me add that, just as alchemy bewitches the featherbrains who believe in it with the promise that solid lead can be turned into gold (only to fill the nostrils with smoke and dust), in a similar fashion printing leads ne'er-do-wells to believe that rag paper and ink can be minted into florins. But in fact they are left stuck out in printing shops surrounded by inky press sheets, eternally to vie with the vain hope of the Jews in the Messiah—and at the mercy of mold.

Lollio: Also I have heard it said that Robert Estienne in Paris, Gryphius in Lyon, Froben in Basel, and many Italians in Venice really have earned thousands of ducats by working in the printing trade.

Coccio: Surely you have also heard of the countless individuals who, working to no avail, have prosecuted this business and squandered vast amounts of money.

Lollio: I know little about such trickery.

Doni, *I marmi*, 1.189; Doni, *A Discussion About Printing*, 39–40; Domenichi, *Dialoghi*, 394. The point is made forcefully as well in the letter "a coloro che non leggono," which begins the second treatise of the *Libraria* and mirrors inversely the letter "ai lettori" of the first treatise (61, 245).

82. Doni, *I mondi e gli inferni*, 54.

83. On which see Masi, "Bibliografia" and "Prospettive."

84. Reproduces Domenichi, *Dialoghi*, 370.

Notes to Epilogue

1. Deborah Parker, *Bronzino: Renaissance Painter as Poet* (Cambridge: Cambridge University Press, 2000).

2. George W. McClure, *The Culture of Profession in Late Renaissance Italy* (Toronto: University of Toronto Press, 2004).

3. Rudolph M. Bell, *How to Do It: Guides to Good Living for Renaissance Italians* (Chicago: University of Chicago Press, 1999).

4. On the intensification of competition among major artists in sixteenth-century Italy, see Rona Goffen, *Renaissance Rivals: Michelangelo, Leonardo, Raphael, Titian* (New Haven, Conn.: Yale University Press, 2002); on professionalism in the sixteenth century, see McClure, *The Culture of Profession*; and Douglas Biow, *Doctors, Ambassadors, Secretaries: Humanism and Professions in Renaissance Italy* (Chicago: University of Chicago Press, 2002), chaps. 3–7, 101–96.

5. Mario Biagioli, *Galileo, Courtier: The Practice of Science in the Age of Absolutism* (Chicago: University of Chicago Press, 1993); admittedly, he is treating a period after that of the authors and artists in this book, but the argument holds. On the importance of courtly etiquette in the sciences of the sixteenth and seventeenth centuries, see in general Paula Findlen, *Possessing Nature: Museums, Collecting and Scientific Culture in Early Modern Italy* (Berkeley: University of California Press, 1994).

6. I draw my characterization of Michelangelo as a superstar from Rab Hatfield, "The High End: Michelangelo's Earnings," in *The Art Market in Italy: 15th–17th Centuries*, eds. Marcello Fantoni, Louisa C. Matthew, and Sara F. Matthews-Grieco (Modena: F. C. Panini, 2003), 195 and *passim*.

7. *Il carteggio di Michelangelo*, eds. Paola Barocchi and Renso Ristori, 5 vols. (Florence: Sansoni, 1965–1983), 2. 253.

8. On Erasmus as a model for Aretino, see Raymond B. Waddington, *Aretino's Satyr: Sexuality, Satire, and Self-Projection in Sixteenth-Century Literature and Art* (Toronto: University of Toronto Press, 2004).

9. Peter Burke, *The Italian Renaissance: Culture and Society in Italy* (Princeton: Princeton University Press, 1986), 87.

Index

Note: Illustrations are indicated by page numbers in *italic* type.

The authorized representative in the EU for product safety and compliance is:
Mare Nostrum Group
B.V Doelen 72
4831 GR Breda
The Netherlands

www.ingramcontent.com/pod-product-compliance
Lightning Source LLC
LaVergne TN
LVHW091037080826
845145LV00002B/529

* 9 7 8 0 8 0 4 7 6 2 1 6 8 *